THE HISTORY

OF THE

Virginia Federal Convention

OF

1788,

WITH SOME ACCOUNT OF THE EMINENT VIRGINIANS OF
THAT ERA WHO WERE MEMBERS OF THE BODY

BY

HUGH BLAIR GRIGSBY, LL.D.

WITH A

Biographical Sketch of the Author

AND

ILLUSTRATIVE NOTES

EDITED BY

R. A. BROCK,

Corresponding Secretary and Librarian of the Society.

VOL. II.

RICHMOND, VIRGINIA.
PUBLISHED BY THE SOCIETY.
MDCCCXCI.

THE HISTORY

OF THE

Virginia Federal Convention

OF 1788.

INTRODUCTION.

Before we proceed to detail the final scene of the Convention, we should leave unperformed an office as useful and instructive as any that devolves on the historian if we failed to glance at the lives and services of some of those patriotic men who composed the body, and whose history is in no unimportant respect the history not only of that great event, which singles out the year 1788 as one of the most important in our annals, but, in some instances, of great epochs of an earlier as well as a later day to which the lives of some of them were extended. It will become our duty to record the names not only of those who took part in debate, but of those who, though they spoke not a word during the session, mainly by their influence and ability effected the ratification of the Constitution. In forming our opinions of the last-named class of individuals, we must be careful to look at the circumstances and the impressions of the time in which they lived. To take the measure of the mental stature and of the political influence of such men from the face of the journals, or from their silence in debate, would not only be unjust to them, but would betray no slight ignorance of the views which prevailed at that conjuncture. Not only were the rules and customs of the British Parliament closely observed in the deliberative assemblies of the Colony, and of the Commonwealth in its earlier days, but the mode of conducting a parliamentary campaign was strictly observed. And in conducting a parliamentary campaign no rule was more generally enforced than that which confined the debate to certain leaders on each side of the House.[1]

The habit of every member making a speech on every subject, which has caused so much prolixity in our public proceedings, had not become the fashion with our public men. Beside the observance of the well known customs of Parliament, there were other considerations which tended to repress much speaking. The sessions of the House of Burgesses were short, rarely exceeding a month, and were usually held in May—a season precious in the eyes of those who derived their sustenance from agriculture. Political considerations also had their weight; for it was in the power of the Royal Governor to prorogue the House at pleasure, and it became important, as difficulties between that officer and the Assembly might at any moment arise, to transact the real business of the Colony with all practicable speed.[2] It should also be observed that the greatest prompter to modern loquacity did not then exist. There were no reporters; and if there had been reporters, there were no papers in which reports could be published. A small weekly sheet afforded to the Colonists the only political nutriment which they could obtain, and that sheet would not hold an entire speech of the ordinary dimensions. Such, too, was the difficulty of public conveyance—such was the infrequency and irregularity of posts—that even that sheet reached very few of the homesteads of the people. Such was, to a certain extent, the case in the Commonwealth. Thus it happened that comparatively few

---

[1] We know from letters cited in the course of this work that the friends of the Constitution had parcelled out their opponents, and held themselves in reserve for them.

[2] Patrick Henry's resolutions against the Stamp Act were adopted at the heel of the session, and so with many other measures likely to offend the Governor.

of the really able members engaged in formal debate in our public bodies; and the remark may be hazarded, that if all those who in the Convention of 1788 engaged in the discussion of the Constitution had been absent, there were able and accomplished men who, as their subsequent career would seem to prove, would have displayed talents of a high order and achieved no mean reputation for statesmanship and eloquence.

ARCHIBALD STUART.

First among the young men west of the Blue Ridge in those qualifications which attract public attention, and which fit their possessor for acting with effect in public assemblies, was Archibald Stuart, of Augusta. He had not that large experience in affairs, civil and military, which was possessed by Thomas Lewis, or even by Andrew Moore, by Darke and Stephen, by William Fleming and Stuart, of Greenbrier; nor had he yet attained that standing at the bar which Gabriel Jones had long held; but he had seen the smoke of battle, was a ready and forcible speaker, was a graceful writer, and, though young, had already served with distinction during several sessions of the Assembly. He belonged to that remarkable portion of the Anglo-Saxon family which had for more than a century cherished on the Irish soil the principles and attachments of the land from which they came, and which under a domestic discipline, partly military and partly religious, were skilful in discerning their rights, and prompt in defending them. The British colonization of Ireland was essentially military. The settlers could be counted by thousands, while the aboriginal population numbered more than a million. Another great element in this, the greatest in English estimation of all the schemes of colonization which England had there developed, was the element of religion. The Colonists were Protestants; the subject caste, ignorant and semi-barbarous, were within the pale of the Church of Rome. Hence the Colonists became in a degree unknown in the mother country—Whigs in politics and Protestants in religion. The history of Irish colonization is intimately connected with the history of our own Colony, and of that freedom which we now enjoy. It was one of those wonderful processes in human affairs, which, though seen even by acute politicians only in their ordinary aspects, was destined in another age and in a distant land to bring about a memorable revolution. To the common eye there seems no connection between the butcheries perpetrated by Cromwell and the cruelties and confiscations wrought by the misgovernment of James the Second, and the passage of the resolutions of Virginia in 1765 against the Stamp Act; yet, it is as certain as any event in history that, if the British policy in Ireland had been other than it was, those resolutions might indeed have been offered, but they would have been rejected by a decisive vote. When it is remembered that those resolutions were carried by the western vote, especially by the vote of the Valley members, the connection is obvious and indisputable. And it may well happen that in the measures of our own day, designed to accomplish limited and definite objects, the historian a century hence may detect the seminal principle which is destined to effect radical changes in existing institutions, and, perhaps, to overturn the present frame of society and to substitute some new system in its stead.

The grandfather of Archibald Stuart emigrated from Ireland in 1727, and settled for a time in Pennsylvania, where in 1735 Alexander, the father of Archibald, was born. In 1739 the family removed to Augusta county in this State, where Alexander, whose lofty stature and uncommon strength were noted even among his neighbors in the Valley, married in due time Mary Patterson. Of this marriage Archibald was the first of many children. He was born at the homestead about nine miles southwest of Staunton, on the 19th day of March, 1757. His boyhood was spent in Augusta; but his father having removed to the neighborhood of Brownsburg, in Rockbridge, Archibald became a resident of that county, and was entered a pupil in the seminary then known as Liberty Hall, now as Washington College. [Now as Washington and Lee University.—ED.] Like his classmates, who derived their instruction from William Graham, he became a devoted advocate of civil and religious freedom, and, in imitation of his illustrious teacher, was ever ready to defend it in battle or in debate.

In the fall of 1779 he attended William and Mary College, and became an inmate of the family of the President, afterwards Bishop Madison. It happened that the institution then contained a large number of youths who were destined to act a conspicuous part in public affairs. Of these Allen, Hartwell Cocke, Eyre, Hardy, John Jones, and Stevens Thomson Mason were his colleagues in the present Convention. Another associate, who, after a long career at the bar, has for more than a third of a century been resting in his honored grave in the yard of St. Paul's in Norfolk, and who was beloved and revered by his countrymen for the incorruptible integrity and unblemished purity of his life, was John Nivison. It is creditable to the standing of Stuart that among such students he was conspicuous. His personal appearance and his address, as well as that accurate scholarship which was characteristic of the pupils of Graham, contributed to his popularity. His erect and sinewy form (which exceeded six feet in height), his placid face and expressive black eyes, his long black hair falling about his neck, the blended austerity and gentleness of his deportment, presented to his young associates one of the finest models of the Western Virginian. There had been lately instituted in William and Mary a literary association, which in its brief life communicated its mystic symbols and its name to a similar association at Harvard, which in its foreign home has flourished with such unexampled vigor as to include on its roll the names of many of the most eloquent and learned men of the whole country for more than two entire generations, which was destined to sudden extinction in the place of its origin, but which was then in its early prime—the Society of the Phi Beta Kappa. Of this association Stuart was elected president. On his return to College, in 1780, he found the eastern part of the State infested by the British. The exercises of the College were suspended, and the public affairs were in an almost desperate condition. Stuart at once hastened to the scene of active war, joined the army as a private soldier in the regiment from Rockbridge, of which his father was the Major, and was promoted to an office in the commissariat department. But when the advance of Cornwallis rendered an engagement certain, he took his station in the ranks, and fought gallantly at Guilford. It was in this battle that he saw his father, who commanded the regiment on that day, fall with his wounded horse, instantly stripped of his clothing by the British Tories, and, suffering from his wounds, conveyed a prisoner within the enemy's lines.[3] During the

---

[3] Dr. Foote, in his second volume of Virginia Collections, page 147, states that Major Stuart was not wounded; but authorities in my possession, which are most authentic, show that he was wounded. Dr.

whole campaign young Stuart had in his possession the official
seal of the Phi Beta Kappa Society, of which he was the president, which, as the Society went down, he retained till his death,
and which, many years after his death, was found in the secret
drawer of his escritoire, where it had remained more than half a
century, and which was transmitted by his son to the Society at
William and Mary, which had been recently revived, where it
now performs its original office.[4]

On the return of Stuart from Guilford he studied law with
Mr. Jefferson, and ever cherished for his preceptor the highest
admiration and esteem. Some of the law-books which he procured from Mr. Jefferson are in the library of his son.[5] What
Wythe had been to Jefferson, Jefferson became to young Stuart:
the adviser, the friend, and the revered associate through life.
In the Stuart papers there is in the handwriting of Mr. Jefferson
a form of a Constitution for Virginia, drawn in 1791. Their
intimacy lasted during the life of Jefferson. When Stuart was
elected judge, his district included the county of Albemarle;
and, in attending the sessions of his court, he regularly spent a
night with his old preceptor. As a politician he sustained his
administration, and was a Republican elector until the series of
Virginia Presidents who had borne a part in the Revolution was
ended.

He began the practice of the law in Rockbridge, and in the
spring of 1783 was brought forward as a candidate for the
House of Delegates, but lost his election by thirteen votes. A

Foote describes the Major as riding on the field a beautiful mare. He
was of gigantic stature. His sword [now in the cabinet of the Virginia Historical Society, and not of unusual size—ED.], which men of
the ordinary size could hardly wield with effect, is in possession of his
grandson, the Hon. A. H. H. Stuart, to whom I am indebted for some
interesting details of his father's life. I would point out to the student
of history the diary of the Rev. Samuel Houston, who was in the
battle of Guilford. It may be found in Dr. Foote's second series,
pages 142-145.

[4] The original MS. proceedings of the Society are in the archives of
the Virginia Historical Society.—EDITOR.

[5] A portion of his correspondence with Mr. Jefferson and others is
in the possession of the Virginia Historical Society, presented by his
son, Hon. A. H. H. Stuart.—EDITOR.

few days after the election in Rockbridge he visited Botetourt on some business with Colonel Skillern, and while he was the guest of the Colonel he was invited to attend a public festival, at which most of the leading citizens of the county were present. At the gathering he was called upon for a speech, which was so well received by the company that he was requested to become a candidate for a seat in the House of Delegates at the election to be held on the following Monday.[6] There was one obstacle to his success, which seemed at first sight difficult to be overcome. He did not possess a freehold in the county; but the prompt generosity of Skillern removed that defect,[7] and on the following Monday he was duly returned. He was re-elected from Botetourt in 1784 and in 1785, when he removed from Rockbridge to Augusta, where he resided until his death. From Augusta he was returned in 1786 and in 1787. But there was no public question in which he seemed to take a greater interest than the ratification of the Federal Constitution. He had sustained in the House of Delegates the resolution convoking the meeting at Annapolis, and the resolution appointing delegates to the Federal Convention that framed the Constitution, and he felt in a certain sense a paternal feeling toward that instrument. In Augusta he put forth all his strength in its support, and, having accidentally learned one day before the election in Botetourt was to take place that the candidates for the Convention were unwilling to pledge themselves to vote for its ratification, he mounted his horse and rode day and night to Fincastle, a distance of seventy-five miles, that he might make an appeal to his old constituents in favor of the Constitution. He arrived at the court-house after the polls had been opened, and requested their suspension until he could address the people. He spoke with such effect that the people were induced to exact explicit pledges from the candidates to sustain the Constitution, which they finally gave, and which they faithfully redeemed.

---

[6] Until 1830 the Virginia elections were held " in all the month of April."

[7] This deed remained on record, overlooked by both parties concerned. Colonel Skillern, indeed, sold and conveyed it to another party. It was improved by the erection of buildings upon it. It was sold a few years ago, and, upon an examination of the title, the defect as above was discovered, and a release was given by Hon. A. H. H. Stuart, as the Editor has been informed by him.

His course in the present Convention, in which he sustained the extreme views of those who upheld the Constitution, has been pointed out already, and may be read in the ayes and noes. In 1797, he was called once more into public life, took his seat in the Senate of Virginia from the Augusta district, and bore a part in the memorable contest which was then waging between the Federalists, who approved the policy of the elder Adams, and the Republicans, who approved the policy of which Jefferson was the representative. Here he voted for the resolutions, which though offered by John Taylor, of Caroline, were drawn by Madison; but before the report of 1799 had reached the Senate he was elected a judge of the General Court, and entered on the duties of his office on the 1st of January, 1800, which he discharged with acknowledged ability and faithfulness until 1831, when, having attained the age of seventy-three, he declined a re-election under the Constitution which had been adopted the preceding year. Though on the bench, he was chosen the Jefferson elector in 1800 and in 1804, the Madison elector in 1808 and in 1812, the Monroe elector in 1816 and in 1820, and the Crawford elector in 1824. Thus far he acted with his ancient colleagues of the Republican party; but, preferring Mr. Adams to General Jackson, he was placed by the friends of Adams on their electoral ticket in 1828, which was defeated by the ticket of the opposite party. He died at Staunton on the 11th day of July, 1832, in the seventy-fifth year of his age.

He possessed an elegant taste in letters, which his contributions to the memoir of Henry, by Wirt, strikingly exhibit; and we are told that he was one of that able cohort of writers who made the Richmond *Enquirer*, then recently established by its late venerable editor, the bulwark of the party to which it belonged and the terror of its foes. Nor were his attainments confined to literature. He was fond of the severe sciences; and such was his reputation in mathematics that he was tendered the professorship in that department in William and Mary College, and was appointed one of the commissioners to run the dividing line between Virginia and Kentucky.[8]

In his latter years he presented to the young generations rising

---

[8] See Revised Code of 1819, Vol. I, page 61. His colleagues were General Joseph Martin and Judge Creed Taylor. The Richmond *Enquirer* came out in May, 1804.

around him a venerable image of the fathers of the Republic. His person to the last was erect; his frame, which was six feet three inches in height, was broad and muscular; his hair, which in youth was black, was white as snow, and was dressed in a queue; but his dark hazel eyes were still bright, and the grave and almost stern aspect of his face was such as one would look for in a statesman who, nearly half a century before, in an hour of trial and apprehension, had assisted in laying the foundation of the government under which we now live, and who had, since that time, been engaged in the honorable but arduous duties of a legislator and a judge. When he visited the hall of the Convention of 1829-'30, and took the seat allotted by the courtesy of the House to the judges, he observed with interest the representatives of a new generation about to frame a new system of government for his beloved Commonwealth, but he could not know the tender regard with which he was beheld as one of the five survivors of that illustrious band which composed the Convention of 1788.[9]

---

[9] In 1829 the survivors of the Convention of 1788 were Mr. Madison, Judge Marshall, and Colonel Monroe (who were members of the Convention of 1829), Judge Stuart, and James Johnson, of Isle of Wight. It was on this occasion I had the honor of forming an acquaintance with Judge Stuart.

I annex portions of a letter received from an intelligent correspondent, which describes the Judge in latter life: "Judge Stuart, in May, 1791, married Miss Eleanor Briscoe, a daughter of Colonel Gerard Briscoe, of Frederick county, Virginia, but formerly of Montgomery county, Maryland. Her two sisters married Dr. Cornelius Baldwin, the father of the late Judge Briscoe G. Baldwin, and Judge Hugh Holmes. In stature the Judge was tall and rawboned, his height was six feet three inches, and he was perfectly erect. He was broad-shouldered, large-boned, and muscular. His eyes were of a dark hazel color and exceedingly expressive. His complexion was dark, but somewhat florid; in manner he was rather stately and reserved. To strangers and on the bench he sometimes appeared austere in his deportment, but amongst his friends he exhibited the kindest and most genial disposition. In his dress he adhered very much to the fashions of the Revolutionary period. His hair was worn combed back from his face and with a long queue behind. Until a short time before his death, he would wear nothing but short breeches with fair topped boots. In the latter part of his life his hair was as white as snow, and I never knew a man of more commanding and venerable appearance. In

GABRIEL JONES.

Another member of the bar, whom the Valley deputed to the Convention, and who holds an important place in its early history, was Gabriel Jones.   To this day some racy anecdotes, everywhere current in the Valley, but too prurient for the public eye, serve to show the peculiarities of this really able but most singular man.   He is said to have opened the first law office west of the Blue Ridge.   He was born in 1724, near Williamsburg, of English parents, who had come over ten years before and had settled in the vicinity of the metropolis.[10]   About 1734 the family returned to England, and in the city of London young

the general aspect of his features he bore a strong resemblance to General Jackson, but was on a much larger scale. The most remarkable characteristic of his mind was his sound judgment. I have often heard Judge Baldwin say that he thought his judgment but little, if at all, inferior to Judge Marshall's, and that, if he had been placed in a position to require the constant exercise of all his faculties, he would have been one of the most eminent judges in his time. He was a generous patron of young men struggling against difficulties, and among those who shared his kindness was the well-known John Allen, the rival of Henry Clay, who was killed at the river Raisin. Another peculiarity of the Judge was his almost intuitive perception of the character of men. The only portrait of him in existence was painted in 1824 by George Cooke, and is in the possession of his son, the Hon. A. H. H. Stuart."

[10] Governor Gilmer, of Georgia, describes Gabriel Jones as "a Welshman well educated, a friend, kinsman, and executor of Lord Fairfax." I have followed the authority of the grandson of Mr. Jones, Francis B. Jones, Esq., as that most likely to be authentic. See Governor Gilmer's "Georgians," page 61. [Gabriel Jones, it is believed, possessed a select, if not a large, library, for his period, in the Colony. Volumes with his book-plate frequently occur in libraries sold at auction. The arms used by him would indicate that he was of English descent, as they are those given by Burk (General Armory), as "Jones, Chilton and Shrewsbury, county, Salop; granted 16th June, 1607. Arms: A lion rampant vert, vulned in the breast, gu. Crest: A sun in splendour, or." Gabriel Jones's plate bore also the motto, "*Pax ruris hospita*," and "Gabriel Jones, Attorney at Law."—EDITOR.]

Jones received his early training. While yet a lad Gabriel returned to Virginia, studied law, turned in due time his course westward, and took up his abode in the Valley, attending the courts of Winchester, Staunton, and Romney. In 1748 he married Miss Margaret Strother, a daughter of William Strother, who lived on the Rappahannock, and whose two other daughters married Thomas Lewis and John Madison, the father of the Bishop. After his marriage, Jones continued to reside in Frederick, but subsequently purchasing a beautiful estate on the Shenandoah in the present county of Rockingham, he removed thither, and there he resided during the remainder of his life. His estate lay directly opposite the estate of his brother-in-law and colleague in the Convention, Thomas Lewis. He died in 1806, in the eighty-third year of his age. He was of small stature and of a nervous temperament, and, having lost his right eye in early life, he always wore a shade to conceal the defect from public observation. He is represented in a portrait at "Vaucluse," the seat of his late grandson, as dressed in the full toilet of a gentleman of the old *regime*, the shade over his eye, and as having a face shrewd and attenuated, and indicative of a high temper. Indeed, with all the discipline of a long life, with all his respect for those restraints which his position at the head of the bar, as the head of a family in an orderly, moral and even religious society, and as a gentleman punctilious in dress and demeanor, he could never turn the cup of provocation from his lips, nor restrain the outbursts of a temper terrible to the last degree. Even in the presence of the court his passions flamed wildly and fiercely. He was the first, and for a long time the only, attorney who practiced in Augusta county, and was generally known as *The Lawyer*. The road by which he travelled to Staunton was called the *Lawyer's Road*. An incident which occurred in Augusta court will serve to show the peculiar temper of Jones, and, at the same time, the temper of the court toward him. He was engaged in a case in which the late Judge Holmes was the opposing counsel. Holmes was mischievous and witty, and contrived to get Jones into a furious passion, when he became very profane. After hearing Jones for some time the court consulted together in order to determine what steps should be taken to preserve its dignity. To think of punishing Lawyer Jones was out of the question; so the presiding judge gave it as the decision of the court, "that if Mr. Holmes did not quit worrying Mr. Jones and making him curse and swear so, he should be sent to jail."[11] Withal he was a most skilful and learned lawyer, indefatigable in maintaining the interests of his clients, and most successful in winning verdicts.

His politics were pitched to the same high key with his temper. He had no fears of a strong government which was, at the same time, a representative government. He thought that the principal defect in popular institutions consisted in their weakness, and that vigor in the administration was the true and the only means of sustaining successfully a republican system. He warmly supported the Federal Constitution, and was to his last hour a thorough, open, and uncompromising Federalist. Looking upon every honor to be conferred upon him as a mark of disgrace if founded on an erroneous view of his opinions, he expressed himself on public occasions with a freedom and a harshness that gave great scandal even to men not ordinarily squeamish. Thus, when he was a candidate with Thomas Lewis for a seat in the present Convention, though his opinions were everywhere known in the Valley, having heard that some of the voters whom he disliked intended voting for him out of regard for his brother-in-law, he declared from the hustings, on the opening of the polls, "that he would not receive the votes of such damned rascals."[12] He had no concealments, in public or in private. He was never worse than he appeared to be. In the relations of private life he was punctual, liberal, and honorable. The man never lived who doubted his integrity. By strict attention to the duties of his profession he accumulated a large estate. In pecuniary matters he was stern, but just. He exacted indiscriminately his own dues from others, but he rendered the dues of others with equal exactness. In an age of wild speculation, he would never buy a bond under par, nor receive more than six per cent. for the use of money. Hence, by the aid of his large capital, his influence was extensive; and that influence was invariably wielded in behalf of suffering

---

[11] I have given this nearly in the words of a writer in the Virginia Historical Register, Vol. III, 17. I have received it from various sources.

[12] I have heard this incident detailed in several ways, but all illustrative of the fearlessness of Jones in the presence of the voters.

virtue, of sound morals, and of public faith. He kept an account of all his expenses; and when he engaged at his own fireside, or at the firesides of his friends, as was the fashion of the times, in a game of cards, he noted his losses and his gains; and a regular account of his luck, kept through his whole life, was found among his papers. When we regard his protracted career, and the influence which his strict veracity, his incorruptible integrity, and his fearless assertion of the right, exerted on the public opinion of a young and unsettled country, rapidly filling up with the waifs of a various emigration, almost beyond the reach of law, his peculiarities, though ever to be pitied and deplored, are softened in the contemplation. He neither sought nor would accept public office; but it is certain that he was elected a member of Congress under the Confederation, and, it is believed, a judge of the General Court.[13]

---

[13] The election of Jones to Congress was made under flattering circumstances. He was at the head of a delegation consisting of Edmund Randolph, James Mercer, Patrick Henry, William Fitzhugh, Meriwether Smith, and Cyrus Griffin. He was elected June 17, 1779. (Journal of the House of Delegates of that date.) He ran against Paul Carrington on the first election of the judges of the General Court, and was defeated by sixteen votes. (Journal House of Delegates, January 23, 1778.) I confess my obligation to Francis B. Jones, Esq., for information concerning his ancestor. There was a portrait of Gabriel Jones at the residence of the late General J. B. Harvie, of Richmond, who was his grandson.

THOMAS LEWIS.

But Gabriel Jones was not the only man of influence and talents whom Rockingham sent to the present Convention. No two men could differ more from each other in physical and moral qualities than Jones and his colleague, Thomas Lewis. Jones was diminutive in stature; Lewis was one of a family of gallant brothers whose height exceeded six feet; and he was large in proportion to his height. Jones, to the extreme verge of a protracted and prosperous life, gave way to an uncontrollable temper; Lewis, though sprung from a fiery race, governed his passions with such deliberate judgment that few even of his intimate friends had ever seen him under high excitement. Jones, when he was furious—and he was apt to be furious on slight provocation—swore with such vehemence as to shock even men of the world; Lewis, though unconnected with any church, was essentially a pious man, and gave instructions in his will that the burial-service of the Episcopal Church should be read by his friend Gilmer at his grave. In the science and practice of law, to which he had devoted for more than half a century the energies of a vigorous mind, Jones was superior not only to Lewis, but to all his rivals west of the Ridge; but in a love of order, in popularity derived from personal worth, and in integrity, Lewis was his equal; and in profound and elegant scholarship, and in a knowledge of political affairs, acquired in the public councils during the earlier stages of those measures which led to the Revolution, he was not only ahead of Jones, but of all the able and patriotic men to whom the West had confided its interests at this critical conjuncture, he was regarded at home and throughout the State as confessedly the first. They were brothers-in-law, lived in a style of liberal hospitality on their princely estates lying on the opposite banks of the Shenandoah, and were personal friends. Lewis was the elder by six years. Both had probably studied at William and Mary, had emigrated in early life to the Valley, with the interests of which they were

fully conversant, and advocated with equal zeal the ratification
of the Federal Constitution. They were descended from different stocks—possibly from the same stock developed under different circumstances. Jones was of English parentage, and though
born in Virginia, spent his youth in England.[14] With the government of that country he was familiar, and he saw nothing in
it to excite remark or to demand reform. In common with the
most conspicuous statesmen of the Revolution, he would have
preferred a safe and honorable connection with England to a
state of independence. He was in favor of an energetic government vigorously administered, and from habit, from policy, and
from principle would have chosen rather to await the full development of bad measures than to assail in the beginning an abstract
principle from which bad measures were likely to follow. Lewis
was the descendant of a Scotch ancestor, who had become an
Irish colonist, and who imbibed the spirit, partly religious and
partly military, which a colonist of the dominant race in the circumstances of his condition could not fail to cherish. Hence
the readiness with which Lewis separated himself from the great
body of the eastern delegation in the House of Burgesses of
1765, and voted for the resolutions of Henry against the Stamp
Act. He well knew that the Colony could bear the weight of a
stamp tax as easily as we now bear the weight of the tax on
letters transmitted through the post; but he saw in the principle
of laying taxes on the people without representation a source of
danger, the extent of which could only be measured by the
cupidity of those who had unjustly assumed the power. Jones,
in common with many eastern members, might have hesitated to
adopt means of resistance until the policy had become fixed;
but Lewis voted to resist the infraction at the outset, and to
incur present difficulty in the hope of forestalling future trouble.
Hence, while many of the eastern men in March, 1775, were
reluctant to proceed to extremities, and were disposed to rely on
the operation of the non-importation agreements as an appeal to

---

[14] Governor Gilmer, already cited, calls Jones a Welshman, and
assigns his reasons for believing that the Lewises were originally from
Wales. I lean to the belief that the Lewises were neither Huguenot
nor Welsh, but were Scotch, and emigrated to Ireland in the time of
James the First, or of Cromwell. [This question grows.—EDITOR.]

the commercial sensibilities of England, Lewis approved the resolutions of Henry for putting the Colony into military array; and in the following year sustained the resolution instructing the delegates of Virginia in Congress to propose independence, and the resolution appointing a committee to report a Declaration of Rights and an independent Constitution. But on this great occasion Lewis and Jones united to attain a common object.

This change in the policy of Lewis did not fail to attract attention. It was from a close observation of his conduct in past years that the opponents of the Federal Constitution counted upon his vote. In the eyes of Henry and his compatriots, who had steadily guarded the right of taxation, not only from the encroachments of the mother country, but from the encroachments of our own Confederation, it seemed monstrous to cede that invaluable right without limitation to any authority whatever, whether that authority was seated on the other side of the Atlantic or on this. The statesmen of whom Henry was the chief were free to declare that the Northern States richly merited their gratitude for their heroic conduct in resisting British tyranny, and that they ardently desired a union with them; but between an expression of gratitude and a love of union, and an entire surrender of the right most precious to freemen, there was an immense interval which it was madness to overleap. Lewis doubtless felt the delicacy of his position. It was painful to part from friends with whom we had long held intimate communion; but it was his deliberate conviction that the difficulties of the crisis demanded a trial of the new system, and he voted with his colleague, who from the first had no doubts on the subject.

Nor was his vote confined to the ratification of the Constitution. On the greatest of all the amendments which were reported by the select committee, and which aimed to secure to the States a modified control over the right of taxation, he again parted from his ancient allies. It may be remarked, as an instructive fact in the history of the Scotch-Irish race which settled in the Valley, and made an impression upon its population likely to last for years and ages to come, that those among them who were attached to the Episcopal Church were eager for the ratification of the Federal Constitution ; and that those who had been dissenters before the Revolution, and were connected with the Presbyterian Church, opposed the adoption of that instrument in its unamended form with all their zeal.[15]

Of the early life of Lewis, of his birth in Ireland, and the circumstances which led to the emigration of his family, of his services as the first surveyor of Augusta, when Augusta extended to the Ohio and to the Mississippi, and of his career in the House of Burgesses, in the early conventions, and especially in the Convention of 1776, when he voted in favor of the resolution instructing the delegates from Virginia in Congress to propose independence, and was a member of the committee which reported the Declaration of Rights and the Constitution, we have already treated in detail.[16] His knowledge of mathematics was held in high repute; and when the boundary line between Virginia and Pennsylvania, an exciting question, which had nearly involved the two States in civil war, was about to be run, he was placed at the head of the commission to which Virginia assigned that delicate duty ; but, as he was unable to be present at the meeting of the commissioners of the two States in Baltimore, and as the arrangement made by his colleagues was not conclusive, he was again called upon by the Assembly to examine the subject in dispute and to report his opinion at a subsequent session.[17] In the intervals of public employments he devoted his time to the cultivation of his estate, and was ever pleased when he could snatch an hour from business and from society to engage in the pursuits of science, or to enjoy the pleasures of literature. He imported the elder as well as the more recent productions of British genius ; and the intelligent visitor from the East, who had come into the Valley in search of a patrimonial land-claim, and was welcomed as a guest at his hearth, saw with unfeigned surprise, on shelves freshly made from trees which had reared for centuries above the waters of the

---

[15] Archibald Stuart and Thomas Lewis on the one side, and William Graham, the Ajax Telamon of the Presbyterians of the Valley, are instances illustrative of the fact stated in the text.

[16] In the discourse on the Virginia Convention of 1776, page 112.

[17] His colleagues in the first instance were the Rev. James Madison and the Rev. Robert Andrews ; and in the second his brother, Andrew Lewis, and Colonel Innes. (Journal of the House of Delegates, June 24, 1779.)

Shenandoah, the most elaborate treatises on the sciences and the most instructive and most elegant performances in history, in theology, and in general literature.[18] His position in the Valley was so prominent that all who sought information or advice on any topic connected with the West either repaired to his house or consulted him through the post.   Washington, who had served with him on many trying occasions in the House of Burgessess and in the Conventions, and who had taken up vast tracts of land on the Kanawha and the Ohio, earnestly asked his aid in the management of his affairs, which Lewis, whose whole time hardly sufficed to manage his own, was compelled to refuse. He had long suffered from a cancer on the face, and on the 31st day of January, 1790, within less than two years after the adjournment of the present Convention, in the midst of his children and grandchildren, and in the seventy-third year of his age, he died on his estate on the Shenandoah, and was buried on its banks.

[He accompanied the commission in 1746 to determine the line of Lord Fairfax's—the Northern Neck grant—from the head spring of the Rappahannock to the head spring of the Potomac. A journal of the expedition, kept by him, is in the possession of his descendant, the Hon. John F. Lewis. It gives the only authentic narrative now extant of the planting of the Fairfax stone.—EDITOR.]

---

[18] In an account of the library of Colonel Lewis, see the discourse on the Convention of 1776, as last cited.

JOHN STUART.

By the side of Thomas Lewis sat his son-in-law, a man of the ordinary height, but of a stalwart frame, whose large head, low, receding forehead, black, bushy eyebrows, small blue eyes, aquiline nose, bronzed features, and stern aspect, presented the beau-ideal of that hardy race, which in the outskirts of the Commonwealth cultivated the earth and worshipped God with a rifle constantly by their side and with a ball-pouch flung across the shoulder. He had learned from his father-in-law to beguile the cares and dangers of a frontier life with the pleasures of literature.

In his rock-built home near Lewisburg, in a cherry case as bright as mahogany, he had collected some of the best authors of the Augustan age of English literature. Nor were his literary amusements unprofitable to his country. He has left to posterity the most accurate and lifelike account of the greatest Indian battle ever fought on the soil of Virginia; and in a neat and truthful narrative has interwoven with charming effect the incidents, of personal and general interest, developed during the settlement of the country west of the Alleghany, of which he was now the representative.

Such was John Stuart, of Greenbrier. He was the son of David Stuart, who was born in Wales in 1710, who married, in 1750, Margaret Lynn, of Loch Lynn, Scotland, and who shortly after his marriage emigrated to Virginia, settling himself in the county of Augusta, where his brother-in-law, John Lewis, the father of Andrew and Thomas Lewis, resided.[19] David died

---

[19] Governor Gilmer says that the name of Colonel John Stuart's father was John; but my information is derived from the family records in the possession of the accomplished granddaughter of Colonel Stuart, Mrs. General Davis, of Fayette. Governor Gilmer states that the father of Colonel Stuart was an intimate personal friend of Governor Dinwiddie, and came over with him in 1752. If this be true, then David Stuart must have come by way of the West Indies. ("Georgians," page 50.) [" The probability is that Stuart had no personal connection

early, leaving two daughters, whose reputable descendants live in the East and in the West, and one son, whose services it is our duty to record. Young Stuart had not the advantages of early instruction; but he was a close observer, a diligent inquirer, and was constant in his endeavors to improve his mind. He acquired a knowledge of mathematics ample enough to qualify him to perform with skill the duties of a surveyor, and was appointed by his uncle, John Lewis, his agent in locating land-warrants in the region now included in the county of Greenbrier. Thither he removed, and there during fifty eventful years he continued to reside. He settled himself on a tract of land four miles from Camp Union, as the present site of Lewisburg was once called, which was presented to him by his cousin, General Andrew Lewis, which he improved and adorned with commodious build-ings, and on which he lived until his death. In the Indian skir-mishes of the times he was frequently engaged, and in the army of General Andrew Lewis, which fought in October, 1771, the memorable battle at the Point, he commanded one of the Bote-tourt companies of Colonel Fleming's division, and acted with distinguished gallantry. In 1780 he was returned to the House of Delegates by the county of Greenbrier, which three years before had been set apart from Botetourt and Montgomery, and in November of the following year was appointed the clerk of the court. For more than a quarter of a century he performed the duties of clerk of all the courts of Greenbrier with scrupu-lous fidelity, and, retiring in his old age from public business, was succeeded by his son, Lewis. He became the County Lieu-tenant at a time when that office was keenly coveted by our fathers. Indeed, the County Lieutenant [20] then held the same honorable office which the Lord Lieutenant held in the parent country, and presided in the court, commanded the militia, and was in all public affairs the exponent of the county. His respon-sible duties were marked out by special enactments. It was not obligatory upon him to take the field; but if he took the field,

---

with Governor Dinwiddie. He certainly settled in the Valley long before Dinwiddie became Governor of the Colony."—*Waddell's Annals of Augusta County*, page 463.—EDITOR.]

[20] For the rank and position of the County Lieutenant, see pages 35-36 of the Journal of the Convention of July, 1775.

the colonel of the regiment became lieutenant-colonel and the lieutenant-colonel became major. It was the experience in civil and military affairs thus acquired, and his long and intimate acquaintance with the wants and interests of the West, that impelled him to approve a vigorous government and to favor the ratification of the Federal Constitution by the present Convention. His sagacity led him to fear that the Indian, though driven beyond the Ohio, might prove a dangerous foe to the West; and he knew that it rested not with Virginia, but with England in the North and with Spain in the West, whether there should be peace or war within our borders; and that a coalition between those two foreign forces might result in the extermination of the settlers west of the Blue Ridge. He viewed both these nations with distrust; yet, if either of them should choose to bring all the Indians within its control into the field, it would require all the resources of the Union to repel the savages and to punish them. With such impressions, he brought all his influence to bear upon his countrymen, and succeeded in securing the vote of Greenbrier in favor of the Constitution. Nor did his affection for the Constitution cease with its adoption. He gave a cordial support to those who were charged with its administration, and upheld the policy of Washington and of Adams with unwavering confidence. As he was earnest and sincere in his political feelings, he maintained his opinions unaltered by the fluctuations of popular passion or by the lapse of time, and died as he had lived—an honest, upright, and consistent Federalist. He rarely spoke with severity of his opponents; but in his letters to confidential friends he handled the foibles of the Democratic leaders without mercy, but without venom; and he showed his antipathy to their doctrines rather by laughing at what he deemed their inconsistencies and absurdities than in fierce and vulgar denunciation.[21] Indeed, the conspicuous trait of his character was a decorous self-command. It was hard to tell what impression a remark made upon him. In mixed companies he was silent and reserved, and his grave deportment and severe aspect were apt to repress the loquacity of others. He

---

[21] The letters of Colonel Stuart, addressed to the Rev. Benjamin Grigsby during the Adams and Jefferson administrations, are in my collections.

never lost his youthful love of the rifle, which to the last he wielded with unerring skill; and it was the delight of his old age to wander through the forest; and he has been seen to halt and carve a date or a name on the bark of a beech, and to sit upon a fallen tree with his rifle on his lap, as he was wont to do in youth when he watched the Indian enemy. Yet, with one or two old friends he would occasionally unbend, and on such occasions it was pleasing to hear him recount the early incidents of his life and his clear and admirable estimate of the Revolutionary statesmen with whom he had served in the public councils. With all his seeming sternness, he was revered by the great body of his fellow-citizens; and his popularity was the more honorable to him, as it arose from no concession to fashionable follies, from no concealment of unpopular opinions, but from the computation of solid worth in the calm judgments of the people. His habit of self-command and the steadiness of his nerves were remarkable even in his last hour. Like many of the early settlers, he had insensibly caught some of the Indian traits. He did not appear to suffer from any particular disease, but seemed, like a soldier on duty, patiently to await the time of his final discharge. On the evening of the 23d of August, 1823, he told his son that his time had come; and, rising from his bed, shaved and dressed himself with unusual care. When he had finished his toilet he rested on the bed, and in five minutes breathed his last. He had reached his seventy-fifth year. He was buried on his estate, not far from the site of a fort which he had erected for protection from the sudden forays of the Indians. A slab with an appropriate epitaph marks the spot.

Taciturn and unbending as this worthy patriot appeared, there was a romance in the courtship of his wife, which has become one of the traditions of the West. About mid-day on the 10th of October, 1774, in the town of Staunton, a little girl, the daughter of John and Agatha Frogge, and the granddaughter of Thomas Lewis, who was sleeping in the room in which her mother was attending to her domestic affairs, suddenly awoke, screaming that the Indians were murdering her father. She was quieted by her mother, and went to sleep again. Again she awoke, screaming that the Indians were murdering her father. She was quieted once more, and was waked up a third time by the same horrid vision, and continued screaming in spite of all the efforts of her mother to soothe and pacify her. The mother of the child was much alarmed at the first dream; but when the same dreadful vision was seen by the child a third time, her imagination, quickened by that superstition which is almost universal among the Scotch, and which the highest cultivation rather conceals than eradicates, presented before her the lifeless form of her husband gashed by the tomahawk of the savage. Her cries drew together her neighbors, who, when informed of what had occurred, joined in her lamentations, until all Staunton was in a state of commotion. It so happened that the bloody battle of the Point was fought on the very day when Staunton was thus agitated, and, what was still more wonderful, John Frogge, the father of the child who had seen the vision, was killed during the engagement.[22] When Captain Stuart, at the close of the Western campaign, visited the Valley, he saw the mother of the affrighted child, who was his first cousin, and, as he had probably seen her husband fall and assisted in committing his body to the grave, communicated to her the melancholy but interesting details of his fate. The sequel is soon told. He was enterprising and brave; she was young and beautiful; and in due time he conducted her as a bride to his mountain home. The offspring of this marriage were two sons and two daughters, who survived their parents, but are now dead, leaving numerous descendants. Mrs. Stuart outlived her husband some years, and saw her grandchildren attain to maturity.[23]

There is one reflection drawn from the life of John Stuart not undeserving our attention. While most of the early politicians east of the mountains, though beginning life with good estates, died poor, or were able to leave but a pittance to their families, which were scattered abroad, their Western colleagues bequeathed to their descendants a princely inheritance. The fine estates on the eastern rivers, the very names of which once imparted to

[22] This incident I have given in almost the identical words of Governor Gilmer. ("Georgians," page 49.)

[23] I knew this venerable lady in my early youth and in her extreme old age. She was active and shrewd to the last. She was somewhat deaf; and her son, Lewis, my early and dear friend, now too gone, used laughingly to say that his mother could not hear ordinary conversation very well, but that if you talked to her about money matters her hearing was perfect.

their owners the dignity of a title, have long been alienated from the blood of their original possessors. During the present century four-fifths of the land on the banks of the James, and of other rivers of the East, have been in the market. Such has not been the case west of the mountains. We should err, however, in ascribing the result to the superior thrift or to the superior skill of our Western brethren. Its explanation will probably be found in the peculiar circumstances of each great section of country. In the East, if a man with ten children dies leaving an old planta- tion worth fifty thousand dollars,[24] as from obvious considera- tions it was incapable of sustaining a division into ten equal and habitable parts, it must be sold for a division. But fifty thousand dollars' worth of landed property in the West, as the West was at the beginning of the present century, could be divided indefinitely into fine plantations abounding in wood and water. Early purchases of land may be said to be the source of Western wealth; and for such purchases the East afforded no opportunity. But Stuart would, under almost any circum- stances, have been a wealthy man. In his temperament were combined in a profuse degree the elements of worldly success. He was systematic, patient, and economical. Debt he held in abhorrence. Whatever progress he made was sure. He did much for himself; but he took care that time should do more. Thus, watching the progress of events, and rising with a rising country, he accumulated vast wealth. Of the quarter of million of dollars at which his estate was assessed at his death, the greater proportion yet remains in the hands of his descendants, and will probably remain for a century to come.[25]

---

[24] Our great Eastern statesmen were as prolific as their Western brethren. If Thomas Lewis brought up thirteen children, Patrick Henry and George Mason nearly averaged a dozen.

[25] The Historical Memoir of Colonel Stuart was among the earliest publications of the Historical Society of Virginia. A portion of it may be found in Howe, in the article on Greenbrier, and in the Historical Register, Vol. V, 181. I read it thirty years ago in the original manu- script, which was taken from the desk on which it was written and handed to me for perusal. I can recall many of the books of the Colonel's library. They were, of course, all London editions, and in calf binding. I acknowledge the kind assistance of Samuel Price, Esq., and of other members of the family of Colonel Stuart.

ANDREW MOORE.

From the mountains of Greenbrier we pass again into the Valley, and recall the name of a patriot who, by birth and race, was one of its peculiar representatives, whose early life was checkered by a various fortune, whose services as a soldier in three arduous campaigns in the North, during which he saw from the heights of Saratoga the surrender of the first British General with his army to the prowess of the American arms—a glorious result, achieved in no small measure by the valor and skill of the corps to which he belonged; who was a member of the Assembly in the latter years of the Revolution, and distinguished himself by his devotion to religious freedom; who was a member of the House of Representatives during the entire term of Washington's administration; who was a leader in the Republican party from the date of the Federal Constitution to the close of the presidency of Jefferson; who was the first native of the Valley elected by Virginia to the office of a Senator of the United States, and who, having lived to behold the second contest of his country with Great Britain and to rejoice in the success of her arms, and, reposing in the midst of his descendants in the shadow of his own vine, went down quietly, in his sixty-eighth year, to his honored grave.

But, great as were the services rendered throughout a long life to his country, his course in the present Convention, which had a controlling influence in effecting the ratification of the Constitution, is not the least interesting incident in his career in the estimation of his posterity. He had been instructed by a majority of the voters of Rockbridge to oppose the ratification of the Constitution; but, after due deliberation, he resolved to disobey his instructions and to sustain that instrument. To obey the instructions of his constituents is the most fearful responsibility which a delegate can assume; and it is questionable whether, in a case that is definitely settled by his vote beyond the possibility of revision, it is susceptible of justification. But the cognizance of the question lies altogether with the constituents whose wishes have been thwarted, and to these Andrew Moore appealed on his return from the Convention, and was sustained by an overwhelming majority of their suffrages.

Andrew Moore was of the Scotch-Irish race, to which Thomas Lewis and John Stuart belonged. His grandfather was one of a family of brothers who emigrated from the North of Ireland and settled in the Valley, and in some of the Southern States. His father, David, took up his abode on a farm in the lower part of Rockbridge (then Augusta), now called "Cannicello." The most remote ancestor of David whom he could remember was a lady whose maiden name was Bante, who in her old age came over to this country, and who used to relate that, when a girl, she had been driven to take refuge under the walls of Londonderry, had seen many Protestants lying dead from starvation with tufts of grass in their mouths, and had herself barely escaped alive from the havoc of that terrible scene.

In 1752, at the homestead of "Cannicello," Andrew was born, and was there brought up, availing himself of the advantages of instruction within his reach so effectually as, before manhood, to become a teacher in a school of his own. He determined to study law, and attended, about 1772, a course of lectures under Wythe, at William and Mary. Fascinated by a love of adventure, he embarked for the West Indies, was overtaken by a tempest, and was cast away on a desert island. To sustain life the shipwrecked party was compelled to live on reptiles, and especially on a large species of lizard, the flavor of which, even in old age, the venerable patriot could readily remember. From this inhospitable abode he was at length rescued by a passing vessel; and he went to sea no more.

The Revolution was now in progress, the Declaration of Independence was promulgated, and Virginia had erected a form of government of her own, and appealed to her citizens to maintain it in the field. Andrew Moore hearkened to the call, and accepted a lieutenantcy in the company of Captain John Hays, of Morgan's Rifle Corps. As soon as he received his commission he attended a log-rolling in his neighborhood, and enlisted in one day nineteen men—being nearly the whole number present capable of bearing arms. Such was the spirit of patriotism that animated the bosoms of his countrymen. He continued in the army three years, and served most of that time in Pennsylvania, New Jersey, and New York. He participated in all the engagements which terminated in the capture of the British army under Burgoyne, and saw that accomplished General play a part in a drama of deeper interest than the one which he wrote for the entertainment of a London audience. At the expiration of three years' service in the army, having attained the rank of captain, he resigned his commission, in consequence of the number of supernumerary officers, and returned to Rockbridge.

In April, 1780, he entered on his legislative career, which he was destined to pursue for nearly the third of a century, and to close with the highest honor which can be attained in that department of the public service. As soon as he entered the House of Delegates he was placed on the Committee of Religion, and it should be remembered forever to his praise that he was from the first the earnest and consistent advocate of religious freedom in all its largest sense. He was a member of the body when Tarleton made his famous effort to capture it in full session at Charlottesville. He acted with the party of which Henry was the head; nor until he took his seat in the present Convention did he depart from the policy marked out by the great tribune of the people. On the 17th day of December, 1785, true to the principles of the race from which he sprung, and, in unison with the spirit of that remarkable era in which he lived, he voted for the memorable act "establishing religious freedom." [26] And

---

[26] As several of the members of the Convention voted with Moore on that occasion, I annex, for the sake of reference, the ayes and noes on the passage of the bill in the House of Delegates:

AYES—Joshua Fry, *Wilson Cary Nicholas*, Joseph Eggleston, *Sam'l Jordan Cabell, Zachariah Johnston,* Michael Bowyer, *John Trigg,* Robert Clark, George Hancock, Archibald Stuart, William Anderson, Hickerson Barksdale, John Clarke (of Campbell), Samuel Hawes, Anthony New, John Daniel, Henry Southall, *French Strother,* Henry Fry, William Gatewood, *Meriwether Smith, Charles Simms, David Stuart,* William Pickett, Thomas Helm, C. Greenup, James Garrard, George Thomson, *Alexander White,* Charles Thurston, *Thomas Smith, George Clendinen,* John Lucas, Jeremiah Pate, Ralph Humphreys, *Isaac Vanmeter, George Jackson,* Nathaniel Wilkinson, John Mayo, Jr., John Rentfro, William Norvell, John Roberts, William Dudley, Thomas Moore, Carter Braxton, *Benjamin Temple,* Francis Peyton, Christopher Robertson, Samuel Garland, Benjamin Logan, David Scott, William

when, on the 16th of January following, the bill came down from the Senate with three amendments, two of which were critical and explanatory, and the third of which proposed to strike out the words, " that the religious opinions of men are not the object of civil government, nor under its jurisdiction," he assented to the two first, but voted against concurring with the last in a minority of twenty-seven; thus affirming in the most positive manner that the religious opinions of men are not within the range of legislation.[27] During the following session—which began in October, 1786, and ended on the 11th of January, 1787—he voted for the appointment of commissioners to meet at Annapolis, and afterwards voted to appoint delegates to the Federal Convention, which should assemble in Philadelphia for the purpose of proposing amendments to the Articles of Confederation.

In the present Convention, as before observed, he sustained the Constitution proposed by the General Convention, and opposed the adoption of the third amendment of the series which was reported by the select committee, and which reserved

---

Pettijohn, Robert Sayres, Daniel Trigg, William H. Macon, Griffin Stith, David Bradford, *James Madison*, Charles Porter, William Harrison, Benjamin Lankford, John Clarke (of Prince Edward), Richard Bibb, *Cuthbert Bullitt*, Daniel Carroll Brent, Williamson Ball, *Andrew Moore*, John Hopkins, Gawin Hamilton, *Isaac Zane*, John Tayloe, John W. Willis, Andrew Kincannon, and *James Innes*—74.

NOES—Thomas Claiborne, *Miles King*, *Worlich Westwood*, John Page, Garland Anderson, Elias Wills, *William Thornton*, *Francis Corbin*, *Willis Riddick*, Daniel Sandford, John Gordon, Edward Bland, *Anthony Walke*, George L. Turberville, William Garrard, John F. Mercer, Carter B. Harrison, Richard Cary, Jr., Wilson Cary, and Richard Lee—20.

The *italics* point out the members of the present Convention who voted on the bill.

[27] As Madison, Harrison, and other prominent men of the popular party voted in the majority of fifty-three, I am inclined to believe that they did so lest, by sending the bill back again to the Senate when the session had only two days to run, they might jeopard its passage. In the negative were the names of Zachariah Johnston, John Tyler, French Strother, Willis Riddick, Andrew Moore, Isaac Zane, and Thomas Mathews, members of the present Convention, all of whom (except Riddick) sustained the original bill. See Journal of the House of Delegates, January 16, 1786.

to the State the privilege of collecting the Federal quotas through her own officers. He was elected to the first Congress under the Constitution ; and it soon appeared that, eager as he was to procure the ratification of that instrument by Virginia, he was resolved to watch its workings with unceasing vigilance, and to insist upon the strictest construction of its powers. On Wednesday, the 18th of March, 1790, he took his seat in the House of Representatives, then sitting in New York, and took an active part in its proceedings. In the arrangement of the new tariff he guarded the interests of the farmer, and contended that, as hemp could be grown in the Southern States, it should receive the same encouragement that was extended to the manufacturers by a tax on cordage. He opposed the heavy duty on salt as being hard upon those who raised cattle, and argued with spirit against the discrimination of pay in favor of the Senators over the members of the House of Representatives as derogatory and unjust. It was on the questions growing out of the treaty negotiated by Mr. Jay with Great Britain that he spoke more at length than he had yet done, and ably defended the rule of the House of Representatives asserting its constitutional rights in relation to treaties ; and exposed the unequal and unjust stipulations of the treaty itself. When in 1793 the proposition was brought forward to reduce the army, he went into a minute history of Indian affairs, and proved what was afterwards established by a severe sacrifice of human life, that regulars, and not militia, were the proper troops for Indian wars.[28] In 1797 he withdrew with Madison and Giles from the House of Representatives, and determined by a vigorous course of measures in the Virginia Assembly to change the current of Federal politics. He supported the resolutions passed by that body in 1798, and the celebrated report presented by Madison at the succeeding session. In 1803 he returned to the House of Representatives, and in the following year was elected for a full term to the Senate of the United States. While he remained in the Senate he upheld the policy of the Republican party, and gave to the administration of Jefferson a cordial and most effective support. On the conclusion of his senatorial term he declined a re-election, and withdrew from public life. He was appointed

---

[28] *Benton's Debates*, Vol. I, 36, 39, 124, 411, 727.

by Mr. Madison marshal of the district of Virginia, and when subsequently the district was divided he remained the marshal of the Eastern district, performing its duties until his death, on the 14th of April, 1821. Some years before his death he was elected by the Assembly a general of brigade, and afterwards major-general. He was of the middle height, stoutly built, and even in old age was capable of enduring fatigue and exposure. In his visits to Norfolk, which he made in the discharge of the duties of his office, he always rode on horseback. He died at Lexington, and was buried there.[29]

---

[29] It was on one of his visits to Norfolk that I saw General Moore for the first and only time. He was then about sixty-six, but in his step and conversation he appeared to my young eyes as a man about the middle age. It was his elder brother William, and not Andrew, as stated by Howe and Foote, who was at the battle of Point Pleasant. When Colonel John Steele was shot during the fight by an Indian, who was about to scalp him, William Moore shot the Indian, and knocking another Indian down with his rifle shouldered Steele, who was a large man, and taking his own rifle and Steele's in the other hand, carried him a hundred yards back, and then returned to the fight. Steele, who recovered from his wound, used to say that William Moore was the only man in the army who could have carried him off if he *would*, or that would have carried him off if he *could*. William was a lieutenant in the militia at the siege of York. He was very strong, and told a nephew that he never drank a pint of spirits in the whole course of his life. He lived to the age of ninety-three. There is a miniature of General Moore in the possession of his widow.

WILLIAM McKEE, MARTIN McFERRAN.

The colleague of Moore from Rockbridge was Colonel William McKee, who was descended from the same Scotch-Irish race, and evinced in a long career in the House of Delegates a firm determination to overturn those institutions, which, however well adapted to embellish and adorn an aristocratic state of society, are out of place in a republic. Hence, he gave a hearty support to the bills reported by the Committee of Revisers, and though he was not one of that illustrious band which, amid the rebukes of the selfish and the prejudices of even wise and honorable men, recorded the act establishing religious freedom on the statute-book of the Commonwealth, he warmly approved the measure. He had been engaged in several encounters with the Indians, had fought gallantly at Point Pleasant, and had acquired a high reputation for integrity, energy, and ability. He was a member of the House of Delegates at the winter session of 1786, and voted to send commissioners to Annapolis, and subsequently to the General Convention, which was summoned to revise the Articles of Confederation. Like his colleague, Moore, he took the responsibility of disobeying the instructions of his constituents, enjoining upon him to oppose the ratification of the Federal Constitution, and received an honorable acquittal at their hands. On the adjournment of the Convention he removed to Kentucky, where he spent the remainder of his days.[30]

The representatives of Botetourt were two men who exerted a great influence on public opinion in the West, and were among the most patriotic and steadfast of their generation. Both Martin McFerran and William Fleming were of Scotch descent. McFerran, who belonged to the great Scotch Irish family that passed from Pennsylvania into the Valley, and who derived his Christian name from a clergyman, who as early as 1759 went forth as a missionary among the Indians, and was, it is believed,

---

[30] For the religious aspects of his character, see *Foote's Sketches of Virginia*, first series, page 447.

slaughtered by them, was for several years before the meeting of the Convention an active member of the House of Delegates, and maintained a prominent place on the committees of that body at a time when a few leading names only were found upon them. He, in common with his more distinguished colleague, was, in the first instance, opposed to the ratification of the Federal Constitution, and it is probable that but for the fervid eloquence of Archibald Stuart on the day of the election of the members of the Convention, which persuaded the voters to elicit pledges from the candidates, would, as in earlier days, have ranged under the banner of Patrick Henry. But he regarded the expressed will of his constituents as a rule of action, and not only voted in favor of the adoption of the Constitution, but opposed the scheme of previous amendments. And when the celebrated memorial to Congress adopted by the House of Delegates of which he was a member, on the 14th day of November following the adjournment of the Convention, which insisted " in the most earnest and solemn manner that a Convention of deputies from the several States be immediately called, with full power to take into their consideration the defects of the Federal Constitution that have been suggested by the State Conventions, and report such amendments thereto as they shall find best suited to promote our common interests, and secure to ourselves and the latest posterity the great and unalienable rights of mankind,"[31] he voted for the milder propo-

---

[31] For the two memorials which strikingly exhibit the temper of the times, see the Journal of the House of Delegates of November 14, 1788. The first memorial was probably from the pen of Henry, and the substitute from the pen of Edmund Randolph. The substitute was lost—ayes 50, noes 72—and then the original memorial was carried without a division. As it is interesting to trace the action of the members of the Convention, some fifty odd of whom were members of the House of Delegates when the memorials were offered, I annex their votes for and against the substitute :

AYES—Mr. Speaker (General Mathews), Wilson C. Nicholas, Zachariah Johnston, Martin McFerran, David Stuart, John Shearman Woodcock, Alexander White, Thomas Smith, George Clendenin, Daniel Fisher, Robert Breckenridge (Kentucky), Levin Powell, William Overton Callis, Francis Corbin, Ralph Wormeley, William Ronald, Walker Tomlin, John Allen.

NOES—William Cabell, John Trigg, Henry Lee (Kentucky), Notlay

sition offered by the immediate friends of the Constitution, which left it discretionary with Congress to act on the amendments proposed by the States in the form prescribed by the Constitution itself, or to submit them to a Convention of the States. Nor should it be omitted in this brief sketch of McFerran that he voted against the schedule of amendments reported by the select committee of the Convention, and adopted by that body.

Conn (Kentucky), Binns Jones, Benjamin Harrison, French Strother, Joel Early, Miles King, John Early, John Guerrant, Thomas Cooper, John Roane, Green Clay (Kentucky), Alexander Robertson, Richard Kennon, Willis Riddick, Burwell Bassett, Patrick Henry, Theo. Bland, Cuthbert Bullitt, William McKee, Thomas Carter, James Monroe, Thomas Edmunds, Samuel Edmiston.

WILLIAM FLEMING.

Colonel William Fleming was not a member of the General Assembly which held its sessions in 1788; but on the first vote by ayes and noes in the Convention he separated from his colleagues and sustained the schedule of amendments proposed by the select committee. The life of this remarkable man richly merits a deliberate record. For forty years he was engaged in the military and civil trusts of the Colony and of the Commonwealth; and signalized himself by his valor, his incorruptible integrity, and his ardent patriotism, all of which qualities were combined with and exalted by a pure moral character, by great domestic virtues, and by a deep sense of religion. He was born on the 18th day of February, 1729, in the town of Jedburgh, Scotland, a little village made familiar to the world by the genius of Scott. He was the son of Leonard and Dorothea Fleming, and was nearly allied to the Earl of Wigton and Lord Fleming. When the title of the earldom of Wigton was in abeyance on the death of the last earl without issue, which happened after the Revolution, Fleming was urged to visit Scotland and claim the succession; but, true to the principles of the memorable event which he had helped to achieve, he preferred to remain in Virginia and bring up his large family in a new country, alleging that he had no wish to make his eldest son, who was already well provided for by his maternal grandfather, a rich man, and his other children poor. When we recall what Scotland was at that time, we are inclined to approve, on grounds disconnected from politics, the wisdom of his choice. That he had no unkind feelings toward his Scotch relations, and that he cherished the memories of his distinguished lineage, is evident from the fact that he called his beautiful estate in Botetourt (now in Roanoke) by the name of " Bellmont," a seat of the Flemings, which he had visited in his early days. That lineage had long been illustrious, and was intimately connected with the unfortunate but beautiful Queen of Scotland, whose character is one of the puzzles of modern history. It will be remembered that, when Mary was prohibited from taking more than two female friends to share with her the solitude of Lochleven, one of the most touching of modern fictions represents one of them to have been a Fleming.

His parents were in moderate circumstances, but were able to afford him the means of a liberal education. He attended the school of a Mr. Totten in Dumfries, a good classical teacher; and, having to make his way in the world by his own exertions, he chose the calling of a surgeon, and prosecuted his studies in the University of Edinburgh. At the close of his terms he entered the British navy as a surgeon's mate; and while engaged in the service was taken prisoner in his vessel by the Spaniards, who took him to Spain, where he was treated with great cruelty. He was strictly confined to his prison, but when his health began to fail he was allowed to walk in a small garden connected with the jail. So scanty was his fare, and of such indifferent quality, he would have perished with hunger but for the benevolence and sympathy of a Spanish lady, whose residence overlooked the garden, and who supplied him at intervals with nourishing food. Her name he could never learn, but her kindness he never forgot; and to the last day of his life he would not allow persons in want, apparent or real, to be turned from his door, lest, as he sometimes said with a smile, they might be descended from the good Spanish lady, but, in truth, from the impulses of his own generous heart. Possibly, too, we may see in this incident an explanation of his tender affection for the female sex which was conspicuous in his character, and of that affectionate devotion to his wife which shines so sweetly through all his letters.

When he was relieved from confinement he was resolved to resign his appointment in the navy, which from the first was uncongenial to his taste, and try his fortunes in the Colony of Virginia. Governor Dinwiddie, a Scotchman, had then been promoted from a berth in the customs of Barbadoes to the office of Lieutenant-Governor of Virginia; and it is probable that, as an intimacy was soon formed between the Governor and young Fleming, the latter had brought over very flattering letters from Scotland.[32] In August, 1755, he landed in Norfolk, and visiting

---

[32] A number of clever Scotchmen came to the Colony in Dinwiddie's time with letters from his relatives in Scotland; and when the young Virginians visited England he was ever ready to introduce them

Williamsburg he determined to embrace the profession of arms. A few days before his arrival, and while he was on his passage to Virginia, the battle of Monongahela had been fought. Braddock, Halket, and Shirley had fallen, and the general route of the army had laid the whole West open to the incursions of the French and the Indians. Under such circumstances it was not difficult for an active and intelligent young man of six and twenty to obtain a commission; and on the 25th of August he was appointed ensign in the Virginia regiment commanded by Colonel George Washington. It may seem strange that he did not choose a place in the medical staff; but he cherished a spirit of adventure, and it is probable that he had already shown a taste for war, as he bore on the bridge of his nose the mark of a sabre cut which he may have received in the fight with the Spaniards. His commission as ensign is printed on a folio sheet, the names and dates filled up in a fine hand, and the ink as bright as it was the day it was used; and bears the large, straggling signature of Robert Dinwiddie, which reminds us of the signature of Stephen Hopkins to the Declaration of Independence.

After serving faithfully in the grades of ensign and lieutenant, he received on the 22d of May, 1762, the commission of captain in the Virginia regiment commanded by Colonel Adam Stephen. This commission, which is also before me, is printed on parchment about the size of a half foolscap sheet, and is signed by Governor Francis Fauquier. The term of the military service of Fleming included one of the darkest periods in the annals of the Colony. The letters of Washington faithfully portray the exigencies of that epoch. Even the heart of Washington, familiar as he was with the cruelties of the Indians, grew sick, and he declared that, if by his death he could restore peace and safety to the frontier, he would lay down his life without hesitation. At this trying time Fleming performed his duty with unfaltering devotion to his adopted country; and it was not until the general pacification took place the following year that he resigned his commission.

---

abroad. Samuel Davies, among others, received this courtesy at his hands, and gracefully acknowledges the attentions he received from Dinwiddie's relatives in Scotland.

He was now to change his mode of life and to resume his old profession. In selecting a new home he came to Staunton, in the county of Augusta, where he settled and engaged in the practice of physic. Here he became acquainted with the family of Isaac Christian, one of the early settlers of the town, who was a prosperous merchant, and was rich in Western lands. The name of Christian is honorably known in the records of the West, and his blood flows in the veins of hundreds now living in Kentucky and in other Southern States. It was William, the eldest son of Isaac, whose name is intimately connected with our early Indian history, and whose murder by the savages, perpetrated with all the subtle refinements of Indian cruelty, has nerved the white man in many a bloody contest with his tawny foes, and will draw tears from generations yet unborn. To Anne, the sister of William, who was then living, and one of the most prominent men of the West, Fleming paid his addresses; and on the 9th of April, 1763, she became his wife.[33]

A few years after his marriage he withdrew from the practice of medicine, and went to reside permanently on the estate in Botetourt (now Roanoke), which he received from his father-in-law, and which, as before stated, he called " Bellmont "; and here he lived, unless when absent in his various public employments, .until his death. At that time the Indians made frequent incursions into the settlements, and his first office was to build a log house or fort (the feudal castle of the West), and to this fortress the people of the neighborhood flocked on the discovery of Indian signs. On one occasion, when the neighbors had collected in the building, one of the sisters of Mrs. Fleming, who was slightly indisposed, had thrown herself on a bed beneath a window; and presently looking up, she beheld the face of an

---

[33] As I write for Virginians and the descendants of Virginians, who are curious in tracing the origin of the settlers of Kentucky and other Southern States, it may be well enough to say that Isaac Christian had one son. William, mentioned in the text, who married a sister of Patrick Henry, and left several daughters, who married in Kentucky: Anne, who married Colonel Fleming; Rose, who married Judge Caleb Wallace, of Kentucky; Mary, who married Colonel Stephen Trigg; Elizabeth, who married Colonel William Bowyer, of Botetourt; and Priscilla, who died early. Fleming, Trigg, and Christian counties in Kentucky were called after the brothers-in-law.

Indian warrior examining the room. She instantly gave the alarm, and a strict search was made, but without success; and it was generally believed, in spite of the earnest protestations of the lady, that there was some illusion or mistake in the case. Some years later, when a deputation of Indians, on their return from Richmond, called at " Bellmont," one of the chiefs observed that he had been there before, and had looked through the window, but finding the whites ready to repel an attack, had quietly departed.

The first important trust that Fleming filled after his removal to Botetourt was that of colonel of the regiment of militia which marched to the Ohio and which performed so gallant a part in the battle of Point Pleasant. Allusions have been frequently made in this work to that battle, and we subjoin in a note the best sources of information on the subject.[34] Suffice it to say, that Colonel Charles Lewis and Colonel Fleming, in the early part of the fight, were ordered by General Lewis to detail a portion of their forces under their oldest captains, and to advance in the direction of the reported enemy. The two colonels, hastening on as directed, sent forward scouts, and while yet in sight of the camp guards heard the discharge of musketry and saw the scouts fall; and in a few moments received a heavy fire along their entire line. Both the colonels fell badly wounded, and were in due time borne into the fort. Lewis died before the fate of the day was decided; but Fleming, though believed to be mortally wounded, joined in the shout of victory. He had received three balls—one in his right wrist, which crushed the bones; another in the same arm, higher up; and the third in his breast. Before reaching the fort the extravasated blood had gathered in the cavity of the chest, which seemed to protrude, and he was in such a state of intense suffering as to preclude all hope of relief. In this emergency, while the surgeons were attending to those who appeared likely to recover, Fleming called to his aid his negro servant, who had frequently assisted him in surgical operations, and instructed him to follow his prescriptions. This ball in the breast was never extracted;

---

[34] *Colonel John Stuart's Historical Memoir, Foote's Sketches of Virginia*, second series, 159–168, and *Charles Campbell's History of Virginia*, 179, first edition.

and from this time to his death in 1795, a period of twenty-one years, he was more or less an invalid. When he exerted his strength—often when he rode on horseback—the ball made itself felt. It would rise up for the distance of two inches, causing at times much suffering, and then fall down again to its old bed. That with such a drawback he persisted in making numerous journeys to Richmond and Williamsburg, and to the extreme West, at a time when the back of a horse was the only means of travel, shows great perseverance and energy.

With great caution, united to medical skill, he was enabled to render material service to his country. Soon after the organization of the State government he became a Senator from the district composed of the counties of Montgomery, Botetourt, and Kentucky, and a member of the Executive Council; and when we reflect that then the Indians were almost as formidable as the British, and were, in fact, subsidized by them, his knowledge of the Indian character, and his military talents which had been trained in many a contest with that wary foe, were eminently useful. His letters and papers show the active part which he took, especially in Western affairs. From some of those letters, written on coarse paper and somewhat mutilated, an interesting picture of the cares and wants, the hopes and fears of that day may be drawn. In a letter to his wife from Williamsburg, dated October the 30th, 1778, and written before the currency had greatly depreciated, he says: "I have sent you half a pound of Hyson tea at forty shillings, half a pound of green tea at twenty shillings, and half a pound of Bohea at ten shillings. I have sent you a pound of pins at three pounds. No coffee to be got. We have nothing new here, except the high price of grain—corn five pounds a barrel, wheat four dollars. I hope this will find you and all the little ones in health. I trust God will preserve them and all the rest of the family. I have much to say, but no time, as Colonel Christian is waiting. God bless and protect you."

Writing to his wife from Williamsburg, May 20, 1779, he describes the taking of Portsmouth, and narrates some instances of British cruelty not to be found elsewhere: "Four ships of force and others (in all seventeen) came to anchor near Portsmouth the 9th instant, and next day landed and took possession of the town; Major Mathews, who commanded a part of the artillery battalion, retiring after spiking the cannon. A large

quantity of tobacco, provisions, and some military stores fell
into their hands.   A party of the enemy marched to Suffolk,
and burned the town.   On hearing that General Scott was
marching against them, they hastily retreated, doing all the
damage they could.   Many of my old friends and acquaintances
have suffered greatly by having their houses burned, and their
negroes and stock taken, and the women made captives of and
exposed to the greatest insults they can be subjected to.
Another party of the British, meeting with some trading French-
men, butchered five of them in cold blood, and strangled three.
The captain of a French vessel informed me that they had taken
two vessels near Gwinn's Island, one of them his own; that a
snow fought them bravely.   The other did not fire; and the
British murdered their crews with shocking barbarity, one man
having his eyes cut out, and his body mangled with worse than
Russian barbarity.   They threaten to visit Hampton and York.
Thank God, we are prepared for them; every day men pouring
in, and a thousand came in to-day.   By the next opportunity I
hope to send you a favorable account of the issue of this affair.
The strength of the enemy is known by deserters to be two
thousand five hundred.   Old Guthridge,[35] James Parker,[36] and

---

[35] A corruption of the name—John Goodrich, ship-owner and merchant ; at first enjoyed the confidence of the Whigs, and was employed
to import gunpowder to the amount of £5,000, with which sum he was
entrusted in advance.   Under this engagement he incurred the dis-
pleasure of Lord Dunmore, who caused him to be seized and confined.
In January, 1776, he petitioned the Virginia Convention for an adjustment of his accounts, which caused much debate in that body, and led
to the development of fraud by himself and sons.   In March, 1776, the
father and his sons—John, William, Bartlett, Bridger, and another
(five)—had abandoned their houses, plantations, negroes, and stock,
and were serving the Crown under Lord Dunmore, who had five of
their vessels in his fleet, under orders to constantly run up the rivers
of Virginia and seize, burn, or destroy everything that was water-
borne.   John Goodrich was captured by the authorities of Virginia,
and was for a time in prison and in chains.   Finally, released, he went
to England, but returned and engaged in fitting out privateers.   His
daughter, Agatha Wells, married Robert Shedden, a loyalist, whose
descendants in England are persons of consideration.   (*Sabine's Loyal-
ists of the American Revolution*, page 480.)   There are many descendants of Goodrich in Virginia.—EDITOR.

[36] Of Norfolk, Va., merchant ; appointed Captain.   (*Sabine.*)—EDITOR.

Parson Agnew[37] are said to be active with them." After recount-
ing these outrages of the British, which were in the same
vicinity in 1812, with equal if not greater brutality, his thoughts
recur homeward: "I am anxious to hear from you and to know
how my dear children are. Is there danger from the small-pox
or from the enemy? If from either, let me know. There is
such a bustle about me I cannot say anything more. I must
suppress the emotions I feel rising, and only say what I have
constantly told you, and what I know you believe, that I am ever
yours."

In November, 1780, when the currency had become depreciated, he writes to his wife from Richmond: "Robert Preston
took up the box, in which you will receive thirty-three pounds
of sugar, a pair of shoes, a pair of breeches and waistcoat; likewise two papers of pins, which cost one hundred and thirty dollars (if you think proper you may spare one of the papers, as I
shall get some pound pins), half a pound of allspice at thirty
dollars, and eight pounds of coffee at thirty dollars a pound, &c."
These items explain the scarcity of those days as well as the
currency. He adds: "Colonel Campbell has the thanks of the
House for his behavior at King's Mountain, and a present of a
fine horse equipped, and a sword." As he is about to close his
letter, recollections of his distant home burst upon him. "O,
my little ones! let me hear how they are, and believe me ever
yours." In this letter he announces the appointment of General
Greene as the successor of General Gates in command of the
Southern army—an appointment of precious memory to this
hour from the Potomac to St. Mary's.

He had received the commission of County Lieutenant of
Botetourt as early as the 1st of April, 1776. This office had
been established anew by the July Convention of 1775, and its
duties were prescribed by the ordinance. During the interval of
1775 and the establishment of the Constitution in July, 1776, the
commission was signed by the Committee of Safety. As the
ordinance contained no form of a commission, as it was careful
to prescribe in the case of the colonel commanding in chief the

[37] Rev. John Agnew, rector of Suffolk parish; became Chaplain of
the Queen's Rangers; died near Fredericton, New Brunswick, in 1812,
aged eighty-five years. (*Sabine.*)—EDITOR.

forces of the Colony, and as it is probable that no copy of a commission of County Lieutenant issued by the Committee of Safety is in existence, with the exception of Colonel Fleming's, now before me, I will recite its words: " The Committee of Safety of the Colony of Virginia to William Fleming, Esq : By virtue of the power and authority invested in us by the delegates and representatives of the several counties and corporations, in General Convention assembled, we, reposing especial trust and confidence in your patriotism, fidelity, courage, and good conduct, do by these presents constitute and appoint you to be Lieu-tenant and Commander-in-Chief of the militia of the county of Botetourt; and you are, therefore, carefully and diligently to discharge the trust reposed in you by disciplining all officers and soldiers under your command. And we do hereby require them to obey you as their County Lieutenant; and you are to observe and follow all such orders and directions as you shall from time to time receive from the Convention, the Committee of Safety for the time being, or any superior officers, according to the rules and regulations established by the Convention. Given under our hands, at Williamsburg, this 4th day of April, 1776."   It is signed by Dudley Digges, Paul Carrington, James Mercer, Thomas Ludwell Lee, William Cabell, and Thomas Walker. An endorsement on the commission is in the following words: " May, Botetourt County Committee, 1776.—I do hereby certify that the within-named William Fleming, Esq., took the oath required by the Convention. Teste: David May, Clerk." The commission is printed lengthwise on a half foolscap sheet. The signatures of the Committee of Safety are all distinct, legible at a glance, and like ordinary writing, except Mercer's, which has an elaborate flourish, strongly reminding us of the times when the old feudal barons found it easier to deal in hiero-glyphics than to write simple words, though those words made up their own names.

In June, 1779, he was placed at the head of a commission consisting of James Steptoe, Edward Lyne, and James Barbour, for carrying into execution an act of Assembly entitled an act for adjusting and settling the title of claimers to unpatented lands under the present and former governments previous to the establishment of the Commonwealth Land Office in Kentucky. This office, which required a minute knowledge of the land laws, and stern personal courage to resist the passions peculiar to squatters, he performed with great credit to himself and to the entire satisfaction of the Executive and the General Assembly. At that time, and long subsequently, the traveller to Kentucky incurred no little personal risk; and on one occasion his party was attacked by the Indians, who were fortunately repulsed.

It was the custom of the patriots who controlled the public councils during the Revolution, when any important duty was to be performed, to select the best man for the purpose, and to throw the responsibility of a refusal upon him. Thus it was that, notwithstanding the inconvenience arising from his wounds, which rendered him susceptible of what he called rheumatic attacks, Fleming was constantly called upon in Western affairs; and his energy and patriotism always impelled him to respond to the call of his country. Accordingly, on the 29th of January, 1782, he was placed at the head of a commission issued by Governor Harrison, composed of Thomas Marshall, the father of the Chief Justice, Samuel McDowell, the ancestor of the late Governor McDowell, and Caleb Wallace, afterwards a judge of the State of Kentucky, "to call to account all officers, agents, commissaries, quartermasters, and contractors, who have been or are in service in the Western country (then extending to the Mississippi), belonging to this State, for all their proceedings, and to liquidate the accounts of all such persons, as well as those who may still have any claim or claims against the Commonwealth, and make a special report thereof to the Executive." The commission was invested with the power of choosing its secretary, of calling and summoning before it all public officers in the Western country, and of doing all things necessary to accomplish its object; and in April of the following year he was appointed by Governor Harrison commissary to the troops that then were in Kentucky, and to the militia that may be sent there, for the purpose of building and garrisoning a fort at the mouth of Kentucky river.

As a member of the Senate from the district made up of Botetourt, Washington, and Kentucky counties he was punctual in his attendance upon its sessions, and gave efficient support in conducting the war and in furthering those domestic reforms which then engaged the attention of the Assembly. It was by the aid of such men as William Fleming that the relics of feudal policy, which disfigured the Colonial *regime*, were extirpated from our new system.

Having thus during the third of a century passed through all the grades of military service, from an ensign to a colonel, and filled the most responsible trusts which his connection with the Senate and the Council entailed upon him, and having seen the humble Colony which he had entered thirty-three years before assume her station as a sovereign member of a great Confedera- tion, he fondly hoped that his public career was ended, and that he would be called abroad no more.   But a great question, which shook the State to its centre, rose suddenly before him, and he was called to the metropolis once more as a mem- ber of the Convention called to consider a new Federal Con- stitution.

His views of a Federal Union were those of a statesman; and he correctly estimated its value in respect of the country at large, but more especially of the distant and thinly-settled West. He knew, as well as any man living, that so long as Spain held Louisiana, and Great Britain held the Canadas, Indian troubles would be frequent, and that all the resources of all the States would be required to repress the hostilities of the Indian tribes in the pay of those foreign powers.   But he also knew the innate dread of the tax-gatherer by a people who had no outlet for the products of their farms, and, of course, no money, and he shrunk from a system of direct taxation by Federal authority. Hence he would have preferred a strictly Federal Union, which would bear upon the States rather than upon the people; and it is probable that, but for the visit of the eloquent and enthusiastic Stuart to the Botetourt election heretofore alluded to, which resulted in instructions to the members of the Convention, he would have sided with the opponents of the Federal Constitu- tion.   But, yielding to those instructions which the Rockbridge delegates did not hesitate to disobey, he voted in favor of ratifi- cation; but at the last call of the ayes and noes in Convention, as has been already stated, he parted from his colleague and sustained the schedule of amendments which were proposed by the select committee, and which were adopted by a majority of twenty.

He saw the intimate relation of knowledge and freedom, and

became an active promoter of education in the Commonwealth. Had it depended upon him, all Mr. Jefferson's schemes of schools would have been in full operation before the close of the war. He aided in providing funds for the benefit of Hampden-Sidney;[38] and he was one of the first Board of Trustees of Washington College. But he knew that academies were quite as useful as colleges; and at a time when elementary education was little thought of in the West or in the East, he used his influence with the General Assembly in the establishment of a literary fund for the great western counties.[39] He cultivated a taste for letters throughout his varied and various career, and he was one of the few residents of the West that had a good collection of books. Beside the leading medical authors which he read professsionally, he possessed some of the best English classics, especially the historians and the theologians. His Tillotson, bearing the signs of thorough reading and annotated by his hand, is, I believe, still in existence. And it deserves to be remarked that, of all his letters to his family, though written hastily, as most of them were—sometimes in the bustle of a tavern, at others in camp or in the wilderness—few there are that do not contain some allusion to a Superintending Power, and a commitment of his family to His care.

In the practical business of life he was, like most Scotchmen who turn their backs upon Toryism and brandy, not only successful, but highly prosperous. He invested largely in Kentucky lands, and was able to provide well for his family. Had his lands been judiciously managed after his decease, they would have conferred great wealth upon all his descendants. His hospitality was always on a liberal scale. The first eight years of his life in Virginia, when he was not engaged in his compaigns, were spent in Williamsburg and in its vicinity; and entering into society with a zest made more keen by the hardships and dangers of a camp, and uniting in his person the qualities (then rare) of a scholar and a soldier, who bore the prestige of noble blood, he acquired a quiet dignity of address and a polished courtesy which were conspicuous in his old age; and his intimate

---

[38] Judge Paul Carrington, Sr., to Fleming, in the Fleming papers.

[39] A copy of the petition to the Assembly may be seen in the Fleming papers.

acquaintance with all the distinguished actors of his time was refreshed by visits from them whenever they came within reach of his house. And the traveller from the East or from the West looked forward with longing to the hospitable mansion at "Bellmont."

The last days of this estimable patriot were now at hand. Writing to a niece in England the year before his death, he says: "I have retired from all public business for several years; am now old, my constitution broken, maimed by several wounds, and am often attacked by violent pains in my limbs, brought on by colds and by many years' severe duty in a military line. I am just able to walk a little, after a month's confinement to my bed and room. When well I am employed in my family affairs, and in the support cf a pretty numerous family in a part of the country where little business is carried on." He lingered to the following year, when on the 5th day of August, 1795, in his sixty-sixth year, he breathed his last. His remains were interred in the burial-ground at "Bellmont" by the side of his deceased children. At a late day the body of his wife was placed by him. A substantial stone wall protects the remains; but, in common with most of our early patriots, no stone tells the passer-by who rests beneath.[40]

---

[40] Colonel Fleming had twelve or fourteen children, of whom seven survived him. Of these Leonard, the eldest son, removed to Kentucky before his father's death, and lived to the age of eighty-four; Eliza, who married first the Rev. Cary Allen, and afterwards the Rev. Samuel Ramsey; Dorothea, who married Mr. James Bratton; Anne, who married the Rev. George A. Baxter, D. D.; Priscilla, who married Mr. Samuel Wilson, and has resided more than thirty years in Alabama; William, who has also lived in Alabama for many years; and John, the youngest son, who died at the age of eighteen, while a student at Washington College. Of these Colonel William Fleming and Mrs. Wilson are the only survivors. Mrs. Fleming long survived her husband, and maintained the wonted hospitality of his house. Consult *Foote's Sketches of Virginia*, second series, page 268. Governor Gilmer, in his "*Georgians*," page 56, states that Colonel Fleming was Governor of Virginia; but he is mistaken. As a member of the Council, he may have acted on some occasion as Lieutenant-Governor. [As a member of the Council, for a time in June, 1781, during the flight, before the enemy, of Governor Jefferson from the capital, Colonel Fleming was the Executive of the State. His acts were legalized by a resolution of the Assembly (*Hening's Statutes*, x, 567):

He is said to have been of medium height, his features strongly marked, his eyes blue, his nose Roman, and his hair, until it became grey, of a dark brown. His teeth were sound to the last. There is no portrait of him extant; for in those days painters never crossed the Blue Ridge, and came very rarely east of it; but there is a small profile likeness of him, which exhibits the outline of a striking head. His address was dignified and engaging; and having received a classical training in early life, and mingled freely in society, passing in a period of more than forty years through all the varieties of public life, and with fair powers of observation, he was always self-possessed in his demeanor, and displayed great facility in pleasing and interesting all who came in contact with him. He wore the dress of the Revolution to the end; and was not inattentive to his person or to the customs of polished society. Even in his Indian campaigns he sealed his letters to his wife with wax on which was impressed the Fleming coat-of-arms. Such was William Fleming, a patriot whose name had almost slipped from the memory of that Commonwealth whose independence he aided in achieving, and whose glory is a part of his work.

There is a strong similarity in the lives of Hugh Mercer and William Fleming. Both were Scotchmen, who emigrated in early manhood to the Colony of Virginia. Both studied medicine in the University of Edinburgh, and exchanged the scalpel for the sword, and were engaged in the Indian wars that ended with the pacification of 1763. Both in high military command and in the midst of battle fell covered with wounds. But here

---

" It appearing to the General Assembly that Colonel William Fleming, being the only acting member of the Council for some time before the appointment of the Chief Magistrate, did give orders for the calling out the militia, and also pursued such other measures as were essential to good government, and it is just and reasonable that he should be indemnified therein—

" *Resolved, therefore*, That the said William Fleming, Esq., be indemnified for his conduct as before mentioned, and the Assembly do approve the same.

"JOHN BECKLEY, C. H. D.

" 1781, June 23.

" Agreed to by the Senate.

"WILL. DREW, C. S."

—EDITOR.]

the parallel ceases. Mercer died in a few days of his wounds; Fleming, though disabled from active command, and at times enduring excruciating pain from his injuries to the hour of his death, which was caused by them, lived more than twenty years, during which he rendered valuable services to his country, saw that country's independence recognized by the proudest nations of Europe, and succeeded in securing the adoption of the Federal Constitution under which we now live.[41]

---

[41] I acknowledge with much pleasure my obligations to Miss Louisa P. Baxter, a granddaughter of Colonel Fleming, for entrusting to my care some valuable papers of her ancestor, and for an admirable letter of her own. Sidney S. Baxter, Esq., formerly Attorney-General of Virginia, is a grandson of Colonel Fleming. The reader of our early journals must be careful not to confound William Fleming, of Cumberland, who was a member of the Convention of 1776, &c., and afterwards a judge of the Court of Appeals, with Colonel William Fleming, of Botetourt.

ISAAC VANMETER, EBENEZER ZANE.

It would be to present an unfaithful portrait of the useful and able men who represented the West in the Convention if we omitted to record the names of Isaac Vanmeter, of Hardy, and of Ebenezer Zane, of Ohio. They were the peculiar representatives of the region from which they came; but in their manners, in their services rendered to their adopted State, and in their eminent fitness for the perilous times in which they acted, would compare favorably with their ablest associates in the body. Vanmeter was the son of John Vanmeter, of New York, who accompanied the Delawares on a war party against the Catawbas; but the Catawbas, anticipating the attack, surprised and defeated the Delawares in a battle fought near where the present courthouse of Pendleton county now stands. John Vanmeter escaped, and returned to New York; but he was so impressed with the fertility and beauty of the lands on the South Branch bottom in Hardy county, particularly those immediately above what was called the Trough, that he advised his sons to migrate and settle upon them. Isaac, the subject of the present notice, shortly set out for the happy valley, and in 1736 made a tomahawk improvement on the lands recently, if not now, owned by his descendants of the same name, lying just above the Trough, where Fort Pleasant was afterwards erected. He then returned to New York, but in 1740 visited his improvement, on which he found a squatter, whom he immediately bought out.[42]

In the mean time emigrants from other quarters made their appearance, and in the names of Hite, Mercer, White, Swearingen, Stephen, Lucas, Vance, Rutherford, Jackson, Morgan, and others, we find the representatives of that region who opposed the measures of the British Ministry which led to the Revolution, and who on the field and in the council sustained

---

[42] I derive my authority for these facts from *Kercheval's History of the Valley of Virginia*, page 72, and *Foote's Sketches of Virginia*, second series, page 15.

with unfaltering fidelity the fortunes of the young Commonwealth through a long and perilous war. It was by the aid of
these and such like gallant sons of the West that Patrick Henry
maintained that majority in the House of Delegates, without
which, according to Jefferson, there must have been a stand-still
in the prosecution of the contest with Great Britain.

Isaac Vanmeter was frequently a member of the House of
Delegates, and in 1786 approved the expediency of amending
the Articles of Confederation, and gave a cordial support to the
resolutions appointing the Convention at Annapolis, and subsequently the General Federal Convention that met at Philadelphia.

During the October session of 1786 a measure of domestic
policy, which has a peculiar interest at the present time, was
brought before the House of Delegates, and from the introduction of the ayes and noes, which, however, were still rarely
called, we have the means of knowing the deliberate opinions of
Eastern and Western men upon it. It appears that Joseph
Mayo had in his will instructed his executors to give freedom to
his slaves, and on the 4th of November, 1786, an application
was made by them for permission to carry the will into effect.
The subject was referred to the Committee of Propositions and
Grievances, and reported reasonable. A motion to lie on the
table was made and failed. It was then moved to postpone the
subject until the next session of the Assembly, which the House
refused to do. A motion was now made to strike out the words
"is reasonable," and insert "be rejected," which also failed.
The main question was then put upon agreeing with the report
of the committee, and decided in the affirmative by a vote of
fifty-three to forty-eight—ascertained by ayes and noes.[43]   A
select committee, consisting of James Madison, Theoderick
Bland, Francis Corbin, John Page, Mann Page, Richard Bland
Lee, French Strother, and Thomas Underwood, all Eastern men,
were appointed by the Chair to draft a bill in pursuance of the
vote of the House. On the 13th of the month, Mr. Madison
reported a bill, which was made the order of the following day,
but which was not reached until the 18th of December, when,
after an animated discussion, it was passed by a vote of sixty-

---

[43] House Journal, November 4, 1786.

seven to forty—ascertained by ayes and noes."[44] Vanmeter voted for sustaining the report of the committee and for the passage of the bill. This question receives additional interest from the fact that few slaves were then owned west of the Blue Ridge.

On the various questions touching the finances of the State, and particularly on those relating to the payment of taxes, he voted with the popular majority which so long ruled the councils of the Commonwealth. When the act to amend an act

---

[44] As many of the members of the House of Delegates at this session were also members of the present Convention, I annex the ayes and noes, the names of the members of the present Convention being in *italics:*

AYES—John Cropper, *Zachariah Johnston, Archibald Stuart, John Trigg,* John Campbell, Thomas Rutherford, *Martin McFerran,* George Hancock, Adam Clement, Paul Carrington, Jr., Henry Southall, William Christian, *French Strother, Merriwether Smith, David Stuart,* Elias Edmunds, Joseph Crockett, John Fowler, Jr., George Thompson, *John Early, George Clendenin, Isaac Coles,* Elias Poston, *John Prunty, George Jackson, Isaac Vanmeter,* Willis Wilson, *John Mann,* William Norvell, William Walker, Richard Terrill, Arthur Campbell, John Lyne, Daniel Fitzhugh, *James Gordon,* Cyrus Griffin, Francis Peyton, Richard Bland Lee, *William White,* James Dabney, Benjamin Logan, John Jouett, *Francis Corbin,* Owen Davis, David Scott, Robert Sayres, Andrew Hines, William McMahon, *James Madison, Jr.,* Charles Porter, Benjamin Lankford, Constant Perkins. Wade Mosby, *Theodorick Bland,* John Thoroughgood, *Andrew Moore, William McKee,* John Hopkins, Isaac Zane, Abraham Bird, Mann Page, *John Dawson,* James Campbell, Robert Craig, Daniel McCarty, David Lee, and *Thomas Matthews.*

NOES—*George Nicholas, John Pride,* Thomas Claiborne, *Binns Jones,* John Cabell, Anthony New, Thomas Scott, Matthew Cheatham, *Miles King,* James Upshaw, John Rentfro, *Samuel Richardson,* Charles Mynn Thurston, *Thomas Smith,* John Lucas, Edmund Wilkins. John Coleman, *Parke Goodall,* John Garland, George Hairston, John Scarbrook Wills, John Lawrence, *William Thornton, Benjamin Temple, Christopher Robertson, James Johnson,* William Curtis, *Willis Riddick,* Anthony Brown, Willis Wilson, Griffin Stith, *Littleton Eyre,* John Gordon, Cuthbert Bullitt, George Lee Turberville, Thomas Ridley, Andrew Buchanan, Lemuel Cocke, and *John Allen.*

Joseph Prentis was Speaker of the House; but it appears that at this time it was not usual for that officer to vote except in the case of a tie. Those who wish to examine the geographical aspect of the vote so far as the votes of the members of the Convention of 1788 are concerned, may do so by turning to the list of the members in the Appendix.

entitled an act for the establishment of Courts of Assize, which
took up much of the time of the October session of 1786,
came before the House with sundry amendments from the Committee of the Whole, he voted to sustain the eleventh of the
series, which virtually enacted a stay-law for a given period in
certain cases, and it is a pregnant illustration of the public
opinion of that age that the amendment was carried by a majority
of one hundred and twelve against ten.[45]   When the engrossed
bill came up, however, there was an even vote on its passage,
and its passage was effected by the casting vote of the Speaker.[46]
Nor should we fail to add that when on the 17th day of December, 1785, the bill "establishing religious freedom" was on
its passage in the House of Delegates, Vanmeter, in common
with his colleagues of the West, gave it a cordial support.[47]

In the present Convention he opposed the policy of previous
amendments, and voted for the ratification of the Constitution.
And when the motion to strike from the schedule of amendments the third article, which stipulated that Congress should
first apply to each State for its quota of taxes before proceeding
to lay any taxes at all, he seems to have been casually absent, as
his name does not appear on the roll of ayes and noes, though
there is no doubt of his opposition to the amendment.

The name of Zane is honorably known in the history of the
West.   The original emigrants who bore it passed from Pennsylvania, it is believed, between 1735 and 1745, into what is now
the county of Hardy, and encountered all the difficulties and

---

[45] See the ayes and noes in the House Journal of December 16, 1786.

[46] House Journal, December 18, 1786.   On the stay-law clause Madison voted in the affirmative, and George Nicholas in the negative.

[47] I annex the vote of the House of Delegates on the bill, so far as the
names of the members of the present Convention are concerned :

AYES—Wilson Cary Nicholas, Samuel Jordan Cabell, Zachariah
Johnston, John Trigg, Archibald Stuart, French Strother, Meriwether
Smith, Charles Simms, David Stuart, Alexander White, Thomas Smith,
George Clendenin, Ralph Humphries, Isaac Vanmeter, George Jack-
son, Benjamin Temple, Christopher Robertson, James Madison, Cuth-
bert Bullitt, Andrew Moore, and James Innes.

NOES—Miles King, Worlich Westwood, William Thornton, Francis
Thorburn. Willis Riddick, Anthony Walke, and Richard Cary. (House
Journal, December 17, 1785.)

dangers that beset a frontier life. As early as 1752 William
Zane and several members of his family were taken prisoners by
the Indians from their dwelling on the South Branch in Hardy,
but regained their liberty. Isaac, one of the sons of William,
who was captured in his ninth year, spent his whole life among
the Indians. He was seen in the town of Chilicothe, as late as
1797 by Kercheval, the historian of the Valley, and detailed to
him his early career. He had married a sister of the chief of
the Wyandots, and had eight children, of whom four were sons
and four were daughters. The sons adhered to the savage life,
but the daughters married white men, and are said by Kercheval "to have been remarkably fine women, considering the
chances they had for improvement." The father, who had
become identified with the Indian race, possessed great authority
among his redskin comrades, and exercised his influence in
behalf of the whites in so marked a manner that the Government of the United States granted him a patent for ten thousand
acres of land.[48]

---

[48] *Kercheval's History of the Valley of Virginia*, page 113.

ISAAC ZANE.

The first of the Zanes who appeared in the public councils was the namesake and relative of the Indian refugee, General Isaac Zane, of Frederick, as Frederick was at its creation. He was probably born in Pennsylvania, and migrated in early life to that part of Virginia then known as Frederick; was successful in the pursuit of wealth, and displayed his enterprise by establishing the first iron-works in that region. As the site of his foundry he selected Cedar creek, a full and bold stream, which winds its way under high cliffs, and affords now and then a stretch of bottom land. The remains of the forge are yet visible, and attest the skill and thorough workmanship of the original structure. The source from which he obtained his ore was distant ten miles from the foundry. Surrounding his establishment he possessed a fine estate of three thousand acres of land.[49]

From this scene of successful enterprise he was called to the March Convention of 1775, which held its sessions in the wooden church [St. John's] on Church Hill, in the town of Richmond. This was the first step of a career which embraced ten years, more remarkable for the number and dignity of the events that transpired during their term than any other similar period in our history. When Zane took his seat in the Convention he thought that the troubles of the times would soon pass away, and that

---

[49] "I rode over for my satisfaction and examined the site of General Zane's old iron-works. I found still standing the remains of the old stack of the furnace, which is still a huge pile of mortar, sandstone, and brick. It was formerly encased with large timbers and walls of limestone on the outer side, to resist the inward expansion of heat. The large arches for the bellows and for the escape of the melted iron are in good preservation. The works afforded employment for a number of persons. It was evident that the structure had suffered more from the hand of man than from the progress of time." (Letter of Francis B. Jones, Esq., March 12, 1857.)

the old good humor between the mother and the daughter would soon be restored. But events, which were soon to dispel all hopes of a reconciliation, were at hand. Though Zane was compelled to travel on horseback through the snows of the mountains, he was early at his post in the Convention. What memorable events in the annals of Virginia soon passed before him! He heard the eloquence of Henry in defence of his resolutions putting the Colony into military array, and was one of that majority which carried those resolutions triumphantly through the house.

In the Convention of the following July he voted for the raising of the two Virginia regiments, and for placing Henry at their head. In the December Convention of the same year he, with his compeers, assumed the direction of public affairs as fully as if Virginia had been an independent State. Still, there was no open talk of an entire separation from the mother country. How impotent are the actors themselves to foretell the progress of events in the tempest of a revolution! Three short months elapse, and the Convention of May, 1776, assembles. Zane, living on the outskirts of our territory, was again among the earliest in his seat. The first stages of the drama of Independence now passed before his eyes. He voted to instruct the delegates of Virginia in Congress to propose independence. He voted for the appointment of a committee to draft a Declaration of Rights and a plan of government for a free Commonwealth; and when those papers were passed from the honest hands of Archibald Cary—who, by the way, like Zane, was a worker in iron—to the Clerk of the House, he gave them an active and cordial support. He voted for Patrick Henry as the first Governor of the new Commonwealth he had aided in establishing, as he had already voted to confer upon him the chief command of the public forces. He now returned home to proclaim his work to the sturdy pioneers who would soon be called upon to sustain it in the field. As he was returning to his mountains he might almost have heard the sound of the simple artillery of his Western compatriot, Andrew Lewis, as it played upon the vessels of Lord Dunmore and drove that weak and faithless man beyond the waters of the new State. And he had just reached his home, when he read in the *Virginia Gazette*, of the 10th of July, a synopsis of that Declaration of Independence which had been brought forward in Congress in obedience to his own vote.

Three rapid months have flown, and he is again in the saddle on his way to Williamsburg to attend the first session of the General Assembly under the Constitution. He had already borne a prominent part in bringing about events which, even at this day, startle and thrill us as we trace their progress on the cold pages of the old journals. But these events, grand and august as they were, were but the first acts of a long and perilous drama which he was to behold to its close. It is known that the Convention of May, 1776, having filled the measure of its labors by the organization of the new government created by its act, adjourned over to October, and became the first House of Delegates under the Constitution which it had framed. Zane was accordingly a member of the first House of Delegates, and was one of that noble majority which, under the auspices of Mr. Jefferson, abolished primogeniture and entails and the collection of church levies; and, besides making active preparations for maintaining the war, laid the foundations of a judiciary system. The creation of the courts caused much discussion in our early Assemblies, and it is worthy of record that it was on a motion made on the 3d of March, 1778, to postpone indefinitely Mr. Jefferson's bill "for establishing a General Court and Courts of Assize," that the ayes and noes were first called in a Virginia Assembly;[50] and on that occasion the name of Isaac Zane

---

[50] As it may interest the curious to see a list of the first ayes and noes ever called in Virginia, I annex the vote on the indefinite postponement of the bill "for establishing a General Court and Courts of Assize." I may add that the motion to postpone was negatived by a majority of six votes, and that the bill passed the House by a majority of two votes. Pendleton was Speaker, but voted in course as a member for Caroline:

AYES—Munford, McDowell, Bowyer, Macklin, Tazewell, Patterson, *Harrison* of Charles City, Edmondson, *Smith* of Essex, Woodson, Underwood, Terry, Syme, Anderson, Wilkinson, Adams, Hairston, Nicholas (Robert Carter), Norvell, Wills, Fulgham, Callaway, Dabney, Meriwether, Crockett, Montgomery, Allen, Godfrey, Porter, Thoroughgood, Robinson, Brown, Gee, and Judkins.

NOES—Jefferson, Talbot, Thomas Hite, Lockhart, *Pendleton*, Upshaw, Strother, Randolph, *Carrington* (Paul), Bird, *George Mason*, *Pickett*, Hugh Nelson, Zane (Isaac), Smith of Frederick, *Burwell*, Abraham

appears in the negative, and in favor of the immediate establishment of the judiciary under the new government. Until the end of the war he united with Henry and his associates in carrying those measures into effect which were then deemed indispensable to the public welfare.

In common with all the Western members he cherished a devoted love of religious liberty, and in 1785 voted for the act establishing religious freedom, and thus invested his name with a glory that will only kindle the brighter for years. A friend to thé Union of the States, he approved the scheme of a Convention at Annapolis and of the General Federal Convention at Philadelphia. With the session of 1787 his public career ended. He had grown old, and he determined to retire from public life. He never married, but a relative bearing his name succeeded him in the public councils. We may add that he lived to hail the adoption of the Federal Constitution, which he greatly admired, and to vote for the re-election of his friend Washington, with whom he had voted in the March Convention of 1775 in favor of Henry's warlike resolutions. In 1795 this venerable patriot was gathered to his fathers.

Hite, Neaville, Braxton, Griffin, *Gordon*, Clapham, Daniel, Duval, Muse, Moore, Fleming, Ruffin, Harrison of Prince George, *Bullitt*, *Thornton*, Carter, Fitzhugh, Richard Lee, Bledsoe, Cocke of Washington, Wright, Prentis, Jett, and Harwood.

It is probable that the ayes and noes were introduced by Mr. Jefferson, with a view of holding up to public responsibility the men who were reluctant to put the courts in motion under the new *regime*. See Journal of the House of Delegates, January 3, 1778. The name of Moore in the above list is that of William Moore of Orange, and that of Fleming is Judge Fleming.

EBENEZER ZANE.

The namesake and relative of Zane who succeeded him in the public councils, and now held a seat in the present Convention, hailed not from Frederick, as Isaac Zane had hailed when he represented that immense principality in the early Conventions, but from the county of Ohio, which had been cut off ten or twelve years from the district of West Augusta.

Colonel Ebenezer Zane was now past middle life, and had long been known as one of the most intelligent, brave, and enterprising settlers of the extreme Northwest. As early as 1760, we are told by Withers, Colonel Zane and two of his brothers, with some friends from the South Branch of the Potomac, visited the Ohio for the purpose of making improvements and of selecting positions for their future residence. They finally determined upon the site of the present city of Wheeling, and, having made the requisite preparations, returned to their former homes, and brought out their families the ensuing year. It was characteristic of the Zanes that they possessed enterprise, tempered with prudence, and directed by sound judgment. To the bravery and good conduct of the three brothers the Wheeling settlement, according to Withers, was mainly indebted for its security and preservation during the war of the Revolution.[51] The defence of Fort Henry, which was built at the mouth of Wheeling creek, was one of the most brilliant exploits of our Indian warfare. One of the handful of men who on that occasion defied and defeated a host of Indians commanded by the notorious Girty, was Ebenezer Zane; and it is delightful to record that, while Zane was firing on the foe, his wife and sister, who were in the fort, were cutting patches and running bullets for those engaged in the fight. Nor should we pass over in silence the heroic courage of this sister of Zane's, who, though

---

[51] *Withers's Chronicles of Border Warfare and Chronicles of Western Virginia.* Clarksburg: 1831.

just returned from a boarding-school at Philadelphia, volunteered during the heat of the action to sally from the fort and fetch from a neighboring house a keg of powder—an achievement she succeeded in accomplishing amid a shower of rifle balls from the Indians who suspected the object of the mission. She escaped without a wound, and lived many years to enjoy the reputation of having performed a deed of daring unsurpassed by man or woman in ancient or modern times.[52]

It is probable that Colonel Zane's intimate knowledge of the Indian character, and of the numbers which the savage warriors could bring into the field, and his conviction of the necessity of the union of all the States in any effort to oppose them with ultimate success, rather than the positive provisions of the Federal Constitution, insensibly led him to sustain that instrument before the people, and to vote for its ratification in Convention. He accordingly opposed the policy of previous amendments, and had he been present when the question was taken (just before adjournment) on striking out the third article of the schedule of amendments proposed by the select committee, which recommended to Congress a resort to requisitions upon the States before that body proceeded to lay direct taxes, he would have followed the example of his colleague and voted in the affirmative.[53]

---

[52] Withers states that she married twice, her last husband being a Mr. Clark, and that she was living at the time of the publication of his work. For an animated account of the battle of Fort Henry (so called after Patrick Henry), see an article which originally appeared in the *American Pioneer*, from the pen of George S. M. Kiernan, and is partly copied in *Howe's Virginia*, page 409.

[53] Journal Virginia Federal Convention, page 37. Colonel Zane some years after the date of the Convention moved to Ohio, and settled the town of Zanesville, in that State. The substance of the article of Mr. Kiernan on the battle of Fort Henry may be found in *Lossing's Pictorial Field-Book of the Revolution*, Vol. II, 292. He entered the House of Delegates in 1784.

GEORGE JACKSON.

Among those adventurous and fearless men to whom Virginia is indebted for the settlement of her northwestern territory, and whose names deserve to be held in lasting remembrance, was George Jackson, who was one of the representatives in Convention of the county of Harrison, which had been created four years before, and had been called in honor of Benjamin Harrison, of "Berkeley." He was the son of John Jackson, who, in 1768, accompanied by his sons, George and Edward,[54] set out from their settlement on the South Branch of the Potomac, and under the guidance of Samuel Pringle, a British deserter, who, as early as 1761, had made a lodgment in the new territory, made an improvement at the mouth of Turkey Run, where his daughter resided as late as the year 1831.[55] An active and intelligent member of the new settlement, he gained the confidence of his associates, and having been returned at the first election of members for the county of Harrison, he took his seat with his present colleague, John Prunty, in the House of Delegates in the October session of 1785.

---

[54] It is an interesting conjecture if the distinguished Confederate chieftain, General Thomas Jonathan Jackson (born in Harrison county, and whose great-grandfather was Edward Jackson,) was of the blood of George Jackson.—EDITOR.

[55] The Pringles, John and Samuel, had deserted from Fort Pitt in 1761, and keeping up the course of the Valley river, observed a large right-hand fork (now Buckhannon), which they ascended some miles, and at the mouth of a small branch, now called Turkey Run, they took up their abode in a large hollow sycamore tree, the remains of which were not long since visible. Fearful of being apprehended and sent back prisoners to Fort Pitt, as was the fate of two companions who had deserted with them, they avoided the settlements for several years ; nor until their powder was reduced to two loads did Samuel Pringle venture into the society of white men ; and on his return he was attended by John Jackson and his sons, and by other residents of the South Branch. See *Withers's Border Warfare*, quoted in *Howe*, 188.

The first important question which he was called to vote upon was one that from the beginning of the Revolution to the adoption of the Federal Constitution more than any other perplexed our councils and laid the foundation of our early parties. Money was wanted to defray the ordinary expenses of government, to meet our own obligations, which were pressing heavily upon the Commonwealth, and to pay the Federal requisitions; and money could not be collected from the people. There was substantially no circulating medium; tobacco had fallen to a nominal price; the old channels of trade had been closed by the Revolution, and no new ones had been as yet effectually opened. Hence the various measures of relief which were brought forward and discussed from time to time. On the 14th of November, 1785, General Matthews reported from the Committee of the Whole a long amendment to the act " to postpone the collection of the tax for 1785," which struck out the whole of the act, declared that from various considerations "it is found impracticible, without involving the people in too great and deep distress, to collect from them one-half tax levied for 1785 by an act entitled ' an act to discharge the people of this Commonwealth from the payment of one-half of the revenue tax for the year 1785,' and that there is reason to believe that by the remitting of the said tax the people will be hereafter enabled to pay the revenue taxes with more ease and punctuality," and concluded with enacting the repeal of the act. On this amendment the ayes and noes were called, and Jackson and his colleague (Prunty) voted in the affirmative. It was agreed to by a vote of fifty-two to forty-two, and the bill as amended was ordered to be engrossed.[56] The following day when the

---

[56] As this was one of the test questions of the October session of 1785, I annex the votes of those who became members of the present Convention:

AYES—Benjamin Harrison (Speaker), John Trigg, Joseph Jones, Thomas Smith, George Clendenin, Ralph Humphries, Isaac Vanmeter, Parke Goodall, George Jackson, John Prunty, William White, Christopher Robertson, Andrew Moore, Richard Cary.

NOES—Zachariah Johnston, Archibald Stuart, John Tyler, David Patteson, Miles King, Charles Simms, David Stuart, Alexander White, Isaac Coles, William Thornton, Francis Corbin, Wills Riddick, James

bill came up on its passage with a rider, "authorizing the Solici-
tor-General to move for and obtain judgment for the penalty of
a bond given by any sheriff or collector who should fail to
render when required an account of the taxes by him already
collected," the vote was again taken by ayes and noes, and
resulted in the defeat of the bill by a majority of two votes;
Jackson and Prunty voting in the affirmative.

On the 13th of November of the same year another great
question was presented to the House, which foreshadowed the
amendment of the Articles of Confederation to such an extent
at least as to invest Congress with a limited control over the
commerce of the several States.   Alexander White reported from
the Committee of the Whole a resolution which it had agreed to,
in substance, "that the delegates of Virginia in Congress be
instructed to propose in that body a recommendation to the
States in Union to authorize that assembly to regulate their
trade under certain stipulations."   One of these required "that
no act of Congress that may be authorized as here proposed
shall be entered into by less than two-thirds of the confederated
States, nor be in force longer than thirteen years.'   A motion
was made to add to these words: "unless continued by a like
proportion of votes within one year immediately preceding the
expiration of the said period, or be revived in like manner at
the expiration thereof."   On this amendment the ayes and noes
were called; and it was rejected by a vote of seventy-nine noes
to twenty-eight ayes; Jackson and Prunty voting in the negative.
The original resolution as reported was then agreed to without
a division, and White was requested to carry it to the Senate
and request its concurrence therein.[57]   But the meditation of

---

Madison, William Ronald, Edmund Ruffin. Cuthbert Bullitt, Anthony
Walke, John Howell Briggs, James Innes, Thomas Matthews.
    This is a most significant record to those who read it rightly.

[57] The votes of those who became members of the present Convention were as follows :
    Ayes—Zachariah Johnston, Archibald Stuart, John Tyler, French
Strother, Charles Simms, David Stuart, Thomas Smith, George Clendenin, Isaac Coles, William Thornton, James Madison, and James
Innes.
    Noes—Benjamin Harrison, Samuel Jordan Cabell, John Trigg, Wil-
liam Watkins, Joseph Jones, Miles King, Worlich Westwood, Alex-

a single night seems to have materially changed the views of the members, for on the following morning, as soon as the House was called to order, a motion was made to rescind the order of the House transmitting the resolution to the Senate, and to resolve itself into a Committee of the Whole to reconsider it. This motion prevailed by a majority of sixty to thirty-three—ascertained by ayes and noes; and several amendments were made in committee which were reported to the House; and the resolution and amendments were ordered to lie on the table. We believe the resolution slept during the session; at all events, the ayes and noes were not again called upon it.[58]

On the 17th day of December, at the same session of the Assembly, there was brought up in the House of Delegates a not less important question, and the vote of Jackson on that occasion has connected his name honorably with one of the most liberal and most glorious enactments recorded in our statutes. On that day the engrossed bill "for establishing religious freedom" came up on its final passage, and was triumphantly carried by a vote of seventy-four to twenty—ascertained by ayes and noes. The name of George Jackson, enrolled among the friends of that measure, is the richest legacy which he could have bequeathed to his posterity.[59] From this period to the close of the session Jackson was absent from his seat.

During the October session of 1786, Jackson voted to sustain the report of the select committee, of which Madison was the chairman, which recommended the manumission of the slaves of Joseph Mayo, deceased, in pursuance of the provisions of his will, with certain restrictions—a subject which attracted much attention at the time; and on the 16th of December he voted for the amendment to the bill establishing Courts of Assize and allowing a limited stay in collecting debts under certain circum-

---

ander White, Ralph Humphries, Isaac Vanmeter, George Jackson, John Prunty, Benjamin Temple, Christopher Robertson, Francis Corbin, Willis Riddick, Edmund Ruffin, Cuthbert Bullitt, Andrew Moore, Thomas Edmunds (of Sussex), John Howell Briggs, Richard Cary.

This vote represents pretty fairly the relative strength of parties on Federal questions before the advent of the Federal Constitution.

[58] House Journal, November 30 and December 1, 1785.

[59] House Journal, December 17, 1785. See ayes and noes, *ante*.

stances—another test question of the times. He also voted on its final passage for the bill emancipating the slaves of Mayo, with certain restrictions, and in favor of the passage of the bill establishing Courts of Assize. He sustained the bill to amend and reduce into one act the several acts concerning naval collectors—a bill which involved in its discussion the litigated question of taxation by imposts, and which caused so much heat at the time that the House of Delegates ordered it to be published for three weeks in the *Virginia Gazette*, with a list of the ayes and noes appended to it! We will only say further that Jackson approved the resolutions convoking the meeting at Annapolis and the General Convention at Philadelphia, both of which passed the House without a division.

Allusion has been made more than once to the great revolution which was effected in the State of parties respecting Federal affairs by the appearance of the new Constitution, and by the able and prolonged discussions which it produced. This change was most sensibly apparent among the public men west of the Blue Ridge, who usually maintained the decided majority of the Assembly for eight or ten years previously on Federal as well as purely domestic questions. This change was to a certain extent, and to a certain extent only, perceptible in Jackson. He opposed, indeed, the policy of previous amendments, and voted for the ratification of the Federal Constitution; but he manifested his adherence to the leading principle of the old Confederation by sustaining the third article of the schedule of amendments, which aimed at the restoration of the ancient systems of requisitions instead of an immediate resort to direct taxation as prescribed by the new scheme; and he was one of the celebrated majority of twenty who retained that distinctive article among the amendments proposed by Virginia.

ALEXANDER WHITE.

Perhaps no member of the able and patriotic delegation which the West contributed to our early councils exerted a greater influence in moulding public opinion, especially during the period embraced by the treaty of peace with Great Britain and by the adoption of the Federal Constitution, than Alexander White, of Frederick. He was the son of Robert White, a surgeon in the British navy, who, having visited, about the year 1730, his relative, William Hoge, then residing in Delaware, fell in love with his daughter, whom he married, and with whom, accompanied by her father, he emigrated to Virginia, and made his home near the North Mountain, on a creek which still bears the name of White. Robert White died in the year 1752, in the sixty-fourth year of his age, and was buried in the eastern corner of the old Opecquon church-yard, in the county of Frederick, distant three miles from Winchester, where a tree marks his grave. He left three sons, of whom the youngest was the statesman whose services it is our duty to record.[60]

In June, 1783, he took his seat for the first time in the House of Delegates, when the body had been in session more than a month; and we find him immediately placed on a select committee, consisting of Joseph Carrington and Cabell (of "Union Hill"), appointed to bring in a bill " to confirm certain proceedings of the court of Cumberland county.'' At that day great vigilance was manifested by the House of Delegates in scruti-

---

[60] I am indebted for these particulars respecting the Whites to *Foote's Sketches of Virginia*, second series, page 23. The father of Robert Carter Nicholas and the father of William Cabell of ("Union Hill") were also surgeons in the British navy. The late eminent Judge Robert White was the nephew of Alexander. [From the following extract there is reason to believe that Alexander White had the advantages of education in England and of legal training : "Alexander White, son of Robert White of Virginia, Esq., matriculated January 22, 1763 ; admitted to the Inner Temple January 15, 1762." (*Gray's Inn Admission Register*, 1521-1889, by Joseph Foster, page 383.)—EDITOR.]

nizing the claims of a member to his seat—a vigilance the more remarkable from the fact that the qualifications were prescribed by law in addition to those required by the Constitution. As White had been an assistant to the county attorney in certain prosecutions, probably about the time of his election, a member moved that his case be referred to the Committee of Privileges and Elections, which made a favorable report. On the 7th of June, 1783, a bill came up for engrossment concerning one Peter Heron, a subject of His Most Christian Majesty, and master of the brigantine Lark, who, being ignorant of the language and misled by his interpreter, had, contrary to law, broken bulk before he had entered his vessel. This would seem to be a plain question at this time; but from peculiar circumstances it elicited warm debates, and the ayes and noes, which up to this date were rarely called during the session, were demanded by Mann Page and seconded by George Nicholas. The proposed amendment was adopted and the bill ordered to be engrossed by a vote of sixty to twenty-five, George Nicholas, William Cabell, Adam Stephen, French Strother, Thomas Smith, Patrick Henry, Joseph Jones, Stevens Thomson Mason, and James Gordon voting in the affirmative; and John Tyler (Speaker), Archibald Stuart, Alexander White, William Ronald, Andrew Moore, and Gabriel Jones in the negative.[61] The bill alternately passed both houses and became a law.

On the 9th of June a select committee was appointed to bring in a bill to amend an act entitled an act declaring tenants of lands, or slaves in tail, to hold the same in fee simple; and White was placed at its head, with Thomson Mason as his associate. At this day we can hardly form an adequate opinion of the intense excitement raised in the early stages of the Republic by every measure relating to sheriffs. There was no coin in the country, the circulating medium had only a nominal value, and nothing could be more arbitrary than the prices affixed in the interior to

---

[61] These gentlemen were all members of the present Convention, and in reporting their votes on the test questions of the session I give the most authentic account of their public conduct. I must caution those who consult our early journals against the remarkable errors in the names of the members. Adam Stephen is always confounded with Edward Stevens, who was also a general, and a gallant fellow. Stevens Thomson Mason's name is never printed correctly, nor Willis Riddick's.

tobacco, hemp, flour, deerskins, and other commodities receivable in kind in the payment of taxes. An astute and unscrupulous sheriff or deputy sheriff, aided by an unprincipled pettifogger, and availing himself of the authority of law, could render the rich uncomfortable and reduce men of moderate means to beggary. Hence the enormous fortunes made by the sheriffs, some of which have descended to our times; and hence the terrible malediction upon the sheriffs which was uttered by Patrick Henry in the present Convention, and which was the fiercest that ever fell from his lips. The orator had doubtless felt the sting of the viper on his own person; and he had seen hundreds of poor and virtuous citizens Iriven from their homes by the rapacity of the legal bloodsuckers, to take refuge in the haunts of the savage. The present bill was evidently designed to modify the existing laws in relation to the collection of taxes, and was sustained by White, Henry, George Nicholas, William Cabell, Zachariah Johnston, Archibald Stuart, Thomas Smith, Isaac Coles, Joseph Jones, Andrew Moore, and Gabriel Jones; Adam Stephen, French Strother, and James Gordon voting in the negative. The measure was carried by a vote of seventy-seven to seventeen.[62]

On the 10th of June an engrossed bill for the relief of the sheriffs was read the third time, and the ayes and noes were called upon its passage.

It was often difficult to procure money for the wages of the members of the General Assembly. At one time, such was the depreciation of the currency, a member would have been compelled to pay fifty dollars for a night's lodging and feeding for himself and horse, and probably feed and dress himself and his horse with his own hands. The difficulty of paying the wages of the members had become less since the termination of the war, but it was still annoying, and had to be encountered at the present session of the body. On the 11th of June a motion was made to appropriate eighteen hundred pounds out of the fund heretofore appropriated for the defence of the Chesapeake, and twelve hundred pounds out of the fund arising from recruiting duties, for the payment of the wages of the members. This proposition involved the important considerations affecting

---

[62] I do not cite the paging of the Journals of Assembly, because the dates are the surest means of reference.

the payment of the debt of the Commonwealth, to which these funds were pledged, and the public defence. These funds were composed of duties collected mainly in the East, which were mainly paid by Eastern men. The debate was long and warm. The motion was carried by a vote of forty-three to forty; White, Stephen, Smith, Coles, Henry, Joseph Jones, Stevens Thomson Mason, Robert Lawson, and Andrew Moore voting in the affirmative, and George Nicholas, Cabell (of "Union Hill"), Strother, and William Ronald, in the negative.

On the 17th of June leave was given to bring in a bill to amend the act concerning the appointment of sheriffs, and White was placed at its head; and on the 22d he was appointed chairman of a select committee, which was instructed to bring in a bill to suspend the operation of so much of any act or acts of Assembly as prohibits intercourse with British subjects, and to legalize such intercourse in certain cases.

A glimmering of a more wholesome public opinion on the subject of debts was seen on the 20th of June. The House postponed indefinitely a bill for the relief of debtors, by the decided vote of sixty-six to twenty-three; White, George Nicholas, Johnston, Stephen, and William Watkins voting in the affirmative, and Archibald Stuart and Strother in the negative.[63] The last topic of general interest during the May session of 1783 was one which at a later day produced much excitement in the public councils—the removal of the seat of government from Richmond. A committee of the House had been appointed to hold a conference with the directors of the public buildings in Richmond,[64]

---

[63] Patrick Henry and Stevens T. Mason were absent when the ayes and noes were called. I wish Henry's name had been forthcoming, but we may judge by White's vote what his would have been, as they rarely separated. That such a cool, clear-headed man as White always upheld Henry, is greatly to the honor of Henry.

[64] On the 24th of June, 1779, when the Assembly determined to remove the seat of government from Williamsburg, they appointed a board of directors of the public buildings to make arrangements for the accommodation of the members of Assembly and the public officers in Richmond. The board was composed of Turner Southall, Archibald Cary, William Watkins, Robert Goode, James Buchanan, and Robert Carter Nicholas. They had accordingly purchased certain lots and tenements, which are specified in the report of the committee of the House of Delegates, and may be learned from the Journal.

and made a report of what had occurred between them, con-
cluding with a recommendation that it was most expedient for
the progress of the settlements on Shockoe Hill that the House
declare its determination to adhere to the site already chosen on
that hill in preference to any other place within the limits of
Richmond. When the question of concurring in the resolution
of the committee came up, it was moved to amend it by striking
out all after the word " Resolved," and by inserting the words
" that the seat of government ought to be removed from the city
of Richmond to the city of Williamsburg." After an animated
discussion the vote was taken by ayes and noes, and resulted in
the rejection of the proposed amendment by a majority of sixteen; Stephen, Thomas Smith, Joseph Jones, Stevens Thomson
Mason, Robert Lawson, and Edmund Ruffin voting in the
affirmative, and George Nicholas, Cabell (of " Union Hill "),
Archibald Stuart, French Strother, William Watkins, Alexander
White, William Ronald, and Andrew Moore in the negative.
The vote was mainly founded on geographical views, but not in
strict relation to East and West. This was the last effort made
to return to Williamsburg. The large appropriations for public
buildings, which soon followed, put an end to the contest between
the ancient and the new metropolis.

There was a vote of the House on a subject connected with
the church establishment, which, though not final, shows the
views of the members on that topic, and claims a passing notice.
The House, on the 24th of June, resolved itself into Committee of the Whole on the bill to amend the several acts
concerning vestries, and the bill was reported without amendment. A motion was then made to postpone the further consideration of the bill to the second Monday in October next,
and was carried by a vote of fifty-two to twenty-eight; John
Tyler (Speaker), Zachariah Johnston, Adam Stephen, William
Watkins, Alexander White, Isaac Coles, Joseph Jones, Stevens
Thomson Mason, and Edmund Ruffin voting in the affirmative,
and George Nicholas, Cabell (of Union Hill), Archibald Stuart,
French Strother, Robert Lawson, and Andrew Moore in the
negative.[65]

[65] This was not equivalent to a vote for the indefinite postponement
of the bill. as the House was really in session in October.

At the October session of 1783 White was late in his attendance. Indeed, from the necessity of travelling on horseback, and in the absence of those helps for protection in bad weather which we now possess, the members of Assembly frequently failed to make a quorum on the first days of the session. Those who were punctual met and adjourned from day to day, and on the organization of the House held the absentees to a strict accountability. The roll was called, the names of the absent were noted, and the sergeant-at-arms was ordered to take them into custody. Nor was this a mere farce. No absent member was then allowed to take his seat without the payment of the fees, unless he could render a substantial excuse for his delinquency. On one occasion the sergeant-at-arms dispatched a messenger to a distant member, who grumbled when called upon to pay fifteen pounds for the adventure. The calling of the roll of absentees had an effect which neither the House nor the absentees dreamed of at the time. It has preserved to posterity the full names of some individuals whose connection with the Assembly could not otherwise have been proved from the Journals. In ordinary times the only appearance of the name of a member was on a regular committee appointed at the beginning of a session, when the Christian name was almost always omitted, or on the list of ayes and noes, where a similar omission frequently occurs. Indeed, the ayes and noes were rarely called from the Declaration of Independence to the peace with Great Britain; and when they were called the members were often absent. To ascertain who were members of our early Assemblies is one of the most laborious offices of the annalist. In many cases it is impracticable. In the case of the House of Burgesses it is impossible.[66]

---

[66] It is impossible to ascertain who were members of the House of Burgesses from the Journals; but the fact can be learned from the clerks' offices, and from the old almanacs. From the absence of a list of the names of members, from the constant omission of Christian names, and from the number of persons of the same surname, it requires great caution in perusing our early records not to confound individuals and even generations. Thus there are Burwells, Carters, Cabells, Bassetts, Harrisons, Carys, Diggeses, Mayos, Carringtons, Masons, Moores, Randolphs, Lees, Taylors, without number. At the present session, and at several previous ones, there was a Benjamin Har-

The first vote which White gave at the October session of 1783 was on one of the most perplexing topics of those days. We have heretofore said that, as there was no coin in the Commonwealth, and hardly a circulating medium of any kind apart from the public securities, the taxes, if paid at all, must be paid in kind. To fix upon the articles which might be taken in payment of taxes was often difficult; but it was also difficult to determine the sections of country to which the act should apply. A man living on tide-water would have a fairer chance of getting money than a man living in the interior at a time when, from many parts of the State to the seat of government, there was no public road at all, when wagons were unknown, and when a man was deemed fortunate who had succeeded in rolling a hogshead of tobacco undamaged to tide. But at the session of 1783 there was the dawn of a new policy, which, at all times admitted to be theoretically sound, might with proper caution be gradually introduced into practice; and that was the payment of taxes in money. Consequently, when on the 19th of November an engrossed bill "to amend the laws of revenue, and declaring tobacco, hemp, flour, and deerskins a payment of certain taxes," there was a most animated discussion in the House of Delegates. It was necessary to determine what taxes should be payable in either of the articles, and the sections of country to which the provisions of the bill should extend. It should seem that all were agreed that the bill should include the country west of the Blue Ridge, but should it also include the counties of the East? Should an Eastern nabob be allowed to pay his taxes in skins? Accordingly, when the bill was on its passage, a rider was offered "to admit payments of hemp in counties on the eastern side of the Blue Ridge in certain cases," which was duly read three times and adopted by the House. The question then

---

rison from Rockingham, while another of the same name was either Speaker of the House, member of Congress, or Governor, and yet another who was a member of the Council or of the House The indispensable necessity of tracing the history of each member of the one hundred and seventy of the present Convention for twenty or thirty years through volumes of Journals that have no regular list of names or indices of subjects, has cost me as much labor as would have sufficed to acquire any European language. Hence I may have made some mistakes, but I trust they are few and unimportant.

recurred on the passage of the bill with the rider, and was decided in the affirmative by a vote of sixty-one to twenty-three (ascertained by ayes and noes). Some of the ablest statesmen of the East were opposed to the mode of paying taxes in kind, now that the war was over; and it appears that nearly every negative vote was given by the members from that section of country. The names of those of the present Convention who then voted in the affirmative were Zachariah Johnston, Archibald Stuart, Thomas Smith, George Clendenin, Patrick Henry, Joseph Jones, and William Ronald; and of those who voted in the negative were George Nicholas, Alexander White, Isaac Coles, and Edmund Ruffin. The vote of White, which was almost the only one from the West, bespeaks his courage in opposing a policy which, in one shape or other, had always prevailed in Virginia, and which, however inconsistent with correct notions of political economy, seemed peculiarly applicable to the condition of the people of the West.[67]

Few questions excited keener debates and roused to a higher pitch the passions of the members who composed the General Assemblies immediately after the peace with Great Britain than those relating to citizenship. At the beginning of the Revolution many persons went abroad and continued to be loyal subjects of England. Such persons on their return to Virginia were plainly not entitled to any other privileges than those which the laws offered to the subjects of any other foreign potentate. There were, however, numerous individuals who remained at home and took no open interest in public affairs, but whose secret wishes, it was well known, were in favor of the success of the British arms. There was a strong desire manifested by others, who were nominally on the side of the Commonwealth, to save their lives and estates in the event of the subjection of the States by Great Britain. These sent a son, a brother, or an aged relative to some British port or colony as an earnest of their own good will towards the mother country, and as a means of procuring immunity from future punishment;

---

[67] In the minority was Henry Tazewell, who was particularly distinguished by his efforts to inaugurate the new system of taxation, until he withdrew from the Assembly on his election to the bench of the General Court.

while they remained themselves at home, showing just so much
fidelity to the State as was necessary to exempt them from the
penalty of treason, or, entering the public councils, they sought to
embarrass by the tricks of Parliament or by specious maneuver-
ing the measures of the patriots.[68]   As for those emigrants
who were not subjects of Great Britain, and who came with the
honest intention of taking up their abode in the Commonwealth,
there was a very slight difference of opinion respecting them.
But the element of British influence entered very generally into
all the discussions on the subject of citizenship, and in no debate
more than the one which occurred on the bill which we shall
now proceed to notice.

On the 2d day of December, 1783, an engrossed bill "for
repealing a former law, and declaring who shall be deemed citizens of this Commonwealth," was read the third time, and after
a protracted discussion, which consumed nearly the whole day,
was rejected by a vote of fifty-five to thirty one—ascertained by
ayes and noes.   The vote on the bill affords a curious study to
the political anatomist.   East and West were blended together
in beautiful confusion.   Some Eastern men had constituents of
great influence at home, who were eager for the return of
friends, and these they were unwilling to disoblige; while other
Eastern men, remembering the trouble which the Tories had
caused during the Revolution, were not indisposed to hold the
rod of terror over the heads of the returning recreants.   Opposing
sentiments were also visible in the Western vote.   There had
been few or no Tories in the West; but Western men had seen
with the deepest indignation in the public councils the policy of
those whom they regarded as the friends of the Tories, and were
not inclined to hold out to emigrants from Great Britain a too

---

[68] I have all needful respect for those Virginians who, at the outbreak
of the Revolution, elected to remain subjects of Great Britain and
withdrew from our territory.   Such a determination was altogether
legitimate.   But for those miscreants who pretended to adhere to the
cause of Virginia, and sought by private letters or advices to entice
the enemy to visit our borders, or who perplexed our early councils
with their treacherous wiles, I have no respect, but rather an unutter-
able abhorrence.   The private papers of Cornwallis, of Tarleton, of
Arnold, and of Matthews ought to be examined for evidences of the
guilt of such wretches.

welcome hand, even on the return of peace; while Western men generally, and especially the holders of vast tracts of land, were eager for the prompt settlement of the country, which could hardly be effected in a single generation without the aid of emigrants from abroad. Hence these were inclined, for the most part, to favor a liberal policy in respect of citizenship. Those who voted for the rejection of the bill were George Nicholas, Zachariah Johnston, French Strother, Alexander White, Isaac Coles, Patrick Henry, Benjamin Wilson, and William Ronald, and those who voted against the rejection were John Tyler (Speaker), Cabell (of "Union Hill"), Archibald Stuart, Thomas Smith, George Clendenin, Joseph Jones, and Stevens Thomson Mason. A few days after leave was given to bring in a new bill on the subject, and George Nicholas, Patrick Henry, Alexander White, and Joseph Jones were placed on the committee to prepare it.

From the position and wants of Virginia, as well as from the variety of her products, a trade with the West Indies on principles of reciprocity has been for nearly two centuries and a half a favorite object. While the States were colonies of Great Britain the commerce between the different settlements of the same empire was comparatively unrestricted. The most friendly relations existed between the West Indies and our ancestors; visits were interchanged, which resulted in marriages; and some names most honorably distinguished during the Revolution, and continuously to this day, were borne either by the original emigrants from the West Indies or by their immediate descendants.[69] Nor

---

[69] General Matthews, who bore arms during the Revolution, was long Speaker of the House of Delegates, a member of the present Convention, and from whom the county of Mathews has been named, was a native of St. Kitts. Howe states that the county was named after Governor Mathews, of Georgia, which is a mistake, as I, who am a townsman of Matthews, have always heard to the contrary; and I find in the chart of the Commonwealth of Virginia, compiled in the year 1790 by William Marshall, clerk of the district of Virginia, the very year of the birth of the county, that it was called after " Mr. Speaker Matthews." I take pleasure in vindicating the just fame of my townsman from the misrepresentations of careless compilers. The Mayos and the Carringtons came from Barbadoes. Farley, a West Indian, visited Colonel Byrd at Westover, and bought from him the vast area of the Saura Town-lands at a nominal price. Byrd had previously sold

when peace was secured with England, reverted eagerly to their old trade, but found it crippled with limitations and restrictions. The subject was immediately brought before the Assembly. It should seem that a British order in Council, passed on the 2d of July previous, prohibited American ships from carrying the products of this country to any of the West India islands belonging to England, and the Virginia merchant was compelled to ship his merchandise in British bottoms, or to give up the trade altogether. The House of Delegates, on the 4th of December, took the matter in hand, and having discussed it at length in Committee of the Whole, came to a resolution which was reported by White as chairman of the committee. This resolution recommended "that Congress be empowered to prohibit British vessels from being the carriers of the growth or produce of the British West India islands to these United States as long as the restriction aforesaid shall be continued on the part of Great Britain, or to concert any other mode to be adopted by the States which shall be thought effectual to counteract the designs of Great Britain with respect to American commerce." It was unanimously adopted, and a select committee, consisting of White, Jones, Henry, Cabell, Ronald, and Tazewell, was appointed to bring in a bill in pursuance of the same. It is creditable to the standing of White—a Western man as he was—that, in a matter referring to the seabord and to the interests of commerce, he should hold such a prominent place on a committee composed of the ablest men of the East. He reported the bill on the 5th, and on the 6th it was discussed and referred back to the committee, and was again reported, when it passed unanimously both houses of the Assembly.

On the 5th of December White reported a bill "to regulate elections, and to enforce the attendance of the members of

---

the lands to a Mr. Maxwell, who visited them during a pest, and was so dispirited that he begged to be excused from his bargain. Some time after the sale to Farley, Byrd's eyes were opened to their great value, and it is said that he grew sick from vexation and took to his bed. In the course of time Farley sent his son from the West Indies to inspect his lands, and the young man, calling at Colonel Byrd's, fell in love with his daughter, married her, and brought the lands, for a third time, into the family. See *Smith's Tour in America*, Volume I, printed in London about 1780.

Assembly,'' and was placed on a select committee, of which
George Nicholas was chairman and Patrick Henry a member,
for granting pardons, with certain exceptions.   On the 8th he
was appointed a member of the select committee to bring in a
bill "instructing the delegates of Virginia in Congress to convey,
by proper instrument in writing, on the part of Virginia, to the
Congress of the United States, all right, title, and claim which
the said Commonwealth hath to the lands northward of the
river Ohio, and upon the terms contained in the act of Congress
of the 13th of September last, with certain restrictions."   On
the 13th a bill prohibiting the migration of certain persons to the
Commonwealth, and for other purposes, was read a third time,
and passed the House by a vote of sixty-nine to eleven; Alexander White, Cabell (of "Union Hill"), Adam Stephen, Strother,
William Watkins, Thomas Smith, Patrick Henry, Joseph Jones,
Benjamin Wilson, William Ronald, and Andrew Moore voting
in the affirmative, and Johnston, Archibald Stuart, and George
Clendenin in the negative.

At the May session of 1784, White again appeared in the
House of Delegates as a member from Frederick.   He was
required on the 7th of June to vote on a question, which, however simple it may now appear, involved considerations, public
and private, of so grave a caste as might well account for the
reception it then met with from the Assembly.   We allude to
the definitive treaty with Great Britain.   A motion was made in
the House of Delegates "that so much of all and every act or
acts of Assembly, now in force in this Commonwealth, as prevents a due compliance with the stipulations contained in the
definitive treaty entered into between Great Britain and America,
ought to be repealed."   This motion appeared in a questionable
shape, and probably came from a questionable source.   It had
not passed through the hands of a committee.   It was absolute.
It made no exceptions or reservations whatsoever.   If it passed
the House in its present shape, and a bill in pursuance of its
spirit became a law, the entire financial system of the Commonwealth for the past ten years would be involved in inextricable
confusion.   Great trouble would fall upon the people.   Every
man who had paid a British debt into the treasury in obedience
to the enactments of good and constitutional laws would be
compelled to pay the same debt a second time, and to pay it in

coin. To make suitable arrangements for encountering such an extraordinary stipulation of the treaty would require great deliberation and consummate judgment, and delay was absolutely indispensable for the purpose. Nor did the British Government show any haste in carrying into effect those parts of the treaty which depended upon itself. There was hardly a member present from the country west of the Blue Ridge who had not seen some individual of his own household, some friend or neighbor, slain by the Indians, who had been supplied with arms and ammunition by the British forts on the frontier, and who were paid by British officers for the scalps of Virginia men, women, and children. Yet, though a year and more had elapsed since the date of the treaty, there was no movement made towards withdrawing from those forts their garrisons and their arms. On the contrary, they were kept in the highest state of preparation for immediate action. It was plain that England regarded the treaty as a mere truce that would separate us from our European allies, and that she held the Western forts in reserve as a part of her insiduous scheme. So long as those forts were retained by Great Britain, the Indians would annoy our frontiers and deluge the cabins of the settlers in blood. Did the treaty absolutely require that the British debts should be paid a second time? And if it did, had not Congress clearly exceeded its powers in acceding to such a provision? To confiscate a debt was as perfect a belligerent right as to burn a house or a ship, to take a negro from his owner, or to pocket the ancient silver flagon of a host who was dispensing to his foes the hospitalities of his house; and yet, there was no mention made of the rebuilding of our homesteads, or a restitution of our negroes, one-fifth of whom had been enticed or forced away, or of that flagon which found its way into the pocket of Cornwallis. Even the negroes on board the British ships at York, who were carried off in the face of the articles of capitulation, were not to be restored or paid for.[70] There was no reciprocity

[70] Mr. Jefferson, in his correspondence with Hammond, held that Congress had performed its duty when it recommended to the States the payment of the British debts. That Cornwallis took a piece of plate from the table of Mr. Bates may be seen in *Randall's Life of Jefferson*, Vol. I, 344. As the ayes and noes on the subject of complying with the

in such a provision; and until it was evident that Great Britain was disposed to withdraw her garrisons from a position which threatened our Northwestern frontier, it was the dictate of common sense, as well as of patriotism, to deliberate well while deliberation was possible.   The result was that the motion to repeal the acts of Assembly in conflict with the definitive treaty prevailed by a majority of twenty—ascertained by ayes and noes; White voting with the minority.[71]

On the 10th of June the House of Delegates went into Committee of the Whole on the subject of the public lands, White in the chair; and two resolutions were reported and agreed to, one of which ordered all the public lands, except such as were

---

British treaty have never been published from the Journals, I annex the full vote, the names of the members of the present Convention being in *italics*:

AYES—*Wilson Cary Nicholas*, *Archibald Stuart*, *John Marshall* (Chief Justice), *Alexander White*, James Wood. Moses Hunter, Thomas Edmunds (of Brunswick), Edward Carrington, George Wray, Bartlett Anderson, William Norvell, Philip Barbour, Larkin Smith, *William Thornton*, Richard Bland Lee, *Francis Corbin*, John Breckenridge, William Armistead, John Watkins, *Littleton Eyre*, Bennet Tompkins, *James Madison*, William Mayo, Jr., *William Ronald*, *Thomas Walke*, John Taylor (of Southampton), Bailey Washington, William Brent, *John Allen*, John Howell Briggs, Wilson Miles Cary, John Langhorne, Richard Henry Lee, Joseph Prentis, Nathaniel Nelson, and Henry Tazewell.

NOES—John Cropper, Jr., Thomas Parramore, Samuel Sherwin, John Booker, Jr., William Meredith, Michael Bowyer, *John Trigg*, Robert Clarke, George Hancock, Thomas Claiborne, Samuel Hawes, Jr.. Thomas Collier, Matthew Cheatham, Carter Henry Harrison, *French Strother*, *Joseph Jones* (of Dinwiddie), Spencer Roane, William Gatewood, Alexander Henderson, John Mosby, *Thomas Smith*, Batte Peterson, *Isaac Vanmeter*, Garland Anderson, Turner Southall, Nathaniel Wilkinson, *Patrick Henry*, Peter Saunders, William Walker, John S. Wills, Edmund Byne, John Heath, John Berryman, *William White*, Anthony Street, John Glenn, John Logan, William Randolph, *Benjamin Wilson*, Francis Worman, *Willis Riddick*, Kinchen Godwin, John Kearnes, *Ebenezer Zane*, Charles Porter, Benjamin Lankford, William Dire, Richard Bibb, *Edmund Ruffin*, Edward Bland, John Ackiss, John Bowyer, Gawin Hamilton, *Thomas Edmunds* (of Sussex), William Russell, James Montgomery, and *Thomas Matthews*.

[71] For repeated instances of the gross violation of the treaty by General Carleton, see House Journal, June 14, 1784.

necessary for the use of government, and except also the lands and houses in and adjacent to the city of Williamsburg, which ought to be given to the masters and professors of William and Mary University for the use of that seminary forever, ought to be sold for money or military certificates; and the other recommended that the lands known by the name of Gosport ought to be laid off into lots and annexed to the town of Portsmouth. A select committee was appointed to draft the bills in pursuance of the resolutions, of which White was chairman and Patrick Henry and William Grayson were members.

The public mind had not yet become reconciled to the removal of the seat of government from Williamsburg to the town of Richmond. The associations connected with the ancient metropolis, with the old House of Burgesses, and with the venerable college, and the delightful society and pleasant accommodations, which did not exist in such a rude settlement as the Richmond of that day was, long exerted an influence on the members of Assembly generally, while a sense of interest impelled the immediate representatives of Williamsburg and of the adjacent counties to make every effort to revoke the precipitate action of the Assembly of 1779. The attention of the House of Delegates had already been drawn to the public lands, as just stated, and a select committee had been appointed to bring in a bill on the subject. But on the 11th of June the House went into committee on the public lands, and a resolution was reported requiring all the public lands in and near Richmond, not necessary for the purposes of the government, to be sold, and the proceeds of the sales applied to the erection of the public buildings in Richmond, in pursuance of the act for the removal of the seat of government. As soon as the resolution was read in the House, a motion was made to strike out all after the word "Resolved," and insert "that proper measures ought to be adopted to obtain the opinion of the citizens of the Commonwealth as to the place that ought to be fixed on for the seat of government." An animated discussion arose; but the ancient city, though sustained by a strong party, was destined to succumb once more. The amendment was lost, and the bill passed by a majority of six votes only in a full House; Wilson C. Nicholas, Trigg, Archibald Stuart, Strother, Joseph Jones (of Dinwiddie), John Marshall, Richardson, Isaac Coles, Vanmeter, Patrick Henry, William White, Wilson, James Madison, Ronald,

William Grayson, and Briggs voting in the affirmative, and Miles King, Alexander White, Thomas Smith, Clendenin, Thornton, Temple, Francis Corbin, Riddick, Littleton Eyre, Gaskins, Ebenezer Zane, Edmund Ruffin, Thomas Walke, Allen, Edmunds (of Sussex), and Thomas Matthews voting in the negative.

A remarkable incident occurred on the 14th of June, which stands alone in our annals, and, as it has been most grossly though facetiously mistated, it may be proper to state the facts of the case as they appear on the Journals of the House of Delegates. It was reported to the House that Mr. John Warden had spoken most disrespectfully of the members who had voted against the repeal of the laws in conflict with the definitive treaty with Great Britain, and the matter was referred to the Committee on Privileges and Elections. The committee reported that Warden had appeared before them, and, waiving the necessity of examining any witnesses as to the charge against him, delivered in the following written acknowledgment signed with his name: "I do acknowledge that, in a mistaken opinion that the House of Delegates had voted against the payment of British debts, agreeable to the treaty of peace between America and Great Britain, I said that, if it had done so, some of them had voted against paying for the coats on their backs. A committee of the House judging this expression derogatory to the honor and justice of the House, I am sorry for the offence I have given, and assure the committee that it never was my intention to affront the dignity of the House or insult any member of it." The House immediately resolved that the acknowledgment was satisfactory, and that John Warden be discharged out of the custody of the sergeant-at-arms. This was the end of the whole affair. He was not personally before the House at all, and could have made no remark about the dust on his knees as he rose from the floor; and the blessed mother of us all has been for more than seventy years laughing herself, and making. her children laugh, at a joke as utterly destitute of a solid foundation as the currency she supplied us with during the Revolution.[72]

---

[72] Warden was a Scotchman, a prominent lawyer, a good classical scholar, and had some generous qualities as an individual, but was classed among "the tainted" during the Revolution. As some of my

Among the difficulties that beset the path of the young Commonwealth was the proper regulation of commerce. To lay uniform duties upon our own and foreign vessels and their cargoes was a simple office—on paper; but there were territorial obstacles which tended greatly to diminish the amount of revenue derived from the customs, and to prevent this easy and effectual mode of taxation from being as profitable to the State as it ought to be. In one aspect the numerous rivers of Virginia, trending from the Northwest and West to the Chesapeake, should seem to afford extraordinary facilities for agricultural success. Most of the products of our soil are bulky, and are difficult to be conveyed by land carriage to market; and the accessibility to water must exert a wonderful influence on the productive capacities of the State. In a purely agricultural view, then, nothing can well exceed the advantages of our position in this respect, and such a natural arrangement unquestionably develops the resources of the State in a greater degree than any improvement that could be contrived by the wit of man. Unfortunately each large stream has its distinctive interests, and its inhabitants are not only anxious to retain their own trade, but seek the trade of the other rivers of the Commonwealth. Hence a rivalry is excited which is fatal to the concentration of commerce in a single mart, and prevents a cheap and speedy collection of the revenue for customs. When we regard Virginia as an independent Commonwealth, such as she then was (1784), it is obvious that she could not derive that profit from the trade which was indispensably necessary for her prosperity and her safety. Commerce, to produce its full effect upon a country, must be concentrated in a single mart. For the sake of economy

---

young readers may not have heard the joke in question, and as I am inclined to indulge them with a spice of the fun that tickled their fathers, I may as well put it down. The story goes that Warden was summoned before the House in full session, and was required to beg its pardon on his knees, which he is said to have done. As soon, however, as he rose from his knees, pretending to brush the dust from his knees, though really pointing his hands toward the House, he uttered audibly in broad Scotch, and evidently with a double meaning: "Upon my word, a *dommed* DIRTY House it is indeed." For a humorous passage between Warden and William Wirt, see *Virginia Historical Register*, Vol. II, 58.

alone, such a concentration was expedient. If the State was compelled to follow the ancient custom, and establish ports of entry and custom-houses at every plantation on the banks of our numerous rivers, the expenses of collecting the revenue from customs might exceed the amount of the revenue itself and involve the public in loss. Moreover, by the multiplicity of offices, the chances of smuggling would be too numerous to be controlled by any police which the State could maintain; and those merchants who were too honest to cheat the revenue, and who deserved the aid of the State, would suffer a loss of their legitimate profits and be involved in ruin. Thus one of the most difficult problems which our early statesmen were compelled to solve was, how they could most effectually concentrate the commerce of the State with the least inconvenience to the people. Unless commercial capital could be fixed in a single mart, the State would not only fail to derive a fair revenue from the customs, but she could form no seamen; and as Virginia then was, a navy was necessary to protect her ships in peace as well as in war. It was also seen that, with the concentration of capital, the arts would prosper, and that we might be able ere long to manufacture common articles for ourselves.

To accomplish such desirable objects, a bill was presented in the House of Delegates which "restricted foreign vessels to certain ports within this Commonwealth." On the 17th of June it came up on its final passage, and was discussed with all the zeal that public and private interests could inspire by the ablest men in the body. Its provisions were closely scrutinized, and it is evident that they must have interfered sensibly with the profit and convenience of many members. Its preamble declared that our foreign commerce would be placed upon a more equal foundation; that expedition and dispatch would be better promoted if foreign vessels in loading and unloading were restricted to certain ports, and that the revenue arising from commerce would also thereby be more certainly collected. The bill then enacted that all foreign vessels shall enter, clear out, load, and unload at Norfolk, Portsmouth, Tappahannock, Yorktown, or Alexandria; and it further enacted that, as the navigating small county craft by slaves tended to discourage free white seamen, and to increase the number of free white seamen would produce public good, not more than one-third part of the persons employed in the navigation of any bay or river craft shall consist of slaves; and if the owner of slaves shall put a greater proportion on board of such craft, he shall forfeit and pay one hundred pounds for each offence. The act was not to take effect until the 10th of June, 1786. The principle on which it was based was sound, and it was a step in advance to reduce the number of ports of entry to five; but even this reduction could not suffice to attain what was practicable. The trade of that day could easily have been managed at a single office, but, divided among five, would enrich neither, and many of the advantages flowing from a concentration of trade would be lost. We should have no controlling mart of trade and money; there would be but a small gathering of people around either of the five commercial centres; the domestic arts and manufactures could not be sustained, and a sickly languor would still pervade our commercial system.

The bill passed in a full House by a majority of six; Patrick Henry, James Madison, Archibald Stuart, Patteson, Strother, King, Thomas Smith, Clendenin, Isaac Coles, Thornton, Temple, John Logan, Francis Corbin, Riddick, Eyre, Gaskins, Ebenezer Zane, Ronald, Thomas Walke, Allen, Edmunds (of Sussex), and Matthews voting in the affirmative, and John Marshall, Alexander White, Wilson C. Nicholas, John Trigg, Watkins, Joseph Jones (of Dinwiddie), Richardson, William White, Wilson, Edmund Ruffin, William Grayson, and Briggs in the negative.

As an illustration of the importance attached to the bill, it was ordered to be inserted at full length on the Journal, and, together with a copy of the Journal of the proceedings of the House thereupon, printed in handbills, and four copies thereof delivered to each member. We have already recorded a solitary instance of the publication of the ayes and noes in the public prints by order of the House of Delegates; but, so far as our researches have extended, we cannot recall an instance in which the bill itself was printed entire by a vote of the body on the face of the Journal.[73]

It is not an uninstructive office to trace the early stages of

---

[73] I have heard old men who had served in the Assembly about the period of the passage of this bill speak of it as " Madison's bill," and " Madison's scheme of building up towns."

great measures which engaged the attention of our fathers, and
which, discussed at long subsequent periods, were finally determined in our own time.   One such measure is that which has
been familiar to the present generation as the Convention question.   The first Constitution of the State was formed simultane-
ously with the adoption of the resolution instructing the delegates
of Virginia in Congress to propose independence.   It was indeed
formed at a perilous time; but it was unquestionably formed with
all the deliberation which so grave a subject demanded.   The
Federal Constitution, which effected the most thorough change
in our Government that ever was made in the institutions of a
free people, was summarily settled during a discussion of twenty-
five days; while the Constitution of the State was deliberately
examined and discussed for nearly two months by the ablest
and wisest men whom Virginia had then or, perhaps, has since
produced.   Of the practical workings of the Constitution there
was no foundation for just complaint, at least on the part of the
West.   Severe complaints had been made by the residents of the
extreme Eastern counties that the rapid creation of new counties before the Declaration of Independence would subject the
property of the State to the control of those who owned but a
small proportion of it; [74] and the statutes show that after the
adoption of the Constitution in 1776 the multiplication of new
counties continued with accelerated rapidity.   Still there was a
dissatisfaction with the existing form of government in the
Assembly, both among the Eastern and Western members; and
a serious design was entertained at the close of the war of forming a new scheme of government by the authority of the ordinary Legislature. [75]   The reasons of this extraordinary movement

---

[74] Letter of Carter to Washington, dated August or September, 1775,
in the American archives.   I have mislaid the exact reference.

[75] George Mason, in a letter to Cabell (of " Union Hill "), dated May 6,
1783, thus writes : " We are told here that the present Assembly intend
to dissolve themselves to make way for a General Convention to new-
model the Constitution.   Will such a measure be proper without a
requisition from a majority of the people ?   If it can be done without
such a requisition, may not the caprice of future Assemblies repeat it
from time to time until the Constitution shall have totally lost all stability, and anarchy introduced in its stead ? "   And on the subject of
the definitive treaty with Great Britain, he writes in the same letter :

were mainly theoretical, and may be seen in the *Notes on Virginia.*[76] It was promptly opposed by George Mason, who was not then a member of Assembly, in letters to the leading men in public life, and by others, and finally defeated. The contest was renewed at the present session by a petition from the county of Augusta praying that further time be allowed for paying hemp in discharge of taxes, and that the government of the Commonwealth be reformed.

On the 13th of June, 1784, Mr. Carter Henry Harrison, from the Committee of Propositions and Grievances, reported that so much of the Augusta petition as prayed farther time for paying hemp in discharge of taxes ought to be rejected; but "that the prayer for the reformation of the government was reasonable; that the ordinance of government, commonly called the Constitution, does not rest upon an authentic basis, and was no more than a temporary organization of government for preventing anarchy, and pointing our efforts to the two important objects of war against our then invaders, and peace and happiness among ourselves; that this, like all other acts of legislation, being subject to change by subsequent legislatures possessing equal power with themselves, should now receive those amendments which time and trial have suggested, and be rendered permanent by a power superior to that of an ordinary legislature." The report concluded with a resolution that "an ordinance pass, recommending to the good people of this Commonwealth the choice of delegates to meet in General Convention, with powers to form a Constitution of government to which all laws, present and future, should be subordinate," and providing that the existing Constitution remain in force until duly superseded by the new system. The House rejected the prayer for farther delay in paying hemp in discharge of taxes; but it referred the subject of the Convention to a Committee of the Whole.

"We are very much alarmed in this part of the country lest the Assembly should pass some laws infringing the articles of the peace, and thereby involve us in a fresh quarrel with Great Britain, who might make reprisals on our shipping or coasts, without much danger of offending the late belligerent Powers in Europe, or even the other American States; but I trust more prudent and dispassionate counsels will prevail."

[76]*Query* XIII, page 128, *et seq.*   (Randolph's edition.)

On the 21st of June the House resolved itself into committee to consider the subject—Henry Tazewell in the chair—and a resolution was reported "that so much of the petition from Augusta county as relates to an alteration of the Constitution or form of government ought to be rejected, such a measure not being within the province of the House of Delegates to assume; but, on the contrary, *it is the express duty of the representatives of the people, at all times and on all occasions, to preserve the same inviolate until a majority of all the free people shall direct a reform thereof.*"[77]   A motion was made to strike out the words in *italics*, and, after an animated discussion, passed in the negative by a majority of fifteen votes; Wilson C. Nicholas, John Marshall, Archibald Stuart, Patteson, Watkins, Clendenin, Thornton, Temple, William White, Logan, Gaskins, Madison, Ronald, and Edmunds (of Sussex) voting in the affirmative, and Patrick Henry, Alexander White, Trigg, Strother, Joseph Jones, Richardson, Thomas Smith, King, Wilson, Eyre, Ruffin, Thomas Walke, Allen, and Matthews in the negative.   A motion was then made to strike out the words "a majority of all the free people shall direct a reform thereof," and insert "it shall be constitutionally reformed," which was rejected by six votes.

The main resolution was then agreed to without a division. The next most prominent movement on the subject of calling a Convention was in 1816, when the measure would have succeeded but for a compromise, which resulted in the re-arrangement of the representation in the Senate on the basis of white population, according to the census of 1810; and it was finally determined, in 1827, to take the votes of the freeholders on the

---

[77] As the vote on striking out the words in *italics* was a test vote, and some of my young readers may be curious to know how certain prominent men voted who were not members of the present Convention, I may as well state that among the ayes were John Taylor (of Caroline), Henry Tazewell, Larkin Smith, Jones (of King George), John Breckenridge, and Joseph Prentis, and among the noes were Spencer Roane, Edmunds (of Brunswick), Turner Southall, Edward Bland, William G. Munford, John Bowyer, and William Russell. The ayes were forty-two, the noes fifty-seven; and this was a full vote, the members being very lax in their attendance throughout the session, and a bill was accordingly passed at the present session to force their attendance.

question, a majority of which was cast in favor of calling a Convention. That Convention was called by an act passed during the session of 1828-'29, and on the first Monday in October, 1829, assembled in the city of Richmond.

There was one act of this session which posterity will ever appreciate, and which was passed with entire unanimity. It was the just and beautiful tribute paid to Washington, in acknowledgment of his services during the Revolution, in the form of an address from both houses of Assembly, and by the adoption of a resolution "requesting the Executive to take measures for procuring a statue of General Washington, to be of the finest marble and of the best workmanship," with the inscription from the pen of Madison upon it, which is now so familiar to us all, and which, we fondly hope and believe, will be as familiar to posterity for generations and ages to come. Thirteen years before, in sadness and in sorrow, Virginia had voted a statue in commemoration of the patriotism of a noble Briton, who had fallen suddenly in our midst while honestly seeking to avert that storm which seemed to threaten the Colony with ruin; and now, when that storm had spent its force, with joy and gladness again she voted a statue in honor of her own son, whose valor and wisdom had defended her from peril and had given her a place among the nations of the earth.[78]

---

[78] The statue to Lord Botetourt was voted by the Assembly July 20, 1771, and, when completed, occupied a position in the old Capitol at Williamsburg very similar to that now held by the statue of Washington—between the two houses. On the removal of the seat of government the statue of Botetourt was presented to William and Mary, and was then unfortunately placed in the open air, which in our climate will soon destroy the finest work of the chisel. Exposure more than violence has marred the beauty of this admirable statue. We need not add that the address and the statue to Washington passed unanimously, though we wish the ayes had been recorded as a memorial for posterity. The committee appointed by the House of Delegates to present the address were Joseph Jones (of King George), William Grayson, Brent, Henderson, and West. From the geographical caste of the committee it is probable that the address was presented to Washington at Mount Vernon. We may add that the Executive was unrestricted in its discretion as to money in procuring the statue; and a resolution was passed on the 30th of June instructing the Treasurer to pay to the order of the Executive, out of the first money that shall

We have alluded already to the report of the committee appointed to inquire into the infraction on the part of Great Britain of the seventh article of the definitive treaty of peace with that Power—a report that shows conclusively that General Carleton had repeatedly refused to deliver to citizens of Virginia and Maryland their slaves and other property under his control in the city of New York, though the application was made by our citizens in persons. On the 23d of June the report, which had been referred to the Committee of the Whole, was debated at length, and three resolutions were reported, the first of which instructed the delegates of Virginia in Congress to lay before that body the subject-matter of the preceding report and resolution, and to request from them a remonstrance to the British Court, complaining of the aforesaid infraction of the treaty of peace, and desiring a proper reparation for the injuries consequent thereupon; that the said delegates be instructed to inform Congress that the General Assembly have no intention to interfere with the power of making treaties with foreign nations, which the Confederation has wisely vested in Congress; but it is conceived that a just regard to the national honor and interests of the citizens of this Commonwealth obliges the Assembly to withhold their co-operation in the complete fulfilment of the said treaty until the success of the aforesaid remonstrance is known, or Congress shall signify their sentiments touching the premises. The second resolution declares that so soon as reparation is made for the aforesaid infraction, or Congress shall judge it indispensably necessary, such acts of the Legislature passed during the late war as inhibit the recovery of British debts ought to be repealed, and payment made thereof in such time and manner as shall consist with the exhausted situation of this Commonwealth. And the third resolution declares, in a spirit of peace, that the further operation of all and every act or acts of Assembly concerning escheats and forfeitures from British subjects ought to be prevented. The first resolution having been read a second time, an amendment was offered to strike out from the word "thereupon" to the end of the resolution, and insert "and

---

arise under the law "for recruiting this State's quota of men to serve in the Continental army," any sum they may direct for the purpose of procuring a statue of General Washington.

that in case of refusal or unreasonable delay of due reparation the said delegates be instructed to urge that the sanction of Congress be given to the just policy of retaining so much of the debts due from the citizens of this Commonwealth to British subjects as will fully repair the losses sustained by the infraction of the treaty aforesaid." A motion was then made to amend the amendment by adding to the end thereof: "and in order to enable the said delegates to proceed therein with greater precision and effect, the Executive be requested to take immediate measures for obtaining and transmitting to them all just claims of the citizens of this Commonwealth under the treaty aforesaid." The question was put on the amendment to the amendment, and reasonable as it appears to us, and merely executive as it was, it was lost by a majority of twenty-two—Madison for the first time in his life calling out for the ayes and noes. Those who voted to sustain the amendment were Alexander White, Madison, Marshall, Wilson C. Nicholas, Archibald Stuart, Watkins, Thornton, Francis Corbin, Gaskins, Thomas Walke, Allen, and Matthews, and those who voted in the negative were Patrick Henry, Strother, Joseph Jones, Richardson, Thomas Smith, Isaac Coles, and Edmund Ruffin. The rejection of this amendment, which purported on its face to procure the materials necessary for conclusive action in the premises, can only be explained on the supposition that it came from a suspicious quarter, and that the delay consequent upon making inquiries would result in the defeat of the scheme for obtaining reparation from the British Government.

The question was then put upon the amendment, and was lost by seventeen votes; Alexander White, Madison, Marshall, Nicholas, Strother, Watkins, King, Thornton, Corbin, Gaskins, Ronald, Walke, Allen, and Matthews in the affirmative, and Patrick Henry, Joseph Jones, Thomas Smith, Coles, Riddick, and Ruffin in the negative. The rejection of this amendment by the so-called opponents of the treaty, who would be anxious to arm Congress with full power on the subject, seems to be susceptible of but one explanation, and that is, that it proceeded from a hostile source, and was designed to convey a menace that would disgust some of the friends of the original resolution.

All the resolutions were then severally agreed to, and a committee, consisting of General Matthews, Judge Tazewell, Judge

Stuart, and Jones (of King George), were appointed to prepare a bill in pursuance of the third resolution relating to escheats and forfeitures by British subjects. When we regard the wanton destruction of our property during the war by the British, and by the Tories in their ranks, in violation of all the rules of warfare observed among civilized nations, and our utter inability to retaliate upon them, the abduction of our slaves in open defiance of the articles of capitulation at York, and the positive refusal of General Carleton to deliver up to our own citizens their slaves and other property in his possession when claimed by them in person and with full proofs in the city of New York, according to the express provisions of the definitive treaty, and the retention of the forts by the British, who might at any moment involve Virginia in a bloody and expensive war with all the Indians of the Northwest and West, we may safely pronounce the conduct of our fathers in relation to the treaty to have been not only temperate and legitimate, but in the highest degree gallant and honorable.[79]

An engrossed bill on the 25th of June came up on its passage, directing the sales of the public lands in and near the city of Richmond, and was decided by ayes and noes (recorded in the Journal). The question which excited debate had not so much a reference to the intrinsic merits of the bill as to the mode and time of sale. A rider was offered directing that all lands sold for certificates should be sold at private sale and before the 1st of October next. The object of the rider was to make a good bargain for the Commonwealth by enabling her to affix a round price for lands when paid in certificates, and if the lands should not be sold for certificates, then to obtain ready money at the public sale. As certificates abounded, and there was but little cash in the treasury, such artifices were not then deemed dis-

---

[79] The case of Thomas Walke, who was a member of the present Assembly, and also of the present Convention, was singularly hard. Carleton not only refused to give up his negroes, who were then in the city of New York, but sent them off before his face to a British colony, not for the purpose of manumitting them, but of selling them for the benefit of British officers. Yet Walke might not only have been called upon, as probably was to pay a British debt which he had already paid in pursuance of law, but to pay it in coin. See the report of the committee, House Journal, June 14, 1784.

honorable, as Patrick Henry, Madison, Grayson, Stuart, Strother, Joseph Jones, Richardson, Coles, William White, Watkins, Wilson, Ronald, and Matthews voted with the majority; while Alexander White, Nicholas, Thomas Smith, Thornton, Temple, Corbin, Eyre, Gaskins, Ruffin, and Allen opposed the bill.

The last topic of the session which required a deliberate record of the opinions of the members on the Journal was the amendment of the several laws concerning marriage. In the Colony no marriage ceremony performed by any other than a minister of the Established Church was valid in law; and as the dissenters had increased to such an extent at the period of the Revolution as to compose, in the opinion of a competent judge, a moiety of the population, it was plain that an amendment of the law was demanded, not only on the faith of the doctrine laid down in the sixteenth article of the Declaration of Rights, but on the still stronger ground of public necessity. Of the ministers of the Episcopal Church who held the livings at the beginning of the war, a large majority had disappeared before its close. One of them entered the military service and attained to the rank of major-general. Another also entered the service and became a colonel.[80] Some of the ministers had taken to secular pursuits; and there were large districts of territory where no minister of the Established Church had ever been seen. To limit the performance of the ceremony of marriage to such men was virtually to interdict it altogether, and to work not only great temporary inconvenience in a new country, but the most permanent and most disastrous results to society; and hence, even before the modification of the old law, some of the patriot chiefs recommended the policy of having the ceremony performed by a clergyman of any religious persuasion, and of trusting to the Assembly to make it valid.[81] On

---

[80] Bishop Meade says that at the beginning of the war the Episcopal Church had ninety-one clergymen officiating in one hundred and sixty-four churches and chapels; at its close only twenty-eight ministers were found laboring in the less desolate parishes of the State. (*Old Churches, Ministers, &c.*, Vol. I, 17.) Muhlenburg and Charles Mynn Thurston were the military priests. Muhlenburg was a member of the December Convention of 1775, and Thurston was a member of all the Conventions except that of May, 1776.

[81] Patrick Henry gave this advice.

the 28th of June the engrossed bill to amend the several acts of Assembly concerning marriage came up on its passage, and, though far from being what it ought to be, made some necessary and important alterations of the existing laws. It passed the House of Delegates by a vote of fifty to thirty—ascertained by ayes and noes. White, who stood on the frontier of religious freedom, opposed the bill, and, demanding the ayes and noes, was sustained by Ronald, who voted for the bill, but who believed that it had gone too far on the road of reform. Those who voted in the affirmative were W. C. Nicholas, John Trigg, Archibald Stuart, Strother, Watkins, Joseph Jones (of Dinwiddie), Richardson, Thomas Smith, William White, Logan, Benjamin Wilson, Ronald, Edmunds (of Sussex), and Briggs, and those who voted in the negative were Alexander White, William Grayson, Coles, Corbin, Ruffin, Allen, and Matthews. Two days later the House adjourned.

The second session of the present General Assembly, which was held on the 19th day of October, 1784, was as remarkable for its deliberations on questions connected with religion as on those which were purely political. John Tyler, who had been nominated by Patrick Henry for the Chair in the spring of 1783, and had been elected by a large majority over Richard Henry Lee, and had been nominated by Richard Lee, and unanimously elected, at the first session of the present Assembly, held over as Speaker of the House of Delegates, and John Beckley, who had succeeded Edmund Randolph as Clerk of the House, still held that position.[82] As was usual, when the same Assembly held two sessions in a single year, there was much difficulty in obtaining a quorum, and it was not until the 30th that the House of Delegates could proceed to business. On that day the standing committees were appointed; and it is instructive to read the

---

[82] The majority of Tyler over R. H. Lee was forty-one. The rule of the House of Delegates in the sessions of the same Assembly was that the Speaker and the Clerk held over, but the term of the other officers ended with an adjournment. If the Speaker at the second session was not forthcoming, a substitute was elected to serve until he made his appearance. Thus, at the October session of 1783, on the declination of George Carrington and Charles Carter, of Stafford, Mann Page, of Spotsylvania, was elected to fill the chair until the arrival of Tyler, who was detained by indisposition.

names of the eminent men who were placed at their head.   Norvell, the colleague of Robert Carter Nicholas in the Convention
of 1776, and long known in the councils both of the Colony and
the Commonwealth, presided in the Committee of Religion;
Patrick Henry, another member of the Convention of 1776,
presided in the Committee of Privileges and Elections; Henry
Tazewell, another member of the Convention of 1776, presided
in the Committee of Propositions and Grievances; Madison,
another member of the same body, presided in the Committee
of Courts of Justice; Richard Lee, another member of the same
body, presided in the Committee of Claims; and Matthews, who
was a gallant officer of the Revolution, who was subsequently
long Speaker of the House, and whose name, conferred on one
of our counties, is fresh in our times, presided in the Committee
of Commerce.

It would not be uninteresting to record at length the legislation of the State concerning the Episcopal Church since the
Revolution, and to present the exact position which it held in
respect of other denominations at the beginning of the present
session; but we must perform this office in a summary manner.
At the first session of the Assembly in October, 1776, an act
was passed which declared "that all such laws which rendered
criminal the maintaining any opinions on matters of religion,
forbearing to repair to church, or the exercising any mode of
worship whatsoever, or which prescribes punishments for the
same, shall henceforth be of no force or validity in this Commonwealth," and "that all dissenters, of whatever denomination, from the said Church shall be totally free from all levies,
taxes, and impositions whatever toward supporting and maintaining the said Church, as it now is or may hereafter be established, or its ministers."   The act further provides that the vestries of the different parishes shall levy and assess upon the titha-
ables, including dissenters, as before, all the salaries and arrearages
due the ministers up to the 1st of the ensuing January.   These
assessments are also directed where the vestries, counting upon
them, have made engagements, and former provisions for the
poor are directed to be continued, conformist and dissenting
tithables contributing.   The fourth section reserves to the Episcopal Church her glebe lands held at the time, her churches and
chapels built or then contracted for, and all books, ornaments,

and decorations used in worship; also all arrearages of money or tobacco then due, and the perpetual benefit and enjoyment of all private donations. The act closes with directions for taking a list of tithables, and enacts that the old law of Twenty-second of George the Second, for the payment and support of the clergy, should be "suspended" until the termination of the next General Assembly. That body continued, by successive acts, to supend the old law until the session commencing October, 1779, when it repealed it entirely, declaring that this and "all and every act or acts providing salaries for the ministers, and authorizing vestries to levy the same, shall be and the same are hereby repealed." The former provisions, however, are made for arrearages of salary, the performance of engagements, and the support of the poor. And thus the case mainly stood until the first session of 1784.[83]

On the 25th of June, of the year last mentioned, the House of Delegates, just before its adjournment, postponed the consideration of a bill to incorporate the Episcopal Church until the second Monday of November following, when the House would again resolve itself into committee on the subject. This interval afforded an opportunity to those who were opposed to the measure of presenting their views to the House. Accordingly several petitions were offered on the subject of a connection of the Church with the State, and of grievances which then existed on the score of religion. On the 11th of November a memorial from sundry Baptist associations held at Dover was presented, complaining of several acts in force which they believed to be repugnant to religious liberty, especially the marriage and vestry act. The following day a memorial from the Presbyterian Church was presented, setting forth that they felt much uneasiness at the continuance of their grievances, which they complained of in a memorial presented at the last session of Assembly, increased by a prospect of addition to them by certain exceptionable measures said to be proposed to the Legislature;

[83] A succinct and accurate abstract of the laws concerning the Church to this date, by John Esten Cooke, Esq., may be seen in Bishop Meade's *Old Churches, &c.*, Vol. II, 437, and in *Foote's Sketches of Virginia* (first series), 319, *et seq.* Those who wish to consult the acts in full will refer to *Hening's Statutes at Large.* The parliamentary record of the acts will be found in the Journals.

that they disapproved of all acts incorporating the clergy of any society independent of their own, or any interference of the Legislature in the spiritual concerns of religion, and that a general assessment for its support ought, they think, to be extended to those who profess the public worship of the Deity and are comprised within the Declaration of Rights. On the 16th the memorial of the Presbyterians, presented at the last session, was referred to the Committee of the Whole.[84] On the 20th the petition of certain citizens of Lunenburg, Mecklenburg, and Amelia was presented, praying that a general assessment for the support of religion be laid, and that an act should pass incorporating the Episcopal Church. On the 1st of December a petition was presented of certain citizens of Rockbridge expressive of their hostility to assessments for the support of religion, and declaring that such legislation was impolitic, unequal, and beyond the rightful sphere of the Assembly, and that religion ought to be left to its own superior and successful influence over the minds of men. These were the only expressions of the public will which were recorded on the Journal of the House; but it is probable that, as the subject had long engaged the attention of the people, especially during the past summer, each member considered himself fully instructed upon it without the formality of a petition.

On the 11th of November the House resolved itself into committee to take the whole subject into consideration, and General Matthews reported, as the opinion of the committee, that the people of this Commonwealth, according to their respective abilities, ought to pay a moderate tax or contribution annually for the support of the Christian religion, or of some Christian Church, denomination, or connection of Christians, or of some form of Christian worship. The question upon agreeing with the report of the committee was then taken, and it was agreed with by a vote of forty-seven to thirty-two. As usual, we record the names and votes of the members who were also members of the present Convention: In the affirmative were Patrick Henry, Jones (of Dinwiddie), King, Thomas Smith, Coles,

---

[84] This and the other memorials of the Presbytery of Hanover, which are written with great ability, may be found in *Foote*, Vol. I, 319, *et seq.*

Thornton, William White, Corbin, Wills Riddick, Eyre, Gaskins, Thomas Walke, Allen, and Edmunds (of Sussex), and in the negative were James Madison, Wilson C. Nicholas, Zachariah Johnston, Archibald Stuart, Strother, Richardson, Clendenin, Humphreys, and Matthews.[85] A committee was ordered to prepare and bring in a bill in pursuance of the resolution, and Patrick Henry, Corbin, Jones (of King George), Coles, Norvell, Wray, Jones (of Dinwiddie), Carter H. Harrison, Henry Tazewell, and Prentis were placed upon it.

It has happened unfortunately for Virginia that, while her religious history has been recorded in minute detail by skilful and zealous sectarians, her political history, from the Declaration of Independence to the present day, has remained wholly uncertain.[86] Hence, her policy in religious matters at an important epoch has been imperfectly understood; and the patriotic and enlightened men who controlled her early councils have been blamed by one class of sectarians for not having gone far enough in reforming our religious institutions, and by another class as having gone too far. And it is mainly in a political aspect that all her enactments on the subject of religion ought to be viewed. Of these perplexing religious questions the observance of a plain maxim will lead us safely through the maze. On the subject of religion, as on every other, the will of the constituent is the rule of the representative. What was the will of the people

---

[85] Among the ayes were Henry Tazewell, Edmunds (of Brunswick), Nicholas Cabell, Carter H. Harrison, Edward Carrington, Jones (of King George), Richard Lee, and Joseph Prentis, and among the noes were Spencer Roane, Jacob Morton, John Breckenridge, William Russell, and Richard Bland Lee.

[86] Burk and his successors stop at the siege of York, as does Charles Campbell. Howison alone embraces the period of which I am now writing, and he candidly tells us that a very general outline only is within the scope of his work. His authorities for this date are *Foote's Sketches*, *The Literary and Evangelical Magazine of the Late Dr. John H. Rice*, and Wirt's *Life of Henry*—all excellent in their proper place; but it seems to me that the true history of our religious measures cannot be fully known without a perpetual reference to the Journals. I do not pretend to supply the omissions of preceding writers farther than is necessary to put the conduct of the members of the Assembly of 1784, who were also members of the present Convention, in its proper light.

on the subject of assessments? The proposition to lay an assessment had been for several years before them, and it was well known that the question would probably be decided by the present Assembly. Memorials expressive of that will were laid before the House of Delegates. Of all these there were two only that opposed the policy of assessments—the memorial of certain citizens of Rockbridge, which only in part related to the subject of religion,[87] and the memorial from the Baptist associations at Dover.

Even the Baptist memorial did not expressly object to an assessment, but laid the burden of its prayer on the marriage and vestry acts;[88] while the citizens of Lunenburg, Mecklenburg, and Amelia, the Episcopal, the Methodist Episcopal, and the Presbyterian Churches favored the measure.[89] There was then a preponderating majority of the people, as well as of the intelligence and wealth of the State, inclined to such a policy. The proposed scheme was also in entire unison with the sixteenth section of the Declaration of Rights, as that section simply declares that all men are equally entitled to the free exercise of religion according to the dictates of conscience; and the bill enacted, at a time when there was neither a Jew nor an infidel in the State, that each individual called upon to pay the assessment might, if he pleased, apply it to a Christian Church, or to the public schools in his own county. The question, then, arises whether the statesmen of 1784 manifested any lack of liberality or good sense in allowing the people, at their own

---

[87] House Journal, December 1, 1784. The other topic of the petition was the calling of a convention.

[88] House Journal, November 11, 1784.

[89] The Presbyterian memorial did not object to the principle of an assessment, but prayed that it should be extended to the Jew and the Mohammedan as well as the Christian, or (in its own words) *on the most liberal plan.* See the memorial at length in *Foote's Sketches,* Vol. I, 337. In the following year a very different view was taken in the memorial of the Presbytery of Hanover, which was drawn with extraordinary ability by Graham, who doubtless drafted the petition of the Rockbridge people, presented at the present session of the Assembly.

solicitation, to tax themselves for the purpose of religious or general instruction, as they might at the time of giving in their lists deem proper.

But it is a great mistake to suppose that the assessment was a religious question at all. It was strictly meant as a matter of police. It had no religious obligation whatever. So far as it may be supposed to have any religious bearing, it was merely permissive. It instructed the tax-gatherer to receive a certain sum of money from a given individual and pay it to any religious society that individual might choose to name, or to appropriate it to the education fund of his county. It was substantially a tax in favor of education, with an alternative that allowed a different application of the money if the tax payer so pleased. It was this option alone which imparted to the measure a religious aspect, and it was in the power of the tax-payer to deprive it of that aspect at his own will and pleasure. It had no more connection with Church and State than the law has which punishes the infraction of Sunday, which prevents a congregation from being disturbed in time of public worship, or which hangs a man who slays a parson.

There was yet another view of this question that presented itself most favorably to the far-seeing friends of religious freedom, which has been wholly overlooked by those who have condemned assessments with such extreme severity. By requiring every person to pay a certain sum towards the religious or literary instruction of his neighbors, the act might indirectly tend, so far as it exerted any religious influence at all, to strengthen, and even to multiply, the various sects in the community, and thus, by dividing the people into schisms, establish a more powerful barrier than law against the ascendancy of any one denomination. Even at this day it is the opinion of our most philosophic statesmen that the greatest obstacle to the establishment of a single church in the State is to be found, not so much in positive law—constitutional or statute—as in the infinite multiplicity of sects. Should a sect include a majority of the people, it may repeal the law and even amend the Constitution; and it is more probable that such a sect might obtain a share in the government than that all the various sects should unite in stripping themselves of their equal privileges and position in the eye of the law and subject themselves to the authoritative and arbitrary rule of a rival denomination.[90]

On the 17th of November the House of Delegates resolved itself into committee on the subject of religion, and when the committee rose General Matthews reported two resolutions, one of which declared that so much of the memorial of the Hanover Presbytery and of the Baptist associations as prays that the laws regulating the celebration of marriages and relative to the construction of vestries was reasonable; and the second, that acts ought to pass for the incorporation of all religious societies which may apply for the same. The first resolution, having been read a second time, was agreed to by the House without a division. On the second resolution there was a difference of opinion, and a vote was taken upon it by ayes and noes, which resulted in its passage by the large majority of thirty-nine. Alexander White demanded that the names of the members be recorded in the Journal, and was seconded by Carter Henry Harrison. Those who voted in the affirmative were Patrick Henry, Archibald Stuart, Watkins, Joseph Jones (of Dinwiddie), King, Richardson, Thomas Smith, Coles, Humphreys, Temple, Wills Riddick, Corbin, Littleton Eyre, Gaskins, Ruffin, Allen, Briggs, and Matthews,[91] and those who voted in the negative

---

[90] I have no means at hand of ascertaining the number of the persons in full communion with the various sects in Virginia, but my general recollection of the numbers would give to the Baptist Church (including the Campbellite and other branches) 100,000; the Methodist Episcopal and the Methodist Protestant, together, 100,000; the Presbyterian (old and new school), about 40,000; the Protestant Episcopal, about 8,000; the Catholics and Jews, united, not more than 5,000. It is thus evident that if the Methodists and Baptists were to sink their distinctive tenets, and unite on a common platform as a single sect, they could call a convention and create a church establishment whenever they pleased. I am aware that the Baptist and Methodist Churches include a greater proportion of our slaves than the Presbyterian and the Episcopal, but any reasonable deduction on this account would still make them all-powerful as a united body. Hence, our protection from a religious establishment is founded more in the multiplicity of sects than in the law or the Constitution.

[91] Among those not members of the present Convention who voted in the affirmative were Spencer Roane, Cropper, N. Cabell, Edmunds (of Brunswick), Wray, Jones (of King George), Richard Bland Lee,

were James Madison, Alexander White, Zachariah Johnston, W. C. Nicholas, Trigg, Strother, and Clendenin. Committees were appointed to prepare and report bills for each of the two resolutions; those composing the committee to report a billl incorporating the Protestant Episcopal Church were Carter Henry Harrison, Patrick Henry, Thomas Smith, William Anderson, and Henry Tazewell. On the 11th of December Mr. Harrison reported the bill to incorporate the Episcopal Church, which was read a first time and ordered to be read a second time. It was before the Committee of the Whole on the 18th and the 20th, and on the 22d it passed the House by a vote of forty-seven to thirty-eight—ascertained by ayes and noes; James Madison,[92] John Marshall, William Grayson, Benjamin Harrison (of Berkeley), Joseph Jones (of Dinwiddie), Miles King, Joseph Jones (of King George), Thornton, Corbin, Willis Riddick, Eyre, Ronald, Ruffin, Edmunds (of Sussex), and Briggs voting in the affirmative, and W. C. Nicholas, Zachariah Johnston, Archibald Stuart, John Trigg, Strother, Clendenin, Humphreys, and Isaac Vanmeter in the negative.[93]

The incorporation of the clergy of the Protestant Episcopal Church was an important incident in the religious controversy which began with the first Assembly in October, 1776, and was terminated, in its legislative aspect, by the passage of the act of 1802, which ordered a general sale of the glebe lands. It tended to infuse a bitterness in the subsequent discussions not before known, and was upheld by one party with all its zeal, and

---

and Richard Lee, and in the negative were John Taylor (of Caroline), Nathaniel Wilkerson, John Breckenridge, and William Russell. Many members were absent.

[92] Madison had recently voted against the resolution which offered the privileges of incorporation to all sects. The reason of his present vote may be inferred presently.

[93] Among those not members of the present Convention who voted for the bill were Cropper, N. Cabell, Edward Carrington, C. H. Harrison, Richard Lee, and Henry Tazewell, and those who voted against it were Spencer Roane, John Nicholas, Jacob Morton, Henderson, R. B. Lee, and Michael Bowyer. John Taylor (of Caroline) was absent. Alexander White had asked and obtained leave of absence on the 20th of November, but was present on the 29th, and voted on that day, as will be seen hereafter.

denounced by all not included in its scope with unusual severity. At this day we may safely regard the question on its own merits, and form a correct opinion of the conduct of our fathers on a trying occasion.

The first question that arises is, whether any act of incorporation ought to be passed by the General Assembly; the second, whether, if an act of incorporation ought to pass, ought an act incorporating a religions society receive the sanction of that body ; and the third, whether the special provisions of the act in question were just and proper. There have always been a few of our earlier, as well as later, politicians who were opposed to the granting of acts of incorporation for any purpose whatever. As late as the Convention of 1829 Mr. Giles presented a proposition on the subject, and intended to have put forth all his strength in demonstrating their dangerous effects;[94] but the measure was not sanctioned by that body. In the opinion of such politicians no association of citizens for any public purpose should be allowed to sue or be sued, or to have a common seal, but must be compelled to conduct their affairs through the cumbrous and perilous machinery of trustees. But no such doctrine was advanced in any petition from the people, or was countenanced by the Assembly. On the contrary, acts of incorporation were as freely sought and as freely granted for any useful enterprise of a public nature, conducted by the joint capital of several individuals, then as now. Perhaps, from obvious reasons, grants of exclusive privileges were then made more readily than at present. During the present session the exclusive privilege of running stage-coaches between Williamsburg and Hampton had been granted to John Hoomes for a term of years, and the exclusive right of constructing and managing certain boats for the term of ten years was conferred upon James Rumsey.[95] So

---

[94] He was prevented by indisposition from a constant attendance during the session, and happened to be absent when his proposition was called up and rejected. But the body was so much opposed to the proposition that it rather ungraciously refused to reconsider their vote on the subject with a view of allowing Mr. Giles to present his views at length.

[95] House Journal, November 15, 1784. The State, however, could at any time take possession of his boats and determine the charter by paying him ten thousand pounds, Virginia currency, in gold or silver.

far, then, as the opinions of the people and of the Assembly were concerned, there was no serious ground for hostility to the bill arising from theoretical views of the nature and effect of incorporations.

The second question is, whether there was anything in the character of religious associations which should exclude them from the privileges which were freely accorded to all others. Without entering into the minute discussion of the question whether the proprietors of a church should not have the privilege of holding their property in the same manner in which a college building or a manufacturing mill is held, and " be relieved from the precarious fidelity of trustees," [96] it is sufficient to say that, although there had been a period of several months allowed by the postponement of the bill for the ascertainment of public opinion on the subject, none of the memorials or petitions from societies or individuals recorded in the Journals objected to the expediency of incorporating religious associations.

It is true that the Presbytery of Hanover of October, 1784, objected to the incorporation of the clergy *as a class* distinct from the people; but it is obvious that this objection extended to the form of incorporation only, and not to the expediency of incorporating the Church as an association. And this view is sustained by the explicit declaration of the same Presbytery, in its memorial of the 19th of May, 1785—drawn by the skilful and unconquerable Graham after the passage of the Episcopal Church bill—that " we (the Presbytery of Hanover) do not desire to oppose the incorporation of that Church for the better management of its *temporalities*." [97] There was then not a single memorial before the Assembly, which specifically objected to the incorporation of a religious society, not excepting the Rockbridge petition, which objected to assessments only, [98] and which,

---

[96] I quote these words from the memorial of the Presbytery of Hanover of May 19, 1784, in *Foote*, Vol. I, 334.

[97] *Foote*, Vol. I, 343. The *italics* are in the printed memorial.

[98] As the Rockbridge petition was evidently drawn by the same hand that drafted the Hanover memorial of 1785, which favored acts of incorporation, had it spoken at all, it would have been in favor of incorporating religious associations. It may be observed that the objection of Hanover Presbytery in their memorial of October, 1784,

had it been opposed to incorporations, would have been out-weighed by the petition from Lunenburg, Mecklenburg, and Amelia, either of which counties equalled Rockbridge in intelligence, and exceeded it in population and resources. When we regard the time that elapsed between the committal of the Episcopal Church bill on the 25th of June, and its third reading on the 22d of December following, the unparalleled excitement produced by the religious disputes in the interval, and the absence of all objections from the people to the policy of incorporating religious associations, it is hard to see on what ground the Assembly could refuse to grant a mere act of incorporation, which was freely offered to all religious sects by a formal resolution, to any one religious body which might apply for the same. So far, then, the conduct of the Assembly was not only free from serious objection, but was in the highest degree liberal, and in perfect consonance with the express and implied wishes of the people.

The third, and most popular, objection to the bill was the nature of its provisions. The bill declared that every minister of the Protestant Episcopal Church, now holding a parish in this Commonwealth, either by appointment from the vestry or induction from a governor, and all the vestrymen in the different parishes now instituted, or which may hereafter be instituted, within this Commonwealth—that is to say, the minister and vestry of each parish, respectively, or, in case of a vacancy, the vestry of each parish, and their successors forever—are hereby made a body corporate and politic, by the name of "The Minister and Vestry of the Protestant Episcopal Church," in the parish in which they respectively reside. Each vestry could hold property not exceeding in income eight hundred pounds per annum, could sue and be sued, and perform all necessary acts of a vestry or corporation, and hold the glebe lands and the churches. A Convention of the Church was to be called, and the government of the Church to be vested in the Convention, both as to its forms and doctrines. Such were the principal enactments of the bill; and so far as the forms are concerned, as

---

against the bill as incorporating the clergy as a class, was removed by including the vestry, as well as the minister, in the name of the corporation.

the same privilege of prescribing forms for themselves was conceded to all churches which would apply for a charter, there was no favoritism in the provisions.   But the Episcopal Church was entitled by this bill to hold all the churches and glebes which it was entitled to hold under the act of the October session of 1776.   And the question arises here whether the churches and glebes held by the Episcopal Church belonged to that Church, as such, or to the people.

Looking at this question with the convictions and feelings of this day, and regarding it as an original question presenting itself for the first time, few would hesitate to say that the people who paid for the building of the churches, and for the purchase of the glebes, were their rightful proprietors.   The Episcopal Church was originally chosen as an efficient instrumentality in conveying moral and religious instruction to the people, and was as essentially an integral part of the Government as a judiciary constructed for the dispensation of justice, or a treasury department for the receipt and disbursement of the public revenue; and it was fair to suppose that the clergy and vestry had no more right to the houses in which they preached and worshipped than a judge possesses to the hall in which he performs his duty, or the treasurer to the room in the capitol in which he keeps his office.   The right of property in the churches and glebes should seem to be in the Commonwealth, and it should appear that to confer upon a single sect the property belonging to all the people would be manifestly unwise and unjust, and, as the Assembly did not propose to confer an equal amount of property upon all the sects, it would be in violation of the fourth article of the Declaration of Rights, which enacts that no man, or set of men, are entitled to exclusive privileges from the community.   Such is the view which persons of the present day are apt to take of the subject when presented as an original question.

But for more than eight years it had ceased to be an original question.   There cannot be a greater mistake than that into which some theoretical writers have fallen, which supposes that when our fathers sundered the tie that bound the Colony to the King we were resolved into a state of nature.   The only change effected in our condition by the deposition of the King was a change of a foreign executive for one of our own making.   The body of our jurisprudence remained just as it had been before. Property in possession of its lawful owners was deemed as sacred as it ever was, and was so declared to be in the Declaration of Rights, and was held by the same tenures. If any property may appear to have been invaded by the Declaration of Rights it was property in slaves; yet, though there were few or no slaves at that time in that vast territory beyond the Blue Ridge, none deemed its tenure less secure after the adoption of the Declaration of Rights than before. All the provisions of that artificial polity, the growth of a thousand years, and the emblem of a high civilization, which were binding before the Declaration of Rights was adopted, were equally sacred after its adoption. Hence, when, after the Declaration of Independence, the rights of individuals or associations were concerned, the question was not what the law of nature said upon the subject, but what were the laws of the land.

There were grave objections to the division of the church property at this time (1784) in the mode just alluded to, which had great weight with the eminent jurists who were to vote upon the bill.[99] Indeed, the question of the disposition of the churches and glebes was far from being an original question. Setting aside all right and title held by the Episcopal Church to its houses and lands prior to 1776, the members of the House knew that the Convention of that year which framed the Constitution not only did not repeal the corporate character of the Church, but sought to make it more efficient by amending its liturgy. At the close of the session of the Convention that declared independence, the Episcopal Church was as much an establishment as she had been from the passage of the act of the

---

[99] The House of Delegates then held as able men as ever appeared in our councils. Among them were James Madison, who was always placed at the head of the Committee on the Judiciary; Henry Tazewell, who was soon after the present date elected a judge of the General Court and then a judge of the Court of Appeals; John Marshall, afterwards Chief Justice of the United States; William Grayson, one of the ablest lawyers as well as statesmen of his age; Jones of King George, and Jones of Dinwiddie, and other distinguished men, who voted for the bill; while the only able lawyer who opposed it was Spencer Roane, then a young man, and Archibald Stuart, then also very young. John Taylor (of Caroline) was absent.

twenty-second year of George the Second. Great changes had
been made in her authority and revenues at the October session
of 1776; but, shorn as she was, she was still an establishment;
and the act of that session distinctly reserved to her her churches
and her glebes.   How far it was just and proper to confirm the
Church in her title to property under existing laws we shall not
discuss here; but it was a grave question with eminent lawyers
whether the act of 1776 did not settle the question of property
forever.   Supposing the Church had not a perfect title, the
right of the Assembly to make donations was unrestricted by
the Constitution ; and, although a donation or confirmation of
title may appear to trench upon the Declaration of Rights, that
instrument was then believed by prominent members of the
Convention that framed it to be no part of the Constitution; nor
had any decision settling its relation to the Constitution then
been made.[100]

In the eye of the law the Assembly was competent to bestow
public property upon literary or religious associations according
to its discretion ; and the act of 1776 confirming the right of the
Church to the property held in possession, was, in its nature
and extent, insignificant when compared with the act of the
same session converting all the lands in the Commonwealth held
by tenants in tail into fee simple.   The members of the Assembly well knew that if they made any new enactment touching
the property of the Church, the subject would immediately be
brought before the courts, and what would be the decision of the
court of the last resort was hardly a matter of doubt.   Indeed,
nine years later, when the Assembly had passed the act of 1802
ordering the glebes to be sold, that court would, but for the sudden death of its chief, have pronounced that act unconstitutional,
and restored the glebes to the Episcopal Church.[101]   With these
facts before them, the members of the House, in a spirit of prudence and peace, made no new provision in the present bill

---

[100] Edmund Randolph denied its authority as a part of the Constitution as late as the year 1788, and that denial was made in the presence
of the present Convention.

[101] The Court of Appeals had heard the argument in the case, and
Pendleton had prepared an opinion in favor of the Church, which he
was to have delivered the day on which he died.

respecting the property of the Church, but simply remitted it to the rights and titles which it enjoyed under the act of 1776—an act made by the identical men who composed the Convention of 1776, and were sitting as the House of Delegates under the Constitution which they had formed. That act was either constitutional, or it was not. If it was constitutional, then the present bill did not confer any right or title to property which the Church did not already possess under the sanction of law; and if it was unconstitutional, then it was the province of the judiciary to decide the question, and the provisions of the present bill in respect to property were of no avail. It will thus appear, from a full view of the case, that the majority which carried the bill incorporating the Protestant Episcopal Church acted with that wise foresight that became a deliberate body, and in the full spirit of religious freedom.

In a historical as well as in a moral view, it is much to be regretted that the religious controversy, which was soon to wage more fiercely than ever, had not ended in our legislative halls with the passage of this bill, or if it was destined to continue, had not been transferred to the cooler arena of the courts. Before the close of the session religious freedom was established as substantially as it was in the following year; and the speedy and successful adjustment of this vexed question might have saved from decay many of those venerable structures in which our fathers worshipped, and which ultimately became the prey of the beasts of the field and the fowls of the air, and the still more brutal spoliation of man; and might have rescued from desecration those noble monuments which the piety of the people had reared to protect and honor the abodes of the dead. It might have prevented the almost entire extinction of an illustrious branch of the Church of Christ, which had achieved great and glorious things in the common cause, and the literature of which is still the pride of the Anglo-Saxon race;[102] and it might

---

[102] The memorial of the Presbytery of Hanover estimated the value of church property at "several hundred thousand pounds"; but the sales contributed the merest pittance to the public funds. The downfall of the Episcopal Church was owing partly to the prejudice arising from its former connection with the British Crown, and the hostility which an establishment, as such, must necessarily excite in any country in proportion that it is free; partly from the large emigration from

have filled the pulpit with learned and faithful ministers throughout a populous region of our country at a time when none other
existed to take their places, and might thus in some measure
have tended to avert that torrent of infidelity which was soon to
sweep over the land and scatter destruction in its train.

We now advert to the action of the committee appointed to
bring in a bill providing for an assessment in pursuance of the
resolution adopted by the House on the 11th of November.
Patrick Henry had been placed at its head, but he had in the
mean time been elected Governor, and Francis Corbin, on the
2d of December, reported a bill "establishing a provision
for teachers of the Christian religion," which was immediately
read a first time and ordered to be read a second time.   On
Friday, the 3d, it was read a second time and referred to a committee of the whole House for the following Thursday.   Finally,
on the 24th the engrossed bill came up on its passage, and a
motion was made that its further consideration be postponed
until the fourth Thursday in November next; James Madison,
Wilson C. Nicholas, Zachariah Johnston, Archibald Stuart, John

---

Eastern Virginia to the upper and western counties and to Kentucky,
but mainly from the irreligious demeanor of its clergy, both before and
after the Revolution.   There was no hostility to the Episcopal Church
as a Church of Christ.   If any man felt that hostility, Samuel Davies
might have been expected to feel it.   That illustrious man was the
father of the Presbyterian Church in Virginia, and was as fearless in
the expression of his opinions as he was able in defending them.
But he candidly declares that, "had the doctrines of the Gospel been
solemnly and faithfully preached, I am persuaded that there would
have been few dissenters in these parts of Virginia, for their first objections were not against the rites and ceremonies of that Church, much
less against her excellent articles, but against the general strain of the
doctrines delivered from the pulpit; so that at first they were not
properly dissenters from the original Constitution of the Church of
England, but the most strict adherents to it, and only dissented from
those who had forsaken it."   One thing our fathers owed to the old
clergy of the Church, who, though they were sometimes tempted to
hunt foxes, fight duels, and to drink hard, were capital scholars, and
and taught Latin and Greek and mathematics quite as thoroughly as
they have been taught since.   It is to this source mainly that we are
indebted for that admirable literary preparation which made the
State papers of our public men worthy of the cause in which they were
engaged.

Trigg, Strother, Clendenin, Humphreys, Isaac Vanmeter, Ronald, Edmunds (of Sussex), Briggs, and Matthews voting in the affirmative, and John Marshall, Benjamin Harrison (of Berkeley), Watkins, Joseph Jones (of Dinwiddie), Miles King, Thomas Smith, Thornton, Corbin, Wills Riddick, Littleton Eyre, Edmund Ruffin, Thomas Walke, and John Allen voting in the negative. The motion prevailed by a vote of forty-five to thirty-eight.[103]

The postponement was expressly designed to submit the question of assessment to the people. Accordingly, the House ordered "that the bill with the ayes and noes on the question of postponement be published in handbills, and twelve copies thereof to be delivered to each member of the General Assembly, to be distributed in their respective counties; and the people thereof be requested to signify their opinion respecting the adoption of such a bill to the next session of Assembly." We have already shown that the question of assessments had no connection with the notion of an establishment, but arose from a conviction that some certain means of support might be afforded to religious teachers of all sects, who might thus be induced to settle in the Commonwealth. The preamble of the bill declares "that the general diffusion of Christian knowledge hath a natural tendency to correct the morals of men, restrain their vices, and preserve the peace of society, which cannot be effected without a competent provision for learned teachers who may be thereby enabled to devote their time and attention to the duty of instructing such citizens as from their circumstances and want of education cannot otherwise attain such knowledge; and it is judged that such provision may be made by the Legislature without counteracting the liberal principle heretofore adopted and intended to be preserved, by abolishing all distinctions of pre-eminence amongst the different societies or communities of

---

[103] Among those not members of the present Convention who voted for the postponement were Spencer Roane, Nicholas Cabell, Jacob Morton, M. Bowyer, Moses Hunter, John Nicholas, John Breckenridge, Charles Porter, John Bowyer, Gawin Hamilton, Isaac Zane, John Hopkins, Mann Page, and William Brent, and against it were Henry Tazewell, Carter H. Harrison, Philip Barbour, Joseph Jones (of King George), R. B. Lee, Richard Lee, and Nathaniel Nelson. The vote shows a very thin House.

Christians." The obvious tendency of the bill was to create
and sustain a variety of sects, and thus most effectually provide
against the predominance of any one of them in particular.
Nor should we overlook, in forming an opinion of the policy of
the bill, the utter destitution of religious services at that day
throughout entire districts of country. The old system of
church supply had gone down, and the new had not taken its
place. A single fact will show the absence of intelligent preaching in some populous parts of the State. More than four years
later two young Presbyterian missionaries from the Valley visited
Petersburg, and there preached the first sermon ever delivered
by a clergyman of their sect in that town.[104]

The only other topic connected with the clergy that was acted
upon during the present session was the amendment of the law
passed at the preceding sessions concerning marriages. It was
now enacted "that it shall and may be lawful for any ordained
minister of the Gospel, in regular communion with any society
of Christians, and every such minister is hereby authorized, to
celebrate the rites of matrimony according to the forms of the
church to which he belongs," and thus placed the law of the
land on that just and equal footing which it now holds.

Among the political questions of the session was one which
has, in some of its forms, maintained an interest to the present
time, and which related to the extradition of fugitives from
justice. The position of the United States between the territories of Great Britain on the north and northwest, and those of
Spain on the west and south, rendered it important that a good
understanding should exist respecting the delivery of persons
who, having committed a crime within the dominions of one of
the Powers, might flee into those of another. On the 26th
of November John Breckenridge, from the Committee of the
Whole, reported certain amendments made therein to a bill "for

---

[104] For the religious condition of the people of that day, even in the
thickly-settled parts of the country, consult the narrative of the two
missionaries mentioned above in the *Life of Dr. A. Alexander of
Princeton*, by his son. Alexander was one of the young preachers,
and the other was Benjamin Porter Grigsby, who afterwards became
the pastor of the first Presbyterian church ever gathered in Norfolk,
who died in the prime of manhood from yellow-fever, and whose
remains now repose in the yard of Trinity church, Portsmouth.

punishing certain offences injurious to the tranquility of this Commonwealth"; and a motion was made to strike out the first amendment and insert in its place an amendment which declared the desire of Virginia, in all cases, to manifest her reverence for the laws of nations, to cultivate amity and peace between the United States and foreign Powers, and to support the dignity and energy of the Federal Constitution; and enacted "that if any citizen of Virginia should go beyond the limits of the United States within the acknowledged jurisdiction of any civilized nation, and should within the same commit any crime for which, in the judgment of the United States, in Congress assembled, the law of nations, or any treaty between the United States and a foreign nation, requires him to be surrendered to the offended nation, and shall thereafter flee within the limits of this Commonwealth, and the sovereign of the offended nation shall exhibit to the United States, in Congress assembled, due and satisfactory evidence of the same, with a demand for the offender, and the United States, in Congress assembled, shall thereupon notify each demand to the Executive of this State, and call for the surrender of such offender, the Governor, with the advice of the Council of State, is hereby authorized to cause him to be apprehended, and conveyed and delivered to such person or persons as the United States, in Congress assembled, may prescribe." This limited law of extradition, which applied to our own citizens, but not to those of any other nation, was discussed at great length. Suspicions of England were rife among our wisest statesmen; and it was also feared by some that Spain might seek to entrap individuals living on our frontiers, and by the instrumentality of such a provision get them into her power. The motion prevailed by a majority of four votes only; James Madison, John Marshall, Johnston, Archibald Stuart, Watkins, Isaac Coles, Humphreys, Littleton Eyre, Ruffin, Thomas Walke, and Matthews voting in the affirmative, and John Tyler (Speaker), Alexander White, Wilson C. Nicholas, John Trigg, Strother, Joseph Jones (of Dinwiddie), Thomas Smith, Clendenin, Isaac Vanmeter, Corbin, Gaskins, Ronald, and Briggs in the negative.[105] Most of the votes on such questions had a geographical

---

[105] Among those not members of the present Convention who sustained the amendment were Henry Tazewell, John Taylor (of Caroline), Jacob Morton, C. H. Harrison, W. Walker, Philip Barbour, Jones

tinge, which the curious eye may detect; and it will occur to the reader that a great man, whose name is second on the roll of ayes, was, a few years later, to make one of the most extraordinary displays of his intellect on a question somewhat similar to the present.[106]

The subject of the British debts was again considered; and a series of resolutions was reported from the Committee of the Whole, the purport of which was a repeal of all acts of Assembly in conflict with the fourth article of the definitive treaty of peace; the recommendation that interest should not be stated between the 19th day of April, 1775, and the 3d of March, 1783; the balance due British creditors should be paid in seven annual instalments, the first of which should become due on the 1st of April, 1786; the suggestion of providing for a more ready collection of the British debts than was practicable under existing laws; and a repeal of the law concerning forfeitures and escheats from British subjects. All of the series were agreed to without a division, and Edward Carrington, Jones (of King George), Madison, Grayson, Carter H. Harrison, and Matthews were ordered to bring in the corresponding bills.

The House soon passed a bill entitled an "act for the enabling of British merchants to recover their debts from the citizens of this Commonwealth." The bill was sent to the Senate, and was returned with many verbal alterations, to which the House would not consent. A conference was granted—Tazewell, Madison, Breckenridge, Stuart, and Henderson acting on the part of the House—and Tazewell reported the result of the conference in

---

(of King George), R. B. Lee, William Russell, and Charles Porter; and those who opposed it were John Cropper, Hunter, Wray, West, Thomas Edmunds (of Surry), Richard Lee, and Joseph Prentis. Charles Porter, last named in the ayes, was the colleague of Madison, and was the person who defeated the great statesman at the spring election of 1777. Mr. Madison told Governor Coles, who told me, that he lost his election because he would not treat; and I am afraid that Mr. Porter, who was a near kinsman of mine, gained his by pursuing a different policy. A venerable friend assured me that Mr. Porter, who ominously hailed from the "*Raccoon Ford*" of the Rapid Ann, was unsurpassed in the tact of electioneering.

[106] I allude to Judge Marshall's speech, in the case of Jonathan Robbins, delivered in the House of Representatives on the 7th of March, 1800. See a pretty full report in *Benton's Debates*, Vol. I, 457, *et seq.*

the shape of an amendment, which was amended by the House. At this stage of the contest, before the action of the Senate was received, the House was compelled, by the absence of a quorum, to adjourn *sine die.*[107]

As an illustration of the pecuniary condition of the State at this time, we may notice an engrossed bill, which came up on its passage on the 30th of December, "discharging the people of this Commonwealth from the payment of the revenue tax for the year 1785." It was debated with much warmth, partly on considerations affecting the true theory of taxation, and partly on those drawn from the necessities of the people. It was carried by a vote of fifty-one to twenty-nine; Madison, Grayson, Marshall, W. C. Nicholas, Archibald Stuart, Benjamin Harrison, Strother, Joseph Jones (of Dinwiddie), King, Clendenin, Humphreys, Eyre, Ronald, Edmunds (of Sussex), Briggs, and Matthews sustaining the bill, and Johnston, Trigg, Thomas Smith, Thornton, Temple, Corbin, Wills Riddick, Ruffin, and Thomas Walke opposing it.[108] The vote was so thin that the House determined to adopt a new method of exposing the negligence of its members. The names of the absent members were recorded on the Journal, and it was ordered that the names of all who were absent without leave should be published in the *Virginia Gazette.* On the following day, however, the House rescinded the order of publication. On the 7th of January, 1785, the House finally adjourned.

It is due to the members who composed the Assembly of 1784 to say that they have not been surpassed in ability and in a liberal patriotism by any who have since occupied their places. They discussed the exciting and complicated questions which arose during their sessions with great skill and learning, and effected, where it was possible, a wise and satisfactory adjustment of them. The subject of religious freedom was managed

---

[107] For the report from the Committee of the Whole on British debts, see House Journal, December 1, 1784; and for the amendments of the Senate and the report of the conference, January 5, 1785, pages 106 and 107.

[108] Judge Roane voted in the affirmative and Judge Tazewell in the negative. It is much to be regretted that John Taylor (of Caroline) was absent when nearly all the best questions of the House were decided.

with as much liberality as at any subsequent session. All Christian societies were placed upon the same footing, and were entitled to the same privileges; and if the Episcopal Church received a charter, it received it under a resolution of the House, which tendered the same privilege to every sect. The marriage question was arranged in a manner agreeable to all denominations; and the bill concerning religious teachers, though called for by petitions and memorials, and its principle determined by a vote of the House, was, nevertheless, in a spirit of deliberation and compromise, submitted to the people for a distinct expression of their opinion upon it.[109] In a purely political view, the action of the Assembly was high-toned and unanimous. It went as far, in relation to the British treaty, as courtesy demanded; for Great Britain had made (and did not make ten years later) no reparation for those infractions of the treaty which bore with peculiar severity upon our own citizens, and still retained, and did retain for ten years to come, the western forts that threatened the safety of our frontier. And, to pass over many important acts which required the utmost deliberation and wisdom in maturing them, but which it would exceed our province to record, the Assembly not only voted an address and a statue to Washington, but bestowed upon him "a certain interest in the companies established for opening and extending the navigation of Potomac and James rivers."[110] Thus, in every respect, the numerous descendants of the members may contemplate the conduct of their ancestors with a just pride and pleasure.

We now proceed to give a brief outline of some of the proceedings of the House of Delegates during one of the most laborious and responsible sessions in its history. It began its session on the 17th day of October, 1785, but did not form a quorum until the 24th. Benjamin Harrison (of "Berkeley"), who had been defeated in Charles City as a candidate for the House, and going over into Surry had been returned one of the members

---

[109] We omitted to mention the petition of Isle of Wight in favor of assessments. It was presented on the 4th of November.

[110] The bill was evidently drawn by Mr. Madison, and was reported by him just as the House was about to rise on the 4th of January, 1785, and was passed unanimously the following day. Mr. Madison was requested to carry the bill to the Senate.

of that county, was elected Speaker by a majority of six votes over John Tyler, one of his successful opponents in Charles City, and the occupant of the chair at the last session. There were some few changes in the members. Tazewell having been appointed by the Executive, before taking his seat in the House, a judge of the General Court, and Joseph Jones (of King George) and John Marshall had withdrawn,[111] but their places were filled by several able men, among whom were Arthur Lee, Meriwether Smith, and James Innes.

The chairmen of the standing committees were selected with evident regard to the nature of the duties which they would be

---

[111] The Executive appointment of Tazewell was confirmed by the Assembly. I cannot tell whether John Taylor, of Caroline, was a member. He was on no standing or other committee during the session; but the name of John Taylor occurs in a collocation on the list of ayes and noes that could not apply to his namesake of Southampton. He certainly did not attend the session more than a day or two. Arthur Lee lost his seat in a few days (November 1st), in consequence of his having accepted the appointment of Commissioner of the Board of Treasury of the United States, since his election to the House, and still held the office. The vote declaring his seat vacant was ayes eighty, noes nineteen. Among the noes was Madison, also Archibald Stuart, who was to lose his own seat as a member from Botetourt before the close of the session on the ground of non-residence, but not until he had borne the burden of the day (December 19th). Harrison ought to have lost his seat on the same ground. After he was defeated in Charles City on the 6th of August, he "carried his bed and some furniture to Surry, where he engaged his rooms and board for a twelvemonth; also a servant and horses, leaving his family in Charles City" (House Journal, November 2, 1785, and was returned on the fourth Tuesday of the same month as a member from Surry. It was palpable that he was not a *bona fide* resident of Surry at the time of his election. If the same justice had been dealt to him that was dealt to Lee and Stuart, he must have lost his seat. But parties had formed in relation to Harrison and Tyler, and it was foreseen that, if Harrison was sent home, Tyler would have been restored to the Chair. Had Harrison been sent home, as he ought to have been, and Tyler chosen Speaker in his place, as he would have been, we should have had another chapter in this amusing rivalry between two old neighbors and esteemed patriots There is a harsh representation of the facts about the defeat of Harrison in the sketch of his life in the work called the *Biographies of the Signers of Independence*, first edition, which is softened in the second. I have the letter of General W. H. Harrison, the son of Benjamin, making the correction.

required to perform.   Zachariah Johnston, the unflinching friend
of religious freedom, presided in the Committee of Religion;
John Tyler, in the Committee of Privileges and Elections; Car-
ter Henry Harrison, in the Committee of Propositions and
Grievances; James Madison, in the Committee of Courts of
Justice; Richard Lee, in the Committee of Claims; and Carter
Braxton, in the Committee of Commerce.[112]

Some able members of the present Convention held seats in
the House.   Beside Harrison, Tyler, Johnston, Madison, and
Innes were Alexander White, Archibald Stuart, French Strother,
Christopher Robertson, Miles King, William Watkins, William
Thornton, John Howell Briggs, Willis Riddick, Joseph Jones (of
Dinwiddie), Wilson Cary Nicholas, Richard Cary, Benjamin
Temple, Samuel Jordan Cabell, John Trigg, Meriwether Smith,
Andrew Moore, George Clendenin, Isaac Coles, Cuthbert Bul-
litt, Henry Lee (of the Legion), Worlich Westwood, Edmund
Ruffin, Parke Goodall, Isaac Vanmeter, Anthony Walke, Thomas
Edmunds (of Sussex), William Ronald, and Thomas Matthews.

It will be remembered that the House had at its last session
distributed among the people copies of the engrossed bill,
establishing a provision for teachers of the Christian religion,
and had invited an expression of their opinions upon its merits.
The bill had been freely discussed since the adjournment, and
numerous petitions were presented throughout the present
session, either approving or condemning it.   On the score of
the number of petitions and of petitioners, the majority was
clearly against the bill.[113]   It was plainly seen, however, that few

---

[112] General Matthews was absent, and could not, consistently with the
rules of the House, be placed on the standing committees.

[113] I annex a list of the counties from which the petitions came.
Where the name of a county appears on both sides, or twice on the
same side, it is owing to several petitions coming from the same
county.   The counties are given in the order of the presentation of
their petitions :

IN FAVOR OF THE BILL—Westmoreland, Essex, Richmond county,
Pittsylvania, Lunenburg, Amelia, Halifax.

AGAINST THE BILL—Caroline, Buckingham, Henry, Pittsylvania,
Nansemond, Bedford, Richmond county, Campbell, Charlotte, Acco-
mack, Isle of Wight, Albemarle, Amherst, Louisa, Goochland, Essex,
Westmoreland, Culpeper, Prince Edward, Fairfax, King and Queen,
Pittsylvania, Mecklenburg, Amelia, Brunswick, Middlesex, Amelia,

or no petitions came from the friends of the Episcopal and Methodist Churches; while the Presbyterians and Baptists, both as societies and individuals, took evident pains to put forth all their strength on the occasion. The memorial of Hanover Presbytery of the 10th of August, 1785, discussed at length, and with great power, the subject of religious freedom, protested against the passage of the bill, and urged a revision of the act to incorporate the Protestant Episcopal Church; with an express declaration, however, that its authors did not object to the incorporation of that Church for the better management of its temporalities, but to its possession of the churches and the glebes. The remonstrance of the Baptist associations, holding their sessions in Orange, went still farther, and objected not only to the bill providing for the payment of religious teachers, and to certain provisions of the act incorporating the Episcopal Church, but to the act granting certain exclusions to the Quakers and Menonists, whose principles would not allow them to bear arms, and who were excused from the muster-field; all which acts the remonstrants deemed "repugnant to sound policy, equal liberty, and the best interests of religion."[114] They do not object to the act incorporating the Episcopal Church on the ground of the

---

Middlesex, Montgomery, Hanover, Princess Anne, Amelia, Henrico, Brunswick, Dinwiddie, Northumberland, Prince George, Powhatan, Richmond county, Spotsylvania, Botetourt, Fauquier, Southampton, Lunenburg, Loudoun, Stafford, Henrico, Chesterfield, James City, Washington, Frederick, Chesterfield, Hanover Presbytery, Baptist Associations, Otter Peak Presbyterian Church, Sundry Presbyterian Societies, Frederick Presbyterian Church, Baptist Associations in Orange.

[114] See House Journal, November 17, 1785. This was doubtless the famous paper drawn by Mr. Madison, which presents on the face of the Journal the meagre outline only which is given above. It is probable that many of the petitions contained the paper of Mr. Madison, as the abstract of most of them is in the same words. As Mr. Madison voted for the bill to incorporate the Episcopal Church, he could not consistently include in his paper the subject of religious incorporations as a grievance. Professor Tucker says (*Life of Jefferson*, Vol. I, 99) that George Mason, George Nicholas, and others of their party, proposed to Mr. Madison to prepare a remonstrance to the next Assembly against the assessment, to be circulated throughout the State for signatures.

impolicy of religious incorporations, but of certain provisions of
the act.

This strong expression of public opinion seems to have settled the fate of the bill providing for the payment of religious
teachers, without the formality of a vote. The Journal of the
present session contains no mention of the bill whatever. It
was not called up at the appointed time, nor was it reported at
all. It is stated by Howison that the bill was rejected by a small
majority; but in his reference to Wirt, who referred to what he
believed had been the fate of the bill at the preceding session,
misses the date by an entire year.[115] Foote says that the bill
was lost in the Committee of the Whole, and the bill concerning
religious freedom was reported to the House. He assigns no
authority for his statement; but if it had been rejected in committee as an independent bill, it would have been reported to
the House, and the question would have been put on agreeing
with the report of the committee. But the Journal makes no
allusion to the bill. It is possible that the bill might have been
offered in committee as an amendment to the bill concerning
religious freedom, and rejected; and it would not then have been
reported to the House. If this supposition be correct, the fate
of the bill was decided, not upon its own merits, but as a substitute for the bill concerning religious freedom; and under the
pressure of such an alternative, many who opposed the prin-

---

[115] *Howison*, Vol. II, 298, refers to Wirt, who says "the first bill"
(meaning the act incorporating the Episcopal Church) "passed into a
law; the last" (providing for religious teachers) "was rejected by a
small majority"; but he distinctly refers to the session of 1784, when
Henry was a member of the House. But he errs in stating that even
then the bill was rejected. It was not rejected at all, Wirt mistaking
the definite postponement of the bill to a certain day of the ensuing
session, with a view of submitting it to the people, for a rejection of
the bill. Professor Tucker, in his *Life of Jefferson*, Vol. I, 99, is disposed to view the postponement as a hostile movement; but it is plain
that, as there was a majority of the House on the test question, some
of that majority must have favored the postponement. The statements
of Professor Tucker, in his *Life of Jefferson*, in relation to this part of
our history, deserves respect, not only from the source from which
they come, but incidentally as having passed under the eye of Mr.
Madison, who perused the proof-sheets of much of the first volume of
that work.

ciple of assessments might have been constrained to vote against it.[116]

In reviewing this period of our history, which is interesting alike in its religious and in its political bearing, it will be the province of the philosophic observer to inquire whether the bill providing for the support of religious teachers was decided on its intrinsic merits, or by the policy of religious sects, or from the financial condition of the country. That the measure of assessments was well received in the first instance is proved by the vote of the House of Delegates—ascertained by ayes and noes. The bill brought forward in pursuance of the vote on assessments passed its early stages without opposition, and was postponed for obvious reasons to the following session. When that session came round, no vote was ever taken directly upon it in the House. If the House of Delegates leaned either way on the bill, it was inclined in its favor. As to the policy of religious sects, as such, it was sustained to the last by the Episcopalians, and almost to the last by the Presbyterians. It was only in the last memorial from Hanover Presbytery that serious objections were taken against the expediency of assessments. The Baptists alone from the first opposed all legislative action in religious matters. The temporal interest of each sect, though it may not have been the result of deliberate design, was in unison with its abstract opinions on the subject. The Episcopalian, who had heretofore received public support, and who knew that the majority of wealth, and probably of numbers, was on his side, could not think hard of a policy which allowed him the privi-

---

[116] The Rev. John B. Smith is said to have spoken three days in the Committee of the Whole. He must have received permission from the committee. If he had received it from the House, some notice of it would have appeared on the Journal. The Rev. Reuben Ford was deputed by the Baptist associations to present their remonstrance to the House. He, too, may have addressed the committee; but the memorial was presented by a member of the House. The authority for the statement concerning the Rev. Mr. Smith is the *Literary and Evangelical Intelligencer*, of which I do not possess a complete set, and especially of the period in question; but Dr. Rice, its editor, though too young to have known Smith personally at the time, lived in his old neighborhood, was intimate with his personal friends, and was eager and cautious in gathering the materials of a history of the Presbyterian Church.

lege of paying his tax in support of his own Church. The Presbyterians, who in intelligence were equal to the Episcopalians, but were surpassed by them in wealth, justly thought that, as all the churches and glebes had been retained by the Episcopalians, a *pro-rata* assessment might tend to strengthen their most formidable rivals, and in the same ratio to weaken themselves. The Baptists, though numerous, were poor, and it was evidently their policy rather to leave the religious contributions of their rivals to private impulse than to enforce them by law.[117]

There was, however, an obstacle to the success of the bill not less difficult to be surmounted than any abstract notion of the nature of assessments. The State was overwhelmed with an unsettled debt. Taxation was severe; and it was manifest, by petitions and other proofs, that it could hardly be borne. The Journal of the present session contains numerous memorials from whole counties, and from counties united in districts, praying for relief. One county prayed that its taxes should be appropriated to the making of a road towards the seat of government— or, in other words, that money should be commuted for labor. Another county prayed that the sheriffs should not distrain for taxes for a certain period, and that facilities for the payment thereof should be granted; and a bill for the purpose passed the

---

[117] The Methodists were as yet regarded as connected with the Episcopal Church. No memorial from them as a body was presented during the session. The relative numbers of the different sects at this time (1785) I suppose to have been in favor of the Episcopalians, next of the Presbyterians, then of the Baptists. Mr. Jefferson, in his *Notes on Virginia*, estimates the number of dissenters to have been two-thirds, and, in his *Memoir*, as a majority of the people at the beginning of the Revolution. But when we remember that all the offices and honors of the Colony, that a seat in the Council, a commission in the militia, or a constable's post could only be held by a member of the Church of England, the amount of wealth owned by its members, and the social caste of the day, it is hardly to be presumed that a majority of the people were in open opposition to the Established Church. Mr. Madison evidently thought Mr. Jefferson's estimate altogether beyond the mark. It may be stated here that Washington, R. H. Lee, Patrick Henry, and some other leading men warmly approved the policy of assessments, while George Mason, Madison, George Nicholas, and others opposed it. *Writings of Washington*, Vol. XII, 404; *Life of R. H. Lee*, Vol. II, 51; *Tucker's Jefferson*, Vol. I, 99.

Assembly, was printed in handbill form, and dispatched by a special messenger to the counties to which it applied. A bill "to postpone the collection of the tax for 1785," was brought forward, and was lost by two votes only. Three counties applied at the same time to be exempted from all taxes for a limited period. Then the unsettled state of the public mind in relation to the payment of British debts, many of which had been paid, and were now to be paid a second time, and in coin, rendered the suggestion of a new *pro-rata* tax highly distasteful. To add to the gloom which hung so heavily at this time above a people thinly scattered over a vast extent of country, and just emerging from an eight years' war, was the loss of the West India trade, by a British order in council. Petersburg, Norfolk, and other ports complained loudly of their loss of business, and called for relief or retaliation.[118] It is nearly certain that no additional tax for any purpose, religious or political, would have been approved at that time by a direct vote of the people.

As several of the remonstrances against the bill, providing for the payment of teachers of the Christian religion, called for a revision of the act incorporating the Protestant Episcopal Church, it may be proper to state in this connection that, on the 29th of December, leave was given to bring in a bill "to amend the act for incorporating the Protestant Episcopal Church," and Wilson C. Nicholas, Meriwether Smith, Alexander White, Zachariah Johnston, Francis Corbin, and Carter Braxton were appointed to prepare and bring it in. It was accordingly brought in, and on the 16th of January, 1786, was read a second time and committed to the whole House; but in the press of business it was postponed from day to day, and was not reached before the final adjournment.

The ever-memorable act of this session was the passage, on the 17th of December, by the House of Delegates, of the bill for establishing religious freedom. As we have heretofore alluded to the bill in detail, we will only add here that it was

---

[118] This order in council was met by the passage of a bill to impose additional tonnage duties on British vessels. The bill was brought in on the last day of the session, and read three times and passed by the House, and the same by the Senate, and enrolled—all in one day.

passed in the House of Delegates by a majority of fifty-four votes—ascertained by ayes and noes. Of the members of the present Convention who voted in the affirmative were Alexander White, James Madison, Wilson Cary Nicholas, Samuel Jordan Cabell, Zachariah Johnston, John Trigg, Archibald Stuart,[119] French Strother, Meriwether Smith, Charles Simms, David Stuart, Thomas Smith, George Clendenin, Ralph Humphreys, Isaac Vanmeter, George Jackson, Benjamin Temple, Christopher Robertson, Cuthbert Bullitt, Andrew Moore, and James Innes, and in the negative were Miles King, Worlich Westwood, William Thornton, Francis Corbin, Wills Riddick, Anthony Walke, and Richard Cary.[120]   As soon as the vote was announced Alexander White was ordered to carry the bill to the Senate and request the concurrence of that body. On the 29th the Senate returned the bill with an amendment, which struck out the whole of the preamble, and inserted in its stead the sixteenth article of the Declaration of Rights. The House refused to agree to the amendment by a vote of fifty-six to thirty-six. As the preamble of the bill was much admired in Europe, and is justly regarded with great favor here, the reader will be inclined to inquire how the members of the present Convention, who were then members of the House, voted upon the subject. In the affirmative—that is, for striking out the preamble—were John Tyler, Alexander White, David Patteson, Thomas Smith, Joseph Jones (of Dinwiddie), Miles King, Worlich Westwood, Parke Goodall, George Jackson, John Prunty, William Thornton, Benjamin Temple, Francis Corbin, Willis Riddick, and Richard Cary; and in the negative—that is, for retaining the preamble—were James Madison, Wilson C. Nicholas, Samuel J. Cabell, Zachariah Johnston, John Trigg, French Strother, Meriwether Smith, Charles Simms, David Stuart,

---

[119] It was not until the 19th—two days later—that the seat of Judge Stuart was vacated, as before mentioned.

[120] King, Thornton, Corbin, and Riddick voted, on the 11th of November, 1784, for the resolution declaring the expediency of assessments, on which the bill providing for teachers of the Christian religion was founded. Westwood was absent when the vote was taken, and Richard Cary was not then a member of the House.

William White, Cuthbert Bullitt, Andrew Moore, and Thomas Matthews.[121]

The bill was returned to the Senate, which held it under advisement until the 9th of January, 1786, when it returned it to the House of Delegates, with the message that that body adhered to its amendment, and desired a free conference with the House on the subject. On the same day the House agreed to a free conference with the Senate, and Madison, Johnston, and Innes were appointed to manage the conference on the part of the House; and Madison was ordered to acquaint the Senate therewith. On the 12th a message from the Senate announced that that body had appointed managers to meet the managers on the part of the House in free conference on the subject-matter of the amendment of the Senate to the bill for establishing religious freedom, and they were attending in the conference chamber. The House immediately ordered its managers to attend, and in due time they reported that they had met the managers of the Senate in free conference, and fully discussed the subject. On the 13th the House considered the report, receded from their disagreement to the amendment of the Senate, and do agree to the said amendment, with amendments. What these amendments were is not stated in the Journal. On the 16th the Senate informed the House that it had agreed to the amendments proposed by the House to the amendments of the Senate, with several amendments, to which that body desires the concurrence of the House. The House, in the course of the day, took the amendments into consideration, and agreed to them by a majority of twenty-six votes—ascertained by ayes and noes. The amendments to the preamble, which the House was compelled to agree to in order to save the bill,[122] may be seen by

---

[121] There were three clergymen of the Episcopal Church, or had been, who voted on the bill establishing religious freedom at some one of its stages—Charles Mynn Thruston, Thomas Smith, and Anthony Walke. The two first were in favor of the bill as it passed on the 17th of December, and the last voted against it. Smith and Walke voted, as above, against the preamble, and Thruston in favor of it.

[122] The original bill, and the bill as amended, may be seen in a single view in the first volume of *Randall's Life of Jefferson*, 219–220, and make an interesting study.

comparing the act of religious freedom as reported by the revisors and the act as it now appears in the Code.

The votes in opposition to the preamble of the bill may be explained on the ground of literary taste, of the supposed unsoundness of its doctrines in a religious view, and of the apparent appropriateness of the sixteenth article of the Declaration of Rights as a preamble to the subject-matter of the bill. Nor does the final vote against the bill necessarily imply any hostility to religious freedom. There prevailed as great a degree of religious freedom in the State before its passage as after, and if at any future time the disposition to connect a Church with the State should exist, the act of religious freedom could as readily be repealed as any other. It is probable that all who voted against the bill approved the policy of assessments, which, though not inconsistent with its provisions, would be indefinitely defeated by its passage.[123] Fortunately an overwhelming majority of the House sustained the bill, not only for the truthfulness and beauty of its reasoning, but as a distinctive and definitive measure in relation to the connection of the State with religion.[124]

The subject of slavery was discussed during the session, and that the descendants may form some opinion of the public sentiment of their fathers at that epoch, we will trace the course of a petition in favor of a general emancipation of the negroes. It was presented on the 8th of November by one of the members, purported to be from sundry persons without place, set forth "that the petitioners are firmly persuaded that it is contrary to the fundamental principles of the Christian religion to keep such a considerable number of our fellow creatures (the negroes) in this

---

[123] The reasoning of the act establishing religious freedom applies only to the impolicy of *compelling* individuals to sustain a plan of religion. The assessment bill made the support of any plan optional, and was only operative in a religious view by the deliberate consent of each tax-payer.

[124] *Howison*, Vol. II, 299, says that "a careful analysis of these documents (the memorials of the Hanover Presbytery) will draw from them every material argument and principle that will be found embodied in the act for establishing religious freedom." This is, in one sense, true and proper praise; but it may be well enough to recall the fact that the act of religious freedom was published far and wide seven years before the Hanover memorials were written.

State in slavery; that it is also an express violation of the principles on which our government is founded; and that a general emancipation of them, under certain restrictions, would greatly contribute to strengthen it, by attaching them by the ties of interest and gratitude to its support; and prayed that an act might pass to that effect." It was the obvious scope of the petitioners not only that the negroes should be emancipated, but that they should be made citizens, and reside within the Commonwealth. As a counter petition was presented at the same time from Mecklenburg, it is probable that the original petition came from that county. The counter petition not only opposed the abolition of slavery, but prayed that the act empowering the owners of slaves to emancipate them be repealed. Both petitions were ordered to be laid upon the table. On the 10th counter petitions were also presented from Amelia, Brunswick, Pittsylvania, and Halifax. All the petitions were referred to the Committee of the Whole on the State of the Commonwealth. In the course of the day, however, the House, waiving the form of going into committee, called up the petition in favor of abolition, and a motion was made to reject it, which passed unanimously. On the 14th of December Carter H. Harrison, from the Committee of Propositions and Grievances, reported that the petition from Halifax, praying that the act to authorize the manumission of slaves be repealed, was reasonable. The question presented by the report of the committee on the Halifax petition was very different from the one just decided. At that day it was evident that public opinion was disposed to allow every man to act on the subject of manumission as he pleased, the law leaning to the side of liberty; and, as at particular seasons in many parts of the State there was a great demand of labor, which could be supplied to a certain extent by free negroes, it does not appear that there was that prejudice against that class of our population which, now, for obvious reasons, exists in a greater or less degree throughout the Commonwealth. As soon as the report of the committee was read a motion was made to strike out the words "is reasonable," and insert "be rejected." After a long discussion the vote was taken by ayes and noes, and it was ascertained there was a tie, when the Speaker gave his casting vote in the negative. Those who were members of the present Convention and voted in the affirmative were Alexander White, James Madison, John Tyler, Zachariah Johnston, Archibald Stuart, John Trigg, David Patteson, French Strother, William Watkins, Worlich Westwood, Meriwether Smith, Charles Simms, David Stuart, George Clendenin, Isaac Vanmeter, William Thornton, William White, Francis Corbin, Edmund Ruffin, Cuthbert Bullitt, Andrew Moore, Thomas Edmunds (of Sussex), John Norvell Briggs, and James Innes, and in the negative were Benjamin Harrison (Speaker), Wilson C. Nicholas, Samuel Jordan Cabell, Joseph Jones (of Dinwiddie), Miles King, Thomas Smith, Ralph Humphreys, Parke Goodall, Christopher Robertson, Anthony Walke, and Richard Cary.

The amendment was lost, and the question recurred on agreeing to the report of the committee, which declared the repeal of the act to authorize the manumission of slaves to be reasonable. On this question another contest took place, the ayes and noes were again called, and the repeal of the act was ordered by a majority of a single vote. Among the ayes were W. C. Nicholas, Cabell, Jones, King, Thomas Smith, Humphreys, Goodall, Robertson, Walke, and Cary, and among the noes were Madison, Tyler, Alexander White, Johnston, Archibald Stuart, Patteson, Strother, Watkins, Westwood, Simms, Meriwether Smith, David Stuart, Clendenin, Vanmeter, Jackson, Thornton, Corbin, Ruffin, Bullitt, Andrew Moore, Edmunds (of Sussex), Briggs, Innes, and Matthews. The Committee of Propositions and Grievances was ordered to report a bill to repeal the act to authorize the manumission of slaves. On the 24th of December the bill was brought in and was read a first time, and, the question being put that it be read a second time, it passed in the negative by a majority of seventeen; Nicholas, King, Thomas Smith, Goodall, Temple, and Cary in the affirmative, and Madison, Tyler, Alexander White, Trigg, Patteson, Strother, Watkins, Westwood, Simms, David Stuart, Clendenin, Vanmeter, Prunty, Thornton, William White, Corbin, Bullitt, Andrew Moore, Briggs, and Matthews in the negative. As soon as the vote was announced a motion was made to bring in a bill to amend the act entitled an act to authorize the manumission of slaves, and Carter Braxton, Richard Bland Lee, Thomson, Tyler, David Stuart, Isaac Zane, Simms, and Nicholas were ordered to prepare and bring it in. On the 17th of January, 1786, within three days of the close of the session, Braxton reported the bill to amend the act in question, and it was read a first time; but on the motion that it be read a second time, the House rejected it without a count, leaving the law of 1782 as it originally stood.

The manumission of slaves was never popular in the Colony. When Jefferson, in 1769, for the first time took his seat in the House of Burgesses, one of the earliest schemes that engaged his attention was the melioration of the laws respecting slavery.[125] He prevailed on Colonel Richard Bland to make the motion in the House; but the scheme was scouted, the learned and patriotic Bland was denounced as an enemy of his county, and Jefferson owed it to his youth that he was not treated with the same severity. But, with the establishment of the Commonwealth, a new spirit began to be diffused among the people, and not only were obstacles to manumission removed, but the policy of the relation of slavery was called in question. The Committee of Revisors unanimously agreed upon the propriety of offering an amendment to one of the bills, declaring that all slaves born after a certain day should be free at a certain age, and then to be deported from the Commonwealth. And though the state of public sentiment did not justify the offering of such an amendment when the revised bills were discussed, there was an evident inclination among the leaders of the Revolution to oppose no obstacle in the way of voluntary manumission. Hence, before the close of the war (1782), the bill to authorize the manumission of slaves was passed, and hence the refusal of the present Assemby to repeal it.

---

[125] What the precise measure proposed by Mr. Jefferson was is rather uncertain. In his letter to Governor Coles, dated August 25, 1814, he says "he undertook to move for certain moderate extensions of the protection of the laws to these people." Professor Tucker, in his *Life of Jefferson*, Vol. I, 46, states that his object was "merely to remove the restrictions which the laws had previously imposed on voluntary manumission, and even this was rejected." The letter to Governor Coles strongly details the views of its author on the present subject, and may be found in print in *Randall's Life of Jefferson*, Vol. III. 643. It is not in either Randolph's or the Congress edition of his writings. Its genuineness is beyond question, as I have seen the original, and have a copy in manuscript, which I owe to the kindness of the venerable gentleman to whom it was addressed.

An interesting event occurred on the 31st of October in relation to the Revised Code. Up to this period no nation in modern times had ever devolved upon a committee the office of deliberately revising its entire jurisprudence, and, embracing the work of the revision in the shape of bills, had proceeded to examine them in detail. It will be remembered that, during the session of the Assembly in 1776, a Committee of Revisors had been appointed, consisting of Thomas Jefferson, Edmund Pendleton, George Wythe, George Mason, and Thomas Ludwell Lee. These gentlemen met in Fredericksburg on the 13th of January, 1777, and divided the task among themselves.[126] In February, 1779, they reassembled in Williamsburg, read and commented on the parts of each, ordered a fair copy to be made of the whole, and deputed two of their number to present their joint work to the Assembly. It was accordingly presented in the shape of one hundred and twenty-six bills. Thus was accomplished the most laborious, the most responsible, and the most delicate undertaking which had then been assigned to three men, and which, if it stood apart from the great deeds of an extraordinary epoch, would make an epoch of its own.[127]

---

[126] At this meeting all the revisors attended, when George Mason and Lee resigned, but not until some most important principles were settled, and the parts were assigned to Jefferson, Pendleton, and Wythe. Professor Tucker says (*Life of Jefferson*, Vol. I, 104, note) that he learned from Mr. Madison that Lee and Pendleton were in favor of codification, Wythe and Jefferson against it, and that Mason gave the casting vote. I use the word revi*sor* because it is the word of the bill. In modern times it is written with an *e*. It is from the mint of Jefferson, and is nearer the original. I may add that the pay of the revisors, as proposed in the House of Delegates in 1785, was three hundred pounds apiece, or one thousand dollars of our present currency. What a theme for the artist, that gathering of the revisors in an attic in Fredericksburg!

[127] It is due to Jefferson and Wythe to say that Mr. Pendleton, not having embraced exactly the views of his colleagues, "copied the British acts *verbatim*, merely omitting what was disapproved; and some family occurrence calling him home, he desired Mr. Wythe and myself (Jefferson) to make it what we thought it ought to be, and authorized us (Wythe and Jefferson) to report him as concurring in the work. We accordingly divided the work, and *re-executed it entirely*, so as to assimilate its plan and execution to the other parts." (Jefferson to Skelton Jones, July 28, 1809.) This explicit statement destroys the

The difficulties and dangers of the Revolution now began to engross the minds of men, and the time and attention of the Assembly was, for years to come, devoted exclusively to the complicated topics of the war, and at the commencement of the present session (1785) nine of the bills only had been enacted into laws.

And we are now to record the next step in this noble work. On the 31st of October Mr. Madison rose in his place in the House of Delegates, and presented from the Committee of Courts of Justice, according to order, one hundred and seventeen of the printed bills contained in the Revised Code, and not of a temporary nature. The titles of the bills alone fill two closely-printed quarto pages of the Journal. The bills were received, read severally a first time, and ordered to be read a second time; and on motion they were read severally a second time and ordered to be committed to the whole House the following day. The order was postponed daily until the 7th of November, when the House, fully appreciating the nature and urgency of revising so many fundamental laws, and the importance of setting apart a specified time for the purpose, resolved "that, during the continuance of the present session, it be a standing order of the House that Tuesday, Wednesday, and Thursday in each week be set apart and appropriated to the consideration of the Revised Code in such manner that no business be introduced, taken up, or considered after twelve o'clock of the day other than the bills contained in the said Revised Code, or such other as respects the interests of the Commonwealth at large, or messages from the Executive or the Senate." The House pro-

---

force of the compliment said by Henry Lee, the son of General Henry Lee, to have been paid by John Wickham to Pendleton on the superior precision of his (Pendleton's) part of the revision; and as we may suppose that Jefferson, being the younger and more ready man, recast much more of Pendleton's part than Wythe, it may be that the very precision praised by Wickham was the merit of Jefferson. Still, eminent credit is due to each of the revisors, and it deserves to be noticed that although the admirable accomplishment of this great work was sufficient of itself to fill the measure of the fame of each, yet such were the numerous and valuable services rendered by each of the revisors to his country that the revision of the laws appears only as one act of the series. See *Randall's Jefferson*, Vol. I, 217.

ceeded in good earnest to perform its duty, and made considerable progress, when, on the 14th of December, it was resolved that the further consideration of the several bills in the Revised Code, from No. 63 to the end, except the bill (No. 68) for the employment, government, and support of malefactors condemned to labor for the Commonwealth; the bill (No. 82) for establishing religious freedom; the bill (No. 105) reforming the proceedings in writs of right; and the bill (No. 123) concerning executors, be postponed till the next session of the General Assembly. And on the 21st the House went into committee " on the residue of the printed bills in the Revised Code of laws enumerated in the order of the 14th instant," and, on rising, it was resolved " that the House would again resolve itself into committee on the 31st of March next on the said bills." When we recall the fact that from 1779 to 1785 nine bills only had been acted on, and that during the present session the number of sixty-eight had been reached in regular progression, we may form an opinion of the dispatch of public business in the days of our fathers.[128]

But, engrossing as were the labors expended in the revision of the laws, the current business of the State would have sufficed to occupy the full time of an ordinary session. Before we relate the memorable proceedings of the House on Federal affairs, we will glance at a few acts which exhibit the courtesy and taste, as well as the sense of justice, of the House. A bill was reported in the early part of the session for the naturalization of the Marquis de Lafayette, which passed rapidly through its several stages, and was passed unanimously into a law. A bill securing to authors of literary works an exclusive property

---

[128] Those who wish to refer to the acts passed at this session will find them in *Hening's Statutes at Large*, Anno 1785. Probably one of the greatest theatres of usefulness, as well as for the display of his great powers of management and reasoning, which was presented in Madison's whole career, was his masterly and triumphant generalship of the revised bills. No man then living but himself—if we except Mr. Jefferson, who always seemed to carry his point by casting a spell over his political associates—could have achieved the work. And the members of the House, who were also members of the present Convention, and who aided him on the occasion, deserve, and should receive, their just and patriotic praise.

therein for a limited term of years was introduced by Mr. Madison, and received the sanction of both houses. The House received with due sensibility, on the 30th of December, the intelligence of the death of the Honorable Samuel Hardy, a delegate from Virginia in Congress, who had died in Philadelphia, paid cheerfully the expenses which his colleague (Grayson) had incurred in conducting the funeral, and entered on their Journal, as a perpetual record, that "the faithful and important services of Samuel Hardy demand this token of his country's gratitude." [129]

---

[129] The bill of funeral expenses was £114 9d. Samuel Hardy died in Philadelphia on the 17th of October, 1785, while attending Congress as one of the delegates from Virginia. His death was announced the same day to Congress, which resolved that the members, as a body, would attend his funeral the following day, with a crape around the left arm, and will continue in mourning for the space of one month. They appointed Mr. Grayson, Mr. Read, and Mr. Kean a committee to superintend the funeral and the chaplains were notified to attend, and one of them to officiate on the occasion; and the committee was ordered " to invite the Governor of the State, the ministers of foreign Powers, the mayor of the city, and other persons of distinction in town to attend the funeral." (*Journals of the Old Congress*, October 17, 1785, Vol. X, 251, edition of 1801.) Hardy was one of the most popular and beloved of our early statesmen. He entered the House of Delegates about the close of the war, and remained an active member until he was sent to Congress in 1783. The Assembly, during the present year [1858], called a county by his name. Monroe and Hardy were about the same age, were in the Assembly together, were on terms of the strictest intimacy, and boarded with Mrs. Ege, in Richmond. When Monroe made his Southern tour as President, he called to see his old landlady, who presently appeared, and, though thirty-odd years had passed since the death of Hardy, as she threw her arms about the neck of Monroe, she sobbed forth, "*Poor Hardy!*" [There is a tradition, which has been regarded as somewhat apocryphal, that the small one-story-and attic building of rubble-stone on the north side of Main, between Nineteenth and Twentieth streets, known as the "Old Stone House," has accommodated as guests Washington, Monroe, and other distinguished men. It is now the oldest house in Richmond, and was probably built soon after the town was laid off in 1737. In the original plan Jacob Ege appears as an owner of a town lot. His descendants occupied the house until a few decades past. The house is too small, and the rooms two few in number, for it to have been used for the entertainment and lodging of guests. Mrs. Ege, the landlady of Monroe and Hardy, was more likely some other than the

The session of the House of Delegates of 1785, in connection with Federal affairs, will always be conspicuous in our annals. It may be said, in a certain sense, to have given birth to the present Federal Constitution. During the century and a half of her colonial existence the commerce of Virginia, except in the interval of the Protectorate, was regulated by Great Britain, either in the form of direct legislation or by the supervisory power which was exercised over the acts of Assembly.[130] After the Declaration of Independence the Commonwealth passed laws for the regulation of her trade; but, owing to the preponderance of the naval power of the enemy throughout the war, our regulations were merely nominal. At the peace of 1783 all obstacles to trade were removed, and Virginia, for the first time since the death of Cromwell, regulated her trade with foreign Powers. It was soon apparent that her geographical position in respect to several neighboring States rendered a commercial compact with them highly expedient, if not indispensably necessary to the prosperity of each. An adroit legislative movement of Maryland, in abolishing a duty on certain articles highly taxed by Virginia, might divert the entire foreign trade of a season from Norfolk to Baltimore or Annapolis. Hence the early indications of a wish in our councils to form an agreement with Maryland; and the object was promoted by the residence on the Potomac of some of the ablest statesmen of that era, who felt sensibly the inconvenience perpetually arising from a conflict of jurisdiction over their immediate waters. But, anxious as Maryland might be to form an agreement with Virginia, she must be controlled, to a greater or less extent, by the policy of Pennsylvania, whose waters mingled with her own, and whose territory, running the whole length of the northern boundary of Maryland, afforded opportunities for smuggling, which nothing short

---

mistress of the "Old Stone House."—EDITOR.]   His remains still rest in Philadelphia, where those of Henry Tazewell, James Innes, Stevens Thomson Mason, Isaac Read, and of other gallant and patriotic Virginians also repose. Should we not gather all the honored dead of the Revolution in a cemetery of our own?

[130] I have before me the Sessions Acts of 1766, [?] in which the acts vetoed by Great Britian are marked by a member of the House of Burgesses. The royal veto was exercised very freely on the acts of that session.

of a strict military police always on the field could fully check. At the present session two years and a half had elapsed since the peace; yet, with every disposition on the part of Virginia to form an equal and amicable commercial league with neighboring States, she had been foiled in her purposes—each State looking to her local interests only, and unrestrained by any feeling of a personal or patriotic nature.[131] Hence a conviction, which had long been felt by our members of Congress, became general among the people at large that the regulation of commerce, under certain restrictions, should be entrusted to the Federal Government.

The nature and extent of those restrictions involved long and angry debates.   Those argue falsely who contend that the acknowledgment of our independence bound the several States to each other, so far as local interests were concerned, more intimately than before.   The main conviction drawn from the struggle with England was that the union of the States was necessary to enable them to resist a foreign foe; but that any one State should subject its business or its trade to the control of another, or of all the States, was a sentiment that was slow to make its impression on the public mind.   The interests of the States were diverse; there was but little communication between them; their institutions were unlike; and few of those considerations that soften national prejudice could act upon the people. It is probable that there was a more intense individuality of feeling and of character among the several States after the peace than before it.   This temper was heightened in Virginia by her weight in the confederacy, produced by her numbers, the extent of her territory, and her wealth, and partly, perhaps, from the fact that some of her most eminent statesmen, who had for thirty years directed the State councils, had never gone abroad, nor had come directly in contact and in friendly association with men of the same class in other States.[132]   The success of the Revolution tended rather to confirm the sense of individuality in

---

[131] John Randolph, of Roanoke, used to say that the exemption by Maryland of certain articles which were taxed high in Virginia gave the first impulse to the trade of Baltimore.

[132] Patrick Henry, George Mason, Joseph Prentis, John Tyler, Henry Tazewell, and many other able men had never been abroad or held seats in Congress—except Henry, for a few weeks—and they opposed the adoption of the Federal Constitution with all their might; while

the States, for it added a moral element to the less exalted ones
of interest and power.   Still, a commercial arrangement with a
neighboring State, whose waters were identical with our own,
was necessary, and its negotiation on fair terms seemed impracticable.   And, as the finances of the States required the successful development of all her resources, it was determined to bring
the whole subject before the Assembly.   Accordingly, on the
7th of November the House of Delegates went into Committee
on the State of the Commonwealth; and, when it rose, Prentis
reported a resolution, which was twice read and agreed to by the
House, declaring that an act ought to pass to authorize the delegates of Virginia in Congress to give the assent of the State to
a general regulation of the commerce of the United States under
certain qualifications.   A select committee, consisting of Joseph
Prentis, James Madison, Henry Lee, Meriwether Smith, Carter
Braxton, William Ronald, James Innes, and Cuthbert Bullitt,
were ordered to bring in a bill in pursuance of the resolution.[133]

Madison, Randolph, Henry Lee, and Pendleton (who occupied a seat
on two occasions in Congress) were friendly to its adoption.   This
distinction was obvious in the Assembly from as early as 1777 to 1778,
and exercised a serious influence upon public measures.

[133] This committee, which was appointed by Speaker Harrison, who
had been a member of Congress and knew the parties of the House,
was composed of four members who had not been members of Congress, and four who had.   Prentis, one of the best of men, the substitute of Wythe in the Convention of 1775, an old member of the House,
and afterwards a judge of the General Court; Bullitt, a member of all
the early Conventions, an old member of the House, of which he was
Speaker, and afterwards a judge of the General Court; John Tyler,
who had been more than once Speaker of the House, afterwards a
judge of the Court of Admiralty, and a district judge under the Federal
Constitution; Innes, who succeeded Edmund Randolph as Attorney-
General of Virginia, was a commissioner under Jay's treaty, and
declined the appointment of Attorney-General of the United States
tendered by Washington; and Ronald, an old and able lawyer, and a
member of the present Convention.   These four members of the committee had never been abroad; while Meriwether Smith, one of our
oldest statesmen, who has claims to the authorship of the first Constitution of Virginia (of which hereafter), Madison, Carter Braxton, who
signed the Declaration of Independence, and Henry Lee, who was
soon to become a member of Congress, had been much abroad in a
public capacity.   All the members of the committee except Prentis
and Braxton were members of the present Convention.

Meantime, the House reconsidered the plan of giving its assent to regulations of commerce by a bill, and resolved to discharge the committee from the office of preparing one, and, constituting the same gentlemen members of a new committee, ordered them to draft and report instructions to the delegates of the State in Congress according to the resolution adopted by the House. On the 14th Prentis reported a preamble and resolution, the preamble setting forth that "Whereas the relative situation of the United States has been found on trial to require uniformity in their commercial regulations, as the only effectual policy for obtaining in the ports of foreign nations a stipulation of privileges reciprocal to those enjoyed by the subjects of such nations in the ports of the United States, for preventing animosities, which cannot fail to arise among the several States from the interference of partial and separate regulations, and for deriving from commerce such aids to the public revenue as it ought to contribute, and whereas such uniformity can be best carried into effect by the Federal councils, which, having been instituted for the purpose of managing the interests of the States in cases that cannot be so well provided for by measures individually pursued, ought to be invested with authority in this case as being within the reason and policy of their institution"; and the resolution declaring "that the delegates in Congress be instructed to propose in Congress a recommendation to the States in union to authorize that Assembly to regulate their trade on the following principles and under the following qualifications: (1) That the United States, in Congress assembled, be authorized to prohibit vessels belonging to any nation which has no commercial treaty with the United States from entering any of the ports thereof, or to impose any duties on such vessels and their cargoes which may be judged necessary; all such prohibitions and duties to be uniform throughout the United States, and the proceeds of the latter to be carried into the treasury of the State within which they shall accrue. (2) That over and above the duties which may be so laid the United States, in Congress assembled, be authorized to collect in manner prescribed by an act 'to provide certain and adequate funds for the payment of this State's quota of the debt contracted by the United States,' an impost not exceeding five per centum, *ad valorem*, on all goods, wares, and merchandises whatsoever imported into the United States from any foreign ports; such impost to be uniform as aforesaid, and to be carried to the treasury of the United States. (3) That no State be at liberty to impose duties on any goods, wares, or merchandises imported by land or by water from any other State, but may altogether prohibit the importation from any other State of any particular species or description of goods, wares, or merchandise of which the importation is at the same time prohibited from all other places whatsoever. (4) That no act of Congress as may be authorized, as hereby proposed, shall be entered into by less than two-thirds of the confederated States, nor be in force longer than — years, unless continued by a like proportion of votes within one year immediately preceding the expiration of the said period, or be revived in like manner after the expiration thereof, nor shall any impost whatsoever be collected by virtue of the authority proposed in the second article after the year 17—.''[134] The instructions were read a second time and were ordered to be committed to a Committee of the Whole on Friday sennight.

When we consider the temper of the times, these stipulations must be regarded as going far beyond the true mark. The uniformity of duties was desirable, and some sacrifice of interest might fairly be claimed for the arrangement. Still it was a concession that went beyond any proposition offered by the States to the Federal authority, and was rendered yet more influential from the source from which it came. The payment of the customs into the treasury of the State in whose waters they were collected was right and proper. But the grant to the Federal Government of the right to laying five per centum on imposts at a time when the average rate of the Virginia tariff was greatly below that figure, and which savored of an entire cession of the customs to the United States, might well create alarm and rouse the suspicions of those who were inclined to view the Federal authority with distrust. If it be alleged that the measures

---

[134] House Journal, November 14, 1785, page 36. Mr. Gilpin, in his note (169) to the "Introduction" of Mr. Madison, refers to the proceedings of the Assembly of the 30th November and 1st of December, 1785, but has overlooked the resolution of the 14th of November, which is the foundation of the whole. I cannot refrain from bearing my tribute to the modesty, accuracy, and unbounded research which characterizes the editing of the *Madison Papers* by Mr. Gilpin.

recommended by the committee excluded those States that did not possess seaports from all benefits arising from the customs, it also relieved them from all expense in their collection; and it was competent to any State, with the consent of Congress, to make any agreement with any seaport State in relation to the customs which might be deemed beneficial. It should be remembered that each State was then responsible for its own debt, foreign and domestic, contracted during the war. The duration of the grant for a term of years, which could not be recalled until they expired, but could be abridged at the pleasure of Congress, was also a concession to the Federal Government.

In the interval an urgent petition was forwarded to the House by the merchants of Petersburg, the business of which town then greatly exceeded that of Richmond, setting forth that they considered the commerce of the State in a ruinous situation from the restrictions and impositions which have been laid upon it by the commercial Powers of Europe, and praying that such measures may be adopted as may tend to re-establish it upon a proper basis; and that due encouragement be given to the building of ships in this State, and to the trade carried on in American bottoms, and owned by American merchants only.[185]

When Friday came the House, as if reluctant to grapple with Federal affairs, ordered that the Committee of the Whole, to which had been referred the instructions to the delegates in Congress, be discharged from further proceedings thereon, and that the instructions be referred to the Committee of the Whole on the State of the Commonwealth. On the 28th the House went into committee to consider the instructions, and, when it rose, Alexander White reported that the committee had come to certain resolutions on the subject, which it had instructed him to present whenever the House should think proper to receive them. On the 30th White reported the original preamble without amendment, and the first and third stipulations of the original resolution, omitting the second, which set apart five per

---

[185] House Journal, November 24, 1785. Norfolk had presented an equally urgent memorial at the last session, referring mainly to the West India trade. I have often conversed with old merchants in the interior who bought their foreign goods at this date in Petersburg, which they paid for in specie or tobacco. The merchants of Petersburg were mostly foreign, as were those at Norfolk.

centum of the imposts for the Federal treasury, and declaring, as a third stipulation, that no act of Congress that may be authorized as hereby proposed shall be entered into by less than two-thirds of the confederated States, nor be in force longer than thirteen years. The Federal party proper had evidently sustained an overwhelming defeat in committee; for no member of that party proposed in the House to amend the report by inserting their favorite stipulation, which had been lost, but merely sought a comparatively immaterial issue by moving to add after the words "thirteen years," in the third stipulation, the words "unless continued by a like proportion of votes within one year immediately preceding the expiration of the said period, or be revived in like manner after the expiration thereof." This amendment was, at best, but a matter of minor detail since the rejection of the grant of five per centum, and could add but little to the power already granted by the stipulation; but, such as it was, the Federal party determined in its support to venture a battle, which resulted in their second entire defeat—the ayes being only twenty-eight and the noes seventy-nine. The members of the present Convention who voted in the affirmative were Madison, Johnston, Archibald Stuart, John Tyler, Strother, Simms, David Stuart, Thomas Smith, Clendenin, Isaac Coles, Thornton, Innes, and Matthews, and in the negative were Benjamin Harrison (Speaker), Alexander White, Cabell, John Trigg, Watkins, Joseph Jones (of Dinwiddie), Miles King, Westwood, Humphreys, Isaac Vanmeter, George Jackson, Prunty, Temple, Robertson, Corbin, Willis Riddick, Ruffin, Bullitt, Andrew Moore, Edmunds (of Sussex), Briggs, and Cary. The third stipulation was then read and agreed to, and Alexander White was ordered to carry the instructions to the Senate.

The following day (December 1st), as soon as the House proceeded to business, a motion was made that, as the resolution including the stipulations respecting commerce, which had been agreed to the day before and sent to the Senate, did not, from a mistake, contain the sense of a majority of the House that voted for the resolution, the direction to send the resolution to the Senate be rescinded, and the House immediately resolve itself into a committee to reconsider the same. This motion was carried by a vote of sixty to thirty-three—ascertained by ayes and noes; Madison, Trigg, Cabell, Watkins, Jones, Westwood,

Simms, David Stuart, Thomas Smith, Humphreys, Vanmeter, Prunty, Temple, Willis Riddick, Ruffin, Bullitt, Andrew Moore, Edmunds (of Sussex), Briggs, Cary, and Innes voting in the affirmative, and Alexander White, Johnston, Archibald Stuart, John Tyler, Patteson, Strother, King, Jackson, Thornton, and Matthews in the negative. The House at once resolved itself into committee on the instructions; and, when it rose, Matthews reported that the committee had taken the resolution into consideration and had made several amendments thereto, which he was directed to present when the House should think proper to receive them. The report was then ordered to be laid upon the table.

The real cause of the recall of the resolution from the Senate can only be inferred; but it is probable that the Federal party proper, having felt the pulse of their opponents since the adjournment of the previous day, were inclined to make another effort to secure the grant of five per centum for the Federal treasury; while their astute opponents, on the other hand, thinking, perhaps, that they might have gone too far, were not unwilling that the resolution should be placed once more within their reach.[136] Its further history may be given at once. The House went into committee on the 4th of December, and, when it rose, Alexander White reported two resolutions on the subject of commerce, one of which declared that no vessel trading to this State, other than such as are wholly owned by American citizens, or the subjects of Kingdoms or States having commercial treaties with the American States, shall be permitted to bring in any goods not the produce or manufacture of the State to which she belongs; and the other allowing a certain drawback on the duties imposed on goods imported into the Commonwealth by her citizens, or by citizens of the United States, in Virginia-built vessels, which

---

[136] It was a clear breach of the privileges of the Senate for the House of Delegates to recall from that body, without its consent, a resolution which had been duly passed by the House and was beyond its power, and which was doubtless referred by the Senate to a committee. The Senate Journal of the 30th of November does not notice the receipt of the resolution, but it notices the receipt of other resolutions or bills which White had been commanded, during the day, by the House to present to the Senate. The Journal was, no doubt, corrected when the turn of the House became known.

shall be wholly owned by such citizens. These resolutions were agreed to, and the Committee of Commerce was ordered to bring in a bill pursuant with their tenor, and at the same time to bring in a bill in pursuance with the resolution instructing the delegates of Virginia in Congress to propose a grant of power over commerce, with certain stipulations, to that body. This was the last action of the House on this famous resolution, which, we are told by Mr. Madison, its peculiar friends cared no longer to sustain; but not until they had presented a resolution, still more famous, which was adopted at a later stage, recommending a meeting of the States to consider their commercial regulations, but which was now voted down.[137]

The brilliant success of the Federal Constitution has cast a halo around those who were active in preparing the public mind for its advent, and has left in shadow the illustrious men, who, devoted to the independence and glory of Virginia, hesitated to strip her of the prerogatives of sovereignty, and bind her up in one homogeneous mass with all the States. And the reputation of the members of the present House of Delegates has been arraigned at the bar of posterity by a venerable statesman, who usually displayed great magnanimity in judging the conduct of his associates, and whose censure, uttered from the verge of the grave, falls with the greater force upon those against whom it

---

[137] Mr. Madison's words are: " The resolution [of the 21st January, of which presently] had been brought forward several weeks before on the failure of a proposed grant of power to Congress to collect a revenue from commerce, *which had been abandoned by its friends in consequence of material alterations made in the grant by a committee of the whole.*" (" Introduction to the Debates in the Federal Convention," *Madison Papers*, Vol. II, 695.) In the same paper (694) Mr. Madison calls the proceedings of the House " wayward," but it is hard to see wherein that waywardness consists. A committee reports to the House a resolution embracing certain stipulations, which the House, after full debate, alters and amends. Surely there is nothing " wayward" in such action. If there was anything openly " wayward," it was the recall of the resolution from the Senate; but Mr. Madison could hardly allude to that subject, as he was one of the majority which sustained that questionable measure. Perhaps it is not going too far to say that Mr. Madison, in writing, so many years later, his " Introduction," could not forget the terrible defeats which he sustained, both in the committee and in the House.

is aimed. What we have already said will show that the majority acted with a degree of prudence as well as of public spirit, which seem to have been wanting to the minority. That majority conceded nearly all that was asked by the Federal party proper, except the grant of five per centum on imports. The members of the majority voted to grant to Congress the right to lay uniform duties, which, when we regard the relative importance of Virginia in the confederation, was evidently a liberal concession. The duties were to be paid into the treasury of the State within which they were collected; for even the partial friends of the Federal Government did not propose to take directly from a State, almost overwhelmed with the embarrassments of a long war, all income from the customs. But it was evident that, if the system of uniform duties worked well in practice, it would supply the State with the means of honoring promptly the Federal requisitions already made or to be made thereafter. The majority did refuse to grant the five per centum duty to the Federal Government; but it was refused because the grant, judging from past experience, seemed nearly equivalent to a total surrender of all revenue from imports, while the expense of collection was borne by the State, and at a time when the State was not only burdened with debt, but when entire regions of country were praying to be relieved from the payment of taxes. On the other hand, the conduct of the small Federal minority was not only "wayward," but it verged to faction. This party received nearly all that it asked, with a single prominent exception. They had obtained the consent of the House of Delegates to cede to Congress the unlimited privilege of laying uniform duties upon imports. If the system of uniform duties had been carried into effect, then, for the first time, would Virginia be able to derive the full benefit from customs; and it is not improbable that the forward impulse immediately given to trade by the tariff laws of the Federal Government under the present Constitution would have been felt under the confederation. But the small Federal minority was stubborn, and, we had almost said, factious; and instead of availing themselves of the advantages proposed by a uniform rate of duties, they rejected the scheme in disgust, and, because they could not mould the majority to all their purposes, determined to do nothing at all. Had it not been for the lucky turn of events

in the following two years, the conduct of the Federal party
proper, in folding their arms when really substantial advantages
were placed within their reach, would have received the severe
condemnation of posterity. Upon a fair view of the case it is
just to conclude that, while the conduct of the minority was
deficient in judgment and in energy, the disposition of the
majority of the House on this as on other occasions was eminently liberal and patriotic.[138]

---

[138] If ever a body of men deserved to be held in grateful remembrance by the friends of civil and religious freedom, it was the majority
which guided the legislative councils of Virginia from 1765 to 1776, and
from 1776 to the adoption of the Federal Constitution. That majority
was formed in the Colony when Virginia had no more legal connection
with any other American Colony than she had with England, Ireland,
or Scotland; or, in other words, when her relation to all was the same.
We are indebted to that majority for the preparation of the public
mind for independence, which it finally achieved. With independence
some of the elder members passed from the scene, and their places
were filled by a set of young and brilliant men who were more forward
in the field and in the cabinet during the war. But as these young
men came upon the stage when the Colony had become independent,
and was bound in a union of offence and defence with the other States,
there was an evident change from the old feeling in their mode of
viewing public affairs, and they were inclined to view Virginia rather
as in connection with the other States than as an independent sovereignty standing on her own bottom. But the feeling of the old
majority still predominated in the Assembly, and especially in the
House of Delegates; and though they were sometimes pressed by
extraordinary emergencies to do some questionable things (of which
hereafter), yet to their spirit and wisdom we mainly owe the blessings
we now enjoy. Lest it might be supposed that we except Mr. Madison
from that majority, it is due to the memory of that illustrious man to
say that he was from his entrance into public life on many occasions
one of the leading members. His services in the House of Delegates
in respect of the revised bills, to omit allusion to his important services in the same theatre in other things, are worthy of all praise. But
he belonged to the later type of that majority. He began his career
in the Convention of 1776 at the age of twenty-five, passed in a year or
two into the Privy Council, which was perpetually engaged with Federal topics, and had served a term of three years in Congress at the
close of the war. He had gradually learned to embrace all the States
in his political periscope; and he was more apt to decide upon a
domestic measure from general than from local considerations. And
though in no human bosom was ever ambition the minister of a purer

Another subject, which ultimately led to important changes in our Federal relations, engaged the attention of the House. On the 28th of June, 1784, the General Assembly appointed four commissioners to meet such as should be appointed by Maryland, and, in concert with them, to frame such liberal and equitable regulations, respecting the jurisdiction and navigation of the river Potomac, as may be mutually advantageous to the two States, and to report the same to the General Assembly.[139] On the 28th of December, of the same year, the House of Delegates resolved that the commissioners appointed on the 28th of June last be further authorized to unite with the Maryland commissioners in representing to the State of Pennsylvania that it is in contemplation of the said two States to promote the clearing and extending the navigation of the Potomac, from tidewater upwards, as far as the same may be found practicable, to open a convenient road from the head of such navigation to the waters running into the Ohio, and to obtain from Pennsylvania certain immunities in her waters and territory.[140] On the 31st of December, of the same year (1784), the commissioners made a report, in part, respecting the opening and navigation of the Potomac, which was read, and referred to Grayson, Madison, and Page, who duly reported a bill for the purpose, which was read a second time, on the 1st of January, 1785, and committed to the gentlemen who brought it in. On the 3d of January the committee reported the bill without amendment, and it was ordered to be engrossed and read a third time. On the following day it passed the House, and on the 4th received the assent of the Senate. On the 13th of December, 1785, George Mason, as chairman of the committee appointed under the resolution of the 28th of June, of the preceding year, and charged with fresh instructions by a resolution of the House, passed on the 28th of

---

patriotism, yet he could not be unconscious of his ample endowments, nor feel indisposed to exert them in accomplishing an object which he thought indispensable to the ultimate safety of all the States, and even of liberty itself.

[139] The commissioners were George Mason, Edmund Randolph, James Madison, and Alexander Harrison.

[140] House Journal, December 28, 1784. The resolution was carried to the Senate by Mr. Madison.

December, of the same year, addressed a letter to the Speaker of the House, "enclosing the proceedings of the commissioners on the compact between the States of Virginia and Maryland respecting the jurisdiction and the navigation of the rivers Potomac and Pocomoke," which were read and ordered to be committed to the Committee of Commerce. On the 26th of the same month Mr. Braxton, from the Committee of Commerce, reported a bill "to approve, confirm, and ratify the compact made by the commissioners appointed by this State to regulate and settle the jurisdiction and navigation of Potomac and Pocomoke rivers, and that part of Chesapeake bay which lieth within the territory of this State"; and the same was received, read the first time, and ordered to be read a second time. On the 27th the bill was read a second time, and committed to Madison, Tyler, Isaac Zane, Corbin, Braxton, and Simms. On the 29th Madison reported the bill, with amendments, which were agreed to by the House, and it was ordered, with the amendments, to be engrossed and read a third time. A few moments after the second reading of the bill a letter from the Governor of New Hampshire was communicated by the Executive to the Speaker of the House, enclosing an act of the Legislature of that State respecting navigation and commerce, which was referred to the whole House, on the bill "for imposing certain rates and duties upon goods, wares, and merchandise imported into this Commonwealth." On the 30th the bill ratifying the Maryland compact was read a third time, and passed without a division; and Madison was requested to carry the bill to the Senate and desire their concurrence, which was given on the 4th of January, 1785, and the bill became a law.

This was a fresh instance of the sincere disposition of the General Assembly of Virginia to adopt the regulations of trade proposed by the Federal party proper, which were not inconsistent with her position as an independent Commonwealth, and, by prudent management of her resources, to maintain her own credit, and incidentally the credit of the Union. The House had already ordered a bill to be brought in conferring on Congress the right to regulate duties for the term of thirteen years; and if from the perverseness of the Federal minority that wholesome and efficient measure was suffered to fall in their pursuit of their more extended schemes, it was no fault of the majority.

A striking illustration of the hostility with which the majority of the House was regarded by the minority may be seen in the statement of Mr. Madison, who seems to charge that the compact between Maryland and Virginia was not communicated to Congress for its sanction in compliance with the Articles of Confederation.[141] The second section of the sixth Article of Confederation certainly requires the assent of Congress before any State can "enter into a treaty" with another State; but a distinction is clear between entering into a treaty—that is, making a treaty—and entering into negotiations which may result in a treaty. If the latter were in violation of the Articles of Confederation, Mr. Madison and his colleagues, who made the compact with the Maryland commissioners, and who, under the excitement of the conversations at Mount Vernon, were inclined to go farther in their negotiations than were warranted by their instructions, were knowingly guilty of a grave error. But it is clear that the second section of the sixth article merely forbids the ultimate execution of a compact between two or more States without the consent of Congress. Now, as the assent of Virginia to the compact formed by Mr. Madison and his colleagues did not make it final until the assent of Maryland was obtained, it is obvious that the refusal of the House of Delegates to communicate the compact to Congress in its incomplete state was fairly justified both by the letter and the spirit of the Articles of Confederation. It was also prudent, as Maryland did not give her full assent to the compact. Thus, if the Assembly erred in entertaining a negotiation, Mr. Madison was blameable for acting as their minister in the premises; but, if the Assembly were right in entering upon the preliminaries, as it takes two to make a bargain, they incurred no blame in declining to transmit to Congress a treaty that, as it turned out, was not "entered into" at all.[142]

---

[141] "Introduction to the Debates in the Federal Convention" (*Madison Papers*, Vol. II, 713). From the position of the charge it appears plainly to refer to the action of Virginia on the Maryland compact.

[142] Mr. Madison's words are : "From the legislative Journals of Virginia it appears that a vote refusing to apply for a sanction of Congress was followed by a vote against the communication of the compact to Congress." (*Madison Papers*, Vol. II, 712.) This charge is vague. It arraigns Virginia before the Union and before posterity as guilty of a

But the majority were now to afford still further proof of their urgent wish to promote harmony among the States, to provide for the full and early discharge of the public debt, and to place the United States on an equal footing with foreign Powers in respect to commercial regulations. On the last day of the ses sion (January 21, 1786,) a resolution was offered in the House

---

most deliberate violation of the letter and spirit of the Articles of Confederation, while it affords no clew by which we may ascertain its date and soften its heinousness or remove it altogether. But its date can be reduced to a narrow compass. It must have happened since 1781, as the Articles of Confederation did not take effect until that year. From that date until 1783, Mr. Madison was in Congress, and his general argument excludes what occurred so early as the war. Indeed, the gist of his argument was that the Articles of Confederation in their last days were not duly respected by the States; and as he was in the Assembly in 1784 and 1785, it is certain that his charge, which must have been founded on what he saw, as the Journals (as we will presently show) contain nothing of the kind, attaches to one of those two years. Now, I affirm, from a minute inspection of the Journals, that I cannot find the slightest foundation of such a charge. On the contrary, I perceive on every page an earnest effort to vest Congress with fresh and larger powers than it already possessed. But as the great compact of those years was the treaty with Maryland, I have traced most critically the progress of the whole affair, and affirm positively that no such record can be found in the Journals of the House and of the Senate, where, if anywhere, it should appear. Still, I am ready to concede, on the authority of Mr. Madison, that the motions in question were made and rejected; but, if they were made, as they only could have been made, respecting the Maryland compact, I think I have shown that they were very properly put aside until it was known whether the compact should be acceded to by the parties to it. So far on the negative side of the proof. But there is positive proof that the Assembly did recognize to the last the binding force of the second section of the sixth article of the Confederation. On the 13th of January, 1786, a series of resolutions was reported from the Committee of Commerce, one of which was in these words: "That this State should concur with the State of Maryland in making a joint application to Congress for their consent to form a compact for the purpose of affording in due time, and in just proportion between the two States, naval protection to such part of Chesapeake bay and Potomac river which may at any time hereafter be left unprovided for by Congress," &c., &c., and "that the delegates from this State to Congress ought to be authorized and *requested* to make such application in behalf of this State. in conjunction with the delegates from the State of Maryland in Congress."

of Delegates, which, if we consider its ultimate results, was one of the most memorable in human history. It was resolved "that Edmund Randolph, James Madison, Jr.,[143] Walter Jones, Saint George Tucker, and Meriwether Smith, Esqs., be appointed commissioners,[144] who, or any three of whom, shall

---

This resolution was doubtless drawn by Madison, as it recognizes the propriety of obtaining the assent of Congress in the initiatory stages of a compact. Now, what was the action of the House on this resolution? It was immediately read a second time, and *was unanimously agreed to;* and, with others of the series, was taken to the Senate by Mr. Braxton, and passed that body, *without amendment,* on the 17th of January So that, if, in some moment of excitement, the motions alluded to by Mr. Madison were rejected, the Assembly nobly redeemed their character in the adoption of this resolution. The series of resolutions, of which this was the first, consisted of seven, *two of which were rejected;* and it is possible that Mr. Madison, after a long lapse of years, relying only on his memory (for there is no record on the Journals in the case that I can find), may have believed that the resolution asking the consent of Congress to a compact with Maryland was one of those that were rejected. (House Journal, January 13, 1786, page 140.) What induces me to believe that the resolution in question was written by Mr. Madison, who had been three years in Congress and entertained the *esprit de corps,* was the use of the word "*requested*" instead of "instructed," which was invariably used in resolutions addressed by the Assembly to the delegates in Congress. Perhaps it may as well be stated here that Curtis, in his *History of the Federal Constitution* (Vol. I, 341), following Marshall, dates the appointment of the Virginia commissioners "in the spring of 1785." As such appointments were only made by the Assembly, which up to this period never sat early in the spring (for the Virginia commissioners met in Alexandria in March), I was led to search the Journals with some care to ascertain the facts of the case, which are as already narrated in the text.

[143] I have invariably omitted the affix of "Jr." to Mr. Madison's name, because, however convenient it was in Orange, it had no significancy in our public bodies.

[144] As all the commissioners, except Saint George Tucker, were members of the present Convention, it is proper to say that the time and place agreed upon was the first Monday in September, 1786, and at Annapolis; that Randolph, Madison, and Tucker alone attended; that five States only—Virginia, Pennsylvania, Delaware, New Jersey, and New York—were represented, and that the commissioners from all the States present addressed a letter, written by Alexander Hamilton, to the States collectively, setting forth the facts of the case, and

meet such commissioners as may be appointed by other States in the Union, at a time and place to be agreed on, to take into consideration the trade of the United States; to examine the relative situations and trade of the said States; to consider how far a uniform system in their commercial regulations may be necessary to their common interest and their permanent harmony, and to report to the several States such an act relative to this great object, as, when unanimously ratified by them, will enable the United States, in Congress, effectually to provide for the same''; and it was also resolved "that the said commissioners shall immediately transmit to the several States copies of the preceding resolution, with a circular-letter requesting their concurrence therein, and proposing a time and place for the meeting aforesaid.'' The resolution was offered by John Tyler, one of the majority of the House, and sustained by him. It was twice read, and agreed to by the House without a division. But it was the last day of the session, and there was no time to lose. General Matthews was immediately ordered to carry the resolution to the Senate and desire their concurrence. This remarkable resolution was drawn by Madison, and had been offered in Committee of the Whole, when the resolution granting five per centum of the customs had been summarily rejected; but "it was," says Mr. Madison, "so little acceptable that it was not persisted in," but "it now obtained a general vote."

A message was soon delivered from the Senate, by Mr. Jones, that the resolution was agreed to, with certain amendments, in which that body desired the concurrence of the House. The House proceeded to consider the amendments of the Senate, some of which were agreed to, and others disagreed to. General Matthews was ordered to acquaint the Senate therewith. That body instantly receded from the amendments which had been disagreed to by the House, and the resolution became a law. This remarkable resolution was drawn by Madison, and had been offered in Committee of the Whole by Tyler, when

recommending an appointment of commissioners from all the States to assemble in Philadelphia on the second Monday in May next, 1787; that Virginia, in a law drawn by Madison (*Madison Papers*, Vol. II, 704, and *Hening*, 1786), was the first to appoint commissioners to the Convention (of which hereafter).

the stipulation granting five per centum of the customs to the Federal Government had been summarily rejected. "It was, however," says Mr. Madison, "so little acceptable that it was not persisted in, but it now obtained a general vote." [145]

---

[145] The resolution, as altered by the Senate, contains the names of David Ross, William Ronald, and George Mason, and requires *five* commissioners, instead of three, to be present. Professor Tucker informed me that Madison told him that he wrote the resolution. The Journal does not mention the name of the mover, nor the fact that it had been previously presented. We learn these facts from the "Introduction" of Mr. Madison to the "Debates in the General Convention" (*Madison Papers*, Vol. II, 696). Some months ago John C. Hamilton, of New York, wrote to ex President Tyler with the view of ascertaining from him the precise relation which his father (Judge Tyler) bore to the resolution The ex-President did me the honor of consulting me on the subject, and I wrote to him in detail the facts of the case, and the reasons which induced the selection of his father as the mover. In the course of the investigation the original resolution, in the archives of the House of Delegates, was examined, and it was ascertained, as I was told by Mr. Tyler, to be in the handwriting neither of Mr. Madison nor Judge Tyler, but of Mr. Beckley, the Clerk of the House. Mr. Madison assigns as the reason for its passage "that it was the alternative of adjourning without any effort for the crisis in the affairs of the Union." Such was, naturally enough, the conclusion of Mr. Madison as the representative of the Federal party proper, who was disposed to consider nothing done unless in correspondence with his wishes; but the *acts* of the majority present a very different case. The majority had, indeed, rejected the five per centum feature of the Federal project; but they cheerfully conceded to the Federal Government the power to establish uniform duties throughout the Union for the term of thirteen years; and when they found it vain to satisfy the Federal minority without what they deemed the virtual subjection of the State at the feet of Congress, they threw the whole responsibility of a general regulation of the customs upon those who, claiming to be the special friends of the Federal Government, had given up the subject in disgust. They accordingly ratified with promptness the compact already made with Maryland, and on the 13th of January, 1786—eight days only before the adjournment—determined to enter into a negotiation with Maryland for the regulation of the commerce of the two States, and adopted the following resolution: "That it is important to the commerce and revenue of the State of Maryland and this State that duties, imports, or exports, if laid, should be the same on both States; and that it is proper for the Legislatures of the said States, at their annual meeting in the autumn, to appoint commission-

Of the course of Alexander White throughout the session, his recorded votes already reported afford incontestible evidence. He was appointed a member of nearly all the select committees to which general topics were referred; and he presided, perhaps, more frequently than any other member in Committee of the

---

ers to meet and communicate the regulations of commerce and duties proposed by each State, and to confer on such subjects as may concern the commercial interests of both States, and within the power of the respective States; and that the number of the said commissioners should be equal—not less than three nor more than five—from each State; and they should annually meet in the third week in September, if required by the Legislature of each State, or the commissioners thereof, at such place as they should appoint." And, to show still further the truly federal spirit of the majority, they ordered the resolution to be sent by the Governor to the Legislatures of all the States in the Union, who were requested to appoint commissioners for the purposes therein expressed. This was a great and definite measure—looking to a general regulation of commerce by all the States—and was altogether in advance of any legislative measure which had then appeared, with the exception of the resolution of Massachusetts adopted during the preceding summer (*Curtis*, Vol. I, 336); and it was referred for the consent of the States. In the mean time the Assembly revised their custom-house regulations, and passed a stringent law for the prompt and economical collection of the customs. They also resolved to resent the hostile regulations of Great Britain by laying an additional tonnage on British vessels. If intentions are to be gathered from acts, we may conclude that the men who adopted this vigorous and catholic policy never dreamed of the "alternative" in question, but thought that they had marked out for the future a most decided and energetic course of action. And this policy received the sanction of the Senate four days only before the final adjournment. With this view of the facts, I am strongly inclined to think that the resolution of the 21st of January, which called the meeting at Annapolis, was adopted after many members had left for their homes, and when, in fact, there was hardly a quorum of the House. At the end of the previous session the House adjourned over one or two days to get a quorum, and was finally compelled to adjourn *sine die* without one. The present House consisted of one hundred and fifty or sixty members, and we have seen from the ayes and noes on important questions during the session that barely a quorum was present; and, as the resolution was offered by Tyler, who was one of the majority, it is not improbable that the members of the majority present may have regarded it as designed to carry out the scheme which had been deliberately agreed on, and which would require, in due time, the appointment of commis-

Whole. And it may be recalled as a pleasing reminiscence by his descendents, that, as chairman of the Committee of the Whole, he reported to the House the bill constituting the State of Kentucky, and the bill for establishing religious freedom.

The General Assembly of 1786–'87 began it sessions on the 16th of October, but the House of Delegates did not form a quorum until the 23d, when John Beckley was appointed Clerk, and Joseph Prentis elected Speaker by a majority of twelve over Theodoric Bland. Bland was placed at the head of the Committee of Religion, Thomas Matthews of Privileges and Elections, George Nicholas of Propositions and Grievances, Richard Lee of Claims, Thomas Matthews of Commerce, and James Innes of Courts of Justice.[146]

The members of the House who were members of the present Convention, besides Matthews, Nicholas, and Innes, were James Madison, Zachariah Johnston, French Strother, Parke Goodall, Thomas Smith, John Pride, William White, Francis Corbin, Edmund Ruffin, Miles King, Archibald Stuart, David Stuart, Holt Richeson, Richard Cary, John Early, John Prunty, George Jackson, Thomas Turpin, John Marr, Christopher Robertson, James Johnson, Willis Riddick, John Allen, John Howell Briggs, Martin McFerran, Littleton Eyre, John Dawson, Andrew Moore, Samuel Jordan Cabell, Joseph Jones (of Dinwiddie), Samuel

---

sioners. On the other hand, it should be remembered that Harrison, who was one of the majority, and who had more parliamentary experience than any other member of the House, was in the chair, and not being on very amicable terms with Tyler, who had defeated him in Charles City and driven him to take refuge in Surry, would have been inclined to have scrutinized closely any independent measure coming from such a source. At all events, the "alternative" mentioned by Mr. Madison, however it may have appeared to him with his peculiar views of Federal policy, does not seem very apparent from the facts as they are recorded in the Journal.

[146] Madison had not arrived, and could not consistently with the rules of the House be placed on any committee; but Innes in the early part of the session was elected Attorney-General in place of Edmund Randolph, who was elected Governor, and withdrew to attend the courts; and Madison acted as chairman of the committee on many occasions. That Madison, who was not a lawyer, was placed at the head of a committee consisting of the ablest lawyers in the House, is a fresh proof of the universality and accuracy of his acquirements.

Richardson, Isaac Vanmeter, William Thornton, Binns Jones, William McKee, George Clendenin, Meriwether Smith, Cuthbert Bullitt, John Trigg, Isaac Coles, Benjamin Temple, and James Gordon.[147]

The financial condition of the Commonwealth was the first important measure that engaged the attention of the House. A motion was made and carried that the Governor be requested to lay before the House an exact statement of all the taxable property of the State, of duties payable on exports and imports, together with the product of said taxes and duties from the 1st day of January, 1783, to the 1st of October, 1786, specifying the amount of specie received in each year, and the amount of the different species of the public securities, the averages of taxes now due, and the sums of money advanced to the several officers of government between the 1st day of January, 1782, and the present time.[148]   This motion was immediately followed by another to appoint a select committee to take into consideration the whole system of finance established by the laws of the Commonwealth, and to report such regulations therein, and such amendments to the laws thereto, as may to them seem best calculated to alleviate the present distresses of the people, and at the same time to preserve inviolate the national faith and honor of the Commonwealth.   This motion was unanimously adopted, and Bland, Corbin, George Nicholas, Innes, Lyne, Griffin, Eggleston, Matthews, King, Zachariah Johnston, Thompson, Richard Bland Lee, Turberville, Strother, Archibald Stuart, Campbell, Webb, David Stuart, and Wills composed the committee.   The number and ability of the members, who were selected from the great divisions of the State, show the sense entertained by the House of the momentous subject entrusted to their charge.   On the 2d day of December, 1786, their

---

[147] Alexander White, a member of the House, did not attend. I have, however, continued my review of the sessions of the Assembly immediately preceding the Convention as necessary to the understanding of the facts of the times and of the history of many members of the Convention.

[148] This interesting report was made on the 25th of November, 1786, and is doubtless on file in the office of the Clerk of the House of Delegates.   It ought to be published in the *Historical Reporter*, and in the *Southern Literary Messenger*.   (House Journal 1786-'87, page 61.)

report was presented to the House by Colonel Bland, and was, perhaps, the most elaborate paper on our financial affairs that had yet appeared.[149] On the 12th General Matthews, from the Committee of the Whole, reported a series of resolutions founded upon the report, recommending an increase of taxes and manifesting a firm determination to maintain the credit of the State. An additional tax of five dollars a wheel was recommended to be laid on all coaches and chariots, three dollars a wheel additional on all other four-wheel vehicles, and two dollars a wheel additional on all riding-carriages with two wheels. Clerks of courts were ordered to account with the treasurer for one-third of receipts from their fees. Every practicing attorney was to pay down to the clerks of the respective courts one-tenth of all the fees allowed by law for the services performed by attorneys. Physicians, surgeons, and apothecaries were required to pay an annual tax of five pounds each. A tax of twenty pounds was imposed on all imported riding-carriages with four wheels, and of ten pounds with two. Houses in towns were taxed five per centum on the amount of annual rent. Merchants, traders, and factors—native and foreign—were required to take out a license to do business, and foreign merchants belonging to a nation in treaty with the Union were required to pay less than those who did not. These recommendations were adopted, with the exception of the tax on imported vehicles; and Matthews, Meriwether Smith, George Nicholas, and others were ordered to bring in bills to carry the scheme into effect. The House had previously ordered a bill to be brought in allowing taxes to be paid in tobacco;[150] but a new issue of paper money, called for by some counties remote from market, was voted down. Bills were brought in and passed to amend and reduce into one act the several acts for the appointment of naval officers, and ascertaining their fees; to place the naval officers on the civil list; to regulate the public offices and the mode of keeping the books therein; to reduce into one act the several revenue laws of the State, and for

---

[149] It fills ten or twelve pages of the quarto Journal of the House. (House Journal of 1786–'87, page 71, et seq.)

[150] November 13, 1786, House Journal, page 36. On the 23d the House rejected the bill on its passage by a vote of seventy-two to thirty-three.

more effectually preventing fraud and abuses in collecting the revenue arising from customs; to call in and fund the paper money of the State; to explain, amend, and reduce into one act the several acts for the admission of emigrants to the right of citizenship, and prohibiting the migration of certain persons to the Commonwealth.   A bill was passed for the construction of a marine hospital, and for preserving the privileges of embassadors.   Kentucky, which had failed from unavoidable causes to comply with the requisitions of the act passed at the last session, was authorized to become an independent State.

A bill was also passed to encourage navigation and ship-building, and to regulate and discipline the militia.   An export duty of six shillings was laid on every hogshead of tobacco, and a bill passed imposing an additional duty of two per centum, *ad valorem*, on all goods imported into the State.   A bill to supply the United States, in Congress assembled, with a certain sum of money was promptly passed.   These measures convey but a faint idea of the number and importance of the subjects that employed the time of the House.   The revised bills, continued from the last session, were still under discussion; but, after many had been disposed of, it was determined to appoint a second committee of revisors to complete an entire revision of the laws; for in the interval of the first appointment of the revisors ten years had elapsed, and the legislation of that period required to be drafted into the Code; and Edmund Pendleton and George Wythe, two of the former revisors, and John Blair were appointed to perform the work.   If no other record of the worth, the ability, and the sterling faith of the present Assembly existed than the Journal of the House of Delegates, the careful historian would pronounce with confidence on their just claims to the gratitude and veneration of posterity.

The leading topics of the session, however, which have singled it out for a place in general history, were those pertaining to the Protestant Episcopal Church, and to the initiatory measures that led to the formation of the present Federal Constitution. And first of the Church: At an early day petitions were presented from various places complaining of the disposition of the churches and glebes, and praying for a repeal of the act to incorporate the Protestant Episcopal Church.   Those in favor of a repeal and a redistribution of the property of the Church, whether we regard the number of the petitions or of those who signed them, greatly preponderated.[151] The petitions, as they were presented, were referred to the Committee of the Whole. On the 2d of November the House went into committee on the subject, and, when the committee rose, a resolution was reported, and agreed to, that the committee be discharged from the further consideration of the petitions; which were ordered to lie on the table. On the 4th of December the petitions were called up and referred to the Committee of the Whole on the State of the Commonwealth. The subject was discussed in Committee of the Whole on the 5th, when Colonel Thruston, who had been, at the beginning of the Revolution, a minister of the Episcopal Church, reported three resolutions, the first of which recommended that a law ought to pass to empower all societies formed for the purposes of religion to hold such property as they are now possessed of, to acquire property of any kind, and to dispose thereof in any manner that may be agreeable to the said societies. The second recommended that so much of all acts of Parliament or acts of Assembly as prohibits religious socie-

---

[151] As a majority of the churches and glebes, in number and value, were in Eastern Virginia, the subject of repeal and redistribution, in its geographical bearing, will be seen by referring to the places from which the petitions came: For a repeal, &c., were Louisa, Henrico, Westmoreland, Brunswick, Mecklenburg, Dinwiddie, New Kent, Gloucester, Albemarle, Lancaster, Nansemond, King and Queen, Orange, Goochland, Pittsylvania, Hanover, Amelia, Halifax, King and Queen, Lunenburg, Augusta, Caroline, Essex, Westmoreland, Cumberland, Gloucester, King and Queen, Cumberland, Buckingham, Hanover, Gloucester, Powhatan, and Chesterfield. Against a repeal, &c., were Richmond county, York, Hanover, Louisa, Northampton, Southampton, Stafford, King George, York, Elizabeth City, Hanover, Albemarle, and Louisa. The Baptist associations presented a memorial in favor of a repeal, and the Convention of the clerical and lay members of the Protestant Episcopal Church presented a memorial against it, which was followed by another from the standing committee of the last-named Church. When the name of a county appears more than once an additional petition was presented by it. I have given the names of the counties in the order in which they sent in their petitions. The latest was presented on the 5th of December. On the 30th of October the Presbyterian Church of Alexandria applied for an act of incorporation, as the Otter Peak Presbyrerian Church had done at the previous session, but their petitions were rejected.

ties from forming regulations for their own government, in any cases whatsoever, ought to be repealed, and that it ought to be declared that all such societies have full power to form regulations for their own government. The third recommended a repeal of the act to incorporate the Protestant Episcopal Church. These resolutions passed without a division, and a committee, consisting of Thruston, George Nicholas,[152] John Page, Corbin, Johnston, Archibald Stuart, Isaac Zane, Madison, Briggs, and Eggleston, was ordered to bring in bills in pursuance with the resolutions. The bill to repeal the act to incorporate the Church was duly presented, was read three several times on different days, and passed the House without a division. On the 9th it was returned from the Senate, with amendments, in which the House refused to concur, and from which, on the return of the bill, it receded. What those amendments were the Journal of neither House affords any means of determining.[153] It is singular that, while the ayes and noes were frequently called during the session on comparatively trivial questions, none demanded them on such a question as this.

The first two resolutions reported by the Committee of the Whole were just and proper. They served to carry out and enforce the doctrines of the act for establishing religious freedom, and to extend to religious associations the protection and aid of legislation. But the passage of the bill to repeal the act incorporating the Episcopal Church was of doubtful right. This extraordinary act can only be accounted for on the ground of a compromise, or of a panic terror which seized upon the House. It might have been contended in debate that, at the same time the resolution recommending a repeal of the charter of the Church was adopted, another resolution authorizing the passage of all laws necessary to enable a religious society to hold and sell its property received the sanction of the House; and that the Episcopal Church, in losing its charter, which it held alone of all the religious sects, would lose nothing, while the repeal would not affect its title to property which it lawfully held. This

---

[152] George Nicholas had reported the bill of the last session to repeal the charter of the Church.

[153] The original engrossed bill, in the office of the Clerk of the House of Delegates, will settle the question.

ground is not tenable unless it can be shown that the Church had approved it; but the memorials of its Convention and of its standing committee (which last was presented just before the resolution recommending the repeal was adopted), so far from approving such a policy, warmly protested against any action in the premises. If, then, there was a compromise in the House, as there probably was, it was a compromise to which the Church did not assent; and without that assent the act of repeal was manifestly unjust and unconstitutional.[154] It has never been alleged that the Episcopal Church had by any unlawful practice forfeited its charter; but even if it had, the mode of redress was not through the Legislature, but through the courts. On the other hand, some allowance should be made for the peculiar views in respect of the extent of the powers of the Legislature then prevalent. On the subject of charters the public jealousy in England and in the Colony for a century and a half then past was directed to the King, and not towards Parliament. The reckless mode of dealing with charters pursued by James the Second did more to weaken his hold upon the intelligent and religious people of England, and especially upon the Church of England, than any other course, which, under the guidance of evil councillors, and in pursuit of his mad scheme of converting England into a Catholic country, he was driven to adopt. The sanctity of charters became one of the slogans of the Revolution of 1688. It was specially dwelt upon in the memorial from The Hague, which prepared the British mind to accept of a new dynasty. But it was the annulment of charters by the King, and not by Parliament, that roused the fears of the English people. The King was the grantor of all charters, but he could not take them away. The authority of Parliament, however, was unrestricted. It could declare the throne vacant, and fill it at its discretion; and it would certainly have appeared to the statesmen of 1688 the height of absurdity to deny to that body the right of amending or annulling a vicious charter which James

---

[154] The fact that the ayes and noes were not called in any of the stages of the bill would seem to indicate some agreement between its friends and the friends of the Church, or that the friends of the Church seeing all contest hopeless, did not care to put their names on record for future animadversion.

may have bestowed upon his minions. It was in this spirit that the General Assembly passed the bill to repeal the charter of the Episcopal Church, more especially as on the subject of charters the Constitution did not expressly prohibit their repeal. The customs and the laws of England from the time of King William had justly great weight with our fathers. In their early troubles they had looked to the Convention Parliament of 1688 as a guide, and, in imitation of that body, had adjourned over from a convention to an ordinary Legislature.[155] It is true the Convention Parliament repealed no charters; but it is equally true that, if King James before his abdication had not, by recalling his new charters and by the restoration of the old, done the work for them, they would have done it for themselves. But, with all the allowances due from the habits and customs of Parliament, the repeal of the Church bill, even on the ground of compromise, when the Church proper was not a party, was indefensible.

Nor is the repeal more defensible on the ground of popular clamor. The voice of the people is truly the voice of God; but it must be uttered in that deliberate and constitutional way which the people themselves have prescribed. No statesman who consents at the bidding of the popular voice to violate vested rights should escape the serious animadversion of posterity. And this censure attaches with equal severity to the opponents as well as to the friends of repeal. No act of legislation during the session appears more unanimous on the face of the Journal than the act repealing the charter of the Church. From first to last—from the day when the resolution recommending its repeal was reported from the Committee of the Whole to the passage of the bill through its several stages— there was not a single division in the House, either on its principle or on its details. All the members are equally responsible for its passage; while the conduct of the minority, if controlled by fear, is still more to be condemned and deplored. Failing to afford posterity the means of knowing, by the ordinary parliamentary signs, who were the supporters of the bill, its oppo-

---

[155] I have already mentioned the fact that the Convention of May, 1776, which formed our first Constitution, became the first House of Delegates under that Constitution, without an appeal to the people.

nents, if such there were, must share the blame with its friends. Moreover, the repeal of the act was a blunder. In the eye of the law it was a nullity. The great aim of those who desired the repeal was the confiscation of the churches and the glebes. Yet it was plain that, if the Church held its possessions lawfully, no act of Assembly, which merely deprived it of its corporate capacity, could rightfully take them away. The course which the Legislature ought to have pursued seems to be simple and obvious. The whole question of property belonged to the judiciary, and the Assembly might have performed its duty by referring the petitioners to the courts, or by instructing the Attorney-General or the solicitor to prepare for the courts a case which should determine the right of the Church to hold the property in question. On the other hand, the course of the Church on the repeal of its charter was equally obvious. Its friends ought to have pressed the bills carrying into effect the two first resolutions of the committee through the House, and thus placed the Church on a platform on which it could sustain itself in a court of justice; but so far from following up the recommendations of the committee, which were adopted by the House, they allowed them to sleep on the table. The Church should, then, have appealed to the courts, and we know, from what occurred when an appeal was ultimately made, what would have been the result. It would have protected itself from the worriment [sic], vexation, and spoliation of the ten or fifteen years that followed the repeal, and retained its property, if held lawfully, under the laws existing prior to the Declaration of Independence, or under the act of the October session of 1776, or under the act of its recent incorporation. And posterity would have had the satisfaction of knowing that the act of repeal was as inoperative as it was ill-timed and unjust.

The subject of Federal affairs will now claim our attention. On the 30th of October, 1786, the Speaker laid before the House of Delegates a letter from the commissioners appointed by the General Assembly at the last session to meet such commissioners as might be appointed by the other States in the Union, to take into consideration the commerce of the United States, with a copy of the proceedings of the meeting.[156] The letter and its

---

[156] The meeting at Annapolis.

enclosures were read, and committed to the whole House on the state of the Commonwealth. On the 3d of November the House went into committee on the subject, and, when it rose, Matthews reported a resolution declaring "that an act ought to pass in conformity to the report of the commissioners assembled at Annapolis on the 4th of September last, for appointing commissioners on the part of this State to meet commissioners on the part of the other States in convention, at Philadelphia, on the second Monday in May next, with powers to devise such further provision as shall appear to them necessary to render the Constitution of the Federal Government adequate to the exigencies of the Union; and to report such an act for that purpose to the United States, in Congress assembled, as, when agreed to by them, and afterwards confirmed by the Legislatures of every State, will effectually provide for the same." It was unanimously agreed to by the House, and Matthews, George Nicholas, Madison, Nelson, Mann Page, Bland, and Corbin were ordered to bring in a bill in pursuance with its tenor. The object of the resolution was evidently to amend the Articles of Confederation in the form prescribed by them.

On the 6th of November Matthews [157] reported a bill "for appointing delegates from this Commonwealth to a convention proposed to be held in the city of Philadelphia in May next, for the purpose of revising the Federal Constitution"; which was received and read a first time, and ordered to be read a second time. On the 7th it was read a second time, and committed to the whole House on the following day. But on the following day something more than a phantom appeared to the eyes of the Federal party. It will be remembered that on the 13th of January, 1786—a few days before the House of Delegates adjourned at the last session—a resolution had been deliberately adopted which required not less than three nor more than five commissioners to meet a similar number on the part of Maryland and adjust the commercial relations of the two States; but that, at

---

[157] Alexander Hamilton, who drafted the circular of the Annapolis meeting to the States, was a West Indian; and Thomas Matthews, who reported the resolution declaring the expediency of appointing commissioners on the part of Virginia to the Convention at Philadelphia, and the bill above mentioned appointing the deputies, was also a West Indian.

the last day of the session, when it is probable a quorum was hardly present, the Federal party had introduced the Annapolis resolution, and appointed delegates to carry its purposes into effect. It was now determined by the majority that, in the face of the preliminaries for calling a General Federal Convention, the commissioners, under the resolution of the 13th of January, should be appointed, and should, without delay, effect the con-templated meeting. It was also determined to seek the concur-rence of Pennsylvania, and to obtain the consent of Congress. This fearful resolution passed without a division, was immedi-ately transmitted to the Senate by Corbin, and received the sanction of that body on the 22d. The House then resolved itself into a committee on the bill to call the General Convention; and, when it rose, Matthews reported the bill with amendments, which were concurred in, and the bill, with the amendments, was ordered to be engrossed and read a third time. And on the following day it passed the House without a division, was carried to the Senate by Matthews, and was concurred in by that body, and communicated to the House on the 23d.[158] On the 25th the commissioners, under the resolution of the 13th of January, were elected by joint ballot, the choice falling on Saint George Tucker, William Ronald, Robert Townsend Hooe, Thomas Pleasants, and Francis Corbin. And on the 4th of December George Washington, Patrick Henry, Edmund Randolph, John Blair, James Madison, George Mason, and George Wythe were elected, by joint ballot of both houses, deputies to the General Con-vention.

At the first glance the appointment of two sets of commis-sioners at the same time for what should seem one and the same object may appear inconsistent, and the game of two opposing parties. That there was deep management on the side of the Federalists proper (headed by Madison) is probably true; but it was not observed by the majority; or, if observed, it was disre-

---

[158] There is another illustration of the respect manifested by the Assembly to Congress, and shows that the case of disrespect alluded to by Mr. Madison must have been isolated, and the result of some casual impulse; if (as we have before intimated) Mr. Madison had not confounded, after a lapse of years, the nature of the votes on a par-ticular occasion. See the proceedings in full in the House Journal, November 23, 1786, page 55.

garded, as the Federal scheme merely pointed to an amendment
of the Articles of Confederation in the form prescribed by that
instrument, and any proposed amendment would be required to
pass the ordeal of the Assembly.   But the truth is, that the
majority were eminently patriotic.   They loved the Union, and
were willing to make it as efficient as was consistent with the
independence of Virginia.   They well knew that some time
would elapse before the meeting of the Convention, and still
more before its work was ended, and yet still more before that
work could be received and approved by every State in the Confederation.   They remembered the delay in ratifying the Articles of Confederation, to which Virginia had promptly assented
as early as 1777, but which did not take effect till 1781.   Meantime, the commercial relations of Virginia with Maryland and
Pennsylvania required immediate attention.   The interests of
those States would be materially advanced by a uniform tariff,
and those of Virginia most of all.

The principal occasion on which the two parties came into
direct collision, and which resulted in the total defeat of the
Federal party proper, occurred on the 2d of January, 1787, on
a motion to amend the bill to amend and reduce into one the
several laws concerning naval officers, by adding a clause in the
following words: "That the before-mentioned duties shall not
be demanded or paid until the commissioners appointed on
behalf of this State to negotiate with commissioners on behalf
of the States of Maryland and Pennsylvania, for the establishment
of similar commercial duties and regulations within this and the
said States, shall have reported to the Executive that the State
of Maryland has imposed duties similar and equal to those
before imposed by this act; in which case, the Executive is
hereby authorized and required to direct, by proclamation, the
said duties to be paid; and in the mean time the present duties
shall continue to be collected in pursuance of the laws now in
force and of this act." [159]   The ayes and noes were called, and the
amendment failed by a vote of seventy-one to thirty-seven;

---

[159] House Journal, January 2, 1787, page 135.   The ayes and noes in
full on this amendment well deserve to be studied, if the historical
student has a wish to note the somersaults which some of the voters
were to turn in less than eighteen months.

Madison, David Stuart, Richardson, Marr, Thornton, Temple, Gordon, Corbin, Turpin, Bland, Bullitt, and Dawson in the minority, and George Nicholas, Pride, Samuel J. Cabell, Johnston, Trigg, McFerran, Strother, Joseph Jones (of Dinwiddie), King, Meriwether Smith, Thomas Smith, Clendenin, Isaac Coles, Goodall, Prunty, George Jackson, Isaac Vanmeter, Robertson, Willis Riddick, McKee, Allen, Briggs, Cary, and Matthews in the majority. On the 4th the bill came up on its passage, when the Federalists ventured another battle, and were again defeated by a vote of seventy-nine to thirty-two. The bill was sent to the Senate by Madison, who was one of the minority of thirty-two, and received the assent of that body on the 9th.

The design of the Federalists proposing the amendment was to postpone any permanent agreement between Maryland and Virginia, which, by facilitating the collection of customs, might render the adoption of any general system less urgent upon this State. The success of the amendment would have laid Virginia at the mercy of Maryland, who might impose what duties she pleased upon imports, while Virginia might remain helpless and without a revenue to meet her ordinary expenses. Moreover, a state of commercial embarrassment was more favorable to the views of the Federalists than a prosperous system of domestic revenue, as it might serve to demonstrate the absence of any stringent necessity for an entire change in our Federal policy. This vote may be taken as a fair exhibition of the policy of both parties and their relative strength.

The question of the navigation of the Mississippi was one of the great topics of the present session. That river once held to Virginia a relation as intimate as the Chesapeake and the James hold at the present time. The account of the Mississippi debate in the Convention, which has been already reported, explains the state of public opinion on the subject. Let it suffice for the present to say that at a moment when the fate of the Commonwealth was believed to hang by a single hair, Virginia had given a reluctant consent to allow the surrender of the navigation of that river to become a subject of negotiation with Spain; but as soon as the imminent jeopardy was removed she returned to her true feelings, and opposed all negotiation on such a question.[160] It had been recently discussed in Congress, and there was an evident design on the part of that body, or of its Secretary for Foreign Affairs, to cede the exclusive navigation of the river to Spain for a term of years, embracing an entire generation. At this crisis the House of Delegates determined to mark out in unequivocal terms the policy which Virginia would maintain; and on the 29th day of November, 1786, discussed the subject in full in Committee of the Whole. When the committee rose, General Matthews reported to the House three resolutions, the first of which set forth that the common right of navigating the Mississippi, and of communicating with other nations through that channel, ought to be considered as the bountiful gift of nature to the United States, as the proprietors of the territories watered by that river and its eastern branches, and as morover secured to them by the late Revolution. The second declared that the confederacy, having been formed on the broad basis of equal rights in every part thereof to the protection and guardianship of the whole, a sacrifice of the rights of any part to the supposed real interest of another part would be a flagrant violation of justice, a direct contravention of the end for which the Federal Government was instituted, and an alarming innovation in the system of the Union. The third recommended that the delegates of Virginia in Congress [161] ought to be instructed in the most decided terms to oppose any attempt that may be made in Congress to barter or surrender to any nation whatever the right of the United States to the free and common

---

[160] See letter of Madison to H. Niles (*Madison Papers*, Vol. I, Appendix, No. IV).

[161] The delegates in Congress elected at the present session were William Grayson, James Madison, Richard Henry Lee, Joseph Jones, and Edward Carrington. Jones having declined, Henry Lee, Jr. (Legion Harry) was chosen in his place. It has been seen in the debates what an important part some of these gentlemen had to perform. By the way, the members of Congress were elected at each session of Assembly by the process of bringing in a fresh bill at every election appointing delegates to Congress. Leave was asked to bring in the bill, and when the bill was reported it passed through the stages of an ordinary bill in both houses. When the bill became a law the election was held by joint ballot of the houses.

use of the river Mississippi, and to protest against the same as a dishonorable departure from the comprehensive and benevolent policy which constitutes the vital principle of the confederacy; as provoking the just resentments and reproaches of our Western brethren, whose essential rights and interests would be thereby sacrificed and sold; as destroying that confidence in the wisdom, justice, and liberality of the Federal councils, which is so necessary at this crisis to a proper enlargement of their authority; and, finally, as tending to undermine our repose, our prosperity, and our Union itself; and that the said delegates ought to be instructed to urge the proper negotiations with Spain for obtaining her concurrence in such regulations touching the mutual and common use of the said river as may secure the permanent harmony and affection of the two nations, and such as the wise and generous policy of His Catholic Majesty will perceive to be no less due to the interests of his own subjects than to the just and friendly views of the United States.   These resolutions were unanimously adopted by the House, and Matthews was ordered to take them to the Senate, which body concurred in them on the 8th, without amendment.

These resolutions record an era in human affairs.   It may be truly affirmed that, if Virginia had cast her weight in the opposite scale, no American boat, not a bale of American cotton, would have rested on the waters of Mississippi for a generation to come.   The West, all hope of profitable agriculture being blasted, would have remained unpeopled; and those strong incentives which, in better days and under the auspices of a new system controlled by Southern statesmen, led to the purchase of Louisiana and the free and perpetual ownership and use of that mighty river, would not have existed, nor that public opinion which was necessary to sustain that magnificent acquisition. Honor to the men who laid the foundation of that great work, and whose names, almost forgotten in the land of their birth, it is our present purpose and ardent desire to make familiar to those who inherit the results of their splendid statesmanship and heroic courage.

A graceful act of the present session was the purchase and manumission of the slave James, the property of William Armistead, of New Kent.   The subject was brought before the House of Delegates by a petition from the slave himself, setting forth, among other things, a certificate from the Marquis de Lafayette, that James had done him essential services while he commanded in Virginia, and that the intelligence which the negro had received from the enemy's camp was industriously collected and most faithfully delivered as a spy; and that he properly acquitted himself in some important commissions which the Marquis had given him. The bill of purchase and manumission passed both houses unanimously. This is the only instance, which at present occurs to us, in which a petition from a slave was presented to the House of Delegates.

On the 15th day of October, 1787, the General Assembly again came together, and a quorum of both houses appeared on the first day of the session. The modest and estimable Prentis, who was soon to be called to the bench of the District Court, was re-elected Speaker of the House of Delegates without opposition—an honor the more valuable as he was nominated by General Matthews, who was eminent as a parliamentarian, and who, at a subsequent date, filled the Speaker's chair for several years, and was sustained by Governor Harrison, who had more than once presided in the House, had been Governor, and had filled the leading posts abroad.

The members of the House, who were members of the present Convention, were William Cabell, Patrick Henry, Benjamin Harrison, William Watkins, Parke Goodall, French Strother, Thomas Smith, Andrew Moore, George Nicholas, Thomas Matthews, Theodoric Bland, Nathaniel Burwell, William Ronald, Francis Corbin, James Monroe, Edmund Custis, John Trigg, Joseph Jones, Meriwether Smith, Samuel Richardson, John Guerrant, Isaac Coles, John Marr, Green Clay, Samuel Hopkins, Willis Riddick, Thomas Turpin, Cuthbert Bullitt, Robert Lawson, John Dawson, John Howell Briggs, Thomas Edmunds, Zachariah Johnston, Archibald Stuart, Martin McFerran, George Mason, David Stuart, John Early, John S. Woodcock, Daniel Fisher, Ralph Humphreys, George Jackson, John Prunty, John Marshall, William Norvell, Benjamin Temple, Levin Powell, Littleton Eyre, James Webb, Archibald Woods, Anthony Walke, Walker Tomlin, William McKee, John Allen, Richard Cary, Samuel Edmison, Bushrod Washington, Miles King, Samuel

Jordan Cabell, David Patteson, William Thornton, Joseph Jones, David Stuart, James Gordon, Edmund Ruffin, and Alexander White.

Madison was in Congress, which was then sitting in New York, as his published letters show; but probably at no period of our history was the House of Delegates composed of an abler body of men. As a characteristic of the times, it may be mentioned that Daniel Boone was a member from one of the counties of Kentucky.

Norvell, whose grave demeanor and weight of public service well fitted him for the post, was placed at the head of the Committee of Religion; Harrison, at the head of the Committee of Privileges and Elections; George Nicholas, at the head of the Committee of Propositions and Grievances; Patrick Henry, at the head of the Committee of Courts of Justice; and Matthews, at the head of the Committee of Commerce.

The Senate was also successful in getting a quorum on the first day of the session, and elected John Jones their Speaker by a majority of one vote over General Edward Stevens.[162]

Stevens Thomson Mason, John Pride, Walter Jones, and Burwell Bassett, members of the present Convention, were also members of the Senate.[163]

The first general business was the re-election of Edmund Randolph as Governor, and the choice of James Madison, Edward Carrington, Henry Lee, John Brown, and Cyrus Griffin as members of Congress for the following year. The new Federal

---

[162] General Edward Stevens and General Adam Stephen were frequently confounded in their own day, and still more frequently in later times. General Adam Stephen was a member of the present Convention, and is noticed elsewhere. General Edward Stevens was almost our contemporary, as he died as late as 1820. He was an excellent man and a gallant soldier. He is buried near Culpeper Courthouse, in this State.

[163] There were two gentlemen by the name of Burwell Bassett in the Assembly at the present session. The one in the Senate, and not the one in the House, was a member of the present Convention. Great care is necessary in deciding on individuals of the same name. Thus there were Cabells and Joneses in both houses, a Paul Carrington on the bench, and another in the House. This care is more imperative, as the Journals have no index.

Constitution, which had been promulgated some days before,[164] was now in the hands of most of the members for the first time, but did not seem to produce any sensible effect on legislation. Several years had elapsed after the ratification of the Articles of Confederation by Virginia before they went into operation; and it is probable that the members thought that a similar lapse of time might occur in the case of the new Constitution.

The House of Delegates soon adopted three resolutions—the first of which instructed the Executive to procure several thousand stand of arms and accoutrements for the use of the militia of the State, and to distribute them in the several counties in proportion to the number of militia; the second provided that a corps of cavalry should be raised out of the militia of each county by voluntary enlistment; and the third repealed the laws obliging the militia to furnish themselves with arms. These resolutions were referred to a committee consisting of Matthews, Nicholas, Henry, Ronald, Harrison, Monroe, Archibald Stuart, and Marshall—nearly all of whom had taken an active part in military service during the late war. Leave was given to bring in a bill declaring tobacco receivable in payment of certain taxes for the year 1787; and Nicholas, Gordon, and Cabell were ordered to bring it in. Leave was also given to bring in a bill to reduce into one the acts imposing duties on imported articles, and another to amend the laws of revenue and provide for the support of civil government, and the regular payment of all the debts due by the Commonwealth; all of which ultimately became laws.

The subject of the new Federal Constitution came up on the 25th in the House of Delegates. The House went into committee, and, after debate, Prentis resumed the chair, and Matthews reported a series of resolutions providing that the proceedings of the Federal Convention, as transmitted to the General Assembly through the medium of Congress, ought to be submitted to a convention of the people for their free and full investigation and discussion; that every citizen, being a freeholder of this Commonwealth, ought to be eligible to a seat in the Convention, and that the people thereof ought not to be restrained

---

[164] The General Convention had adjourned on the 17th day of September.

in their choice of Delegates by any of those legal or constitutional restrictions which confine them in the choice of delegates to the Legislature; that it be recommended to each county to elect two delegates, and to each city, town, or corporation entitled by law to representation in the Legislature to elect one delegate to the said Convention; that the qualifications of the electors be the same as those established by law; that the election for delegates aforesaid be held at the several places appointed by law for holding the elections for delegates to the General Assembly, and that the same be conducted by the officers who conducted the elections for delegates, and conformably to the rules and regulations thereof; that the election of delegates shall be held in the month of March next, on the first day of the court to be held for each county, city, or corporation, respectively, and that the persons so chosen shall assemble in the State House, in the city of Richmond, on the fourth Monday of May next; that two thousand copies of these resolutions be forthwith printed and dispersed by the members of the General Assembly among their constituents; and that the Executive transmit a copy of them to Congress and to the Legislature and Executive of the respective States. These resolutions were read a second time, and the vote was taken upon them. The first, which required the Constitution to be submitted to an independent convention, was adopted unanimously; the remaining ones were adopted, though not unanimously; but no division was called for. Matthews was ordered to take them to the Senate, which body sent them back by Stevens Thomson Mason on the 31st with amendments, which were concurred in by the House. A bill containing the substance of the resolves was duly reported in the House, passed that body and the Senate, and on the 12th of December became a law.[165] This act was ordered to be sent to the several States in like manner with the resolves. Thus was Virginia not only the first to call the General Convention and to appoint delegates to attend it, but was the first to provide by law for the submission of the work of its hands to the people of a State.

---

[165] What the amendments of the Senate to the resolves were does not appear in the Journal of either house. It is probable that the change of the time of meeting to the first Monday in June was the most important.

A great blunder was committed by the opponents of the Constitution in allowing the first resolution of the series to be adopted. If they ever designed to assail that instrument as exceeding the powers of the body which framed it, as was palpable on its face, then was the time to act. The submission of it to the people at once removed all such objections, and established its legitimacy. Motives of delicacy may have operated in producing unanimity on the subject; and it is not improbable that its opponents relied upon their strength in the proposed convention—which was substantially the General Assembly under another name—in which body they had long been ascendant; and it may have been that parties, at this early stage, had not been distinctly organized.

This session was distinguished by the number and variety of the topics of legislation which were discussed and settled. No opinion seemed to have been entertained that a great change was impending. On the contrary, the acts embraced the whole subject of customs, the construction of a fort,[166] the building of a marine hospital for sick and disabled seamen, and other measures of a commercial character. One of the leading measures, which passed and repassed between the houses more than once, was the establishment of district courts. Under its provisions Joseph Prentis, Gabriel Jones, Saint George Tucker, and Richard Parker were elected judges. An act passed to amend the county courts. Appropriations were made to the lunatic hospital, and one-sixth of the surveyors' fees in the Kentucky district were devoted to the support of the Transylvania Seminary. A company was chartered to connect the waters of the Elizabeth river with those of the Pasquotank; and the Dismal Swamp canal, which has long contributed to the wealth and prosperity of Virginia and North Carolina, has been the result. A safety fund was provided for the gradual extinction of the public debt. All acts which prevented the speedy collection of British debts were repealed; and this was done when our negroes, who were carried off at York and from the city of New York, were unpaid for, and when the Western posts, from which the Indians on our borders were supplied with arms, were still retained, in spite of

---

[166] This fort was built by a man named Richard Chinwith. [A corruption, probably, of Chenowith.—EDITOR.]

the definitive treaty by Great Britain. Certain persons were invested with the exclusive right of running stage-coaches on particular routes; and Fitch was allowed the exclusive privilege of navigating the waters of the State, by steam, for fourteen years. Acts for regulating the customs and the duties of naval officers, carefully prepared, were passed, and for the payment of all arrearages into the treasury. Tobacco was made receivable in payment of certain taxes; and, either by the enactment of new laws or by the amendment of the old, the State was never before so invigorated in her military, financial, and judicial departments. The adjournment of both houses took place on the 8th of January, 1788.

A glance at the Treasurer's account of his receipts during the year, extending from the 12th of December, 1786, to November the 30th, 1787, will afford a safe means of comparison with the revenues accruing to the Commonwealth under the new Constitution. The sum total of receipts from all sources was not far from one million and a half pounds—Virginia currency.[167] This sum was made up of arrears of taxes of previous years, amounting to over thirty-three thousand pounds; the revenue taxes of 1786 were one hundred and forty-one thousand five hundred and twelve pounds; the amount of revenue from the customs, including the export duties on tobacco, was near eighty-seven thousand pounds. Of course, there was a large amount of certificates of the public debt received in payment of taxes; but in a few years this source would have been exhausted. There were also payments for public lands sold at Gosport, for public property, and for public lands generally. When we recall the fact that the duties were almost nominal—rarely exceeding five per cent., and oftener under, owing to the position of Virginia in respect of the custom-houses of Maryland and Pennsylvania just beyond her lines—it is evident that the revenue from customs, which was not far from three hundred thousand dollars, must have represented a vast commerce for those days.

Between the adjournment of the General Assembly, in January, 1788, and its meeting on the 23d of June following, the

---

[167] $3.33⅓ to the pound. The Treasurer's account may be seen in the Senate Journal of January 2, 1788, and in the House Journal of December 13, 1787.

Federal Convention held its sittings. The bodies came together, for the Convention did not adjourn until the 27th of June, and the Assembly met on the 23d. It was, by the proclamation of the Governor, made on the 14th of May last, that the Assembly was called together. On the first day (23d) neither house formed a quorum. The members generally were doubtless attracted by the proceedings of the Convention; and the members of the Assembly, who were members of the Convention, were unable to leave their seats in the latter body. A single vote might settle important questions; and it was not until the 26th that the final vote on the ratification of the Constitution was taken. On the 25th the Senate obtained a quorum, and Humphrey Brooke, a member of the Convention, was appointed Clerk; and John Jones, a member of the Convention, was, on motion of Stevens Thomson Mason, a member of the Convention, unanimously re-elected Speaker. The members of the Senate, who were also members of the Convention, were, besides Mason and John Jones, Burwell Bassett and John Pride and Joseph Jones. Joseph Jones had long been a member of the House of Delegates, had been a member of Congress, and held a front rank among the statesmen of his day.

The House of Delegates failed to get a quorum on the first day, but on the second a number sufficient to organize the House assembled, when Colonel Monroe nominated the accomplished Grayson as Speaker. This nomination, which at this day we should suppose would have been received by acclamation, was by no means satisfactory; probably, at first sight, because both Monroe and Grayson had warmly opposed in debate the adoption of the Constitution, the fate of which was not yet settled, but rather, I am inclined to think, because both gentlemen had been mainly prominent in military and civil stations abroad, and were not in the direct line of succession to honorary posts at home, especially in the Assembly. Meriwether Smith nominated General Thomas Matthews, whose entire public life had been spent within the Commonwealth, and who had been long deemed one of the best parliamentarians in the House. But it seems there was to be be another formidable nomination. Cabell of ("Union Hill"), who had long known Benjamin Harrison, and had served with him in public bodies for almost thirty years, determined to bring him forward for the chair. The House determined to vote by ballot, and, upon a count, it was ascertained Matthews had received a majority of the whole House, and was declared Speaker. It should seem that our worthy fathers did not make party politics an exclusive test in filling the office of Speaker, as Smith, who was a decided opponent of the Constitution, nominated Matthews, who, coming from a commercial town, was one of its warmest friends, and voted the day after his election by the House of Delegates—a majority of which opposed the Constitution—for the ratification of that instrument. There was also perceptible at all times in the House an *esprit de corps* which prompted its members to confer its honors on those whose terms of public service were spent on its floor. Hence it was that Richard Henry Lee, who was the impersonator of patriotism, eloquence, and honor, though brought forward for the chair repeatedly in the range of thirty years, was always defeated by large majorities.

The members of the Convention who were members of the House were—besides Monroe, Grayson, Smith, Matthews, Cabell, and Harrison—Patrick Henry, Zachariah Johnston, Theodoric Bland, William Ronald, Cuthbert Bullitt, Miles King, French Strother, Francis Corbin, John H. Briggs, Wilson C. Nicholas, William Thornton, Levin Powell, Thomas Smith, John Dawson, David Stuart, Daniel Fisher, Ralph Wormley, William O. Callis, Alexander White, John Early, John S. Woodcock, George Clendenin, John Allen, Samuel J. Cabell, Bushrod Washington, Andrew Moore,[168] Walker Tomlin, John Trigg, Henry Lee (of Bourbon), Binns Jones, John Guerrant, William McKee, Robert Breckenridge, Green Clay, C. Robertson, John H. Cocke, Richard Kennon, Thomas Cooper, John Roane, Thomas Carter, and Samuel Edmiston.

One of the first questions that arose in the House was whether the members of the Convention, who were members of Assembly, should receive double mileage and double *per diem*. This matter, which was quite important in a financial view from the numbers of those who held seats in both bodies, and from the lean state of the treasury, was gravely discussed; and a resolution was passed by both houses prohibiting the payment of double mileage and double pay. So the double members were

---

[168] Who was elected during the session a member of the Council.

no better off than their single brethren. Forty years later this question was again started in relation to those who were members of the Convention of 1829, and who were at the same time members of the Assembly. The Convention of that year ran for a month and a half into the session of the Assembly, and both bodies were hard at work at the same time. But the question, though propounded in private, never reached the ear of either house, each member deciding it for himself.[169] The fact is, that the law passed by the Assembly of 1788 was *ex post facto*, and a nullity. Every member of the Assembly and of the Convention was entitled under existing laws to his mileage and *per diem*, and, having rendered the service, was entitled to receive the wages prescribed by law. How far the Assembly would have been justifiable in increasing the pay is another question; but it is plain they could no more reduce or abolish the pay of a member for services actually rendered than they could reduce or abolish the pay of any other officer under similar circumstances. But the double members were numerous, the treasury was scant of coin, and a law as clearly as unconstitutional as was ever enacted passed both houses with apparent unanimity.

A file of the Richmond papers for the year 1788 is not in existence; and, as the Journals of neither house contain a copy

---

[169] The *double* members of the Convention and Assembly of 1829 were some twelve or fifteen. I was one of them; but we needed no law to prevent us from receiving double pay. It was a question of equity and honor, and but one member asked and received his double pay, and he has long since passed to a realm where, it is to be hoped, *constructive* journeys are unknown. That we were not compelled to do right by a special law passed in the very teeth of the Constitution and Declaration of Rights, at a time when there was quite a plethora in the treasury, shows that we were at least as patriotic as our worthy predecessors were forced to be. I remember the state of the treasury in 1829 from a little incident that happened on the day of the publication of the Treasurer's report in the papers. I met with the late Judge Philip P. Barbour, the President of the Convention, at our breakfast-table at the Eagle, and seeing him tickled at something in the morning's paper, inquired about the cause of his mirth He said that he was amused at the felicitations of the Treasurer over a surplus of fifty or sixty thousand dollars; that in Congress they made nothing of voting a hundred thousand, or even half a million, at a single breath; and that when he thought what would be the effect of such a vote on the keeper of the Virginia fisc, he could not resist a smile.

of the Governor's proclamation calling them together, I am unable to state positively the reason of the call. It was certainly not on account of the Convention, as the previous Assembly had passed all the necessary laws upon the subject, and the houses would meet in course in October, and the action of the houses had no reference, during their session, to the Convention.[170] I am inclined to believe that the call grew out of the remonstrance of the judges of the Court of Appeals to some details of the new District Court law; for both houses immediately passed the bill to suspend the operation of the law for the present. They, however, kept its bench full; for on being informed of the declinature of his seat by Gabriel Jones,[171] one of the new judges, they supplied the vacancy by the election of Edmund Winston.[172]

On the 30th of June, after a session of six days, the Assembly adjourned. Although the Convention had adjourned three days before, and so many of its leading members were members of the Assembly, it does not appear that any allusion was made to its proceedings. Certainly no action was had on the subject.

Both houses reassembled on the 20th of October, 1788; but, as was usual, when two sessions of the Assembly were held in the same year, no quorum appeared in either house on the first day. The Senate did not succeed in obtaining one until the 28th, but the House of Delegates was able to proceed to business on the second day. The Speaker held over. Johnston was put at the head of the Committee of Religion; Harrison, of Privileges and Elections; Cabell (of "Union Hill"), of Propositions and Grievances; Patrick Henry, of Courts of Justice; Richard Lee, of Claims; and John Page (taking the post of Matthews, who was Speaker), of the Committee of Commerce.

An incident occurred on the third day of the session (24th) which showed the feelings of the House on Federal affairs.

---

[170] They made a slight alteration in the fund, from which the expenses of the Convention were to be paid; but this was purely accidental.

[171] Gabriel Jones twice declined a judicial office and once a seat in Congress.

[172] As Governor Randolph had doubtless made up his mind before the date of the proclamation to quit the anti-Federalists, it is not likely that he would have convoked an anti-Federal Legislature without some paramount consideration.

Colonel Edward Carrington, who had been elected a member of Congress the preceding November, and had taken his seat in that body, was returned to the present House at the April following from the county of Powhatan. It was proved that he did not hear of his election as a member of the House until the last of June, during which month a session of the House was held, and that he had resigned his seat in Congress some days before. The Committee of Elections reported in favor of his holding the seat, but the House reversed the report, and declared his seat vacant.[173] This distrust of servants who were called to serve two masters was manifested at an early period, and was altogether wise and proper. Our early legislation on this subject merits a passing review. As early as 1777 an act was passed declaring members of Congress ineligible to either house of Assembly; but in 1779, evidently for some temporary purpose, it was enacted that, should any person holding an executive, legislative, or judicial office in the Commonwealth be appointed a delegate to Congress, his office shall not thereby be vacated. In 1783 an act passed declaring it improper that a delegate to Congress should at the same time be a member of Assembly, and that if a member of Assembly should accept a seat in Congress his seat in the Assembly should be vacated. Before the passage of the act of 1777 members of Congress were almost invariably members of Assembly, and, when Congress was not sitting, took their seats in the houses—an arrangement which was at that early day extremely convenient and beneficial to the public service. No newspapers worthy of the name were then published in the States; and if there had been, the proceedings of Congress, which were secret, could not have been found in them. The presence of a member of Congress in the Assembly might have a good effect upon legislation; for, although he could not directly reveal the proceedings of Congress, unless required by a direct vote of the houses, his advice and suggestions were valuable and welcome. This policy, however, was put an end

---

[173] He was sent back immediately by the people of Powhatan, and voted throughout the session with the Federal minority. This distinguished patriot, after serving faithfully during the Revolution, particularly as the quartermaster-general of Greene, and filling many civil offices, and declining more (especially a seat in the Cabinet of Washington), died in Richmond, October 28, 1810; aged sixty-one.

to by the jealousy with which a majority of both houses regarded Richard Henry Lee, and which led to the momentary ostracism of that illustrious patriot.

On the 27th of October, 1788, both houses for the first time held their sessions "in the new Capitol on Shockoe Hill," and have continued to hold them there, with the exception of a single session, ever since.

The name of Robert Carter Nicholas, the old Treasurer of the Colony, and the first Treasurer of the Commonwealth, was brought up on the 30th to the consideration of the House. It appeared that he had been appointed by one of the Conventions in 1775 one of a committee to procure gunpowder for the use of the Colony; and for this purpose borrowed of Messrs. Norton & Sons, of London, the sum of five thousand six hundred pounds sterling, for which he gave—at a time when the Colony, not having declared independence, had no name of her own—his private bond, with a number of gentlemen as his securities. The collection of the bond was now pressed upon his executor, who was his oldest son, George, a member of the House, and relief was asked of the Assembly. It is credible to all parties that the bond was instantly ordered to be paid, with six per cent. interest until it was paid.

The absorbing topic which was likely to employ the time of the Assembly, and which filled the public mind with doubt and apprehension, and even with serious alarm, was the Federal Constitution. Both parties were not indisposed to propose amendments to that instrument; but the stress was on the mode of making those amendments. The Federal party proper contended that the true mode of amending the Constitution should be in accordance with its fifth article; while the opponents of that paper urged that the most efficient and thorough means of attaining an end deemed desirable by all was the call of a new Convention of the States for the purpose. On the 30th the House of Delegates went into Committee of the Whole on the State of the Commonwealth, and, when the Speaker resumed the chair, reported the following preamble and resolutions:

" Whereas the Convention of delegates of the people of this Commonwealth did ratify a Constitution, or form of government, for the United States, referred to them for their consideration, and did also declare that sundry amendments to exceptionable parts of the same ought to be adopted; and whereas the subject-matter of the amendments agreed to by the said Convention invokes all the great essential and unalienable rights, liberties, and privileges of freemen, many of which, if not cancelled, are rendered insecure under the said Constitution till the same shall be altered and amended—

"*Resolved*, That it is the opinion of this committee that, for quieting the minds of the good citizens of this Commonwealth, and securing their rights and liberties, and preventing those disorders which must arise under a government not founded in the confidence of the people, application be made to the Congress of the United States, so soon as they shall assemble under the said Constitution, to call a convention for proposing amendments to the same, according to the mode therein directed.

"*Resolved*, That it is the opinion of this committee that a committee ought to be appointed to draw up and report to this House a proper instrument of writing expressing the sense of the General Assembly, and pointing out the reasons which induce them to urge their application thus early for the calling the aforesaid Convention of the States.

"*Resolved*, That it is the opinion of this committee that the said committee should be instructed to prepare the draft of a letter in answer to one received from his Excellency George Clinton, Esq., president of the Convention of New York, and a circular-letter on the aforesaid subject of the other States in the Union, expressive of the wish of the General Assembly of this Commonwealth that they may join in the application to the new Congress to appoint a Convention of the States as soon as the Congress shall assemble under the new Constitution."

When the resolutions were read a motion was made to amend the same by striking out from the word "whereas" in the first line to the end, and inserting the following words:

"Whereas the delegates appointed to represent the good people of this Commonwealth in the late Convention held in the month of June last, did, by their act of the 25th of the said month, assent to and ratify the Constitution recommended on the 17th day of September, 1787, by the Federal Convention for the government of the United States, declaring themselves, with a solemn appeal to the Searcher of hearts for the purity of their intentions, under the conviction 'that whatsoever imperfec-

tions might exist in the Constitution ought rather to be examined
in the mode prescribed therein than to bring the Union into danger by a delay, with a hope of obtaining amendments previous to
the ratification'; and whereas, in pursuance of the said declaration,
the same Convention did, by their subsequent act of the 27th of
June aforesaid, agree to such amendments to the said Constitution of government for the United States as were by them
deemed necessary to be recommended to the consideration of
the Congress which shall first assemble under the said Constitution, to be acted upon according to the mode prescribed in the
fifth article thereof, at the same time enjoining it upon their
representatives in Congress to exert all their influence and use
all legal and reasonable methods to obtain a ratification of the
foregoing alterations and provisions in the manner provided by
the fifth article of the said Constitution, and in all congressional
laws to be passed in the mean time to conform to the spirit of
those amendments as far as the said Constitution would admit:

"*Resolved, therefore,* That it is the opinion of this committee
that an application ought to be made in the name and on the
behalf of the Legislature of this Commonwealth to the Congress
of the United States, so soon as they shall assemble under the
said Constitution, to pass an act recommending to the Legislatures of the several States the ratification of a bill of rights,
and of certain articles of amendment proposed by the Convention of this State for the adoption of the United States, and that,
until the said act shall be ratified in pursuance of the fifth article
of the said Constitution of government for the United States,
Congress do conform their ordinances to the true spirit of the
said bill of rights and articles of amendment."

A second resolution instructed the Executive to transmit a
copy of the foregoing resolution to the Congress and to the
Legislatures and Executives of the States.

By these resolutions the issue was fairly made up between the
two great parties, and they were probably debated with unusual
warmth and ability on the floor; but we can know nothing certain on the subject. The question on the amendment was taken
at once, and it was lost by a vote of thirty-nine to eighty-five;
showing a majority in favor of the opponents of the Constitution of more than two to one. The members of the House
who had been members of the Convention, and who voted for

striking out, were Johnston, McFerran, David Stuart, Wood-cock, Thomas Smith, Clendenin, Fisher, Thornton, Powell, Callis, Corbin, Wormeley, and Allen; and those who voted with the majority against striking out were Custis, William Cabell, S. J. Cabell, John Trigg, Henry Lee (of Bourbon), Conn, Binns Jones, Harrison, Strother, John Early, Joel Early, Guerrant, Cooper, Roane, Clay (of Madison, Ky.), A. Robert-son, Kennon, Patrick Henry, Bland, Bullitt, Grayson, McKee, Carter, Monroe, Dawson, Briggs, Edmunds, and Edmiston.

The main question was then put of agreeing to the preamble and resolutions as reported by the committee, and was agreed to without a division. Briggs, Henry, Harrison, Grayson, Bullitt, William Cabell, Monroe, Bland, Dawson, Strother, and Roane, all of whom were members of the Convention, were appointed a committee to prepare the instrument called for by the report.

On the 14th of November the House again went into Com-mittee on Federal Affairs, and, when the Speaker resumed the chair, Bullitt reported a resolution, which, as a deliberate reflec-tion of the purposes of the majority of that day, should be read by the student of history. Here it is:

"*Resolved*, That it is the opinion of this committee that an application ought to be made in the name and on behalf of the Legislature of this Commonwealth, to the Congress of the United States in the words following—to-wit:

"The good people of this Commonwealth, in Convention assembled, having ratified the Constitution submitted to their consideration, this Legislature has, in conformity to that act and the resolutions of the United States, in Congress assembled, to them transmitted, thought proper to make the arrangements that were necessary for carrying it into effect. Having thus shown themselves obedient to the voice of their constituents, all America will find that, so far as it depends on them, the plan of government will be carried into immediate operation.

"But the sense of the people of Virginia would be but in part complied with, and but little regarded, if we went no further. In the very moment of adoption, and coeval with the ratification of the new plan of government, the general voice of the Conven-tion of this State pointed to objects no less interesting to the people we represent, and equally entitled to your attention. At the same time that, from motives of affection for our sister States, the Convention yielded their consent to the ratification, they gave the most unequivocal proofs that they dreaded its operation under the present form.

"In acceding to a government under this impression, painful must have been the prospect had they not derived consolation from a full expectation of its imperfections being speedily amended. In this resource, therefore, they placed their confidence—a confidence that will continue to support them, whilst they have reason to believe they have not calculated upon it in vain.

"In making known to you the objections of the people of this Commonwealth to the new plan of government, we deem it unnecessary to enter into a particular detail of its defects, which they consider as involving all the great and unalienable rights of freemen. For their sense on this subject we refer you to the proceedings of their late Convention, and the sense of this General Assembly as expressed in their resolutions of the [30th] of [October] last.[174]

"We think proper, however, to declare that, in our opinion, as those objections were not founded in speculative theory, but deduced from principles which have been established by the melancholy example of other nations in different ages, so they will never be removed until the cause itself shall cease to exist. The sooner, therefore, the public apprehensions are quieted and the Government is possessed of the confidence of the people the more salutary will be its operations, and the longer its duration.

"The cause of amendments we consider as a common cause; and since concessions have been made from political motives, which we conceive may endanger the republic, we trust that a commendable zeal will be shown for obtaining those provisions which experience has taught us are necessary to secure from danger the unalienable rights of human nature.

"The anxiety with which our countrymen press for the accomplishment of this important end will ill admit of delay. The slow forms of congressional discussion and recommendation, if, indeed, they should ever agree to any change, would, we fear, be less certain of success. Happily for their wishes, the Constitu-

---

[174] These two blanks for the date were omitted to be filled by an oversight.

tion hath presented an alternative by admitting the submission
to a Convention of the States.   To this, therefore, we resort as
the source from whence they are to derive relief from their present
apprehensions.   We do, therefore, in behalf of our constituents,
in the most earnest and solemn manner, make this application to
Congress, that a convention be immediately called of deputies
from the several States, with full power to take into their consideration the defects of this Constitution that have been suggested
by the State Conventions, and report such amendments thereto
as they shall find best suited to promote our common interests,
and secure to ourselves and our latest posterity the great and
unalienable rights of mankind.''

A draft of a letter to Governor George Clinton, of New York,
the President of the Federal Convention of that State, was presented and read, as follows:

"Sir,—The letter from the Convention of the State of New
York hath been laid before us since our present session.   The
subject which it contemplated had been taken up, and we have
the pleasure to inform you of the entire concurrence in sentiment between that honorable body and the representatives in
Senate and Assembly of the freemen of this Commonwealth.
The propriety of immediately calling a Convention of the States
to take into consideration the defects of the Constitution was
admitted, and, in consequence thereof, an application agreed to,
to be presented to the Congress as soon as it shall be convened,
for the accomplishment of that important end.   We herewith
transmit to your Excellency a copy of this application, which we
request may be laid before your Assembly at their next meeting.
We take occasion to express our most earnest wishes that it
may obtain the approbation of New York, and of all other sister
States.''

A draft of another letter, which was addressed to the States,
requesting their concurrence with Virginia in calling the Convention, was also reported.

As soon as the resolution and the drafts of letters were read,
a motion was made to amend the same by substituting in lieu
thereof the following form of an application and draft of letters—
to-wit:

"The Legislature of Virginia to the Congress of the United
States, sends greeting: The Convention of the representatives of

the good people of this Commonwealth, having on the 25th day of
June last ratified the Constitution, or form of government, proposed by the Federal Convention on the 17th of September,
1787, and having declared, in their act of ratification, that any
imperfections that might exist in the said Constitution ought
rather to be examined in the mode prescribed therein for obtaining amendments than by a delay, with a hope of obtaining previous amendments to bring the Union into danger; and, in order
to relieve the apprehensions of those who might be solicitous
for amendments, having resolved that whatever amendments
might be deemed necessary ought to be recommended to the
consideration of Congress, which should first assemble under
the said Constitution, to be acted upon according to the mode
prescribed in the fifth article thereof; and, on the 27th day of
the same month of June, agreed to certain amendments to the
said Constitution, which were transmitted, together with the ratification of the Federal Constitution, to the United States, in
Congress assembled, which amendments the said Convention
did, in the name and behalf of the people of this Commonwealth,
enjoin it upon their representatives in Congress to exert all their
influence, and use all legal and reasonable methods, to obtain a
ratification of in the manner provided by the said Constitution;
and, in all congressional laws to be passed in the mean time, to
conform to the spirit of the said amendments as far as the said
Constitution would admit:

" This Legislature, fully concurring in sentiment with the said
Convention, and solicitous to promote the salutary measures by
them recommended, do, in consideration of the unanimity with
which said amendments were agreed to, and a just sense of their
utility, earnestly call upon the Congress of the United States to
take the said amendments under their immediate consideration,
and also those which may have been submitted by the Conventions of other States, and to act thereupon in the manner prescribed by the fifth article of the Federal Constitution, either by
proposing the necessary alterations to the consideration of the
States, or by calling a convention to deliberate on the subject,
as to them shall seem most likely to promote the peace and
general good of the Union. We pray that Almighty God in
His goodness and wisdom will direct your councils to such
measures as will establish our lasting peace and welfare, and

secure to our latest posterity the blessings of freedom; and that
He will always have you in His holy keeping.''

The draft of a letter to the States on the subject was in these
words:

" We beg leave to submit to your consideration a copy of our
answer to the circular-letter from the Convention of our sister
State of New York, and also a copy of an address, which we
think it our duty to make to the Congress at their first meeting.
We flatter ourselves that you will not hesitate in making a similar application, the object being to establish our rights and liberties on the most immutable basis.   May God have you in His
holy keeping.''

This amendment was drawn with greater tact than that which
was offered on the 30th of October, and which was rejected by
such an overwhelming vote.   It proposed to make the mode of
obtaining amendments discretionary with the Congress; while,
with the view of enlisting the sympathies of some pious members from the West, who, like McKee, had shown a strong
inclination to side with the anti-Federalists, and who might consider a reference to a Superintending Power on such an occasion
altogether wise and becoming, a religious tinge was given to the
whole.   The anti-Federal majority of two to one of the 30th of
November fell to twenty-two, which, though a fair majority in a
house of one hundred and twenty-two members, was a considerable falling off.   The vote on the amendment, which was to
strike out the report of the Committee of the Whole, and insert
the Federal programme in its stead, was ayes fifty, noes seventy-
two.   So the amendment failed; and the question recurring on
the adoption of the original report, was decided in the affirmative, without a division.

As the names of the members who had been members of the
Convention may explain the character of the vote, we will state
that those who voted for striking out the report of the committee
and inserting the amendment in its place were the Speaker
(General Matthews), Wilson Cary Nicholas, Johnston, McFerran,
David Stuart, Woodcock, Alexander White, Thomas Smith,
Clendenin, Fisher, Breckenridge, Powell, Callis, Corbin, Wormeley, Ronald, John Stringer, Tomlin, and Allen, and those who
voted against striking out and in favor of the report of the committee were William Cabell, John Trigg, Henry Lee (of Bour-

bon), Conn, Binns Jones, Harrison, Strother, Joel Early, King, John Early, Cooper, Guerrant, Roane, Green Clay, A. Robertson, Kennon, Riddick, Patrick Henry, Bland, Bullitt, McKee, Carter, Monroe, Edmunds, and Edmiston. As soon as the vote was declared Bullitt was ordered to carry the instrument to the Senate, and request its concurrence.

There was no difficulty in passing all the laws necessary for setting the Constitution in operation. The bill for appointing electors to choose a President passed unanimously. The bill for electing representatives pursuant to the Constitution of government of the United States passed unanimously, after a smart skirmish in the House before its engrossment, on a motion to strike out the words: "being a freeholder, and who shall have been a *bona-fide* resident for twelve months within such district," which was rejected by thirty-two ayes to eighty noes; the members of the House who had been members of the Convention voting as follows:

AYES—Johnston, McFerran, David Stuart, Woodcock, Fisher, Powell, Callis, Wormeley, Ronald, Tomlin, and Allen.

NOES—William Cabell, John Trigg, Binns Jones, Harrison, Strother, Joel Early, King, Alexander White, John Early, Thomas Smith, Guerrant, Cooper, Breckenridge, Roane, Green Clay, A. Robertson, Kennon, Corbin, Riddick, Patrick Henry, Bland, Bullitt, McKee, Carter, Monroe, Briggs, and Edmiston.

The striking out the word "freeholder" had no reference to the right of suffrage, which has been discussed so freely within the last third of a century, but that word, with the qualification of residence, was introduced into the bill to prevent prominent men from being chosen elsewhere than in the district of their domicile. The opponents of the Constitution had been defeated by the policy of choosing delegates at large, and were determined to put a stop to it; while many of the members present, who might aspire to a seat in Congress, probably thought that there would be, as there was, plenty of candidates at home, without inviting others from abroad. A similar motion was made in the Senate, and failed by a vote of three to twelve—Burwell Bassett in the minority, and Pride and Joseph Jones in the majority. Stevens T. Mason happened to be out of his seat at the calling of the names.

The election of the senators of the United States in Congress was held on the 8th of November. Richard Henry Lee, William Grayson, and James Madison were nominated, and, on counting the ballots, the first two gentlemen named were declared to be chosen. The election of Lee, whose letter opposing the adoption of the Constitution was one of the charts of the times, and of Grayson, whose exertions in resisting its ratification on the floor of the Convention were exceeded by those of none other, shows the temper of the Assembly. The result, only of a vote by ballot, is to be found in the Journals; but it is stated by Wirt, who evidently obtained his information from some of the members, that these gentlemen were nominated together by Patrick Henry, and received a large majority of the votes. But, while the Assembly preferred Lee and Grayson to Madison, it was from no feeling of pique against the last named. The decision was made on just parliamentary grounds. To show that Madison was still held in high esteem by the majority which declined to send him to the Senate, when the election of members to the old Congress was held a few days before he was chosen one of a delegation, consisting of Cyrus Griffin, John Brown, John Dawson, and Mann Page, for the term beginning the following November and ending the following March, which constituted the congressional year.

A resolution was adopted requesting the Executive to make known, by proclamation, the times and places for appointing electors to choose a President of the United States; and an act was passed concerning the credentials of the senators in Congress. All the courts of the State were passed in review. An act was passed reconstructing the High Court of Appeals; and Edmund Pendleton, John Blair, Peter Lyons, Paul Carrington, and William Fleming, the former judges, were put through the forms of a re-election. The right of the Assembly to determine the judicial tenure, by repealing the act establishing a court, seems to have been taken for granted by both houses, and, in the absence of all protests by the judges, we may infer that they were of the same opinion. The same men were re-elected the judges of the new court; but the wrong, if wrong there was, was as flagrant whether the judges were re-elected or not. That there could not have been a secret understanding with the judges, we may safely conclude from their fearlessness in resisting unconstitutional legislation, and especially on a memorable occasion when a law interfering with the Court of Appeals was pronounced unconstitutional. They would have deserved to be cashiered if, believing the judicial tenure could not be determined by a repeal of the act creating the court in which the judge held his seat, they had quietly allowed themselves to be set aside, though assured of a re-election to a seat in a new court. But no such assurance could be given, or was given, in the present case; for, in the Senate alone, Henry Tazewell, James Henry, James Mercer, and Edmund Winston, able and trustworthy men, all of whom at one time or other held seats on the bench, and two of whom were elected judges of the Court of Appeals not long after, were duly nominated in opposition to the old judges, and, as their names were not withdrawn, were doubtless voted for. What imparts an interest to this election of judges is the fact that Stevens Thomson Mason, who was a few years later to play such an important part in the Senate of the United States in repealing the judiciary act of 1800,[175] was at present a member of the Senate of Virginia, was at the head of its Judiciary Committee, and voted for the new Court of Appeals; and that Wilson Cary Nicholas, who was to be the colleague of Mason in the Senate of the United States when the Federal judiciary law was repealed, was a member of the House of Delegates, and voted for the reconstruction of the Court of Appeals. The District Court bill, which had not yet gone into effect, was amended; and Richard Cary, James Henry, and John Tyler were elected judges of the General Court. An act concerning the Court of Admiralty, and the judges thereof, was also passed. As a proof of the unanimity with which these necessary changes in the courts and judges was received by all parties, it may be mentioned that, while such acts as the act disabling certain officers under the Continental Government from holding offices under

---

[175] General Mason, in his speech on the bill to repeal the judiciary act of 1800 in the Senate of the United States, in February, 1802, alluded to the present action of the Assembly in respect of the judges, and said: "Our judges, who are especially tenacious of their rights, did not complain. They thought, as I think, that they should not be removed from their offices that others might be placed in them, and that while they did continue in office their salaries should be continued to them." (*Report of the Senate Debates*, Bronson publisher, Philadelphia, 1802, page 83.)

the authority of this Commonwealth, and an act for the relief of
certain citizens, were subjected, on their passage, to the stringent
curb of the ayes and noes, the judiciary bills passed without
even a division.

One subject bearing upon Federal politics was taken up in
good earnest by the Assembly. The resolutions which had
been made in the late Convention on the subject of the surrender of the right of navigating the Mississippi had alarmed the
people of the West; and, that Congress might be duly impressed
with a proper sense of the importance of that interest to the
Southern States, and to Virginia and Kentucky in particular, the
Assembly unanimously and solemnly resolved that the citizens
of the United States have an absolute right to the navigation of
the Mississippi river; that by the principles of the Federal compact those States more immediately interested in it have a just
claim upon the National Government for every effort in their
power for the accomplishment of that important object; and that,
to merit the confidence and preserve the harmony of the confederacy, the most early measures should be .taken by the said
Government, after it shall be organized, to obtain an acknowledgment of the said right on the part of Spain, or otherwise
remove the obstructions that may prevent the free use of it. It
was also ordered that a copy of the resolution, together with the
resolutions of the General Assembly of the years 1786 and 1787,
in support of the said right, be transmitted to the representatives
of this State in the said Government, and that they be *instructed*
to use their unceasing efforts until the free use of the said river
shall be obtained. This was the first instance in which the
Assembly undertook to instruct the representatives of Virginia
in Congress under the present Federal Constitution. If any
member of the House had risen in his place and denied the
right of the Assembly to instruct all the representatives of Virginia in Congress, he would have been hooted out of the House.
The right to instruct under the confederation was perfect, and
the members could be recalled at pleasure; but the Assembly did
not foresee that a distinction would soon be taken between the
senators and the representatives in Congress—a distinction, it
is palpable, that can only be sustained on the ground that the
present is no longer a *federal* union.

Cash was scarce in the days of our fathers; and Virginia, like a tender mother, as she ever was, about to send a child from home, looked into the pockets of her sons, who, as senators and representatives, were deputed to inaugurate the new government in the city of New York, and finding them empty, or at least large enough to hold a little more than was in them, advanced to each one hundred pounds, and took his bond for the same. This movement must have been made by the Federal party, which might have been sought to keep their opponents in good humor at least until the government was set up, or while the money lasted.[176]

The House adopted a resolution, without a division, requiring the Executive, the chancellors, and the judges to report at each session the defects they may discover in the laws when reduced to practice. An honest and cordial co-operation of the Executive and the judges in the amendment of the law would prove a great blessing to the people; but the Senate, probably thinking that conflicts in high party times might occur between the judges and the Assembly, and, as the right of a mere majority of the Assembly to repeal the judiciary system and to set the judges adrift was conceded and acted on, rejected the resolution.

An instance was given at a previous session of the liberation of a slave by the Assembly as a mark of meritorious conduct during the war. A similar instance occurred at the present session. It appears that a slave named Timothy had rendered valuable service during the Revolution, and it was resolved unanimously by both houses that the Executive be instructed to purchase his freedom at any reasonable price, and to grant him an instrument of emancipation.

The House of Delegates was refreshed by the introduction of a new member toward the latter part of the present session. Edmund Randolph, having retired from the Executive, was returned to the House, evidently with a view to counteract any intemperate legislation in respect of the Federal Government. He was placed on leading committees, and performed his part with his usual ability; but the Federal test questions had been decided before he took his seat. The act concerning the credentials of the senators, and the act concerning incestuous mar-

---

[176] House Journal, December 23, 1788, and Senate Journal, December 24th.

riages, were reported by him, and are evidently from his pen. General Andrew Moore received from the House a cordial recognition of his services lately rendered in the Cherokee country, and the Executive was instructed to award him an adequate compensation. The Senate gave its assent to the measure.

Besides the acts remodelling the courts, and others already noticed, there were some of general interest. Richmond was, for the first time, empowered to send a delegate to the Assembly. The militia laws were amended. Acts to punish bigamy and to prevent bribery and corruption, and to incorporate academies, were passed. The act authorizing Kentucky to become an independent State, which was enacted at a preceding session, but which, from some informality could not be carried into effect, was amended, and that young Commonwealth soon assumed an independent position as one of the United States.

A sketch of the proceedings of the General Assembly at this important epoch may fitly conclude with a glance at the finances of the past year. The sum total of receipts into the treasury from all sources, from the 1st day of December, 1787, to the 24th of November, 1788, was four hundred and seventeen thousand four hundred and ninety-eight pounds nine shillings and eight pence halfpenny, and the disbursements were three hundred and seventy-three thousand nine hundred and twenty-one pounds three shillings and three pence—leaving a balance of forty-three thousand five hundred and seventy-seven pounds. The arrearages of taxes for past years reached one hundred and forty three thousand pounds. The receipts from the customs were seventy-four thousand and twenty-nine pounds.[177]

Too much honor cannot be accorded to the worthy patriots who composed the present Assembly. It commenced its sessions on the 20th of October, 1788, and adjourned on the 30th of December; and the whole time was incessantly devoted to public business. Its general legislation was judicious, firm, and thorough, and embraced many interesting topics. The ability and the judgment with which the entire judicial system was remodelled were conspicuous. But it was in the conduct of Federal affairs that it merits more particularly the grateful praise of succeeding times. Although there was an overwhelming

<hr>

[177] House Journal, December 20, 1788.

majority of the members who had been opposed to the adoption of the Constitution, and who honestly and truly believed that its ratification was in violation of the wishes of a large majority of the people, yet they united most cordially with the friends of that instrument in passing the necessary laws for carrying it into effect. Their hostility to that instrument was not at all abated, and they were anxious to secure the call of another Convention of the States for its revision; but their schemes were open, candid, and honorable. Had such men as Henry, Grayson, and Monroe been factiously disposed, the necessary laws for organizing the new government would not have been enacted, and the new scheme, so far as Virginia was concerned, would have fallen still-born. A blast of war from Henry, sustained by the plausible and comprehensive reasoning of Grayson and by the sterling sense of Monroe, would have swept away all opposition, and would have rung and been responsively re-echoed from the Atlantic to the Mississippi. But the patriotism and wisdom of our great orator were equal to his more splendid qualities; and he sought to attain his ends rather by the forms of a law which his opponents could not censure, and of which they might approve, than by any questionable and precipitate procedure. Such, too, were his illustrious colleagues. They were as far-seeing as they were able in debate, and for the mode in which, at a time of intense excitement, they sought to secure for posterity those blessing of peace and freedom which they regarded as in jeopardy, they deserve the gratitude of their country.

The year 1789 has not only a peculiar significancy in our own history, but relatively in that of the world. The Government under the new Federal Constitution had been organized in the city of New York in the spring of that year, the President had been duly inaugurated, and the Congress had held its first and most important session. That session began nominally on the 4th of March, and ended on the 12th of August; and during its continuance laws were enacted which materially changed the domestic legislation of the States. The subject of the customs, which was the theme of innumerable State laws, and formed one of the most perplexing topics of the period intervening between the Declaration of Independence and the establishment of the new Government, was no longer within their reach. The subject of foreign affairs was also transferred beyond the direct action of the States; and our relations with the Indian tribes, then a subject of a hundredfold greater interest than at present, had been assigned by the Constitution to the Congress. Here-tofore the members of Congress had been elected annually by the General Assembly, but henceforth they were to be elected by the people; and the only remnant of the plenary power wielded by the Assembly over Congress was in the election of two senators at the interval of six years.

In this altered aspect of affairs the General Assembly began its session on the 19th day of October, 1789. The Senate obtained a quorum the second day, and John Pride, a member of the present Convention, was nominated for Speaker by Stevens Thomson Mason, a member of the present Convention, and was elected by a majority of five votes over Charles Carter, who was nominated by Burwell Bassett, a member of the Con-vention. The majority was large, when the numbers of the body are remembered, for the vote of Pride was nine and that of Carter was four. Humphrey Brooke, a member of the Con-vention, was appointed Clerk. The member of the Senate who had been a member of the Convention—beside Mason, Pride, and Bassett—was Joseph Jones.

The House of Delegates had a quorum the first day, when George Hay—then a young man, whose name during the third of a century following was connected with Federal affairs as district attorney and judge of the Federal Court—was appointed Clerk, and General Thomas Matthews, a member of the Conven-tion, was re-elected Speaker without opposition; Richard Lee presenting his name to the House, and Francis Corbin, a mem-ber of the Convention, seconding the nomination.[178]

Norvell was made chairman of the Committee of Religion; Benjamin Harrison, of Privileges and Elections; Edmund Ran-dolph, of Propositions and Grievances; Patrick Henry, of Courts of Justice; and Richard Lee, of the Committee of Claims. One eloquent change was apparent: The Committee of Commerce, which had for thirteen years guarded with zealous care an

---

[178] So many members of the Convention were still members of the Assembly that, in order to avoid repeating in the memoir of each the same facts and votes, I shall continue to present them in one view as they appeared in the Assembly.

interesting department of our affairs, was no longer called into existence.

The members of the House who had been members of the Convention—beside Matthews, Corbin, Harrison, Randolph, and Henry—were Miles King, Tomlin, McKee, Jackson, Robertson, Edmiston, Carter, John Marshall, Wilson Cary Nicholas, Briggs, Henry Lee (Legion Harry), Hopkins, Allen, Samuel Jordan Cabell, Temple, Riddick, Wormeley, Thomas Smith, Kennon, Crockett, Edmunds, Guerrant, Conn, Binns Jones, Logan, Woods, Richardson, Gaskins, McClerry, Bell, Green Clay, Prunty, Strother, Stringer, Custis, John Trigg, Cooper, John Roane, A. Robertson, Walton, and Vanmeter.

Formal messages from the Governor to both houses had not yet come into fashion; but that officer usually transmitted a letter to the Speaker of the House of Delegates, informing him of any circumstance which might be deemed worthy of public attention. When the House was organized the Speaker announced that he had received a letter from the Governor, stating various matters for the consideration of the houses; and another letter from that officer, enclosing one from Richard Henry Lee and William Grayson, senators from the Commonwealth in Congress; and it was ordered that they lie on the table. On the following day the letters were referred to a Committee of the Whole on the State of the Commonwealth.

A graceful act marked the session of the second day in the House. A resolution was unanimously adopted appointing a committee to prepare an address to the President of the United States, "declaring our high sense of his eminent merits, congratulating him on his exaltation to the first office among freemen, assuring him of our unceasing attachment, and supplicating the Divine benediction on his person and administration." Henry Lee, Turberville, Harrison, Edmund Randolph, Corbin, Edward Carrington, Dawson, and Nicholas were appointed by the Chair to prepare the address on the part of the House. The Senate promptly approved the resolution, and appointed Carter, Bassett, Hugh Nelson, and Southall to unite with the committee of the House. The address was reported by Henry Lee on the 27th, was recommitted, and reported on the following day without amendment, and was unanimously adopted. It is short; its topics are judicious and well-timed; but the last clause is not wholly free from objection. Old men do not care to be told that they are soon to die, and still less do they like to be told that the people are already laying in a stock of consolation for the event when it occurs.[179]

On the 21st the House went into committee on the letters from the Governor; and, when the Speaker resumed the chair, Miles King reported progress, and asked leave to sit again. The following day the House again resolved itself into committee; and, when the Speaker resumed the chair, Turberville reported several resolutions, which were twice read and agreed to. One of them recommended that an address be prepared to the President of the United States, expressing the confidence of the House in the measures taken by him for the defence of the Western frontiers of this State, and containing the information given by the representatives of those frontiers on the subject of Indian hostility; and, to demonstrate the anxiety of the Assembly to co-operate with the Federal Government in the most vigorous exertions against the savages, declaring their readiness to share in those expenses which may be incurred in prosecuting the same. And a committee was appointed, consisting of Turberville, Patrick Henry, McClerry, Edmund Randolph, Corbin, Scott, Briggs, Jackson, Robert Randolph, Larkin Smith, Dawson, and Wormeley. The tenor of this resolution will strike those acquainted with the present mode of transacting Federal affairs. It is addressed to the President, and not to our senators in Congress; it proposes to furnish the President with information on Indian matters, and it pledges the co-operation of Virginia in the efforts to repress Indian incursions, and her readiness to bear a part of the expense. The address was duly reported and adopted by both houses. Other resolutions were reported with the above mentioned by the Committee of the Whole; but, with the exception of one requiring a bill to be brought in conformity to a resolution of Congress for the safe-keeping of the prisoners of the United States in the jails of the Commonwealth, are not within the range of this review.[180]

---

[179] House Journal, October 27, 1789.

[180] Committees were appointed to draft the bills called for by the resolutions, and Turberville was placed at the head of them all. When we recall the fact that Patrick Henry, Edmund Randolph, John Mar-

The first question which involved a very decided difference of opinion in the House was the propriety of furnishing the Chickasaw Indians with two thousand pounds of powder, and lead in proportion, to enable them to repel the attacks of the Creeks. It seems that a warm friendship existed between the Chickasaws and the Virginians; that the former had been wantonly attacked by the Creeks, who menaced them with further hostilities; and that, as the distance to the seat of the Federal Government was too great for them to travel at that advanced season, they applied to Virginia for assistance. The vote was taken on the resolution by ayes and noes, and carried—eighty-one to thirty-four. Those who had been members of the Convention and who voted in the affirmative were Patrick Henry, Edmund Randolph, Custis, John Trigg, Conn, Binns Jones, Bell, Strother, King, Richardson, Guerrant, Cooper, Roane, Green Clay, Hopkins, Kennon, A. Robertson, Wormeley, Walton, Gaskins, Woods, Tomlin, Carter, Dawson, Edmunds, and Henry Lee; and those who voted in the negative were Samuel J. Cabell, Harrison, Prunty, Jackson, Corbin, McClerry, Stringer, and Allen. A second resolution was adopted, instructing the committee appointed to address the President on Indian affairs to represent to him that the Assembly had interposed under the circumstances with a full conviction that their course would be acceptable to the Federal Government, and that the Federal Government would not be averse to make restitution for the advances on the occasion. Patrick Henry, who probably advocated the resolution on the floor, was ordered to carry it to the Senate and request its concurrence, which was duly granted.

The change effected in our institutions by the establishment of the Federal Constitution rendered many acts of Assembly of no avail; and the opportunity was embraced of including all our laws in a general revision. On the 24th of October the subject was discussed in Committee of the Whole; and, when the Speaker resumed the chair, Edward Carrington reported a resolution which set forth that many penal as well as other statutes of the

---

shall, Corbin, Wormeley, and such men were on the committees, it is a striking proof of the wealth of our early councils in able men that Turberville was placed in such a position; and yet, of those who read this paragraph, such is the oblivion into which the names of our early statesmen have fallen, how few has ever heard of the name of George Lee Turberville.

English Parliament, though in force in the Commonwealth, have never been published in any collection of the laws thereof; and some of them, having been improved by other statutes subsequent to the fourth year of James the First, remain, with respect to Virginia, as they stood before that era; that the acts of the General Assembly contained in the revisal of 1768 are difficult to be procured, and a large majority of those acts do not exist at all, or have been partially repealed, or are of a private and local nature; that a considerable proportion of the ordinances and acts in the revisal of the year 1783, and of those acts which have been passed since, either do not exist at all, or have been partially repealed, or are of a private and local nature; that the bills of the Revised Code having been drawn without special repealing clauses, from an expectation that a general repealing law would be passed, and a part only of those bills been adopted, there was great danger of misconstruction; that many entire laws are, from the present circumstances of the Commonwealth, unfit to be continued; that the rolls and printed copies of those laws which were private, local, temporary, or occasional have been lost or destroyed by the accidents of war, or other causes; and that a great variety of laws upon the same subject, which ought to be reduced to one, are dispersed in different books; that the rule which prescribes that the repeal of one law which repeals another, revives that other without express words, may revive obsolete laws not in the meaning of the Legislature; that laws passed during the same session are often found to clash; that resolutions of a public nature have been seldom published with the laws, &c. This preamble ended with a resolution to appoint a committee to make special inquiry on the subjects mentioned, and to report the same to the House. The labor enjoined by such a resolution was enormous, and might well employ the time of many men for many days. It was referred to Edward Carrington, Edmund Randolph, Henry Lee, Turberville, Hopkins, Dawson, Wormeley, Stringer, Riddick, John Marshall, Burnley, Ludwell Lee, Page, Buchanan, Preston, Briggs, and Thruston.[181]

On the 31st Carrington made an elaborate report, of which

---

[181] As a proof of the fact that the history of the members of the Convention may be best traced in the Assembly, it will be seen that nine members of this grand committee were members of the Convention.

our limits will only afford room for a very general review. The committee say that they have attentively examined the British statutes, which are either penal in their nature or relate to penal proceedings, and are in force in the Commonwealth; and they furnish a catalogue of fifty-one acts of Parliament anterior to the fourth year of James the First, and running back to the times of the Richards, the Henrys, and the Edwards—under the operation of which the citizens of this Commonwealth are in danger of capital executions, attainders, corruption of blood, escheats and forfeitures of estates, imprisonment, pecuniary mulcts, and other punishments, without scarcely a possibility of access to those immense folios, in which their fate is concealed from the eyes of all but professional men. The committee then consider the different heads of the subjects entrusted to them at great length and with extraordinary research, and conclude by recommending the appointment of a committee to take the subject in hand, and report to a subsequent Assembly.

The report and resolutions were referred to the Committee of the Whole House on the 2d of November; and, when the committee rose, Booker reported that no amendment had been made to them, and they were adopted without a division. Those parts of the report which were recommended to be carried into effect immediately were referred to Booker, Edmund Randolph, Briggs, Henry Lee, Johnston, Lawson, Hopkins, Preston, Walker, Breckenridge, Philip Pendleton, Turberville, Buchanan, Brent, Holmes, and Bassett; and during the session bills were accordingly reported and became laws.[182]

The authorship of the report, reflecting as it does abilities of a high order and a fullness of research which, if not made at second-hand, must have consumed many days of severe toil, may be fairly attributed to the brilliant and accomplished Edmund Randolph. Carrington, who was more of a soldier than a civilian, was placed, from courtesy, at the head of the select committee;[183]

---

[182] House Journal, October 31 and November 2, 1789, where the report and resolutions may be seen in full. It was stated in the report that certain gentlemen were willing to arrange and revise the laws free of expense to the State, but the House seemed to have thought it inexpedient at that time to refer the subject to them.

[183] It was customary to make the chairman of the Committee of the Whole the chairman of the committee to draft bills called for by the report.

and the name of Marshall, who was five years younger than
Randolph, would have been prominent, had he been the author
of the report, on the committee which was charged with the
office of drawing the bills.   It is evident that Randolph, in the
spirit of true patriotism, and under the impulse of a generous
ambition, had prepared his work long before the beginning of
the session.

The circulating medium was the source of constantly concurring difficulties in our early legislation.   Gold and silver were
hardly to be seen, and, when offered in payment of the public
taxes, were received by weight into the treasury.   Certain certificates of the public debt were also received in payment to the
Commonwealth, but with the people at large taxes in kind were
most heartily approved.   On these last the annual loss to the
State, from accidents and depreciation, was always large, and
they afforded the means of most profitable speculation to the
collectors of the revenue.   During the war, when there was no
outlet by sea, and when there was no specie in the Commonwealth, it was a matter of necessity that the taxes should be paid
in the products of the labor of the people.   Patrick Henry had
the credit of being the author of a scheme, which was evidently
the dictate of necessity rather than the result of invention; and
he certainly was its foremost champion.   At the expiration of
the war, however, there was a small party which sought to bring
about gradually the payment of taxes in specie, and which had
increased in numbers with the development of the resources of
the State.   Now that a new Federal Government was established,
the duties under which must be paid in coin or its equivalent, it
was believed by the friends of a sound currency that Virginia
should make a serious effort to require specie or its equivalent
in payment of taxes.   The subject was discussed in Committee
of the Whole, and Briggs reported, as the opinion of the committee, that the taxes of the present year ought to be paid in
specie only, or in warrants equivalent thereto, and that the taxes
on lands, slaves, and other property, and the taxes imposed by
an act entitled "an act imposing new taxes," ought to be reduced
in the proportion of one-fourth less than the last year.   A
motion was made to strike out the specie clause and insert that
"hemp and tobacco ought to be made commutable in the payment of the public taxes for the year 1789," and was lost by a
decisive vote—the ayes being fifty-one and the noes eighty-eight.

As this was a strict party question for many years, I annex the votes of the members of the House who had been members of the Convention:

AYES—Patrick Henry, Binns Jones, Bell, Strother, King, Richardson, Temple, Pawling, Green Clay, Wormeley, Gaskins, Briggs, Henry Lee (Legion Harry), and Dawson.

NOES—Edmund Randolph, John Marshall, Johnston, John Trigg, Benjamin Harrison, Guerrant, Prunty, Jackson, Vanmeter, Smith (of Gloucester), Hopkins, Kennon, Corbin, McClerry, Crockett, Riddick, Stringer, McKee, Carter, Allen, Edmunds, and Edmiston.[184]

The resolution was then adopted without a division. The vote deserves to be studied as showing that geographical considerations did not wholly control the members. The truth was that the State was in such a condition that she could not be relieved from it without the adoption of a measure which must necessarily press with greater or less severity upon all the people. The only question was a question of time; and we are bound to believe that a majority of both houses decided wisely. Still we hazard little in saying that the exaction of the taxes in specie gave an additional impulse to that fearful emigration of our people, which took place at this time, to Kentucky and other Western territories. What would be the effect of the exaction of taxes in specie in distant counties may be inferred from the fact that the rich counties of Cumberland and Buckingham presented

---

[184] As many of the members of the House, though not members of the Convention, afterwards became distinguished, I will give the votes of some of them for future reference :

AYES—Peter Randolph, Sterling Edmunds, Robert Bolling, Jr., George Booker, Richard Banks, Robert Randolph, William Payne, Jr., Mordecai Cooke, Henry E. Coleman, William Terry, Miles Selden, Abner Field, William Roane, John Taliaferro, Sterling Niblett. Samuel Taylor, Burwell Bassett, Jr., John Macon, George Lee Turberville, John W. Willis, and Robert Shield.

NOES—Hugh Caperton, Clement Carrington, Francis Walker, William Cabell, Jr., Philip Pendleton, James Breckenridge, John Clarke, Robert White, Samuel Hairston, Isaac Miller, William Heath, Francis Boykin, Francis Preston, John Giles, Willis Wilson, John Hodges, Edward Carrington, Henry Washington, Alexander Henderson, Dennis Dawley, Thomas Lawson, John Bowyer, George Baxter, Andrew Cowan, George Brent, Thomas West, and William Tate.

petitions setting forth that, in consequence of the great scarcity of specie, the low price of produce, and the unfortunate destruction of the crops of tobacco and corn in the fall, they believe that it will be impossible for them to pay their present taxes.[185]

It is not an unprofitable task to record the action of our fathers on religious questions, which, at intervals, are still discussed in the South, and in the South only. Congress had requested the President of the United States "to issue a proclamation to the people to set apart a day of thanksgiving and prayer for the many signal favors of Almighty God, especially by affording them an opportunity peaceably to establish a form of government for their safety and happiness"—and the 26th day of November was specified for the purpose. The House acceded to the proposition without a division, and resolved that its chaplain be requested to perform divine service and to preach a sermon in the Capitol before the General Assembly, suitable to the importance and solemnity of the occasion, on the appointed day.[186] The public and formal recognition of an over-ruling Providence was frequently made by our fathers during the Revolution; and if the measure (as we know it was in one instance at least) was proposed by politicians for effect, it plainly showed their conviction of the religious sensibilities of the people.

It was resolved at the last session to build a marine hospital at Norfolk, and certain funds accruing from the customs were set apart for that purpose.[187] But the regulation of commerce had been committed to the new Government, and neither the anticipated revenues for the construction of the building were forthcoming, nor had the State any further need for such a structure. A sum of five hundred pounds had already been appropriated

---

[185] House Journal, November 16, 1789, pages 64, 65. The crops had been destroyed by a terrible gust in September.

[186] This probably was the first instance of a religious meeting being held in the Capitol, and was a very proper inauguration of the new building. It afterwards became a regular place for preaching before churches were built in Richmond.

[187] This hospital, beautifully situated at the head of the harbor of Norfolk, was forthwith constructed. During the period when my friend, Dr. E. O. Balfour, was its surgeon, it was greatly improved by his energy and taste—trees were set out, and the grounds were enriched and adorned.

on the subject, and the senators from this State were requested to communicate the facts to Congress.

The amendments of the Federal Constitution, which had been recommended by Congress to the adoption of the States, were discussed in Committee of the Whole on the 13th of November, when it was agreed to ratify the first twelve of them as being in accordance with those recommended by the Convention; and it was also resolved that the procceedings of the House upon them should be published and distributed throughout the Commonwealth. The resolutions of the House were sent to the Senate. That body immediately read them the first time and referred them to the Committee of the Whole, in which they were discussed daily until the 8th of December, when the committee rose and reported an amendment, which was in substance that the third, eighth, eleventh, and twelfth amendments be postponed till the next session of the Assembly for the consideration of the people. A warm debate had evidently been held in committee on each vote striking out a specific amendment, and the votes were repeated in the House by ayes and noes. Those in favor of striking out the third amendment were John Pride, Turner Southall, John S. Wills, Mathew Anderson, Stevens Thomson Mason, Joseph Jones, William Russell, and John Pope, and those in the negative Alexander St. Clair, John P. Duval, Nicholas Cabell, John Kearnes, Levin Joynes, James Taylor, and Hugh Nelson. Five times in quick succession the roll was called; and when the questions were carried, the majority made a request which, as far as my researches have extended, stands alone in our records. The request was that they might be allowed to record in the Journal the reasons which induced them to postpone the amendments in question, and their opinion of those amendments. This request was granted by a majority of one—ascertained by a call of the roll; the ayes seven, the noes six. On the 12th the majority recorded their opinions at length upon the Journal, signed with their names. This step was immediately followed by a protest from the minority against the right and policy of the majority to put their opinions on record, which was signed by the members composing it. The House of Delegates refused to concur in the amendments of the Senate, and the Senate refused to recede; and a committee of both bodies met in the conference chamber.

Mason, Pope, and Anderson represented the Senate, and Edmund Randolph, Henry Lee, Corbin, John Marshall, Johnston, Edward Carrington, Zane, and Wilson Cary Nicholas appeared on the part of the House of Delegates.[188]   The discussion was doubtless animated and eloquent; but the conference could not agree, and the Senate resolutely adhered to their amendments by a majority of one—the vote being seven to six. Against this decision the minority of the Senate protested on the technical ground that the bill and amendments had not been returned from the House of Delegates, were presumed to be under the consideration of the House, and were not open to a vote by the Senate.

On the 5th of December the House of Delegates again went into committee on the subject of the amendments proposed by Congress to the Federal Constitution; and, when the Speaker resumed the chair, two resolutions were reported, the first of which set forth "that the General Assembly, in obedience to the will of the people, as expressed by the Convention by which certain alterations in the Constitution of the United States were recommended, ought to urge to Congress the reconsideration of such as are not included in the amendments already adopted by this Commonwealth"; and the second, which declared that a representation ought to be made to Congress in pursuance of the foregoing resolution.   As soon as the first resolution was read a motion was made to strike out from the word "resolved" to the end of the resolution, and insert in lieu thereof the following words: "That a communication from the Legislature of this State to the Congress of the United States ought to be made, expressing their ardent desire that such of the amendments of

---

[188] Randolph and Mason, as the representatives of their respective houses, must have made a brilliant display.   The reader is reminded of the famous committee of conference of the British Parliament on the resolution of 1788 declaring the throne vacant, in which Nottingham on the part of the Lords, and Somers and Maynard on the part of the Commons, put forth their strength.   Had the manuscript history of Virginia, written by Edmund Randolph (which was destroyed by fire in New Orleans some years ago), been in existence. we might have learned the details of the conference meeting. [This MS., the property of the Virginia Historical Society, has been committed by it to the well-known writer, Moncure D. Conway, for publication.—EDITOR.]

the Virginia Convention as have not been proposed by the Congress to the several States, to be established as a part of the Constitution of the United States, be reconsidered and complied with." The motion to strike out was lost by a tie vote, the Speaker declaring himself with the noes. The members of the Convention who voted in the affirmative were John Trigg, Binns Jones, Benjamin Harrison, Strother, A. Robertson, Riddick, Richardson, Guerrant, Temple, Pawling, Hopkins, Carter, Briggs, Edmunds, and Edmiston. Those who voted in the negative were Wilson Cary Nicholas, Johnston, King, Prunty, Vanmeter, Corbin, McClerry, Tomlin, McKee, Allen, Henry Lee, Edmund Randolph, and John Marshall. The distinction between the reported resolution and the proposed amendment is apparently slight, the latter being somewhat more peremptory in its tone; but the majority of the House, hitherto easily triumphant, sustained a defeat.[189] The second resolution prevailed without a division.

The legislation of the Assembly on domestic topics was judicious and extensive, and apparently unanimous. Many of the irregularities and deficiencies in the laws, which had been pointed out in the able report already described, were corrected by special acts. Among these were acts concerning the benefit of clergy; against fogery; repealing a part of an ordinance by which certain British statutes were allowed to be in force in Virginia; concerning jeofails and certain proceedings in civil cases; to provide against an appropriation of money by a resolution of the two houses; concerning perjury; directing the mode of proceeding in impeachments; for the manumission of certain slaves for good conduct during the war, and to amend the act preventing the further importation of slaves. The act offering to Congress a territory for the seat of government passed without a division, as well as an act ceding to the United States the site of a light-house. The resolution instructing the senators in Congress to vote for admitting the people to hear the debates in

---

[189] The vote was sixty-two to sixty-two, making a House of one hundred and twenty-four members, when the full number was about two hundred. In the absence of Patrick Henry the eloquence of Randolph and Marshall prevailed.

their body was also unanimous.[190]   Kentucky, which had for
several sessions received an act authorizing the formation of an
independent State, was again empowered to carry that object
into effect.   Liberal appropriations were made for the comple-
tion of the Capitol in Richmond.

On his return from France, Mr. Jefferson had reached the city
of Richmond.   Both houses passed a resolution congratulating
him on his return and expressive of their high sense of the services which he had rendered to his country, and appointed a
committee to wait upon him.   He received the deputation most
graciously, and made a handsome acknowledgment, which was
reported to the House.[191]

A memorial from the Baptist associations was presented to the
House, praying that a law might pass to authorize the free
use of the Episcopal churches by all denominations; but, after
the subject had been fully discussed, it was determined on the
9th of December, by a vote of sixty-nine to fifty-eight, to postpone the further consideration of the memorial to the 31st of
March next.[192]

A remarkable resolution on the subject of a call of a Convention to revise the Constitution of the State was presented by a
member to the House.[193]   It was offered by a friend of the Federal Constitution.   The recent action of the Assembly on Federal
affairs was attributed by the minority to the basis of representation on which that body rested; and the conduct of the Senate,

---

[190] The Assembly had received the Journals of Congress, and ordered
five hundred copies to be printed for distribution in the State.   Among
the elections made during the session were that of James Mercer to
the Court of Appeals, in place of John Blair, who had been appointed
a judge of the Supreme Court of the United States; Beverley Randolph
was re-elected Governor, and Jaquelin Ambler, Treasurer; and Cyrus
Griffin, John Howell Briggs, Thomas Madison, and Charles Carter as
members of the Council.

[191] House and Senate Journals, December 8 and 9, 1789.

[192] Consult the House Journal of November 27, 1789, where an argument, in the shape of an amendment to the report of the Committee
of the Whole, in defence of the right of the Episcopal Church to its
houses of worship, will be seen.

[193] House Journal, December 8, 1789.

which had postponed the adoption of several of the amendments
to the Federal Constitution that had been adopted by the House,
excited the wrath of some of the prominent upholders of that
instrument. The resolution was elaborated with uncommon
skill; it analyzed the departments of the government, as established by the Constitution of the State, with stern severity; and
concluded with a recommendation that the people take the subject into consideration, and instruct their delegates to act upon
it at a subsequent session. When the resolution was read, a
motion was made to strike out all after the word "resolved" and
insert the words "that the foregoing statement contains statements repugnant to republican government and dangerous to
the freedom of this country, and therefore ought not to meet
with the approbation of this House, or be recommended to the
consideration of the people." While this amendment was pend-
ing a motion was made to postpone the subject to the 31st of
March next, and was carried without a division.[194]

A glance at the proceedings of the General Assembly which
met on the 18th day of October, 1790, will show the gradual
development of parties in the Commonwealth, not so much in
respect of the true nature of the Federal Constitution as of the
legislative measures adopted by the new government. The
Senate again chose John Pride as their Speaker. Beside Pride
and Humphrey Brooke (the Clerk of the House), the members
of the Senate who had been members of the Convention were
Stevens Thomson Mason, Burwell Bassett, and Thomas Gaskins.
The House of Delegates re-elected General Matthews Speaker
without opposition; and Norvell, Harrison (of Charles City),
Henry Lee (of the Legion),[195] John Marshall, and Richard Lee

---

[194] This resolution presents an analysis of the Constitution, which fills
more than two of the quarto pages of the Journal, and is done in a
masterly manner. Its obnoxious feature, as denounced in the amendment, was probably its protest against annual elections of members of
the Assembly, which it enforces by the same arguments that brought
about our present biennial sessions. From the views expressed
respecting the clashing of the Declaration of Rights and the Constitution, as well as from internal evidence, it is evidently the production
of Edmund Randolph.

[195] As there were two Henry Lees in the Convention, and as few
readers would identify them by the names of the counties from which

were placed at the heads of the standing committees. Some of
the members of the last House, who had been members of the
Convention, had withdrawn from the scene. Edmund Randolph
had been appointed the first Attorney-General of the United
States (as he had been the first Attorney-General of the Com-
monwealth); but, beside Matthews, Harrison, Henry Lee, and
John Marshall, already named, were Patrick Henry, Johnston,
McFerran, Westwood, Prunty, Logan, McClerry, Ronald, Tom-
lin, McKee, Carter, John Trigg, Conn, Binns Jones, John Jones,
Bell, Strother, John Early, Thomas Smith, Jackson, Cooper,
Roane, Kennon, Walton, Edmunds, and Andrews.

The assumption of the debts of the States by the Federal
Government was the first act of legislation which called forth a
distinct expression of political opinion from the people of Virginia. The senators of the State in Congress had transmitted
a copy of the assumption act to the Governor, who enclosed it
in a letter to the Assembly. It was immediately referred to the
Committee of the Whole, and on the 3d of November, 1790, the
House of Delegates took it into consideration. When the committee rose, Selden reported a resolution declaring "that so
much of the act of Congress, entitled 'an act making provision
for the debt of the United States,' as assumes the payment of
the State debts, is repugnant to the Constitution of the United
States, as it goes to the exercise of a power not expressly
granted to the Federal Government."

As soon as the resolution from the committee was read, a
motion was made to strike it out and insert in its stead an amendment which contained an ingenious and elaborate exposition of
the injustice and impolicy of the assumption act, but which
adroitly avoided the constitutional question. This amendment
was rejected by a vote of eighty-eight to forty-seven—ascertained
by ayes and noes. The members of the House, who had been
members of the Convention, voted on the question to strike out
and insert as follows:

AYES—John Marshall, Johnston, McFerran, Westwood, Prunty,
Logan, McClerry, Ronald, Tomlin, and McKee.

NOES—Thomas Matthews (Speaker), Patrick Henry, John

---

they came, I have thought it best to give Henry Lee (of Westmoreland) his Revolutionary cognomen.

Trigg, Conn, Binns Jones, John Jones, Bell, Strother, John Early, Thomas Smith, Jackson, Cooper, Roane, Kennon, Corbin, Walton, Edmunds, and Andrews.

The main question was then put, and was decided in the affirmative by a vote of seventy-five to fifty-two—ascertained by ayes and noes. As the vote to strike out merely tested the sense of the House on the constitutional question, and might have been given on parliamentary grounds by some who approved the policy of assumption, I annex the result of the call of the roll:

AYES—Mr. Speaker (Matthews), Patrick Henry, John Trigg, Conn, Binns Jones, John Jones, Bell, Strother, John Early, Jackson, Cooper, John Roane, Kennon, Corbin, Walton, Edmunds, and Henry Lee.

NOES—John Marshall, Johnston, McFerran, Westwood, Thomas Smith, Prunty, Logan, McClerry, Ronald, Tomlin, McKee, Carter, and Andrews.

The resolution was carried to the Senate, and was in due time adopted by that body; but, as the roll was not called, the ayes and noes cannot be given.[196]

---

[196] As this was the most memorable party vote in our early annals, and was frequently referred to in party contests, I annex some of the names of the members that were afterwards prominent:

AYES—John Cropper, James Upshaw (of Caroline), Peterson Goodwyn, Robert Bolling, Jr., George Booker, Pickett, Cooke, Henry E. Coleman, Miles Selden, Joseph Martin, Francis Boykin, John Campbell, John Taliaferro, Sr., George William Smith (afterwards Governor, and burned in the theatre), John Clopton, Richard Evers Lee, Travers Daniel, Jr., Richard Lee, Charles Scott, John Craig, and Robert Shield.

NOES—Francis Walker, William Boyer, C. H. Clark, James Breckenridge, John Clark, Mathew Page, W. Norvell, John Miller, A. Crockett, John Jouett, Benjamin Johnson (of Orange),* William Patton, Matthew Clay, John Macon, Richard S. Blackburn, George Baxter, Benjamin Blunt, Francis Thornton, Jr., William Digges, William Nelson, and David Talbot.

For the memorial to Congress, drawn in pursuance to the resolution (which was from the pen of Corbin, and presented by him), see House Journal, December 16, 1790. It is well done, and has a peculiar flavor as coming from Corbin, who was a trenchant friend of the Federal Constitution.

---

*Subsequently represented by his accomplished grandson, Benjamin Johnson Barbour, of Orange.

The death of the lamented William Grayson made a vacancy in the Senate of the United States, which was to afford another test of the State strength of parties, and which the Assembly, on the 9th of November, proceeded to fill. James Monroe and John Walker were the only candidates, and, upon counting the ballots, Monroe was declared to be duly elected to fill the unexpired term of Grayson in the Senate of the United States. He was afterwards elected for the full term.[197]

I now conclude my review of the members of the Convention as they appeared in a group in the legislative councils immediately subsequent to the adjournment of that body, and will proceed to treat in detail the life and services of a statesman, who, in war and in peace, achieved a reputation which during his life was the pride of Virginia, but which, sharing the fatality that has befallen the memory of nearly all his contemporaries, has been allowed to fade almost insensibly away. Descending the Blue Ridge eastwardly, and almost in its shadow, we approach the home which he inherited from his father, in which he spent most of his days, and from which he went forth at the call of his country.[198]

---

[197] Some of my readers, who have numbered their three-score years and ten (and I hope I may have many such), may recall the ballad which was written on the occasion of the election of Monroe over Walker. I remember the chorus, but it is rather too pungent for modern ears. As I now close my review of the sessions of the Assembly, I state the fact, lest I might lead astray, that Kentucky was still represented at the present session when several acts were passed respecting her, and George Nicholas was elected her attorney-general in place of Harry Innes, declined. But I must leave this matter to others.

[198] Near Leesburg.

THOMSON MASON.

Stevens Thomson Mason was the senior representative of Loudoun in the Convention. His ancestor, George Mason, the first of the name, had held a seat in the British Parliament; had commanded a troop of horse in the army of Charles at the battle of Worcester, which sealed the fate of the Stuart dynasty during the life of Cromwell; had emigrated with a younger brother to Virginia, and landed, in 1651, in Norfolk, then even a flourishing town, which had been honored not long before with a royal charter, and which, with its domestic and foreign shipping, presented a cheering appearance to the eyes of an industrious and enterprising emigrant. In the vicinity of the town his younger brother, William, selected a home, and lived and died and was buried on the banks of a creek, which still bears his name.[199] George, however, removed to Accohick creek, which flows into the Potomac near Pasbitaney, where, with the remains of his once ample estate in Staffordshire,[200] he purchased a farm, settled it, and, with his family that shortly came over to Virginia, spent the remainder of his life upon it. In 1676, the year of Bacon's Rebellion, he commanded a volunteer force against the Indians, and held a seat in the House of Burgesses.[201] It is to him that

---

[199] He intermarried with the Thoroughgoods, a respectable family for more than a hundred years in Norfolk and Princess Anne counties, though the name is now almost extinct. A son of his removed to Boston, where, or in other parts of New England, some of his descendants are still living.

[200] The family was originally from Worcestershire, not Warwickshire, as the *Old Churches, &c.*, have it. So say the Mason manuscripts. [There is a grant of land, of record in the State Land Registry, of 1,250 acres, in Elizabeth City county, to Francis Mason, dated August 31, 1642. Captain George Mason was granted 900 acres in Northumberland county March 25, 1656.—EDITOR.]

[201] See the account of "T. M." in the *Virginia Historical Register*, Vol. III, 61; *Rice's Magazine*, Vol. III, 128. I first saw this valuable tract in the Richmond *Enquirer* of 1804, September 1, 5, 8. It is also published in *Force's Tracts*, Vol. I.

Stafford county owes its name. He had a son called George, who married Mary, a daughter of Gerard Fowke, of "Gunston Hall" in Staffordshire, England. The eldest son of this marriage was also called George, the third of the name, and lived and died, and, with his grandfather and father, was buried on Accohick creek. He had a son called George, who married a daughter[202] of Stevens Thomson, of the Middle Temple, Attorney-General of the Colony of Virginia in the reign of Queen Anne. He was drowned in the Potomac by the upsetting of a boat, but his body was found and buried at Doeg's Neck. He left two sons and a daughter—George Mason, the author of the Declaration of Rights and of the first Constitution of Virginia (of whom I have already spoken, and shall speak at length hereafter), and Thomson Mason, the father of Stevens Thomson Mason of the present Convention.

Before we speak of the son, the patriotism and worth of the father, now almost forgotten, should not pass wholly unrecorded. Thomson Mason was born at Doeg's Neck, on the Potomac, in 1730, was taught at home by the rector of the parish or by a private tutor; entered the College of William and Mary, and thence passed to London, where he studied law at the Temple. His abode in England gave a decided impulse to his character, for his associates in the Temple, and the illustrious men then on the stage of active life, were well calculated to inspire a clever young man with a love of eloquence and learning. He probably heard the brilliant but fated Yorke in his first efforts at the bar. Lord Hardwicke was then on the woolsack, and was expounding daily, in the marble chair, that code of equity which has made his name immortal.[203] The Earl of Mansfield and the Earl of Chatham—then plain William Murray and William Pitt—were waging their life-long struggle in the House of Commons; and Pratt (afterwards Lord Camden), Yorke, Thurlow, Wedderburne,

---

[202] She was a niece of Sir William Temple.

[203] It may have been through the influence of Mason that the Earl of Hardwicke was elected Chancellor of William and Mary College. Unfortunately the appointment did not reach England until after the death of the Earl. It is noticed by one of his biographers, but has escaped Lord Campbell. Before this period it was common to elect the Bishop of London the Chancellor of William and Mary, evidently from the influence of Commissary Blair.

and Dunning were leaders at the bar. He attended, beyond doubt, sedulously the courts and the Parliament; and, if we may judge from subsequent developments, he rather sided with Pitt, Pratt, and Dunning than with Murray, Wedderburne, and Thurlow.

Returning to Virginia, he began the practice of his profession, both in the county courts and at the bar of the General Court. In February, 1766, he signed the stringent and strenuous resolutions of the Westmoreland Association, and in the following May took his seat for the first time in the House of Burgesses, and was one of that majority which separated the office of Treasurer from that of the Speaker. He rose gradually in reputation and in position, and in 1769 he was placed on nearly all the standing committees of the House. During this session he voted for those four memorable resolutions [204] which embraced the great questions of the times, and which caused a dissolution of the Assembly by the Governor; and when the members adjourned to the Apollo and adopted the non-importation agreement, which had been drawn by his brother (George), and brought to Williamsburg by Colonel Washington. In 1774 he was again a member of the House of Burgesses; but he must have retired at the close of that session, as he was not a member of the Convention of 1775, or of that of 1776, which were but another name for the House of Burgesses, and which were illumined by the genius of his illustrious brother.

Before I proceed further, I ought not to omit a more distinct allusion to the services of Thomson Mason, in the year 1774, in opposition to the policy of taxing America. Allusion has already been made to the Westmoreland memorial, [205] which was drawn by Richard Henry Lee, and signed by the most respectable

---

[204] For a copy of the four resolves, see *Burk*, Vol. III, 343; and for a copy of the Articles of Association, which were signed by every member, and the names of the signers, see page 345.

[205] It may be seen in the *Virginia Historical Register*, Vol. II, 15, and in *Bishop Meade's Old Churches, &c.* As Mason was a member of the House in 1769, and as we are told all the members of that House were returned at the following election, he must have been a member in 1770, and, it is probable, continuously until 1774, where we again begin to trace him. My set of the Journals of the House do not include the period from 1769 to 1774.

citizens of the Northern Neck and of the neighboring country. There, in company with the names of William Grayson, Meriwether Smith, the Washingtons, the Lees, the Monroes, the Carters, the Roanes, Parker, Turberville, Woodcock, and others, then and still respectable for the patriotism of those who bore them, stands the name of Thomson Mason. But Mason was determined to do something more than pledging his name to the sound doctrines contained in that paper, and he wrote a series of letters at a time when the issue was drawing near (1774), which defended the right and duty of resistance to Great Britain, upon principles of law as well as of right, and which denounced, with all the force of argument and with great vigor of expression, the injustice and the impolicy of taxing the Colonies by the legislation of the mother country. These articles were published under the signature of "A British American," and attracted great attention from their intrinsic value; but, willing to assume all the responsibility of their authorship at a time when England was placing her mark upon the froward men of the Colony, and to give to the letters the sanction of his name (which then stood in legal matters second to none other), he concludes the last number with this honorable avowal:

"And now, my friends, fellow-citizens, and countrymen, to convince you that I am in earnest in the advice I have given you—notwithstanding the personal danger I expose myself to in so doing; notwithstanding the threats thrown out by British aristocracy of punishing in England those who shall dare to oppose them in America; yet, because I do not wish to survive the liberty of my country one single moment; because I am determined to risk my all in supporting that liberty, and because I think it in some measure dishonorable to skulk under a borrowed name upon such an occasion as this—I am neither afraid nor ashamed to avow that the letters signed by 'A British American' were written by the hand and flowed from the heart of Thomson Mason." [206]

He did not hold a seat in the first General Assembly under the Constitution which met in Williamsburg in October, 1776, as that body—or rather the House of Delegates—was, in fact, the

---

[206] The letters may be seen in the *American Archives* (fourth series), Vol. I, 418, 495, 519, 541, 620, 654.

Convention of 1776 held over by adjournment; but, in 1777, he was a member of the House of Delegates. As he did not take his seat until the 17th of November, when the House had been nearly a month in session, and had been absent at a call of the roll, he appeared, as was usual under such circumstances, in the custody of the sergeant-at-arms; but, upon showing that he had been engaged in the interval in the service of the House, he was excused without the payment of fees.[207] As soon as he took his seat he was placed on a committee to examine and report the state, progress, and expense of the salt-works belonging to the State, and he was assigned (with his brother George) to the committee for preparing a bill to establish a Court of Appeals.

The Articles of Confederation had just been framed by Congress and submitted to the States; and on the 9th of December those articles were received by the House and spread in full on the Journal. After a deliberate investigation of the articles they were unanimously approved by the House, and the delegates of the State in Congress were instructed to ratify them in the name and in behalf the Commonwealth.[208] On such an occasion, which was so congenial to his character and talents, he probably bore a conspicuous part in debate; but there is no notice of the scene that is extant. One of the great topics of the session was the establishment of the General Court and the Court of Appeals; and Thomson Mason, Joseph Jones, John Blair, Thomas Ludwell Lee, and Paul Carrington were appointed judges of the General Court. At the session of the House in October he appeared in his seat, and engaged with great zeal in furthering the measures for defence and for local purposes. It is believed that he drafted the bill establishing the county of Illinois—now the State of that name—and on the passage of the bill he was

---

[207] The expense incurred by the sergeant-at-arms in sending for George and Thomson Mason was sixteen shillings and ten pence each. Cuthbert Bullitt, Edmund Ruffin, and Willis Riddick were not so fortunate as to have a good excuse for absence, and had to pay their fines.

[208] The Journal of the House states that the articles were agreed to *nemine contra dicente ;* but Patrick Henry says, in a letter addressed to R. H. Lee, dated December 18, 1777: "The Confederation is passed *nem. con.*, though opposed by those who opposed independency." The Senate were also unanimous.

requested by the Speaker to carry it to the Senate and request their concurrence.

He seems now to have changed the place of his residence and become an inhabitant for a short time of Elizabeth City county. He was through life at intervals a martyr to the gout, and it is not improbable that he chose his new place of abode from its proximity to the sea, as a salt atmosphere and salt bathing have been frequently found beneficial to the health of invalids suffering from that disease. At all events, his great reputation had preceded him, and he was immediately returned to the House of Delegates from Elizabeth City. He took his seat in May, 1779; but having since his election again removed to another county, he addressed a letter to the Chair, in which he stated the fact of his removal from Elizabeth City since his election, and that the House had decided in the case of Peter Poythress that a member under such circumstances could not hold his seat, he tendered his resignation; which, however, the House, in courtesy to his extraordinary abilities, declined to accept, and he remained a member during the session.[209] At the October session he found himself unable to attend; and, to make his resignation certain, he accepted the office of coroner, which, *ipso facto*, vacated his seat in the House. As he was appointed a judge of the General Court at a previous session, he must either have delayed to qualify or resigned the appointment.

At the session of May, 1783, he was returned to the House of Delegates from Stafford, and was placed at the head of the Committee of Courts of Justice, on which was also placed his son, Stevens Thomson Mason, the present session being the last but one of the father and the first of the son. A smart debate arose on a motion to strike out from the tax bill the word "November," and insert the word "October" as the time to which distress to be made for the public taxes was proposed to be limited; and the question was taken by ayes and noes, and decided in the negative—the father in the negative and the son in the affirmative. His skill in the law was often called into requisition, and when it was determined to bring in a bill to amend an act declaring tenants in lands or slaves in tail to hold the same in fee simple,

---

[209] House Journal, June 9, 1779, where the letter is spread upon the Journal.

he and Alexander White were appointed to draft it. The bill was reported, and became a law. A test question was made on the passage of a bill for the relief of sheriffs, and he voted in a minority of seventeen—the ayes and noes having been asked by himself. Another test question of the session was a motion to postpone to October the bill declaring who shall be deemed citizens of the Commonwealth, when father and son voted in rather a meagre minority—the House deciding to postpone by a vote of fifty-six to twenty-seven. On a motion to strike out that part of a resolution concerning the public buildings, which fixed their site permanently on Shockoe Hill, and to insert "that the seat of government ought to be removed to Williamsburg," father and son voted with the majority against striking out.[210] When the vote was called on several occasions he was not in the House; but the frequent recurrence of his name in presenting reports and bills from the Committee of Courts of Justice and on select committees leads us to believe that, though temporarily absent, he was closely engaged in his duties as a member of the House.

At the opening of the October session of 1783 he was placed second on the Committee of Elections and at the head of Courts of Justice, of which last his son (Stevens) was also a member. On the 11th of November a bill was reported, and read the first time, to explain and declare the privileges of members of the General Assembly. This has ever been a mooted question in the history of parliaments; and the present Lord Chancellor of Great Britian [211] has expressed the opinion that such a bill in respect of the British Parliament is an impossibility. The present bill, however, was sustained by Henry Tazewell, John Taylor (of Caroline), and others, was opposed by Thomson Mason, Patrick Henry, and Archibald Stuart, and was defeated by a majority of two to one. When the engrossed bill to repeal the act declaring who shall be citizens of the Commonwealth was read a third time, Mason, whose policy was to invite emigration, and to bury the local feuds kindled by the past war in families

---

[210] There is an error in the House Journal in recording this vote, the words "affirmative" and "negative" being transposed, and leading to error without a close inspection.

[211] 1859.

and neighborhoods, voted in its favor along with his son, with John Tyler, with Joseph Jones, and with the Speaker; but the measure was at that moment unpopular.   Some of our patriots thought it too soon to allow those who had quitted their country in the hour of trial to come in and enjoy the fruits of the labors of a brave and devoted people, and enter at once upon all the rights and privileges of citizenship; and of this opinion was Henry, and Tazewell, and Alexander White, and Isaac Coles, and George Nicholas, and the fearless French Strother.   The bill was lost by a majority of nineteen.   At this day the decision would be pronounced wrong; for, as the treaty of peace had established a political amnesty between Great Britain and the United States, it was unwise to cherish a domestic feud in direct contravention of its spirit, and to turn away an intelligent and wealthy set of people, connected with us by blood and association, which, though deluded in the past, was now deeply repentant, and ready to come and aid us in clearing our woods and in paying our taxes.   The same subject was discussed on the 13th of December, on the passage of a bill to prohibit the migration of certain persons to this Commonwealth, which was passed by an overwhelming majority.

The health of Mason, which was affected by the same disease which, at intervals, worried his brother George, who led an active life (and which we may fairly presume to have been inherited), was becoming seriously impaired, and at the close of the present session he withdrew finally from public life.

We wish it was in our power to record many acts of usefulness performed by this worthy man, and a life of learned repose enjoyed by him in his retirement; but the curtain was soon suddenly to fall.   He died in 1785 at " Chippawamsic," his seat in Stafford, near Dumfries, at the early age of fifty-five.   He inherited nothing from his father beyond the means of obtaining the best education then within his reach; but this was enough for Mason.   Had such a man been blessed with health, he would at that day have made a splendid fortune.   But he was not entirely deprived of an inheritance, as he and his sister received from his mother large tracts of land in Loudoun,[212] which,

---

[212] A part of this land is still owned by the Hon. Thomas Swann, of Baltimore, a direct descendant of the only sister of Mason, and by Mr.

though bought originally for a small sum, became valuable; and he added to his possessions by his own industry and skill. He was rather above than below the ordinary size, with blueish-grey eyes and dark hair, and an embrowned complexion. He was a ready and exact speaker, eschewing embellishment, and relying on the force of logic for effect. His great excellence was his skill in the law, and he stood somewhat in the same relation to his contemporaries as that held by Theophilus Parsons toward his associates at the bar of New England. *Laudari a laudato*, especially when the praise comes from a competent and unprejudiced judge, and is uttered long after its object has been consigned to the tomb, is no unfair measure of worth; and we are told by Saint George Tucker, the eldest of the name, who had a near observation of all the great lawyers of the Revolutionary epoch, and who held a seat on the bench of the Court of Appeals near the time of the death of Mason, that " Thomson Mason was esteemed the first lawyer at the bar." [213]

He was buried in a clump of trees on " Raspberry Plain," his estate near Leesburg; but no stone marks his grave. A venerable descendant, still living, says that he had blue eyes. He was married a second time to Mrs. Wallace, of Hampton, formerly Miss Westwood. When the old gentleman—who, by the way, was not more than forty at the time—married his second wife, his son, John Thomson, used to say jocosely that his father had brushed his hair and burnished himself so sprucely that he could hardly recognize *the old fellow*. This lady long survived him, and died in 1824,[214] preserving to the last those endearing qualities of mind and character that fascinated the great lawyer. She was accustomed to say that she was just sixteen when her future husband took his seat in the House of Burgesses, and that he was the handsomest and most eloquent member of the House. She delighted to describe him as a devoted husband, sitting by

---

Temple Mason, a son of Thomson Mason. It was from the fact that he received his property from his mother that her maiden name of Thomson was given to all his children. By the law of entails the property of his father descended to the eldest son.

[213] Letter to Wirt in *Kennedy's Life*, Vol. I, 317. The Judge, in the same letter, states that Peyton Randolph was President of Congress to the day of his death ; in which, however, he is mistaken.

[214] For a description of this lady, see *Old Churches, &c.*, Vol. II, 230.

her side and recognizing in her fading features the beauty that
adorned them in youth.   She spoke with grateful warmth of
his excellence as a stepfather.   He wrote a paraphrase of the
Song of Solomon, adapted to the praise of his wife, which was
much admired, and is still in existence.   A venerable descendant, still living,[215] says he always contributed liberally to the
army in provisions and by the hospitalities of his house; that he
was one of the kindest of men, but was apt to be regarded with
fear by those who did not know him well.   He had a stern eye,
which it was not pleasant to look at when he was in a severe
mood.   Dr. Wallace, his stepson, says that during the Revolution a quartermaster's deputy came to his room when he was ill
with the gout and asked for a contribution of corn.   Mason
instantly directed his servant to give him half of all the corn he
had.   The deputy tauntingly replied, "Half, indeed! I must
have the whole."   Mason, forgetting his gout, leaped from the
bed, seized the poker, and cudgelled the fellow out of the house.
The Doctor remembers that he was fond of his gun, and on one
occasion, being short-sighted, blazed away at some stumps nearly
covered with water, which he mistook for wild ducks.

I have thus endeavored to recall some of the details of the life
of Thomson Mason.   To have said more would not have been
justified by the scope of this work, or by the materials in my
possession, perhaps in existence; to have said less would have
been ungenerous to the memory of a pure and intrepid patriot, of
a great lawyer, and of one of the wisest statesmen of the Revolutionary era.   I now pass to his accomplished son.

---

[215] Mrs. Emily Macrae, a granddaughter.

STEVENS THOMSON MASON.

Stevens Thomson Mason, who was destined to invest his honored patronymic with a brilliancy it had not yet known since the emigration of the first George, was born at "Chippawamsic," in Stafford county, in the year 1760, and was the eldest of a family of five sons and one daughter.[216]

I am unable to say what were his opportunities for improvement in early youth; but the school of the parish was the common resort in those days, and the rector was commonly a graduate of an English or Scotch college; and, if not altogether such a priest as James Blair or Jarratt, was almost invariably a good classical scholar, was moderately versed in mathematics, and cherished a taste for polite letters not at all incompatible with an occasional fox hunt, or with a game at dominoes or cards, or with the love of a glass of old wine. Young Scotchmen were at that time easily obtained as tutors, who, unversed in the common decencies of society, were enthusiasts in classical learning, and who, in their almost servile condition, inspired their pupils with a love of excellence that often led to the most favorable results. These were the men whose teachings formed those educated and able men whose eloquence shone in our early councils, and whose skill drafted the State papers of that age. It may be presumed that, when the oldest son was the favored child, the father was frequently his guide and instructor.

When Stevens entered William and Mary College he was quite as well prepared, as is shown by the result, as any modern matriculate, and engaged with zeal in the prosecution of his studies. He was quickened in his career by one of those accidents which are sometimes more important in deciding the destinies of young men than the mastery of the immediate studies that constitute their chief work. Our clever Virginians almost always appear in groups; and Mason was at once introduced to

---

[216] The day of the month, or the month, I cannot find out. His mother's name was Mary Barnes, of Maryland.

a number of young men of bright parts, with some of whom he
preserved pleasant and intimate relations, personal and political,
during the whole of his future career. Of this group William
Branch Giles, the amiable and lamented Hardy, Littleton Eyre,
John H. Cocke, the Carters (of Shirley), William Cabell (the
son of the patriarch of "Union Hill"), John Jones (of the Senate and of the present Convention), Richard Bland Lee, William
Nelson (the future Chancellor), John Allen (of Surry), John
Brown (a member of the Senate and of the old Congress), Spencer Roane, William Short (*Chargé* at the French Court, and
Minister to Spain and to The Hague), the Brents (of Maryland
and Virginia), Richard Booker (of Amelia), Beckley (who was
continuously the Clerk of the Senate, the successor of Edmund
Randolph as the Clerk of the House of Delegates, and the first
Clerk of the House of Representatives of the United States):[217]
these, and others, were his contemporaries at college. Of this
number no less than six were members of the present Convention.

In regarding this collection of young men we are reminded
of another that nearly trod upon their heels in the same venerable institution, and intermingled with them in public life. Littleton Waller Tazewell, Robert Barraud Taylor, John Randolph,
James Barbour, William Henry Cabell, and the lamented John
Thompson caught the mantles of their predecessors as they fell.
Poor Thompson held the same painful relation to his group that
Hardy held in his—brilliant, profound, and suddenly snatched
away. And hardly had this group disappeared ere another,
which was destined to strive with them for the honors of an
entire generation, appeared in their places. I feel as if I were
pressing the sod of new-made graves when I pronounce the
names of Benjamin Watkins Leigh, of Chapman Johnson, of
Robert Stanard, of Philip Pendleton Barbour, and of Henry
E. Watkins. When the fame of all these gallant young men
is to be weighed, who can estimate the effect of association
with their fellows in the same institution?

Young Mason had a strong military turn, and, after leaving

[217] Beckley served during the eight years of Washington's administration, was turned out during Adams's, and was reinstated in 1801,
serving till 1807—fifteen years.

college, determined to take a part in the war, which was not yet concluded. He served with credit through several grades, and commanded a Virginia brigade at the evacuation of Charleston.[218]

In the year 1783, as stated in the memoir of his father, he became a member of the House of Delegates from the county of Loudoun, and continued to hold his seat for two or three sessions, when he withdrew, and never held a seat in that House again. His votes on leading questions have already been detailed elsewhere.[219]

His legislative career, which was almost unsurpassed in splendor and effect, was now about to begin. After a short interval he was returned to the Senate of Virginia from the counties of Loudoun and Fauquier, and took his seat in that body for the first time at the October session of 1787. His first act was to vote for Edmund Randolph as Governor, with whom he was soon to be intimately connected with in the present Convention, in the House of Delegates, and as Attorney-General of the United States, of which he was ere long to be a senator; and to send his quartermaster-general (Edward Carrington), Henry Lee (his colleague in the war of the South), and his classmate (John Brown) to the Congress of the Confederation, along with James Madison, with whom he acted in unison in Federal affairs to the day of his death. Another classmate (Thomas Lee) was his colleague in the Senate.

On the 26th of October the Senate received from the House of Delegates a series of resolutions declaring that the Federal Constitution, which had been published to the world the month preceding, and which had been forwarded by Congress to the Assembly, should be submitted to a Convention of the people of the Commonwealth, and entering into other specifications on the subject.[220] These resolutions were critically examined in the Senate, were amended in several respects, and on the 30th were

---

[218] Mason manuscripts.

[219] In the review of the legislative sessions, and in the preceding sketch of his father.

[220] See the review of the session of 1787, *ante*. These resolutions were afterwards embodied in a bill which passed both houses, and may be seen in *Hening*.

adopted by the body.   Mason was ordered to carry the amended
resolutions to the House of Delegates, which adopted them
forthwith.   This was his first prominent movement in Federal
affairs, which he may be said to have controlled almost entirely
in both houses as long as he remained in the Senate.

The subjects discussed during the session included many
grave and perplexing questions, which were managed by Mason
with tact and ability.   Some of those questions have partially
lost their interest; but it is easy to see, in tracing the progress
of measures through the Senate, that many fierce battles
were fought between their friends and opponents.   Such measures as the establishment of the boundary line of North Carolina; the construction of the Dismal Swamp canal; the acts
declaring tobacco receivable in payment of the taxes of 1787 (a
subject which involved a discussion of the currency); establishing a district court on the western waters; concerning moneys
paid into the public loan office in payment of British debts; providing a sinking fund for the redemption of the public debt;
repealing all acts preventing the collection of the British debts;
discriminating commercially in favor of those nations which had
acknowledged the independence of the United States; prescribing
the mode of proving wills; imposing duties and regulating the
customs : such acts, and many others equally intricate and
embarrassing, passed under his review, and were, in many
instances, essentially modified by him.   And when a conference
was called by the houses, as was often the case at this period,
the honor and the responsibility of representing the Senate most
commonly fell upon him.   His decision of character, his knowledge of human nature, his ready elocution, his skill in law, and
his familiar acquaintance with the military and political measures
of the Revolution, made him uncommonly apt and useful in
settling those multitudinous and anomalous questions which
sprang up between the close of the war and the adoption of the
Federal Constitution, and which seriously perplexed the bench
as well as the Senate.

The Senate adjourned on the 8th day of January, 1788, and,
on the first day of the following June, he took his seat in that
Federal Convention which forms the theme of the present work.
Although he had discussed in public the true nature of the Federal Constitution, and was one of the readiest, most able, and

most fertile speakers of the day, he did not participate in the debates of the Convention; for, as before observed, it was then not deemed incumbent upon any man of mark to make a speech, partly because, as is the custom of the British Parliament, it was usual to defer to the prominent leaders, whose effective aid was thought sufficient to attain the end in view; partly because, from the habits of the Colony, in which there were neither reporters, nor papers large enough to hold reports, the incitements to much speaking had not become chronic; and, I may add, because the duration of the session of the Convention was limited by the approaching session of the Assembly.[221]

Yet, such was the wealth of the Convention in talent, had the members who made speeches not been present, others would have arisen on both sides of the House who would have filled their places, would have commanded the respect and the applause of the people, and would have given a new cast to the reputations of that epoch. Mason, who was skilful as a parliamentarian (then fresh from the task of revising the rules and orders of the Senate), was doubtless consulted by the opponents of the Constitution, and he manifested his opinions by voting in favor of previous amendments and against the ratification of that instrument without them.[222]

When the Convention adjourned he passed at once into the Senate, and performed the grateful office of nominating his class-mate, John Jones, to the chair of that body, and of seeing him elected by a unanimous vote. When the subject of the district court bill was settled, the Senate, after a session of six days, adjourned.

The Assembly met on the 21st of October following, but the Senate did not form a quorum till the 28th. The first business

---

[221] The Assembly had been convoked by a proclamation of the Governor to meet on the 23d of June. It accordingly met on that day, and, after adjusting some difficulties in the bill establishing district courts, adjourned on the 30th, to meet on the third Monday of October following. The approaching session of the Assembly had an effect, whether designed or not, in shortening the session of the Convention; for the members of the latter body had not the audacity of the Convention of 1829, which sat a month and a half alongside of the Assembly.

[222] See his votes on the ayes and noes, *ante*.

relating to Federal affairs was the appointment of members to
the old Congress; for it was necessary that the old organization
should remain entire until it was superseded by the new.
Strange as it may appear, there were more candidates for the
five seats in the old Congress at the present session than at any
previous one; and the explanation may be found in the excited
state of parties, each being anxious to gain the influence of
Congress, whatever it might be, in its favor.   The candidates in
nomination were Madison, Cyrus Griffin, John Brown, John
Dawson, Ralph Wormeley, Mann Page, John H. Briggs, John
Page (of "Rosewell"), Wilson Cary Nicholas, and John Marshall.   Wormeley was withdrawn before the balloting began.
The result was that Griffin, Brown, Madison, Dawson, and Mann
Page were chosen.   On the 8th of November the Senate proceeded for the first time to choose senators of the United States.
Three persons only were in nomination in either house—Madison, Grayson, and Richard Henry Lee; the first named representing the friends of the Constitution, the two last its opponents.   Lee and Grayson were easily elected.[223]

The Senate received from the House of Delegates, on the 10th
of November, the bill "for the appointment of electors to choose
a President, pursuant to the Constitution of government for the
United States"; which was referred to the Committee of the
Whole, was discussed on the 11th, 12th, and 13th, and, having
received several amendments, was ordered to be read the third
time; and on the 14th it passed the body without a division.
Hugh Nelson was ordered to convey it to the House of Delegates, which agreed to all the amendments of the Senate except
one, from which that body receded.

The bill for the election of members of the House of Representatives was received by the Senate on the 11th, was read the
first and ordered to be read the second time.   On the 15th it
was read a second time, and committed to the whole house on

---

[223] It is well known that Patrick Henry nominated Lee and Grayson
at the same time, but the Journals merely give the names of the persons nominated.   It has been frequently said that George Mason was
elected a senator of the United States on this occasion, and declined.
His name was not mentioned.   (House Journal, and particularly Senate
Journal, November 8, 1788.)

the 18th, when it was discussed; but the Senate declined receiving the report of the committee till the following day, when it was duly received, and a motion made to strike out the words "being a freeholder, and who shall have been a *bona-fide* resident for twelve months within such district." The design of the bill as it stood was to prevent, partly, the selection of a group of men from the metropolis, and, partly, the choice of a member by another district who had been, or was likely to be, excluded from his own. The motion to strike out failed by a vote of twelve to three.[224] The bill and amendments were then agreed to without a division, and Thomas Lee was requested to return them to the House of Delegates; which body, on the 20th, concurred in them all.

The Senate also proposed amendments to the bill calling a new Federal Convention, in which the House of Delegates concurred. The bill authorizing the Executive to make known, by proclamation, the times and places of appointing electors to choose a President was likewise amended by the Senate; and in all its amendments the House of Delegates concurred, with the exception of one, from which the Senate receded. The resolutions respecting the navigation of the Mississippi, which had especial reference to the debate in the Convention on the subject, were agreed to by the Senate, as well as by the House of Delegates, unanimously.

Mason was one of the first of our early statesmen to condemn the policy of insufficient salaries for the highest functionaries of the State—a policy which prescribed as a fit reward for the services of a Wythe a sum a modern day laborer might earn in the course of a year.[225] When the bill allowing travelling expenses

---

[224] As this vote shows the political complexion of the Senate at that time, I annex it:

AYES—Burwell Bassett, John Page, and Hugh Nelson.

NOES—John Pride, Turner Southall, John S. Wills, John Coleman, Matthew Anderson, Robert Rutherford, Joseph Jones, John Pope, John P. Duval, Paul Loyall, Nicholas Cabell, and Thomas Lee.

Mason was out of the house when his name was called. Of these Joseph Jones, Pride, and Bassett were members of the present Convention.

[225] The policy of low salaries for judges prevailed in Massachusetts also until Story gave it a death-blow in the House of Representatives of that State, and the genius of Parsons settled the question.

to the judges of the General Court, &c., was before the Senate,
he voted to amend it by enlarging the *per diem* of the judge
while holding his court, and by raising the standard of remune-
ration in other respects.   He was sustained by a large majority
in striking out sixpence and inserting a shilling; but the other
amendments prevailed by a single vote.   The bill and amendments were returned to the House of Delegates, which refused
its concurrence, and sent the bill back to the Senate.   Mason,
who had only carried the amendments by a single vote, saw that
all further effort at that time was vain; and they were receded
from without a division.

  This session was memorable for the remodelling of the Court
of Appeals and the displacement and re-election of all of its
judges.   The subject has already been alluded to,[226] and is only
mentioned here as bearing upon the course which Mason followed
in the Senate of the United States on the repeal of the judiciary
bill of 1800.

  At the October session of 1789 he appeared in his seat on the
20th, and nominated John Pride—with whom he had served in
the Convention—as Speaker of the Senate, and was sustained
by a majority of the House.   He took an active part in all its
proceedings; but I shall allude at present only to his course on
the resolutions ratifying the amendments proposed by Congress
to the Constitution of the United States, which were sent to the
Senate from the House of Delegates on the 2d of December.
They were read a first time and ordered to be committed to the
whole House on the following day.   They were put off from day
to day till the 5th, when they were discussed in committee, which
rose before a decision was made respecting them; and on the
following day they were considered with the same result.   On
the 8th they were reported to the House; and a motion was
made to strike out sundry words and insert that "the third,
eighth, eleventh, and twelfth amendments adopted by Congress
be postponed to the next session of the Assembly for the consideration of the people."   A vote was taken *seriatim* on each
amendment, and recorded in the Journal.   There was a majority
of one in favor of the first, of two in favor of the second, of one
in favor of the third, of six in favor of the fourth, of one in
favor of the fifth, and of six in favor of the sixth; the vote on

---

[226] In the review of the session of 1788, *ante.*

the seventh was unanimous. And the question recurring that
the Senate agree to the resolutions as amended, it was agreed to
without a division. On each vote Mason was with the majority.
The resolutions as amended were returned to the House of
Delegates.

Mason was fully conscious of the weight of responsibility
which devolved upon him; and he knew that his conduct would
be not only critically scanned in his own time, but would be
examined by posterity when the passions of the day would be
forgotten, and when it would stand on its own merit alone.
Hence, he was altogether conservative. He did not seek to
reject the proposed amendments ferfunctorily and finally, but to
subject them to the deliberate examination of the people. So
solicitous was he do right, and so anxious that in future time his
reasons should be fairly known and not left to inference, he and
those with whom he acted made the extraordinary request, which
was granted, that the views of the majority might be recorded in
the Journal.[227] On the 12th a paper containing the reasons of
the majority, and signed by Mason, Pride, Anderson, Wills,
Joseph Jones, Russell, Southall, and Pope, was presented and
recorded in the Journal of that day. It is evidently from the
pen of Mason, and forcibly maintains those doctrines which
Virginia has upheld ever since. After analyzing the several
amendments which he sought to postpone, he concludes by saying " that of the many and important amendments recommended
by the Conventions of Virginia and other States, those propositions contain all that Congress is disposed to grant; that all
the rest are by them deemed improper, and these are offered in
full satisfaction of the whole; that, although a ratification of part
of the amendments that have been prayed for by Virginia would
not absolutely preclude us from urging others, yet we conceive
that, by the acceptance of particular articles, we are concluded as
to the points they relate to. Considering, therefore, that they
are far short of what the people of Virginia wish and have asked,
and deeming them by no means sufficient to secure the rights of
the people, or to render the Government safe and desirable, we
think our countrymen ought not to be put off with amendments

---

[227] Senate Journal, December 8, 1789; and for the reasons of the
majority, see December 12th, which deserve to be studied.

so inadequate; and, being satisfied of the defects and dangerous tendency of these four articles of the proposed amendments, we are constrained to withhold our consent to them; but, unwilling for the present to determine on their rejection, we think it our duty to postpone them till the next session of the Assembly, in order that the people of Virginia may have an opportunity to consider them.''

The House of Delegates sent back the amendments to the Senate on the 11th, having disagreed to the first, second, and third, and agreed to the fourth. The Senate insisted on their amendments, and Mason was sent to carry their determination to the House of Delegates. On the 14th the House determined to adhere to their disagreement.

The acts referring to the judiciary establishment—especially the bill to amend the District and General Court—which were passed during the session, brought about some clashing between the two houses, and were mainly under the control of Mason, who was the first lawyer of the body.

We will pass rapidly over the proceedings of the Senate, which began its next session on the 18th day of October, 1790. The Federal Congress had held its sessions, and a sadness was cast upon the Assembly by the unexpected death of Colonel Grayson, who had been one of the two first senators of the United States, and was performing the duties of his office with diligence and ability, when, after the close of the second session, he was about to resume his seat, he died on the way.[228]

James Monroe was elected over John Walker for the unexpired term, and for a full term of six years thereafter. The first and leading question on Federal affairs at the present session, as heretofore detailed,[229] was in relation to the act of Congress assuming the debts of the States. The House of Delegates passed resolutions declaring the act repugnant to the Constitution of the United States, unjust, and impolitic. These resolutions assailed alike the constitutionality and expediency of

---

[228] Grayson's humor brightened to the last. I have heard very old men say that, when the proper title for the Vice-President was discussed in the Senate at its first session, he proposed that it should be "His Limpid Highness," or "His Superfluous Excellency."

[229] Review of the session of 1790, *ante*.

the measure; and were conveyed to the Senate, on the 21st of November, by Henry Lee (of the Legion). They were referred to a committee of the whole house on the following Monday, when they were put off to Wednesday, and then to the following Monday, and thenceforth were discussed and postponed till the 21st of December, when they were amended and agreed to. As soon as they were passed, Mason asked and obtained leave of absence for the remainder of the session. What Chapman Johnson—*clarum et venerabile nomen*—was in the Senate of Virginia at a subsequent day, Stevens Thomson Mason was, during the time he held a seat in that body, perhaps with this distinctive difference springing from the temperament of the two men, from the caste of their characters, and from the peculier circumstances of the respective eras in which they lived, that Johnson devoted his critical skill and his wide experience of affairs to the domestic legislation of the Commonwealth, and that Mason, who also watched with the strictest vigilance the development of our judicial and general policy, and who was a foremost champion at an extraordinary crisis, believed that the rights and liberties of the people were placed in jeopardy by the refusal of Congress to accept the amendments to the Federal Constitution proposed by the Convention of Virginia, and that the sternest rule of the interpretation of the powers of that instrument was the only peaceful remedy.

The course pursued by Mason on Federal topics was altogether acceptable to the people of Virginia, and when a vacancy occurred in the Senate of the United States by the appointment of Mr. Monroe to the Court of France, he was chosen to fill his .place.[230] On the 9th of June, 1795, he appeared in his seat in the Senate at the opening of the session; and although some of the measures of the administration most obnoxious to the South had already been disposed of, others were soon to follow which placed him in a delicate and responsible position. In common

---

[230] November 18, 1794. Henry Tazewell was elected a senator the same day in place of John Taylor (of Caroline), resigned, and took his seat on the 29th of December following, and on the 20th of February was chosen President of the Senate. I have no copy of the Journal of the Senate at hand, but I do not see the name of Mason in *Benton's Debates* till the time specified in the text. He must, however, have taken his seat when Tazewell took his.

with all Virginians, and especially with those who had been
engaged in military service during the Revolution, he cherished
the warmest love and veneration for Washington; but he had
been impelled by a sense of duty to oppose, with a large
majority of the people of Virginia, many of the leading measures of his administration.   He was now to oppose with all his
ability a measure which at the time was deemed by its friends a
hard one in its effects upon the whole country, but which was
believed to be exceedingly injurious to the interests of the Southern States, and to those of Virginia in particular.   The famous
treaty with England had been signed by Mr. Jay and the British
Minister in London the day after Mason's election by the Assembly to a seat in the Senate, had been received by our own Government on the 7th of March following, was communicated to a
called Senate on the 8th of June, and was ratified on the 24th
by a bare constitutional majority.   A single vote would have
defeated it.   Every motion made by the Republican minority to
amend the objectionable articles of the treaty was voted down;
the enormous losses sustained by Virginia and other Southern
States in the abduction of slaves, in the face of solemn treaties,
were not only not recognized by the present, but were virtually
abjured forever; and the West India trade, which had always
been a source of profit to Virginia, was substantially sacrificed.
Both these last topics were sore subjects to Virginia.   Some of
the members of the present Convention had repaired to New
York before the evacuation of that city by the British, and had
earnestly beseeched the British general to surrender to them
their slaves in his possession; but, so far from granting their
requests, he had sent the negroes off while the Southern claim-.
ants were present in the city; and the West India trade, which
had been affected by orders in council soon after the peace of
1783, and which had been brought before the Assembly for
several years by the petitions of our merchants, had become a
subject of sensitive interest to the people at large.   Of these
important interests the treaty was regarded as a final sacrifice.
Even after its ratification by the Senate, Washington was in
serious doubt respecting the course he ought to pursue.   The
exact stipulations of the treaty were not as yet generally known,
but enough had got abroad to excite the most serious apprehensions.

But, apart from the specific provisions of the treaty, there was a well-founded conviction in Virginia that it was one of a series of measures calculated, if not designed, to injure the South and materially check her future development. A bold and well-nigh successful movement had been made a few years before by some of the same men now in power, and especially by Mr. Jay (the negotiation of the obnoxious treaty to surrender the right of navigating the Mississippi to Spain for a period of thirty years), and this fatal scheme might be renewed at any moment, and with the certain prospect of success. Moreover, the practical measures of Federal policy, which had resulted in concentrating a vast moneyed capital in the Northern States, had been injurious to the South, and were likely to prove more fatal in the process of time. Added to these considerations, was a deep sense of wrong felt by Virginia in the stern refusal of the Northern States to accept those amendments to the Federal Constitution which Virginia had pressed both by her Convention and by her Assembly in the most solemn manner, and without a belief in the ratification of which that instrument would have been rejected by a decisive majority.

When the treaty was before the Senate two propositions were made by its opponents—one from the North (by Burr), the other from the South (by Henry Tazewell)—and both were rejected. The resolutions of Tazewell—which received the sanction of Mason, and were softened and modified to conflict as tenderly as possible with the views of the majority—were as follows:

"That the President of the United States be informed that the Senate will not consent to the ratification of the treaty of amity, commerce, and navigation between the United States and his Britannic Majesty, concluded at London on the 19th of November, 1794, for the reasons following :

"1. Because so much of the treaty as was intended to terminate the complaints flowing from the inexecution of the treaty of 1783 contains stipulations that were not rightfully or justly requirable of the United States, and which are both impolitic and injurious to their interest; and because the treaty hath not secured that satisfaction from the British Government for the removal of negroes, in violation of the treaty of 1783, to which the citizens of the United States were justly entitled.

"2. Because the rights of individual States are, by the ninth article of the treaty, unconstitutionally invaded.

"3. Because, however unjust or impolitic it may generally be to exercise the power prohibited by the tenth article, yet it rests on legislative discretion, and ought not to be prohibited by treaty.

"4. Because so much of the treaty as relates to commercial arrangements between the parties wants that reciprocity upon which alone such like arrangements ought to be founded, and will operate ruinously to the American commerce and navigation.

"5. Because the treaty prevents the United States from the exercise of that control over their commerce and navigation, as connected with other nations, which might better the condition of their intercouse with friendly nations.

"6. Because the treaty asserts a power in the President and Senate to control, and even annihilate, the constitutional right of the Congress of the United States over their commercial intercourse with foreign nations.

"7. Because, if the construction of this treaty should not produce an infraction of the treaties now subsisting between the United States and their allies, it is calculated to excite sensations, which may not operate beneficially to the United States.

"Notwithstanding the Senate will not consent to the ratification of this treaty, they advise the President of the United States to continue his endeavors, by friendly discussion with his Britannic Majesty, to adjust all the real causes of complaint between the two nations."

The vote rejecting these resolutions was the same as that by which the treaty was ratified.[231]

Up to this period, while Washington, excited by some recent acts of the British Government, was hesitating about the course which he ought to pursue, Mason forwarded, on the 20th of June, an abstract of the treaty to the editor of a Philadelphia paper; and in an instant there was an explosion of public sentiment against the treaty, then without a parallel in our history,

---

[231] The vote was twenty to ten—exactly two-thirds. Neither the resolutions of Tazewell nor the more downright and pungent ones of Burr are to be found in *Benton's Debates*, but may be seen in the Senate Journal, and in a small volume containing the treaty and the memorials and documents appertaining to it, published by Matthew Carey at the date of the treaty.

and only equalled by the exasperation excited at a later day by the attack of the Leopard upon the Chesapeake.[232] For a time public opinion appeared to be unanimous against the treaty.[233] Public meetings were not as common then as now, but all the commercial cities protested against the treaty as fatal to the prosperity of the country. In Virginia there seemed to be but one opinion on the subject, and the treaty was denounced as unjust and injurious; for it not only deprived her merchants of a trade which they had enjoyed in a greater or less degree for more than a hundred years, but compelled them, with others, to pay their debts to the British in coin, while the British were relieved virtually of all counter claims founded upon the negroes carried off, not by the prowess of war, but in the face of the treaty of 1783.

There was, after a season, a slight reaction in favor of the treaty, and Mason was denounced as a man who had violated the decencies of life, had wantonly dishonored himself by violating the pledge of secrecy as a senator, and had made any future effort to secure an advantageous treaty with a foreign power impracticable.

On the other hand, his course was applauded with equal zeal by the opposition. Boston, Baltimore, Trenton, and Norfolk not only applauded the act, but bestowed on its author the loftiest panegyric.[234] Mason was sustained by the General Assembly of

---

[232] Judge Marshall thus alludes to the publication of the treaty : "Although common usage, and a decent respect for the Executive and for a foreign nation, not less than a positive resolution, required that the seal of secrecy should not be broken by the Senate, an abstract of this instrument, not very faithfully taken, was given to the public; and on the 29th of June a senator of the United States transmitted a copy of it to the most distinguished editor of the opposition party in Philadelphia, to be communicated to the public through the medium of the press." (*Life of Washington*, revised edition, Vol. II, 364.

[233] Judge Marshall says : "In fact, public opinion did receive a considerable shock, and men, uninfected by the spirit of faction, felt some disappointment on its first appearance." (*Ibid*, 364.) The intensity of party feeling at that day may be judged by the fact that so cool a man as the Chief Justice, in revising his account of the affair forty-five years afterwards, could brand with the epithet of *factions* a large majority of the statesmen and of the people of the last century.

[234] Boston, in a special resolution, offered by Mr. Austin, extolled Mason's "patriotism in publishing the treaty"; Baltimore gave a vote

Virginia by a direct vote and by a re-election to the Senate
of the United States.   His conduct was approved not only by a
large majority of the people of Virginia, but of the Union; and,
as the subject was fully canvassed, the decision was as deliberate
as it was almost unanimous.

While the judgment of a man's contemporaries is an important element in deciding upon his worth, still, as the subject is
as interesting now as it was sixty-four years ago, the question
recurs whether Mason was excusable for disclosing the outline
of the treaty to the people in violation of the rules of the Senate.   None will deny that, as a general principle, the rules of a
deliberative body—especially in relation to the provisions of a
treaty not yet definitely concluded—should be faithfully observed;
and none probably will deny that a case is possible when it would
become the duty of a patriot to expose the proceedings of a
body which were, in his opinion, in manifest violation of the
Constitution and hostile to the integrity of the States, though an
order of that body enjoined secrecy upon its members.   Mason
was a Virginian, and was intimately acquainted with the practice
of Virginia on such a subject.   She had, again and again, called
her members of Congress before the Assembly, and required
them to discourse of public affairs in Congress, when the proceedings of that body were always as strictly secret as were those
of the Senate on particular occasions; and the members appeared
and made their representations without scruple: A vote of
thanks was given to Meriwether Smith on such an occasion.
But the most remarkable case occurred during the session of the
present Convention.   The right of the navigation of the Mississippi had been placed in imminent jeopardy by the Congress;
and the Convention, regarding the question as of vital interest
to Virginia, whose borders were washed by that stream, in the
waters of which she claimed the right of use, called upon the
members of Congress to state their proceedings in full, and they

---

of thanks "to the virtuous minority in the Senate, and to Stevens
Thomson Mason, for the patriotic service rendered his country by the
disclosure"; Norfolk declared that Mason "is entitled to the thanks
of every good citizen and real friend to the Constitution of the United
States for his patriotic and independent conduct in rending the veil of
senatorial secrecy," &c.; Trenton resolved that Mason "is entitled to
the highest veneration, respect, and esteem of his countrymen" for
making the disclosure, &c., &c.

disclosed them without hesitation.[235]   The question, then, would seem to have been decided in Virginia that a representative is bound, at the bidding of his constituents, to disclose all his doings in their behalf, even though a rule of the body to which he belonged might be violated by the disclosure.   It may be alleged that Mason was not called upon by the Assemby to make a disclosure, but acted on his own responsibility.   But if a disclosure at the bidding of the constituent body is justifiable, it is justifiable on the ground of extreme necessity; and of this necessity it may happen—as in the present case—that the representative only can be the judge.   He alone can know exactly the impending dangers; and, if he believe the danger to be so imminent as to involve the dearest rights of his constituents, the mode of proclaiming that danger to them is, at best, a choice of means, and may be as well—perhaps more effectually—done by a publication in a paper of wide circulation as by a letter to the Governor at a time when the Assembly was not in session, and when a day's delay might be fatal.   That the stipulations of the treaty were believed seriously to impair the rights and interests of Virginia, has already been shown; and Mason might fairly presume that, if a rule of the Senate were regarded as an obligation incapable of being annulled but by a vote of the body itself, no danger menacing a right or possession of the South could be disclosed until the treaty had become a law, and the disclosure was vain.   None will wish that such cases should become frequent; but when they do occur, the great and essential interests of a whole community will more completely control the action of a representative than the rules of the body to which he belongs.   Each case must be decided on its own merits.   Certain it is that the course of Mason was sanctioned by those to whom he looked for justification and approval.

When the British treaty was ratified by the Senate, an article was added providing that so much of the twelfth article as

---

[235] Madison boggled, as he knew the disclosures might seal the fate of the Constitution in the Convention, but made the disclosure.   It is plain that, in a strictly federal system, it would be absurd to deny the right of the Government to ask explanations from its ministers and servants in relation to a public matter.   An inviolable rule of secrecy would sever all connection between the representative and the constituent body.

related to the intercourse with the West Indies should be suspended, and that fresh negotiations should be entered into on
the subject.[236]   At the same time Gunn (of Georgia) offered a
resolution requesting the President further to negotiate concerning the payment of the value of the slaves carried off by the
British army in violation of the treaty of 1783.   This resolution
was so modified as not to interfere with the treaty; but it was
promptly rejected.   The result was, as was predicted at the
time, that the West India trade would never more be placed on
its old footing, at least for a generation to come;[237] and that the
stolen negroes would never be paid for; nor have they been to
the present hour.[238]

At the December session of 1795 the Senate proceeded, as
was then customary, to prepare a response to the President's
communication—a practice borrowed from the British Parliament
and long since disused, and ever ill-timed, as calculated to anticipate opinions and to stir party feuds on the threshold of a
session.   The address inclined to take too favorable a view of
our foreign affairs, and Mason moved to strike out the fourth

---

[236] When Mr. Jay made the treaty he was not aware that cotton had
become an article of export from the United States.

[237] It was secured during General Jackson's administration.

[238] My maxim in respect of foreign powers is that of the Declaration
of Independence, "Enemies in war, in peace friends"; and that of
still higher authority, " Peace on earth and good will to men "; but it is
the province of history to record the delinquencies of nations, and
those of Great Britain towards us have been formidable.   If a bill with
accruing interest were made out of the value of our slaves purloined
in the face of a solemn treaty, of our commerce sequestered by orders
in council which the British tribunals have since pronounced illegal, of
the labor of our seamen pressed on board of British ships, of the
amount of losses sustained by our embargo and non-intercourse regulations into which England forced us, and of the expenses of the war
which she compelled us to wage in defence of the common rights of
human nature—if all these sums with interest were made into a bill,
and that bill placed into the hands of some future senator from Oregon,
fresh from his jaunt of five thousand miles by land or fifteen thousand
by water, it is quite probable that, to simplify matters, he would pro-
prose at once to take possession of the little island, substitute a Territorial Legislature for her Parliament, make her a coaling-station for our
steamers, and award her, as a matter of extreme grace, the privilege
of sending a territorial delegate to Washington.

and fifth paragraphs. Pierce Butler was disposed to go further, and contended not only for striking out, but for inserting a counter statement. The motion failed by a vote of eight to fourteen ; and the entire address as reported was adopted by the same vote. The slight synopsis which has come down to us of the debates of this session shows several instances in which the roll was called; but Mason does not appear to have been present at the time.

On the 12th of January, 1797, he took his seat in the Senate, and was immediately placed at the head of a committee to which the notification of the House of Representatives of the election of Mr. Jefferson as Vice-President of the United States was referred, and he drew a form which the President was requested to forward to that gentleman, stating his election to the office in question. On the 21st of February a bill to accommodate the President was discussed and passed by a vote of twenty-eight to three, Mason in the minority and Tazewell in the majority.

When the proposition was made in May, 1798, to allow General Thomas Pinkney, our Minister to Spain, to receive the customary presents from His Catholic Majesty on the negotiation of a treaty, it was carried by a vote of seventeen to five—Mason and Tazewell in the negative. On the 25th of June, when the bill to declare the treaties between the United States and the Republic of France null and void was on its passage, Mason opposed it; but it passed by a vote of fourteen to five. On the 27th, when the notorious bill to define more particularly the crime of treason, and to define and punish the crime of sedition, came up, a motion was made to commit it, which prevailed—Mason and Tazewell in the negative; and on the 29th a motion was made to amend the bill authorizing the President to prevent and regulate the landing of French passengers and other persons who may arrive in the United States from foreign places, so as not to prohibit the migration or importation of such persons as any State may think proper by law to admit. Mason voted in the affirmative in a minority of three. The bill passed the Senate with the usual majority. When the bill from the House of Representatives providing for the valuation of lands and dwelling-houses, and the enumeration of slaves was discussed, Mason moved to add to the end of the eighth section the words: "except such slaves as from fixed infirmity or bodily disability may be incapable of labor"; and his amendment prevailed by a vote of eleven to eight. When the treason and sedition bill again came up Mason moved to expunge the words: "Or shall in manner aforesaid traduce or defame the President of the United States or any court or judge thereof, by declarations tending to criminate their motives in any official transaction"; but he lost his motion by a vote of fifteen to eight; and when the second and leading section of the bill was read, a motion was made to strike it out, which failed by a vote of eighteen to six. And the question on the final passage of a bill, which was destined to overthrow an administration and to blast for years the popularity of its supporters, was carried by a vote of eighteen to six, Mason, Tazewell, Anderson, Brown, Howard, and Langdon constituting the minority.

The bill for encouraging the capture of French armed vessels by armed ships or vessels owned by citizens of the United States was opposed by Mason; but, like its kindred measures, it prevailed by a vote of sixteen to four—Mason, Tazewell, Brown, and Langdon being the minority. On the passage of the bill for making further appropriations for the additional naval armament, he was in a minority of three—his colleague, Tazewell, and Anderson alone standing by him.

One of the first duties which Mason was required to perform on taking his seat at the December session of 1799 was to commit to the grave the remains of his esteemed colleague and friend, Henry Tazewell, who died on the 24th of January. Tazewell had taken his seat in the Senate three days before, but was suffering from an inflammatory attack which had seized him on his route from Virginia. He was seen to be ill, but none believed that his end was near. He was in his forty-eighth year. He entered the Convention of December, 1775, and had continued in that body till the Declaration of Independence by Virginia and the formation of the first Constitution of the Commonwealth. Throughout the war and after its close he remained in the House of Delegates, always maintaining an eminent position in the debates of the House and in the deliberations of the early patriots, until he was called to the bench of the General Court. On the bench of that court he acquired the reputation of an able and learned judge, and had been elevated to the Court of Appeals a short time before he was called upon by the Assembly to take a seat in the Senate of the United States. His reputation had preceded him; and during the first session of his attendance he was chosen its president *pro tempore*, an honor which was conferred a second time upon him at the following session.

When the death of Tazewell was announced to the Senate Mason was associated with Brown and Marshall (of Kentucky) in superintending his funeral, which was attended to the place of interment by the Senate in mourning. As he wept at the grave of Tazewell,[239] how little did Mason dream, radiant with health as he then was, and quickened by the intellectual contests in which he was daily engaged, that in less than four years he was to die in the same city! But we must not anticipate.

The act further to suspend commercial intercourse with France (from the House of Representatives) came up in the Senate on the 6th of February, but, after several ineffectual motions by the Republicans to amend it, it passed by a vote of eighteen to ten— Mason, of course, in the minority. On the 23d he opposed the bill to augment the salaries of the principal officers of the executive departments, which prevailed by a vote of twenty-two to three; Langdon and Livermore voting with him. I wish, he had voted with the majority, as the salaries were very low, that of the Secretary of State not exceeding three thousand dollars, though three thousand dollars then were equal to six thousand now.

The session of the Senate of the United States—beginning in December, 1799—was occupied for many days by a subject which tended as much, perhaps, as any other to precipitate the downfall of the party which governed its deliberations. At this day it seems wonderful that a party consisting of so many pure, able, and honorable men should have been so completely controlled by leaders who thought that in a free country conciliation was no part of the policy of statesmen, and who believed that the best mode of securing the affections of the people was by

---

[239] Judge Tazewell was buried in Christ church yard, corner of Fifth and Arch streets, Philadelphia, a few feet from the western wall, and about a fourth of the distance of the entire length of the wall from Arch. A white marble slab, formerly on pillars, but now on the surface, protects his remains. The grave of Colonel Innes is near by. For a notice of Judge Tazewell, see my work on the Virginia Convention of 1776, page 79, *et seq.*

inspiring them with the terrors of the law. Had the Federal party acted with ordinary prudence during the period when the publication of the correspondence of our Envoys to France had made a general impression in their favor, it is probable that John Adams would have been re-elected, and its members—who were soon to be scattered to the winds—might have received a new lease of life. But the war upon foreigners seeking our shores, and upon the press, alarmed intelligent men, who saw that, under the guidance of such leaders, the liberty of speech, of person, and of the press would soon be as much endangered in a free country as in the despotisms of Europe. The great and absorbing event of the present session was the persecution of an editor. It appears that Colonel Duane, of the *Aurora* (newspaper), had written and published an article which was distasteful to the ruling majority of the Senate; and that body summoned him to appear at its bar to answer for the contempt. He appeared once; but, as the Senate refused him the full aid of counsel, he declined to appear a second time. This case, in its various stages, consumed a great deal of time, and without any definitive action. It is to the credit of Mason that he opposed this effort to gag the press in all its stages, and on the final passage of the order. On one of its phases Mason uttered these words of warning:

"He recommended to gentlemen to explore well the ground which the motion of the gentleman from Connecticut had taken, and consider seriously the consequences to which they would be led in pursuing their object. What was to be the course of their proceeding? What were the embarrassments likely to arise therein? He called the House to view the delicacy of the situation in which they would be involved while defining their newly-discovered privileges and subverting the old acknowledged privileges of the liberty of the press—he said the delicacy of their situation, because he considered it a delicate one; for he was far from believing that the privileges of the Senate were as unlimited as the gentleman from Connecticut contended they were; if so, and they proceed to touch the liberty of the press—which they may discover in the end to be secured against the invasion—they will be compelled to retrace every step they are now taking, which will redound neither to their honor nor their discernment. They should be careful how they expose themselves to popular scrutiny in cases respecting their own power for the public mind had already been considerably agitated at what many believed to be an unconstitutional exercise of power. If, session after session, attempts were made to fetter the freedom of the press, the people of the United States would watch with anxious regard every movement of this body. A measure which originated in the Senate, and was subsequently acceded to by the other branch of the Legislature, had been just ground of alarm. It is no wonder they watch our bills as well as our laws; for it must be recollected by many of the gentlemen who hear me that the bill called the Sedition Bill was first introduced here, and that, instead of being what it afterwards became, it was a bill more particularly to define treason and sedition. The good sense of the House—during the time it was upon the table and undergoing a political dissection—cut off from it many of those monstrous excrescences which at first disfigured it, and at last trimmed it into a shapely form; but, after all, it was removed below stairs in a condition not fit to meet the eye of our constituents—even obliged to undergo a decapitation; the head or title of it was struck off, and instead of being a bill defining treason—which is a thing totally out of our power, the Constitution having declared in what alone treason should consist—instead of being denominated a bill against sedition, it took the obnoxious head of being a bill to amend the law for punishing certain crimes against the United States.''

As Duane would not appear, and as the majority were determined to punish him, it was resolved on the eve of adjournment, by a vote of thirteen to four, that the President of the United States be requested to instruct the proper law officers to commence and carry on a prosecution against William Duane, editor of the newspaper called the *Aurora*, for certain false, defamatory, scandalous, and malicious publications tending to defame the Senate of the United States.

The famous judiciary act—the repeal of which will be presently recorded—was discussed by the Senate at the present session. When the bill to permit slaves, in certain cases, to be brought into the Mississippi territory was on its final passage, it does not appear that there was much discussion on its merits; but it was rejected by a vote of five to fourteen—Mason one of the majority.

At the session of the Senate in December, 1800, the first bill on which Mason was called to vote was a bill to erect a mausoleum to Washington. He sustained it in company with his new colleague, Wilson Cary Nicholas. The vote was not unanimous, for there was a minority of nine; the choice between a statue and a tomb making the difference among the members. He consistently opposed the policy of shrouding the proceedings of public bodies in secrecy; and when it was proposed in the Senate that no person should be admitted into the gallery while the votes for President and Vice-President were counted, he objected to the proposition, but was left in a minority. The debates of the Senate are so meagre, as reported by Colonel Benton, that we cannot say anything about the course of Mason during the session. Its great event was the election of Mr. Jefferson to the Presidency; and when, on the 3d of March, the Senate adjourned in its legislative capacity it was convoked in its executive; and Mason had the pleasure of voting into office his old colleagues who had fought with him against such formidable odds ever since the adoption of the Federal Constitution. From the time when he took his seat in the Senate to the close of the present session, he was in a small minority, but his ability and courtesy conciliated the respect of his opponents, while his heroic devotion to his party, which he believed to be the party of freedom and of union, received the cordial applause of a majority of the people.

In the evening of his honored life, when Thomas Jefferson was led to recount those acts by which he had rendered essential service to his country, he referred with confidence to the term of his presidency in the Senate of the United States, during which he was compelled to endure in silence a course of proceedings which he believed to be in open violation of the spirit and letter of the Constitution. Let others apply the same test to the services of Mason, who, for a longer term than four years not only beheld those unconstitutional acts in question, but grappled with their supporters, and who, though voted down at the time by a "steady, inflexible, and undeviating" majority,[240] made the victories of his enemies distasteful to them at first, and ultimately disastrous, and his measure of fame will be full.

We are now to regard Mason as the leader in the Senate of

---

[240] Mason's own words.

the great party of which Mr. Jefferson was the chief; and I only regret that my materials as well as my limits will enable me to do him but small justice. His first grand effort was on the repeal of the judiciary act of 1800. On the 8th of January, 1802, the Senate proceeded to consider the resolution offered by Breckenridge (of Kentucky) on the 6th, in the following words: "That the act of Congress passed on the 13th day of February, 1801, entitled an act to provide for the more convenient organization of the courts of the United States, ought to be repealed." That gentleman opened the debate on his resolution with a speech of uncommon power and massive strength, in which he sought to demonstrate the utter inexpediency of such a bill as the one in review, by referring to the decreasing number of suits in the Federal court, and from the certainty of a further decrease; and he sustained the constitutional power of Congress to repeal the act in question. He was followed by Jonathan Mason, of Massachusetts, in reply; and when J. Mason resumed his seat, Governor Morris rose and with consummate tact endeavored to break the force of Breckenridge's speech. When Morris ended, the Senate adjourned. On the 12th the discussion was renewed by a frank and argumentative speech from General Jackson, of Georgia, in favor of the resolution, who, with Tracy, occupied the floor for that day. On the 13th the discussion was continued by Stevens Thomson Mason, who made one of the most brilliant displays of his parliamentary career. He was present when the act passed the Senate and was familiar with all its details; and he not only upheld the inexpediency of its passage at the time, and the right and duty of Congress to repeal it, but brought the charge of unconstitutionality, if such a charge was just, home upon the authors of the act which abolished a court, set the judges adrift, then took them up and placed them in another court, much to their inconvenience and discomfort.

After dwelling for some time on this view of the subject, we can imagine the effect, the tone, and the gesture with which he rebuked his opponents as he uttered these words:

"Where, then, were these guardians of the Constitution, these vigilant sentinels of our rights and liberties, when this law passed? Were they asleep on their post? Where was the gentleman from New York (Morris), who has on this debate made such a noble stand in favor of a violated Constitution? Where was the

Ajax Telamon of his party—or, to use his own more correct expression, of the *faction* to which he belonged? Where was the hero with his seven-fold shield—not of bull's hide, but of brass—prepared to prevent or punish this Trojan rape which he now sees meditated upon the Constitution of his country by a wicked *faction?* Where was Hercules, that he did not crush this band of robbers that broke into the sanctuary of the Constitution? Was he forgetful of his duty? Were his nerves unstrung? *Or, was he the very leader of the band that broke down these constitutional ramparts?"*

After tracing in detail the history of the passage of the bill through the Senate, he continued:

"Various amendments were offered, some of which were admitted to be proper. But they were not received. One, indeed, proposed by a member from Connecticut, who was chairman of the committee, and was then hostile to the plan, did pass in the early stages of the bill; but on the third reading it was expunged. All amendments proposed by the minority were uniformly rejected by a steady, inflexible, and undeviating majority. I confess that I saw no passion, but I certainly did see great pertinacity; something like what the gentleman from Connecticut had termed *a holding fast.* No amendments were admitted; when offered, we were told no. You may get them introduced by a rider or supplementary bill, or in any way you please, but down this bill must go; it must be crammed down your throats. This was not the precise phrase, but such was the amount of what was said. I will say that not an argument was urged in favor of the bill—not a word to show the necessity or propriety of the change. Yet we are told that there was great dignity, great solemnity in its progress and passage!

"But there is something undignified in thus hastily repealing this law—in thus yielding ourselves to the fluctuations of public opinion! So we are told. But if there be blame, on whom does it fall? Not on us who respected the public opinion when this law was passed, and who still respect it; but on those who, in defiance of public opinion, passed this law after that public opinion had been decisively expressed. The revolution in public opinion had taken place before the introduction of this project; the people of the United States had determined to commit these affairs to new agents; already had the confidence of the people been transferred from their then rulers into other hands. After this exposition of the national will, and this new deposit of the national confidence, the gentlemen should have left untouched this important and delicate subject—a subject on which the people could not be reconciled to their views, even in the flood-tide of their power and influence; they should have forborne until agents, better acquainted with the national will, because more recently constituted its organs, had come into the government. This would have been more dignified than to seize the critical moment when power was passing from them to pass such a law as this. If there is error, it is our duty to correct it; and the truth was that no law was ever more execrated by the public. Let it not be said, postpone the repeal till the next session. No; let us restore these gentlemen to private life who have accepted appointments under this law. This will be doing them greater justice than by keeping them in office another year, till the professional business which once attached to them is gone into other channels.'' [241]

This speech, the technical part of which we have omitted, produced a sensible effect on the body and on the public, and called forth a deliberate reply from Morris, which exhibited great ingenuity and afforded at its close a fine specimen of declamation; but he was unable to turn the edge of a single fact or argument urged by Mason, and the speaker seemed more inclined to defend the reputation of the Federal party in relation to the act than the act itself. The question was taken on the 3d, and the bill founded on the resolution passed by a vote of sixteen to fifteen. [242]

---

[241] The best report of Mason's speech will be found in the small volume printed in Philadelphia by Bronson in 1802. But all the reports are synoptical, and convey but a feint impression of his logical vigor and of the fire of his eloquence. All pass over with a mere allusion that admirable part of his speech in which he portrayed the action of Virginia on a similar occasion.

[242] As the ayes and noes will show who Mason's colleagues were in this great debate, I annex them :

AYES—Anderson, Baldwin, Bradley, Breckenridge, Brown, Cocke, Ellery, T. Foster, Franklin, Jackson, Logan, S. T. Mason, Nicholas, Stone, Sumter, and Wright.

NOES—Chipman, Calhoun, Dayton, D. Foster, Hillhouse, Howard,

On the real worth of the judiciary act of 1801 it is a delicate subject to pass an opinion. Great confidence ought unquestionably to be placed in the judgment of the statesmen who repealed it and in the public opinion which sustained the repeal. With our present knowledge of the extent of our country and its unparalleled development in population and resources, the small number of the district judges and their meagre salaries seem almost insignificant. The act increased the number of judges to sixteen, and the cost of maintaining the system slightly exceeded thirty thousand dollars; and the propriety and even necessity of establishing Federal courts for the convenience of the people in the various sections of a thinly settled country should seem to be apparent. Even Mason stated of his own knowledge that his friend, Judge Innes, one of the old judges promoted to be one of the new, would be compelled to travel hundreds of miles through a region beset by Indians in the performance of his duties. And Mason knew the country, for he had lately travelled through it, had lost his baggage, which was stolen by the Indians, and had narrowly escaped a fight with the savages. When, too, we consider that direct taxes were then an important part of the Federal revenue, and that land titles might require to be settled in Federal courts, the expediency of an extended judiciary would appear to be obvious. The hostility which caused a repeal of the act was evidently founded as much on the circumstances of its progress and passage as of its expediency. One good result may have flowed from the repeal. No political party has since attempted to perpetuate itself or to provide for its supporters by wholesale legislation on judicial subjects.[243]

J. Mason, Morris, Ogden, Olcott, Ross, Sheafe, Tracy, Wells, and White.

Of these able men I knew personally but one—the venerable Hillhouse—whose fame is almost lost in that of his son, the great dramatic poet of his country, whom I also knew, and who has passed away.

[243] The judges appointed under the act were Richard Bassett, Egbert Benson, Benjamin Bourne, William Griffith, Samuel Hitchcock, B. P. Key, C. Magill, Jeremiah Smith, George Keith Taylor, William Tilghman, and Oliver Wolcott. On the 27th of January, 1803, they presented to the Senate a memorial, in which they state that the law of 1801, under which they were appointed, had been repealed; that no new law

While the bill to purchase a place of deposit near the mouth of the Mississippi was before the Senate, a series of resolutions on the same subject was introduced by Ross (of Pennsylvania). The mover was an opponent of the administration; and the obvious effect, if not the true design, of his resolutions was to embarrass the Executive in its action in pursuance of the bill which had received the sanction of the Senate. They set forth that the United States have an indisputable right to the navigation of the Mississippi and to a place of deposit on its banks; that the late infraction of their right[244] is hostile to their interest and their honor; that it did not consist with the dignity and safety of the Union to hold so important a right by so frail a tenure; that it concerned the people of the West and the dignity and safety of the Union; that the United States obtain complete security for the full and peaceable enjoyment of their absolute right; that the President be authorized to take immediate possession of such places on the said island of Orleans or elsewhere as he may deem proper, and to adopt such other means of attaining the object as he might think expedient; that he be authorized to employ fifty thousand militia to be drafted from certain contiguous States, together with the whole military and naval forces of the United States, for effecting the objects above mentioned, and that the sum of five millions of dollars be appropriated for the purpose. This was a most ingenious scheme for

---

has since passed assigning to them judicial functions; that they are judges of the United States, and entitled to their salaries during good behavior; and that they desire a review of the existing laws that their duties may be properly defined. The paper is marked by self-possession and dignity. It was referred to a committee, of which Governor Morris was chairman, and which reported a resolution requesting the President of the United States to cause an information, in the nature of a *quo warranto*, to be filed by the Attorney-General against Richard Bassett, one of the petitioners, for the purpose of deciding judicially on their claims. The resolution was discussed fully, and was rejected by a vote of thirteen to fifteen. If the judges possessed the talents and the worth of George Keith Taylor, they would have been, and doubtless were, worthy of their stations. My love for the memory of Taylor leads me to wish that I could make a more pleasant mention of him.

[244]Spain had ceded Louisiana to France without any allusion or acknowledgment of our right to a place of deposit, &c.

defeating the policy of the administration. The resolutions plainly pointed to an immediate war with Spain and France; and while they would receive the unanimous support of the Federal party, they were calculated to excite the warmest sympathies of the Western and Southern States, on which the Government mainly depended for parliamentary support. The speech of Ross on moving them was highly imprudent and inflammatory; and his speech was echoed by Governor Morris in a still more warlike tone. Breckenridge made a strong speech against the resolutions, and concluded by offering a substitute which left substantially any act of reprisals and the calling out of the militia at the discretion of the Executive, and which appropriated funds for the purpose. DeWitt Clinton then rose and made, perhaps, what was his maiden speech in the body, in which he admitted the importance of the right of deposit and the free navigation of the Mississippi; but demonstrated that the resolutions offered by Mr. Ross involved an immediate declaration of war, and the inexpediency of such a measure at that time. General James Jackson followed in a bold and sensible speech, in which he showed that the honor of the country, on which his opponents had laid such a stress, was the true interests of the country; and narrated with admirable effect the anecdote of Count D'Estaing, who, having been wounded at the attempted storm of Savannah, was visited in his chamber by Governor Rutledge and others, who told the Count that his own honor and the honor of France were concerned in his remaining and taking the city; when the Count mildly replied: "Gentlemen, if my honor is to be lost by not taking the city, it is lost already; but I deem my honor to consist in the honor of my country, and that honor is my country's interest." Jackson was followed by Wells (of Delaware), who, in a speech in which sophistry was ingeniously mingled with sound argument and passionate declamation, was fierce for war. Anderson followed in reply to Wells, and when he closed Mason rose to speak. The subject of the Mississippi he was well qualified to discuss. He had spoken upon it more than once in the Assembly and in Congress, and he always regarded it, and now more than ever, as Virginia had no longer a direct interest in its decision, not as a local or party question, but on principles of the broadest statesmanship. But, unfortunately, he was indisposed, and stated in the outset that his physical condition would not suffer him to go as much at length into the discussion as he otherwise would have done. After a short preamble he said that he had heard in the debate many professions of confidence in the Executive. He was very glad to hear such unusual expressions of confidence from that quarter. However, it was entitled to its due weight—what that was he would not inquire; but this he would say, that this unexpected ebullition of confidence went very much farther than he should be disposed to carry his confidence in any man or President whatever. Gentlemen tell us that they are willing to entrust to the Executive the power of going to war or not at his discretion. Wonderful, indeed, is this sudden disposition to confidence! Why do not gentlemen give away that which they have some authority or right to bestow? Who gave them the power to vest in any other authority than in Congress the right of declaring war? The framers of this Constitution had too much experience to entrust such a power to any individual; they early and wisely foresaw that though there might be men too virtuous to abuse such a power, it ought not to be entrusted to any; and nugatory would be the authority of the Senate if we could assume the right of transferring our constitutional functions to any man or set of men. It was a stretch of confidence which he would not trust to any President that ever lived or ever will live. He could not as one, without treason to the Constitution, consent even to relinquish the right of declaring war to any man or men beside Congress.[245]

"We are told," he said, "that negotiation is not the course which is proper for us to pursue. But to this he should reply that such was the usage of all civilized nations; and however gentlemen might attempt to whittle away the strong ground taken by his friend from New York (Clinton), he had shown,

---

[245] This argument was not answered in the debate, but it is not sound. The assent of Congress to a measure which it was obvious would lead to war, and which was to be carried into effect by arms, and the equipping of the President with men and money for the purpose, is in itself a declaration of war. If there was a precise formula on the subject of a declaration of war, Mason's argument would be good; but there are as many ways of declaring war as there are for prosecuting the war when it is begun. The President was instructed to do a certain thing, peaceably if he could, but to do it at all events.

in a manner not to be shaken, that negotiation, before a resort to the last scourge of nations, is the course most consistent with good policy as well as with universal practice. The gentleman from Pennsylvania had indeed told us that Great Britain had departed from that practice; unfortunately for Great Britain and the gentleman's argument, he told us at the same time that she had sustained a most serious injury by her injustice and precipitation. She went to war to seek restitution, and after fighting a while she left off, and forgot to ask the restitution for which she went to war. And this is the example held up for our imitation! Because Great Britain violated the laws of nations, we are called upon to do so too!

"We are also told that Great Britain commenced war during our Revolution against the Dutch without any previous notification; that she did the same in the late war with France, and in both cases seized on their ships in her harbors—that is, like a professional bully, she struck first, and then told them that she would fight them. And this is the gracious example held up to us.

"The merits of the different propositions consisted in this, that by the amendments we propose to seek the recourse of pacific nations—to follow up our own uniform practice; we pursue, in fact, the ordinary and rational course. The first resolutions go at once to the point of war. This was openly and fairly acknowledged by the gentleman from New York (Morris). The gentleman from Pennsylvania told us, indeed, that it is not war; it was only going and taking peaceable possession of New Orleans. He did not before think that the gentleman felt so little respect for the Senate, or estimated their understandings so much inferior to his own, as to call such measures an act of peace. How did the gentleman mean to go, and how take peaceable possession? Would he march at the head of the *posse comitatus?* No; he would march at the head of fifty thousand militia, and he would send forth the whole naval and regular force, armed and provided with military stores. He would enter their island, set fire to their warehouses, and bombard their city, desolate their farms and plantations, and, having swept all their habitations away, after wading through streams of blood, he would tell those who escaped destruction: We do not come here to make war upon you; we are a very moderate,

tender-hearted kind of neighbors, and are come here barely to
take peaceable possession of your territory! Why, sir, this is
too naked not to be an insult to the understanding of a child.

"But the gentleman from New York (Morris) did not trifle
with the Senate in such a style: he threw off the mask at once,
and in a downright, manly way fairly told us that he liked war;
that it was his favorite mode of negotiating between nations;
that war gave dignity to the species; that it drew forth the most
noble energies of humanity. That gentleman scorned to tell us
that he wished to take peaceable possession. No. He could not
snivel; his vast genius spurned huckstering; his mighty soul
would not bear to be locked up in a petty warehouse at New
Orleans; he was for war—terrible, glorious havoc! He tells you
plainly that you are not only to recover your rights, but you
must remove your neighbors' from their possessions, and repel
those to whom they may transfer the soil; that Bonaparte's
ambition is insatiable; that he will throw in colonies of French-
men, who will settle on your frontier for thousands of miles round
about (when he comes there); and he does not forget to tell you
of the imminent dangers which threaten our good old friends,
the English. He tells you that New Orleans is the lock, and
you must seize the key and shut the door against this terrible
Bonaparte, or he will come with his legions, and, as Gulliver
served the Lilliputians, wash you off the map. Not content—in
his great care for your honor and glory—as a statesman and a
warrior, he turns prophet to oblige you (your safety in the present year, or the next, does not satisfy him); his vast mind,
untrammelled by the ordinary progressions of chronology, looks
over ages to come with a faculty bordering on omniscience, and
conjures us to come forward and regulate the decrees of Providence at ten thousand years' distance.

"We have been told that Spain had no right to cede Louisiana to France; that she had ceded to us the privilege of deposit,
and had therefore no right to cede her territory without our consent. Are gentlemen disposed to wage war in support of this
principle? Because she has given us a little privilege—a mere
indulgence on her territory—is she thereby constrained from
doing anything forever with her immense possessions? No
doubt, if the gentleman (Morris) were to be the negotiator on
this occasion, he would say: You mean to cede New Orleans?

No, gentlemen; I beg your pardon, you cannot cede that, for we want it ourselves; and as to the Floridas, it would be very indiscreet to cede them, as, in all human probability, we shall want them also in less than five hundred years from this day; and then, as to Louisiana, you surely could not think of that, for in something less than a thousand years, in the natural order of things, our population will advance to that place also.[246]

"If Spain has ceded those countries to France, the cession has been made with all the encumbrances and obligations to which it was subject by previous compact with us. Whether Bonaparte will execute these obligations with good faith, he could not say; but to say that Spain had no right to cede is a bold assertion indeed. The people of America will not go along with such doctrines, for they lead to ruin alone. We are also told that the power of the Chief Consul is so great that he puts up and pulls down all the nations of the Old World at discretion, and that he can do so with us. Yet we are told by the wonderful statesman who gives us this awful information that we must go to war with this maker and destroyer of governments. If, after the unceasing pursuit of empire and conquest—which is thus presented to us—we take possession of his territory, from the gentleman's own declarations, what are we to expect? Only that this wonderful man, who never abandons an object—who thinks his own and his nation's honor pledged to go through with whatever he undertakes—will next attack us? Does the gentleman think that this terrible picture—which his warm imagination has drawn—is a conclusive argument for proceeding to that war which he recommends?

"The Senate, Mr. President, at this moment presents a very extraordinary aspect; and, by those not acquainted with our political affairs, it would appear a political phenomenon. Here we see a number of people from the Eastern States and the seaboard filled with extreme solicitude for the interest and rights of

---

[246] If Mason had survived twenty years he would have seen, not only the Floridas, but all Louisiana, belonging to the United States ; but his argument is honorable to him as showing that he thought the Ten Commandments were still binding, and that nations no more than individuals should covet their neighbors' possessions. Had he survived six months he would have read and ratified the treaty of Paris, which ceded to the United States the territory of Louisiana.

the Western and inland States; while the representatives of the Western people themselves appear to know nothing of this great danger, and to feel a full confidence in their government—the former declaring that the Western people are all ready for revolt and open to seduction; the latter ignorant of any such dispo· sition, and indignant at the disgrace which is thrown on their character.   In their great loving kindness for the Western people, these new friends of theirs tell them that they are a simple people, who do not know what is good for them, and that they will kindly undertake to do this for them.   From the contiguous States of South Carolina, Georgia, Tennessee, and Kentucky (those States from which the gentleman from Pennsylvania proposes to draw the militia), every member of this House is opposed to war; but from the East (and one can scarcely refrain from laughing to hear the all-important representatives of the State of Delaware, in particular), such is the passion for the wonderful or the absurd, there prevails the liveliest sensibility for the Western country.''

The question was put on striking out the resolutions of Ross, and decided in the affirmative by a vote of fifteen to eleven; and the substitute of Breckenridge was then adopted by a unanimous vote—ascertained by ayes and noes.

The course of the Federal party on this occasion deserves severe censure.   To force the nation into a war with France and Spain without a resort to negotiation was as unwise and impolitic as it was suicidal to those who proposed so rash an expedient. It was unwise, as the object in view might be accomplished—as it afterwards was—by the ordinary means of settling difficulties among nations; it was impolitic, as it committed the Federal party to the most violent measures which the Administration might be induced to adopt, and would thereby deprive that party of a legitimate ground of attack at the future stages of the proceedings; and it was suicidal, as the boisterous vehemence of their orators would be used argumentatively abroad in aid of those negotiations which it was their wish to embarrass, and as they had placed themselves, by their harangues, in the wrong before the country, and particularly before the very people whose rights and interests they assumed to defend against their own representatives, and whose influence they sought to win.   It is a subject of congratulation that Mason and Nicholas—the senators from Virginia in Congress—took the ground in this debate which posterity, with one accord, pronounces to be just, honorable, and wise.

And when the States which rest or depend on the Mississippi shall begin to rear statues in commemoration of the past, they will be sadly unmindful of truth and history if the marble image of Virginia, who among the earliest, through good and evil report, upheld the right of navigating their noble stream, and whose great son finally confirmed that right gloriously and forever, is not the first to adorn their halls.

Mason made this speech under bodily suffering; and, roughly reported as it is, it serves to show the vigor, the sprightliness, and the freedom which marked his style of debate. It compares favorably with the speeches of the most eloquent British speakers of the era ending with the American Revolution, as those speeches are reported in the public debates, and it has much of their freshness and savor. It was essentially the speech of a debater, who seizes at once upon the salient points of his adversary's arguments, and turns them against their authors. Like most of our great statesmen who flourished, or who begun their career during the last century, Mason never wrote or wrote out a speech before or after delivery; but, in the remains of his speeches that are left us, it is apparent that he spoke well and readily, holding back nothing, fearing nothing; and, if not weaving for himself a living crown of oratory with posterity, yet accomplishing all that could be accomplished by eloquence in his then day and generation.

It was on the 25th of February that Mason made his speech just quoted, and in less than three months later he was laid in his grave. He had probably inherited from his paternal ancestry a gouty diathesis, which developed itself in a dropsy, for the relief of which he sought the city of Philadelphia, where he died on the 10th of May. Thus, in his forty-third year, in the prime and pride of his intellectual powers, passed away a statesman whose memory ought to be cherished with fond affection by his country at large, and by Virginia in particular. He belonged to a class of statesmen who were born at the early stages of the troubles with the mother country, who have all passed away, and who can never appear again. They were old enough to have engaged in the latter part of the war of the Revolution, to have

served in the Assembly in the interval between the close of the
war and the adoption of the Federal Constitution, to have
fought the great battle in the public councils and on the rostrum
to which that Constitution led, to have watched its operation
with the strictest scrutiny, and in due time to bear a conspicuous
part in the practical administration of the Federal Government.
Mason's political beau-ideal was Virginia as a free, independent,
and intelligent Commonwealth, committing, for the sake of convenience, her foreign affairs to her Federal agents, but retaining
unimpaired all the rights and privileges of an integral empire.
It was in this spirit he refused to accept the amendments to the
Federal Constitution proposed by Congress, because, though
some of them were better than nothing, yet they were not those
that Virginia had proposed, and which she had a right to demand
and to receive.   Not having been abroad in the Federal councils anterior to the adoption of the Constitution, his affections
were entire, and he had not been broken to the tune of a strong
central government, which fascinated the ears of some of his
compatriots and which insensibly led them to regard without
much aversion the trenching of the new government upon the
rights of the individual States.   Hence, on all interesting Federal
questions, though courteous and respectful of the opinions of
others, he leaned towards the States, and opposed some of the
prominent measures of the Washington and Adams administrations.   He bore along with him throughout his career the
almost unanimous approbation of the Assembly and of the people, who delighted to express their confidence in his abilities, in
his integrity, and in his patriotism by the usual marks of public
favor.   In his thirty-fourth year he had been elected to the
Senate of the United States, in which he remained till the hour
of his death, his finest effort on the floor of that House being
his last; participating in all interesting discussions of foreign or
domestic topics with an effect that was acknowledged by a hostile and exulting majority; and, latterly, swaying at will the
decisions of his own party under the fire of a strong opposition,
led by a wily, unscrupulous, but uncommonly able statesman.
His last scene on the floor of the Senate was a great triumph.
It required unusual prudence on his part to prevent the flame
kindled by the Federal party in favor of the supposed rights of
the Western States from spreading among the representatives of

the West, and the loss of a single vote might have settled the
question; while he grappled directly and openly with Morris,
whose abilities as an orator were formidable, whose knowledge of
foreign affairs was exact and comprehensive, and whose hatred
of the administration of Jefferson impelled him to seek its overthrow by plunging the country, without necessity and in violation of the usages of nations, into a war with the greatest military power then or now existing.   Mason succeeded.   The
policy of his opponents was prostrated; his own favorite scheme
was adopted even by his enemies; and, when he passed the
doors of the Senate for the last time, the whole country was
applauding his eloquent harangue, little dreaming that it was his
last.[247]

In stature Mason was below six feet.   He was very stout,
and is said to have attained his full growth at a very early age.
His countenance, as presented in his portrait, was open and
manly; his hair was dark, his eyes were large and of a deep
gray color; his nose and chin regular and good.   His mouth
was very large and the lips compressed—a characteristic trait of
the Masons, it is said.   His forehead was very broad, open, and
intellectual.   He was neat in his apparel; and, as he wore silk
stockings, he might have taken in a somewhat personal sense
the reflection of the Northern man on the silk-stocking gentry.
His hair was well dressed, with the usual queue closely bound
with a black ribbon.   His appearance on canvas is highly
imposing, and is not unbecoming his general reputation.[248]

One trait of Mason, which, if not the secret of his great popularity, contributed to its diffusion and to its intensity, was his

---

[247] Mr. William Brent said that Mason was distinguished for his eloquence and wonderful powers of sarcasm.   He once heard him in
Philadelphia reply to a Northern man who uncourteously alluded to
the Southern members as "the silk-stocking gentry"; and he said he
should never forget the effect of his oratory and the force of his sarcasm.
It was terrific.   Had Mason lived six months longer he would have
read the treaty of Paris, which ceded to the United States the whole
of Louisiana.

[248] There is a portrait of General S. T. Mason in the possession of his
granddaughter, Mrs. Emily Mason; and there is one of his father, T.
Mason, in the possession of Judge John T. Mason, of Baltimore.   The
portrait of Thomson Mason presents a countenance remarkably benign,
regular features, and compressed lips.

fearless and cordial support of his political friends, especially when they were in trouble. He sat by the side of Judge Cooper when that extraordinary man was prosecuted under the sedition law during the whole of his trial; and when that sentence of fine and imprisonment was pronounced against him, Mason instantly rose in open court and congratulated his friend. Fenno, the Federal editor, animadverted with stern severity upon the conduct of Mason, whom he charged with committing an outrage *on the face of Justice;* but Duane, of the *Aurora,* came to the rescue, and twitted Fenno for mistaking the *bacon face* of the presiding judge for the face of Justice.[249]

The following account of the funeral of Stevens Thomson Mason, Esq., is taken from the Philadelphia *Aurora* of Saturday, May 14, 1803, and has reached me through the kindness of the Hon. William J. Duane—the son of the editor—who was present at the burial as the adjutant of the Militia Legion, under General Shee:

"On Tuesday evening last the remains of the late General Stevens Thomson Mason, of Virginia, were interred in the burying-ground of the Protestant Episcopal church, in Arch street, between Fourth and Fifth streets, and deposited near those of the late Henry Tazewell, Esq., a senator of the same State, and in his lifetime a colleague of General Mason. At 5 o'clock P. M. the procession moved from the house of Mr. James O'Ellers, corner of Fourth and Spruce streets, in the following order:

"1. The Militia Legion, commanded by General Shee, with reversed arms, in advance of the whole.

"2. The clergy of the city, of every denomination.

"3. The corpse, borne by watchmen and supported by six pall bearers; magistrates and officers under the Federal and State governments.

"4. The chief mourners, immediately following the hearse.

"5. Private friends of the General as mourners, with the attending physicians.

"6. The Governor of Pennsylvania, the Minister of Spain, and other diplomatic characters now in the city.

"7. Officers of the General Government.

---

[249] On the authority of Mr. Dickerson, of New Jersey, who sat on the other side of Cooper during the trial.

" 8. Officers of the State Government.

" 9. Corporate councils of the city.

" 10. The members of the Board of Health.

" 11. Officers of militia, in uniform.

" 12. Private citizens.

"Every degree of respectful attention was paid by the concourse of citizens who attended and followed the procession during the movement to the place of interment and the performance of the burial service by Bishop White; and there has been seldom witnessed in this city a more solemn and affecting scene, evincing a general testimonial of respect for the exalted virtues, public and private, which so conspicuously marked the character of the deceased.''

I sincerely trust that the relatives of General Mason will cause a plain slab to be placed over his remains.[250]

---

[250] As to the personal appearance of Stevens Thomson Mason, Mr. Temple Mason did not think him handsome, but his granddaughter, Mrs. Mason, thought that he was ; "that he had the bulk, with the spirit of a king," and that he had "a princely crest." Both agree that he was very large. His uncle, Colonel John Barnes, of Maryland, saw none of the poetry of person or of bearing that struck the female eye, but described his nephew as "being blown up like a bladder."

ARMISTEAD THOMSON MASON.

Mason left a widow, three sons, and three daughters. The maiden name of his widow was Mary Armistead, daughter of Robert Armistead, of Louisa county. She survived him twenty years.[251] His eldest son was Armistead Thomson Mason, who was born in 1786, was educated at William and Mary College, served with credit in the second war with Great Britain, and was elected a senator of the United States by the General Assembly of Virginia in 1815. In 1817 he resigned his seat in the Senate to become a candidate for the House of Representatives, in opposition to Charles Fenton Mercer, and was defeated. Out of this contest sprang the difference which brought on his duel with his cousin, Colonel John Mason McCarty, in which he fell at Bladensburg on the 6th day of February, 1819, at the age of thirty-three. His death Virginia bemoaned with no passing grief. In his character he united in a singular degree the qualities of an orator, a soldier, and a statesman; and he was the idol of the Democratic party, to which he belonged. All the honors which Virginia could bestow he had either received, or they awaited him. He was a major general, had been a senator of the United States, was a member of the Board of Public Works, and would have been the next Governor had he survived. His death was lamented by the press throughout the Union. The Leesburg *Genius of Liberty* echoed the general voice when it said: "All who knew him mourn his fate and lament his loss. As a citizen, neighbor, and friend he stood unrivalled. As a warrior he was firm and undaunted, deliberate and humane. As a statesman he was deep, clear, and penetrating. In short, he bade fair to become one of our brightest ornaments, both as a private citizen and public officer." The same journal adds: "In the fall of General Mason Virginia has lost one of her most esteemed sons.

---

[251] She died on the estate of her husband, near Leesburg, on the 12th of February, 1824; aged eighty-four years. Her obituary may be seen in the *National Intelligencer* of that date, in which she is described as a very remarkable woman.

Although he had numbered but thirty-and-three years, he had risen high in popular favor. On the military list he had been promoted to the office of major-general, and the highest civil appointment, that of a senator of the United States, had been conferred upon him." It describes his burial as follows: " On the day of his funeral the most heartrending scenes were witnessed. His numerous and faithful blacks crowded around his grave, dissolved in tears and frantic with despair. The tender sensibilities of those tawny sons and daughters of Africa would have done honor to whiter complexions. To see an aged nurse, whose head was blossoming for the grave, approaching the corpse through the crowd, crying 'Oh, my master, my master!' must have awakened sympathetic feelings in the most adamantine heart. We have seldom witnessed in this town on any occasion so numerous a concourse of the people as were present at the funeral obsequies of this excellent man. Distinguished by his energy, his firmness, and activity, General Mason enjoyed that confidence and favor of his native State, which he appeared to inherit from his ancestors."

He fell on the 6th of February, and on the 9th of the same month both houses of the General Assembly passed resolutions, in which they say "that they esteem the death of General Mason a public loss, and entertain the deepest sympathy on that untimely event."

Just before Mason took the field he wrote to his uncle—Judge John Thomson Mason, of Hagerstown, Md.—the following letter, the original of which is before me:

"MY DEAR UNCLE,—I have just time to recommend my unhappy and helpless family to your paternal care. You have been a father to me; I know you will be one to them.

"I am your most sincerely affectionate nephew,

"ARMISTEAD T. MASON.

"*City of Washington*, 5th February, 1819."

One incident connected with the descendants of General Mason and his opponent—Colonel McCarty [252]—would seem to

---

[252] A full account of the duel between General A. T. Mason and Colonel McCarty may be seen in the January or February No. of *Harper's Magazine* for 1858. [See, also, *Sabine's Notes on Duelling* and *Truman's Field of Honor.*—EDITOR.]

protract a painful catastrophe to a second generation. Each of them had an only son—a pair of promising and noble young men. The son of Colonel McCarty was on a hunting excursion, and for the first time in his life, impelled by the pursuit of game, crossed over on General Mason's land. In alighting from the fence his gun was accidently discharged and killed him instantly. When the war with Mexico broke out young Stevens Thomson Mason, the son of the General, entered the service, and at Cerro Gordo, while commanding a company of mounted rifles, fell mortally wounded. Thus have these two families become extinct in the male line.

General Mason was about five feet eleven inches in height, rather stout in stature, of florid complexion, light eyes, free and easy in his manners, and was usually generous, mild, and amiable in his intercourse with every one. He was quick and impetuous in temper—as ready to forgive as to resent an injury. He is buried in the Episcopal grave-yard at Leesburg, where his only son reposes by his side. Each grave is marked by a slab.

JOHN THOMSON MASON.[253]

Besides Armistead, who so richly inherited the virtues of his father, General S. T. Mason left two other sons—John Thomson and Thomson.[254] The last-named died young. John Thomson settled in Kentucky, and became a public man. He was Secretary of the Territory of Michigan, and a commissioner to adjust claims with the Indians. He left an only son, Stevens Thomson Mason, who was born at Leesburg on the 27th of October, 1811, was educated at Transylvania University, at an early age removed to Michigan (then a Territory), and was elected, when the Territory became a State, the first Governor, and re-elected in 1837. He had served two gubernatorial terms before he was twenty-eight years of age. He married an accomplished lady of the city of New York, and removed thither in 1840, where he was very successful at the bar; but after an illness of four days he died on the 4th of June, 1843, leaving an only son, who has since died. Thus has every male representative of General Stevens Thomson Mason passed away.[255]

---

[253] Thomson Mason wrote on a blank leaf in *Burrows's Reports* "that he had often heard it said that a child at two and a half years old was just half as tall as he ever would be. My son, John Thomson Mason, is this day just two and a half years old, and is two feet ten inches and a half high; and I can thus ascertain the truth of the remark." John became about five feet nine, or thereabouts.

[254] General S. T. Mason also left three daughters, the eldest of whom married George Howard, territorial Governor of Missouri, but at the time of his marriage member of Congress from Kentucky; the second married Colonel William T. Barry, afterwards Postmaster-General and Minister to Spain; and the youngest married her cousin, William McCarty, subsequently the representative of the Loudoun district in Congress, and who is still living (August, 1859).

[255] Thomson Mason, the father of General S. T. Mason, had two other sons—John Thomson and Temple. The last-named is still living in Washington (August, 1859), in his eighty-fifth year, and has reached a greater age than any of those who have borne the name. John Thomson was born in Stafford county in 1764, and was educated at William

ALEXANDER WHITE—SUPPLEMENTAL.[256]

In the review which I have made of the sessions of the Assembly the name of Alexander White has been used as a thread of connection through the whole; but, as so many members of the Convention were also members of the Assembly, and as the votes and opinions of public men on the great questions of their times, which were discussed and settled by them in the public councils, are their most faithful biography, I have presented at the same time the votes of his colleagues in the interval in question. In the course of the session just concluded White was conspicuous in all its proceedings. He was not present—as was

and Mary. In early life he removed to Maryland, and settled at Hagerstown, where he intended to practice law, but for three years he did not obtain a single client. This was thought at the time an unlucky omen, but it turned out to his advantage, for he made himself a good lawyer. He afterwards removed to Georgetown, where his practice is said to have included one or the other side of every case on the docket. There and in Maryland he maintained many a hard-fought battle with Chase, Pinkney, Martin, Key, Harper, Winder, and others, and acquitted himself handsomely. In the celebrated case of Hampton *vs.* Harper, said to be one of the hardest-fought legal battles in Maryland, he gained great *éclat*. The counsel on one side were Mason, Pinkney, and Johnson, and on the other Martin, Key, and Harper. On one occasion, when Pinkney had been written to for an opinion in a case in which Mason had furnished a carefully-prepared one, he returned the following answer: "If my opinion should concur with that of Mr. Mason, it could add no force to it; and it would be extremely hazardous for any one to venture an opinion in opposition to one from so profound a source." He was appointed Attorney-General of the United States by Mr. Jefferson, and afterwards by Mr. Madison, but declined the appointment on both occasions. He was chosen Chief Justice of Maryland; but, though he held the appointment a few weeks, did not take his seat on the bench, and resigned it.

[256] [The perplexity of the editor in arranging in just connection the manuscript of this volume may be imagined in the statement that the author used paper of different colors, and not only neglected to number his pages, but was not uniform in his use of the paper—writing

too often the case with members who lived at a distance from Richmond—at the beginning of the session, and could not be placed on the standing committees at the time of their organization; but he was assigned to the most important on his arrival, and was a member of various select committees, the drafting of whose reports generally fell upon him.   His votes may be found in the list of the ayes and noes already recorded.   It will there be seen that on the test question of striking out the report of the Committee of the Whole, which presented the anti-Federal programme for obtaining amendments to the Constitution, he voted in the affirmative; but on the motion to strike out the qualifications of members of Congress, in respect of freehold and residence, he voted with the majority, of which Henry was the chief.   On several calls of the ayes and noes he was not in his seat—as, indeed, was almost invariably the case with at least one-fourth of the House.

His term of service in the House of Delegates closed with the present session.   He was returned to the first House of Representatives of the United States from the Frederick district, and was the only member of the House from Virginia who was present in his seat on the 4th day of March, 1789—the first day of the session.   An oath must be drawn up to be taken by the members, in pursuance of the sixth article of the Constitution, and White was appointed chairman of a committee—of which Madison was a member—to report a proper form.   When Madison proposed (April 6th) to regulate duties according to the scheme presented in 1783 by the Congress, White, under the

---

sometimes on single leaves, sometimes on sheets, and at other times upon several sheets continuously, as held together in book form. Many sheets and half-quires of paper had been reversed in their arrangement by being folded in the opposite way.   The whole mass had become disarranged, and, to aggravate the torture of rearrangement, many sheets, from the dampening of the sizing, adhered together. This last evil was occasioned by the manuscript having been buried during the war of 1861-'65, to ensure its safety from destruction by the Federal army.   Portions of the manuscript had to be soaked apart. The sequence of all was as justly fixed as the apprehension of the editor enabled.   It may be inferred that Mr. Grigsby intended to revise and readjust his matter before committing it to press.   This is offered in explanation of the resumption of the consideration of the career of a character so lengthily treated before.—EDITOR.]

impression that an immediate vote was desired by the mover, urged delay for a more full consideration of the subject, and was told by Madison that he did not desire an immediate decision. On the following day he objected to the variety of articles subjected to specific duties, and upheld the policy of Madison in opposition to the scheme proposed by Fitzimons. He urged, with his colleague (Andrew Moore), the propriety of a duty on hemp, as that article could be cultivated to any extent in the South and West, and the lands of the Shenandoah and its consecutive streams could produce the article in abundance. He argued that a duty on hemp would do more to promote ship-building than a bounty on ships.

He was inclined to favor the laying a duty on salt; but as that article was consumed to such an extent by the poor he thought it good present policy to let it pass free; that, as it was used by all, all would feel the tax, and some might deem it oppressive; that some taxes were odious from opinion, and as government was founded upon opinion it should abstain from laying those taxes which were offensive to the people.

On the 18th he made a report from the Committee of Elections, which declared that every member was duly returned.

On the 15th of May he presented to the House an important resolve of the General Assembly of Virginia, offering to the acceptance of the Federal Government ten miles square of territory, or any lesser quantity, in any part of that State which Congress may choose, to be occupied and possessed by the United States as the seat of the Federal Government; which was read and ordered to lie on the table. That he was selected to present the resolution to the House is an honorable mark of the estimation in which he was held by his distinguished colleagues.

Although he voted to ratify the Federal Constitution, he was determined to confine its practical working to the strictest letter of its meaning. He saw that if discretion or policy was to be the rule of its interpretation, the restrictions and limitations which it contained were not worth the paper on which they were written. Hence, when the engrossed bill laying a duty on imports was reported to the House from the committee, a motion was made by Madison that a clause limiting the time of its continuance should be added at the end. The object of Madison was altogether practical; for he knew, from his acquaintance with commercial affairs, that if the merchant was not assured that there was stability in the tariff he would not send his ships on a distant voyage and subject their cargoes to a rate of duty which might be ruinous on their return. But White, who also saw the practical bearing of the proposition, took another view of the case. He argued that he had no jealousy of the Senate or of the Executive; but that, as the House alone had the power of originating money bills, we should be careful in parting with the power for any long period; that, as the Constitution declared that no appropriation should be for a longer term than two years, it virtually limited the duration of a revenue law to that period. The following day the amendment offered by Madison again came up, and the ayes and noes were called upon it. White, after expressing himself sarcastically on the policy of calling the ayes and noes in the stages of a bill,[257] went into a masterly argument against the amendment, which, near seventy years later, was applauded by an able parliamentarian and politician for its ability and wisdom. Madison, with his usual tact, substituted another amendment in the place of the one he had offered, and which was in substance that the act should not continue in force after a certain day, unless otherwise provided in the act for the appropriation of the revenue. This proposition, although it recognized the propriety of limitations, yet, if the duration of the act exceeded two years, did not entirely accord with the sound doctrine laid down by White; but, in a spirit of compromise, he voted for it, and it prevailed by a vote of forty-one to eight.[258]

The right of the President to remove public officers, whose tenure of office is not prescribed by the Constitution, was discussed at an early day, and the doctrine advanced by White in the first day's debate has been sanctioned by the uniform prac-

---

[257] But for the calling of the ayes and noes what would have become of the name of Alexander White? Posterity would hardly have known that he ever was a member of the Assembly, as the Journal of the House of Delegates contains no other record of the full names of its members, or any other obvious means of identifying them, than the ayes and noes.

[258] See the note of Colonel Benton on White's speech, in which are enumerated the difficulties that have arisen since the adoption of the Federal Constitution by a departure from the rule advocated by White.

tice of the Government to this time.   He said that the President
appointed the officers, and that he conceived that the party who
appointed ought to judge of the removal, always excepting those
cases specified in the Constitution.   At a later day, when the
bill establishing a department for foreign affairs was discussed,
he reiterated the sound doctrine that the appointing power had
the right of removal; but, confounding the advisory power of
the Senate in relation to the appointment, which is mainly for the
purpose of record and identification, with the power of appointing, he argued that the Senate ought to be associated with the
President in removing incumbents from office—a doctrine that
strikes at the very root of executive vigor and availability.
At a still later day he seconded the motion that impeachment
was the only mode of removing a public officer.   He said that
impeachments were to be employed in the case of officers who
held their employment for a term of years or during good
behavior.   He intimated that they might be used when the President insisted on retaining an officer who ought not to be retained.
The judges were to be removed by impeachment.   These, he
said, were the three cases in which impeachment was the remedy.
I am afraid that, if his views on the subject of removal had prevailed, he would have made a very considerable deduction from
the good which would have arisen had his opinions respecting
the limitation of public acts been acted upon.   To bring a tide-
waiter from Oregon or California across the Isthmus or by the
Cape to be impeached by the House and to be tried by the
Senate, with the train of witnesses, and to consume the public
time and money in the trial, would involve so much inconvenience
and expense that we would soon find it a better plan to send the
culprit a check for fifty thousand dollars, and beseech him to
make for parts unknown.   As he ultimately voted against a similar bill on constitutional grounds, I wish he had argued that as
the appointing power was vested by the Constitution in the
President, and with it the power of removal, the conferring upon
the President by act of Congress a right which he possessed
under the Constitution might lead to mistakes in our future
legislation and furnish a bad precedent.   Such was doubtless
the view of Madison; but, seeing the temper of the House, and
anxious for the passage of so important a bill as that estab-

lishing a State Department, he was willing to regard the clause conferring a power upon the President which he already possessed as mere surplusage, and voted for the bill.

He opposed a fixed salary for the Vice-President, contending that he should be paid according to the amount of public service rendered. Accordingly, he moved to strike out a clause in the bill concerning that officer, which fixed the salary at five thousand dollars; and said that if his motion prevailed he would move an amendment allowing that officer the pay of the President when he acted as President, and a daily pay during the time that he acts as President of the Senate. During the debate he said that the Vice-President had personal advantages from his position, which holds him up as the successor of the President. The voice of the people is shown to be considerably in his favor, and, if he be a deserving person, there will be but little doubt of his succeeding to the presidential chair.[259] His motion to strike out failed, and so did the motion of Page, who moved to strike out five thousand dollars with the view of inserting eight thousand dollars.[260]

He strenuously opposed the distinction between the pay[261] of the senators and that of the members of the House of Representatives, and was joined by his colleague, Andrew Moore (and opposed by Madison), on the ground that as the Constitution made no distinction on the score of services between one mem-

---

[259] The succession of the Vice-President to the chair of the President continued in the two instances of John Adams and Thomas Jefferson; then the State Department became within the line of safe precedents. Now that is eschewed, and, perhaps, at present the chances of selection are in favor of those who hold no office at all.

[260] It was on the motion of John Page that the President's salary was fixed at twenty-five thousand dollars. He had previously moved to fill the blank with thirty thousand dollars.

[261] In all the early debates about fixing the wages of a member of Congress no other mode than that of a *per diem* was hinted at. When many years later an annual salary was allotted to the members, the scheme was scouted by the people. Any other mode than that of a *per diem* is plainly against economy and the very nature of a Parliament. Yet the rate of an annual salary has recently been adopted. The remedy is to raise the *per diem*, but still cling to the *per diem* as the life and substance of a representative system.

ber of Congress and another, legislation should make none, and that the members of both houses ought to be paid in proportion to the service rendered by them.   Here he has been sustained by the public opinion of our own times.   He opposed the proposition of Vining for a home department, and argued with great plausibility against it.   In this opinion, however, though he was probably right in his day, he is not upheld at the present time, as the comparatively recent creation of the Department of the Interior clearly shows.

A question of intense interest at the first session of the Congress was the location of the seat of government.   The House of Representatives had, by a decisive majority, selected some place on the banks of the Susquehanna; but at the heel of the session the Senate sent back the bill with an amendment striking out the Susquehanna, and proposing " a district of ten miles square, bounded on the south by a line running parallel at one mile's distance from the city of Philadelphia on the east side of the river Delaware, and extending northerly and westerly so as to include Germantown."   The amendment kindled a blaze in the House.   The Southern members opposed it in a body.   Theodoric Bland thought that the bill was so materially changed by the amendment as to warrant the House in postponing its consideration, and he made a motion to that effect.   He said that he trusted the House would not be affected by the fact that the Senate had kept back the appropriation bill as a hostage for the passage of the bill before them.   Page seconded the motion to postpone.   White objected to the Senate's amendment, as virtually changing the tenor of the bill and as introducing a new subject; and, as the House would not allow the introduction of a new subject by one of its own members at this late hour, so the rule should apply to the new measure, though it proceeded from the Senate.   Madison, with exquisite skill, opposed the introduction of an entirely new place for the seat of government, on the ground that it had not been named before the people; that all the other places had been deliberately brought to the notice of the country; that two of them had been examined by the old Congress and had received a favorable decision, and that to adopt in a moment a rival place never before contemplated was risking an improper and a dissatisfactory decision.   The question on

Bland's motion was taken by ayes and noes, and was rejected by a vote of twenty-nine to twenty-five—all the Virginia members voting in the minority.[262]

At the beginning of the second session of Congress, in January, 1790, the members from Virginia were nearly all in their seats. One of the first questions discussed in the House was respecting the reporters. During the previous session these useful gentlemen, to whose labors history is more indebted than to the labors of the professed historians, were placed behind the Speaker's chair, whence they could see and hear to great advantage; but at the present session they had been removed to the gallery. Page brought the subject up informally before the House, spoke very handsomely in favor of the reporters, and thought that they ought to be restored to their old seats. White acknowledged the general fidelity of the reported debates and the readiness of the reporters in obtaining from the speakers their exact expressions in debate, and thought that it was well enough to admit them within the bar of the House; but he said that if the House went further it would seem to give an official encouragement to the reporters, and to hold the House in some degree responsible for their reports. No question was taken, but the cheerfulness with which the members approved of the publication of the debates is the more praiseworthy, as the old Congress always sat with closed doors, and as the Senate followed their example, and it was not long before that the publication of the debates in the House of Commons had ceased to be a breach of privilege. Even at this day, in the House of Lords, there are some restrictions on the right to publish without the consent of their House.[263]

---

[262] The Virginia members were Isaac Coles, James Madison, Theodoric Bland, Alexander White (who were members of the present Convention), John Page, Richard Bland Lee, Samuel Griffin, Josiah Parker, and John Brown. Bland died during the second recess of Congress, and was succeeded by William Branch Giles.

[263] Lord Campbell says that before he could venture to offer to the world his *Lives of the Lord Chancellors* he was legally estopped by a standing order of the House of Lords, of ancient date, which declared "that no one should presume to publish the lives of any lords, spiritual or temporal, deceased, without the permission of their heirs and execu-

The discrimination among the public creditors was another of the difficult problems of our early legislation. That a capitalist who had purchased from a poor soldier his certificate of one hundred dollars for five or ten should receive the original amount was monstrous; and the report of the Secretary of the Treasury recommended a modified discrimination. When that report came up in Committee of the Whole, Madison proposed a scale of modification, which was earnestly and ably supported by White. His speech on the occasion was probably the ablest he ever delivered in Congress, and displays a perfect knowledge of his subject, clear and conclusive argumentation, and no inconsiderable learning. Moore also supported the motion of Madison at great length, and with a seriousness in keeping with the magnitude and the delicacy of the subject. But the arguments of White, Moore, and Madison are too much in detail for our present purposes.[264]

The report of a committee on a Quaker memorial concerning slavery was discussed (March 17th) in the Committee of the Whole, when White moved to strike out the first proposition, because he was opposed to entering at that time into the consideration of the powers of Congress on the subject. He objected to other propositions contained in the report, which he proposed to offer in a different form.[265] He concluded by observing that his wish was to promote the happiness of mankind, and among the rest those who were the subjects of the present consideration; but this he wished to do in conformity to the principles of justice and with a due regard to the peace and happiness of others. He would contribute all in his power to the well-being and comfort of slaves; but he was fully of opinion that Congress had no right to interfere in the business any further than he proposed by his two propositions as modi-

---

tors"; and as he was about to publish the lives of Thomas á Becket, Michael de la Pole, and other early Chancellors, and, as he could hardly think of hunting up their heirs and executors, he was led to move a repeal of the order. This was within the last ten or twelve years. (*Lives of the Lord Chancellors*, Vol. V, 88.)

[264] Consult in the index of the first volume of *Benton's Debates* the names of White, Moore, Madison, &c.

[265] The *Debates* do not give the report, and I cannot state the exact nature of its recommendations.

fied. If Congress had the power to interfere, he did not think
the essential interests of the Southern States would suffer.
Twenty years ago he supposed the idea he now suggested would
have caused universal alarm. Virginia, however, about twelve
years since, prohibited the importation of negroes from Africa,
and the consequences apprehended were never realized. On the
contrary, the agriculture of that State was never in a more prosperous condition.[266]

In the course of a debate on the subject White expressed his
views of the policy of bounties on the occupations of individuals.
A bill had been reported entitled an act for the encouragement
of the bank and other cod fisheries, which allowed a bounty of
so many dollars on the tonnage of the vessels engaged in the
trade. Giles moved to strike out the first section of the bill, and
made a strong speech on the impolicy of granting bounties to
any particular class of persons. White, conscious of the necessity of building a commercial marine, had no objection to give
the trade a proper degree of encouragement; but he did not
relish the idea of granting bounties; but he said that if any gentleman would prepare an amendment, so as to make them draw-
backs in fact as well as in words, he would consent to the
measure.

He was in his seat at the opening of the session in November,
1792, and was called on to give a vote on a subject which has been
long since settled, but which was then not decided. A motion
was made to inform the Secretary of the Treasury and the Secretary of War that the House of Representatives would on the
following Wednesday take into consideration the report of a
committee appointed to inquire into the causes of the failure of
the late expedition under General St. Clair, to the end that they
may attend the House and furnish such information as may be

---

[266] This testimony of an able and honest friend of the Federal Constitution in favor of the prosperity of Virginia at the period of the ratification of that instrument is in strong contrast with the gloomy pictures
of decay and desolation which were held forth by his associates in the
Federal Convention of Virginia. White's attention had probably been
called recently to this subject, as he had been appointed a year or two
before one of a committee to inquire whether the number of slaves in
the State had increased or diminished since the passage of the act
prohibiting the importation of slaves.

conducive to the due investigation of matters stated in said report.   Williamson moved to strike out that part of the resolution requiring the presence of the Secretaries, and Venable followed in a short and decisive speech in support of the motion. White followed Venable, and took the ground that would be taken at the present day.   Madison and Giles followed on the same side, and the motion to strike out prevailed.[267]

He voted in the majority with Andrew Moore, against Madison, Giles, Venable, and Parker, in favor of preventing a reduction of the army at that time, which was one of the party questions of the day.   He voted against the bill to create the Department of Foreign Affairs, on the ground heretofore mentioned; his colleagues (Isaac Coles, Josiah Parker, and John Page) voting with him, and Madison, Moore, Lee, and Griffin against him.   He voted in common with the whole Virginia delegation against the scheme for fixing the seat of the Federal Government on the Susquehanna, and with Madison, Giles, Moore, and Parker against the bill incorporating the Bank of the United States.   When the President returned the bill for apportioning representatives among the several States to the House of Representatives, with his reasons for not assenting to its passage, he voted with his colleagues (Madison, Giles, Griffin, Brown, and Moore) in the negative, and defeated that measure. He approved the famous act respecting fugitives from justice and persons escaping from the service of their masters, and voted in the majority of forty-eight to seven.   In the minority of seven were two of his colleagues—John Francis Mercer and Josiah Parker; but the grounds of their vote it is impossible now to ascer-

---

[267] While the presence of the secretaries in the House of Commons is the life and soul of the British polity, it is wholly inapplicable to our institutions.   In the colonial government of Virginia the Treasurer always held a seat in the House of Burgesses; indeed, the Treasurer and the Speaker were usually, though not invariably, the same person, until 1765, when the two offices were prohibited by law from being held by the same person.   The Treasurer continued to be a member of the House, and afterwards of the Conventions held prior to Declaration of Independence.   At the first session of the General Assembly (October, 1776), it was decided that the Treasurer could not hold a seat in either house, and Robert Carter Nicholas, who had been regularly re-elected since 1766, preferring to hold his seat in the House of Delegates, resigned the office of Treasurer.

tain. When several test questions were taken he appears to have been absent from his seat.

Having served four years in Congress, he withdrew from public life, maintaining to the last a high place among the most distinguished members of the body. He does not seem to have been a partisan on either side, but voted with either, according to his sense of propriety and his views of the Constitution. Eager to organize the new government, he opposed the act to establish the Department of Foreign Affairs, because it contained, in his opinion, an unconstitutional provision; and on the same ground, though favorable to the eminent man at the head of the Treasury, he opposed the favorite scheme of a bank of the United States.

His long and honorable career was drawing to a close. He had devoted the prime of his life to the public service, and in his latter days he was assigned the duty of supervising the construction of the buildings which were designed to accommodate the Federal authorities in the new city of Washington, which had been established by his vote on the banks of the Potomac.[268] And at Woodville, in the county of Frederick, in the year 1804, and in the sixty-sixth year of his age, he departed this life.

The character of White must be determined by his acts, and these we have endeavored to lay before the reader. In all the public bodies of which he was a member, whether at home or abroad, his ready information, his eloquence, and his decision placed him in the front rank. His public qualifications were enhanced by his virtues, among which were a deep and ever-present sense of an overruling Providence, and a firm belief in the truth of the Christian religion.

---

[268] A letter from General Washington to White, dated March 25, 1798, would lead me to believe that the latter held the trust mentioned in the text. (*Writings of Washington*, Vol. IX, 334.) In *Lanman's Dictionary of Congress*, Alexander White is confounded with a person of the same name from North Carolina, who was a member of the old Congress in May, 1786, but who was not a member of Congress during Washington's administration. White of Virginia was never a member of the old Congress.

GEORGE NICHOLAS.

Continuing our course in the shadow of the Blue Ridge, we enter the county of Albemarle, the red soil of which is reputed to be fertile of official dignitaries, and which certainly contributed to the Convention two very remarkable men in the persons of George and Wilson Cary Nicholas. They were brothers, and acted together in political affairs while they both lived; but, for twenty years after the death of George the name of Wilson Cary, in his capacity as a member of the House of Delegates, of the Senate, and of the House of Representatives of the United States, and as Governor of Virginia, was well known and read daily from one end of the country to the other.

And first of George. Allusion has been repeatedly made already to his course in the Assembly in our review of the sessions to the adoption of the Federal Constitution, and the striking figure which he made during the debates in the present Convention has been exhibited at full length; but such was the force of his character, such was the vast influence in Virginia and in Kentucky until the close of the last century, that a more deliberate notice of his character is due to his memory; and I perform this office with the less reluctance, as there is not, so far as I know, any record of his career in print, and as if neglected now it may be overlooked hereafter.

He was the son of Robert Carter Nicholas and of Anne Cary, his wife.[269] Of the father it may suffice to say that he was esteemed for his abilities as a lawyer, for his sterling qualities as a statesman and a patriot, and, at a time when religion in its devotional aspects had almost faded away among the great, for his pure and ardent piety. He was a member of the House of Burgesses from the county of York as early as 1758, holding a place on all the important committees, and in 1766, on the death of Speaker Robinson, when the office of Treasurer was separated from that of the Speaker, he was chosen by the House of Bur-

---

[269] R. C. Nicholas married Miss Cary in 1754.

gesses to the former office. He performed the duties of his
office with great satisfaction to the public until the first session
of the General Assembly held in October, 1776, when, in consequence of a decision of the House of Delegates, of which he was
a member, that the offices of a delegate and of the Treasurer
were incompatible, he resigned the latter in a short address to
the House, in which he said that he resigned his office "with
honest hands—at least with empty ones," and received the unanimous approbation of both houses of the Assembly for his integrity, fidelity, and honor in the discharge of his duties.   On the
first organization of the judiciary he was elected one of the
judges of the General Court; but, as the war kept the courts
closed, it is probable that he did not take his seat on the bench,
or, if he did, that it was but for a short time that he performed
the duties of a judge, which he was so well qualified to discharge.
It was at the bar and in the House of Burgesses that he acquired
the great reputation which he enjoyed among his contemporaries, and which was acknowledged by his appointment to the
office of Treasurer, and to the office of President of the Convention of July, 1775, on the retirement of Peyton Randolph.   That
he was the equal and rival of such men as Thomson Mason,
Wythe, Pendleton, Peyton Randolph, and his brother John, and
others of a similar stamp, is praise enough with posterity.   He
did not live to hail the recognition of the independance of his
country by Great Britain, but died at his seat in Hanover, in
1780, in the fifty-second year of his age.[270]

---

[270] In the *Discourse on the Convention of 1776*, page 67, where a fuller
account of Robert Carter Nicholas may be seen, I state erroneously
that he died in his sixty-fifth year; but since the publication of that
work I have received from one of the descendants of Nicholas a small
slip of paper, being a copy of the original, which contains the date of
his birth, and which was obtained by Nicholas himself from Robert
Fry, the clerk of Bruton parish, on the 26th of December, 1777.   The
slip is endorsed by Nicholas, and has these words: "Robert Carter
Nicholas, son of Dr. George and Elizabeth Nicholas, was born January
28, 1728."   This paper had been laid away seventy years and more,
when it was found by a fair correspondent of mine and transmitted to
me.   And I must confess here that I have received much valuable aid
from the female descendants of my characters; and their zeal in behalf
of the memory of their ancestors gives me a livelier notion of what
their grandmothers were than I had before I began this work.

It is said that clever men may be traced to their mothers; and, although in a physiological view the notion cannot be sustained, it is certain that George Nicholas is not an exception to the rule. His mother was Anne Cary, daughter of Colonel Wilson Cary, of "Richneck," and sister of Colonel Archibald Cary, who, as chairman of the Committee of the Whole, reported to the Convention of 1776 the memorable resolution instructing the delegates of Virginia in Congress to propose independence, and who was the chairman of the select committee which reported the Declaration of Rights and the first Constitution of a free Commonwealth. She is said to have been of small stature, to the eye exceedingly fragile, but possessed of untiring energy. A correspondent, whose sources of information are unquestionable, thus describes her: "Fully imbued with the spirit of the times in which she lived, she early instilled into her sons that republicanism and love of country which had distinguished their father; and, herself a woman of high cultivation, she beguiled the tedium of an almost constant confinement to her couch by awakening in them a thirst for knowledge and a love of reading, more necessary to be roused at a period when war had closed all the institutions of learning. Her labors were requited by the celebrity of four of her five sons. When the war broke out, in 1775, Mrs. Nicholas retired to the country, probably to avoid the excitement and the alarms of which the seat of government was the scene. Her place of retreat was a farm of her husband's in Hanover, called the 'Retreat,' where, in 1780, her husband died and was buried. Here she resided when Lord Cornwallis, crossing the James, fixed his headquarters in the immediate neighborhood of that estate. On the report of the enemy's approach, she concealed her plate and jewels in the chimney; but one of the children disclosing the place of deposit, Cornwallis,[271] who was present, entreated her with a smile not to feel any alarm on the score of her property—a subject which, how-

---

[271] I record with pleasure the liberal conduct of Cornwallis on this occasion, but it is in strong contrast with his doings at other times in Virginia. And even here there is another version of the story, which renders it probable that the plate was carried off after, as is stated by Bishop Meade (*Old Churches, &c.*, Vol. I, 185). where may also be found the capital advice addressed by Mrs. Nicholas to her son, Wilson Cary.

ever engrossing at another time, then hardly occupied her thoughts, as she had just observed from her door a chase in which her son, John, thanks to the fleetness of his horse, had made his escape from the British dragoons. She had no reason to complain of the treatment received from Lord Cornwallis; but, being wholly unprotected, she moved to Albemarle, where her husband had purchased large estates on James river. She lived to see her sons rise to distinction, and to address to one of them about to embark in public life some sage advice, which may well be heeded even at the present day."

Robert Carter Nicholas and Anne Cary had five sons—George, John, Wilson Cary, Lewis, and Philip Norborne; and two daughters—Elizabeth, who married Edmund Randolph, and another who married John H. Norton, of Winchester. George Nicholas, the subject of this sketch, was born in Williamsburg in or about the year 1755,[272] attended the grammar school of William and Mary College, and in 1772 entered the college as a regular student, having for his associates James Innes, with whom he served in the army, in the Assembly, and in the present Convention; William Nelson, the future chancellor; St. George Tucker, the future commentator of Blackstone, and judge of the Court of Appeals; James Madison, the future bishop; Beverley Randolph, the future Governor; Samuel Jordan Cabell, the future member of the present Convention and member of Congress; Benjamin Harrison, of "Brandon," and other young men who became conspicuous in after life. At the breaking out of the war he obtained a captain's commission, and conducted himself with credit at Hampton. He attained the rank of colonel in Bay-

---

[272] All the genealogies in my possession make George the oldest son; and if he was, he must have been born a year or so after the marriage of his parents, which took place in 1754; but in the catalogue of William and Mary College, under the year 1766, there is a Robert Carter Nicholas, "son of the Treasurer." If this youth was the son of the Treasurer, he could only have been eleven or twelve in 1766, when in college. I make no doubt the error is in the catalogue, and that if there was such a person at that time he must have been the son of another man. It is hardly probable that the name and memory of such a youth, if he was the son of the Treasurer, should not appear in the family records. If, however, the youth was a son of the Treasurer, he was the oldest son, and we must put the birth of George in 1756 or 1757.

lor's regiment; and it was at a ball given to the American officers in Baltimore, in 1778, when he had reached the rank of colonel, that he saw for the first time Mary Smith, the lady who was to become his bride. She was the sister of General Samuel Smith, then a colonel, long distinguished as a member of the Senate of the United States, and of Robert Smith, who was successively Secretary of the Navy and of the State Department. Courtships were rapid during the Revolution; and during the same year, in which he saw her for the first time, Mary Smith became the wife of Colonel Nicholas. Withdrawing from the army, he studied law and entered the Assembly.

During the session of 1781, at a time when the cavalry of the enemy were roving through the State and driving the Assembly before them, and when immense losses were suffered from hostile depredations, Nicholas, then a young man of five-and-twenty, and the representative of the county in which the Governor of Virginia resided, moved an inquiry into the conduct of that officer. It is easy to imagine the feelings of a gallant young patriot in beholding the whole Commonwealth at the mercy of a squad of dragoons, and it was his first impulse to move an inquiry into the conduct of the Executive. Such an investigation might be right and proper, whatever may have been the innocence or guilt of the Governor. It was due to all parties that the facts of the case should be fully known; and it is certain that, if a becoming investigation had then been held, and the results committed to paper, we should have had a valuable contribution to our history. The inquiry was properly postponed to the following session, when Mr. Jefferson appeared in the House of Delegates as a member from Albemarle. On the day set apart for the investigation that gentleman rose in his place and avowed his readiness to answer any questions on the subject. Nicholas was absent, but Mr. Jefferson read the objections received from Nicholas and his own answers. No further proceedings followed, and both houses of Assembly adopted a resolution, in which they declare the high opinion which they entertained of Mr. Jefferson's ability, rectitude, and integrity as Chief Magistrate of the Commonwealth, and that they mean, by thus publicly avowing their opinion, to obviate and remove all unmerited censure.

When Nicholas became convinced, upon mature deliberation,

that his motion for an inquiry was founded on a misapprehension of the true state of affairs, he made the *amende honorable;* which was the more magnanimous, as it was already seen that the same intrepid spirit which impelled him to originate the inquiry was not to be swayed by fear or favor.[273]

In the interval between the close of the war and the adoption of the Federal Constitution he was frequently a member of the House of Delegates, and by his skill in law and by his vigorous powers of debate exerted great influence in all its decisions. With the subject of the Western lands, most of the laws respecting which he aided in framing, he was most intimately acquainted; and when Kentucky became a State he removed to that country, and connected his destinies with the new Commonwealth.

He took up his residence in his new home about 1790, not leaving Virginia until the adoption of the Federal Constitution had been secured. It was in the present Convention, called to decide upon that instrument, that he displayed in the greatest perfection his wonderful ability in debate, and reared for himself the most durable monument of his fame. His general course in that body has been detailed with some minuteness. To say that it was distinguished would convey a faint impression of its efficiency. He was the *Ulysses* as well as the *Ajax Telamon* of the hosts which upheld the Constitution. Tongue and tact, as well as brawn and vigor, were his characteristics. Clear as was the logic, convincing as were the ample and apt illustrations of Madison, their effect was equalled, probably surpassed, by the exhibitions of Nicholas. His powerful voice, which could be heard with ease over the hall, and even at the head of a battalion (a rare quality in a close reasoner); his profound acquaintance with the intricate local legislation of the State, in which he had so large a share; his perfect knowledge of his opponents— of their plans and of their modes of thought and action—derived from long experience at the bar and in the Assembly; his familiarity with law and with British political history, which enabled him to detect unerringly any incongruity in the arguments urged

---

[273] For a masterly review of this subject, consult *Randall's Life of Jefferson,* Vol. I, 349, *et seq.* The eighth and ninth chapters of the first volume will richly repay the student of the Revolutionary history of Virginia.

in debate; the advantages resulting from an intimate association with the people, whose manners, habits, and prejudices had been observed minutely by him ever since his entrance into public life; the wonderful readiness with which he marshalled his resources, and the utter fearlessness with which he ventured into the field of debate with his strongest adversaries—qualities in which he was not excelled by friend or enemy—fully justified the choice of his party in consigning to him the province of opening the grand discussion on the practical merits of the new Constitution. He bore the brunt of the battle, assisted, indeed, by eloquent and powerful colleagues, and by none more than by Madison, whose sphere, exalted as it was, was rather in a forum of philosophers than in a vast congregation of planters, whose passions and prejudices were to be cunningly soothed or dexterously assailed, not only by pure reasoning, but by strength of utterance, by vehement gesticulation, and even by personal daring.

Having thus given an outline of the life of Nicholas, I turn to particular parts of his career as detailed by a venerable man, who, having studied law in his office, and observed him critically in his public and private relations in Kentucky, undertook, in his eightieth year, when he had lost his sight and wrote by the hand of an amanuensis, to reduce his recollections to writing.[274]

After some prefatory remarks concerning the ancestry and birth of Nicholas, which have been treated more at large and more accurately already, our reminiscent continues:

"At the close of the war of the Revolution Colonel Nicholas removed to the village of Charlottesville, in Virginia, and commenced the practice of the law in that place and in the surrounding courts. He soon rose to a high eminence, and became the most distinguished lawyer wherever he practiced. He was particularly successful and distinguished at the bar of Staunton, a place then at which much legal business concentrated, and where the celebrated Gabriel Jones resided, and had long been monarch at the bar. Jones soon became a great admirer of Nicholas and his talents, and threw his patronage upon him. He (Jones), having accumulated a large fortune by the practice, had deter-

---

[274] Robert Wickliffe, Esq., of Kentucky, whose death is announced in the Richmond papers received while I was writing this memorandum—September 7, 1859.

mined upon withdrawing from it altogether; and Colonel Gamble relates an anecdote that one of Jones's old clients and friends, having a suit depending of much interest, he directed his client to associate Nicholas with himself in the prosecution of it.   In the argument of the case Nicholas displayed great ability, and the cause was gained; on which Jones's client asked Nicholas his charge, and was told he must pay him a guinea. Jones, meeting his client, asked him what he had paid Nicholas. He informed him, and Jones said, 'Go and give him two more.' The man accordingly went and told Colonel Nicholas what Jones had said; but the Colonel refused to take the two guineas, saying to the man, 'You have paid me my charge.'   The man informing Jones that Nicholas would accept no more, he told the man to deliver him the guineas, and that Nicholas should accept them.   This anecdote not only illustrates the character of Nicholas's mind, but also the principles on which he practiced in the early part of his career.

"When the reminiscent, a student of Nicholas's, a few months before his death, was about to return to his home to enter upon the practice of law, he waited upon Colonel Nicholas to take his leave, and found him in his office, alone.   Nicholas, before he took his final leave, said to him: 'You are about to practice where you will find the courts often ignorant and incompetent. You will owe it to your own personal respect, as well as to your interest, to treat the judges with a deference and respect due to the judiciary of the land, and never to wound the feelings of a judge by intimating that he is incompetent from ignorance. With your clients be ever candid and sincere, and never, by exciting their fears or hopes, extort an additional farthing to your fee.   Some lawyers, after bargaining for a fee, and getting their clients in their power, refuse or fail to do their duty until their fees are enlarged.   Such conduct is base, as well as unlawful.   A lawyer should be reasonable in his charges and faithful in his duties, and no honorable gentleman of the profession will ever make the size of his fee dependant upon the ignorance or credulity of his client; in fine, he should consider himself the friend and the trustee of his client.   Make no enemies, if you can help it, and do not depend with too much confidence on the professions of friendship for your success in life; but while friends may wish you well, and are certainly necessary to success in life, when it comes to a question whether a friend will give his business to a competent or incompetent lawyer, he will not be long in deciding to give it to a competent lawyer.'

"Colonel Nicholas, while he practiced law in Kentucky, was the most moderate lawyer in his charges and the most laborious in his duties to his clients. His regular fee in chancery was five pounds, Kentucky currency, and in a common-law case about three.

"About the year 1787 (1789 or 1790) Colonel Nicholas removed from Charlottesville to the county of Mercer, and settled on a farm near Danville, then the seat of justice of the Supreme Court for the district of Kentucky. He was no sooner settled than he was crowded with business, and considered decidedly the best lawyer in the county so long as he remained at the bar. His competitors at the Supreme Court for the district were of the best talents the country then afforded. When the district was turned into a State, and the Supreme Court was substituted by the Court of Appeals, in civil cases, and the court of Oyer and Terminer, in criminal cases, here Colonel Nicholas met not only the first men of the bar of Kentucky, but competitors equal to those of any bar in the United States. Among them were the late John Breckenridge, James Hughes, William Murray, Thomas Todd, James Brown, and Joseph Hamilton Daveiss. These men were not only distinguised for learning, but for their eloquence and highly honorable bearing as a bar. At the head of this bar was George Nicholas. All his brethren deferred to him; and the courts as well as the people at large listened and were instructed in the great displays which he often made in the important causes with which the Court of Appeals was crowded.

"Colonel Nicholas seems to have commenced his political life and services at the close of the Revolutionary War, always taking a decided and active part in the political questions that agitated his native State, as well as those that concerned the Confederation of the States, and when he was always the advocate for a more strong and energetic government than the Confederation States had. So that when the present Constitution of the United States was submitted to a Convention of the people of Virginia for ratification, it found in him an able and active advocate. In defence and explanation of it he often addressed the people at large, before his election to the Convention. On the assembling of the Convention, though believed to be the youngest member elected,[275] he took the lead in opening the debate in favor of the adoption of the Constitution. His speech upon the subject has been preserved among the debates of that distinguished body, and has ever been considered an able exposition and defence of the Federal Constitution.

"Shortly after the ratification of the Constitution in Virginia Colonel Nicholas, as before stated, removed to the district of Kentucky, where he found the district in a state of great excitement upon the subject of the separation of the district from Virginia, and an election of a Convention to form a Constitution for the new State. He brought with him a great reputation, both as a lawyer and a statesman, which induced several of the leading gentlemen of the district to apply to him to become a candidate for the Convention about to be elected. He expressed his willingness to do so, but his doubts of the propriety of his becoming a candidate on account of his non-acquaintance with the people, and the weight of private and professional business that was pressing upon him. To this the applicants replied that he need not have any apprehension of his election, nor waste his time in becoming acquainted with the people before his election; that they would advocate his claims, and had no doubts of being able to secure his election. He was accordingly announced a candidate, and, instead of making a canvass, he devoted his time, from his becoming a candidate to the meeting of the Convention, in drafting a form of a Constitution for the proposed State. On his being elected and taking his seat he laid before the Convention his plan of a Constitution, which was finally adopted, and passed by the Convention with scarcely an alteration. While his draft was being discussed an incident arose in the Convention which serves in some measure to illustrate the character of Colonel Nicholas's mind. Some one of the Convention had the indelicacy to intimate to him that he was a stranger to the people, and had come in under the popularity and influence of others; upon which he arose, tendered his

---

[275] There were many much younger. If born in 1755, he was thirty-three in 1788—the same age of John Marshall, and a year older than Legion Harry Lee.

resignation, and went home. The Convention proceeded no longer with the Constitution, but ordered a new election in a few days. The people of the county in which he lived, spontaneously and without any exertion of his own, re-elected him; and he again took his seat, and remained in the Convention until it not only adopted his Constitution as offered, but closed its entire business.

"The people of Kentucky were the first that applied to be separated from a mother State and become an independent State, and the Constitution drafted by Nicholas is believed to be the first Constitution formed for a new State. Happy would it have been for the people of Kentucky had they perpetuated its existence. It was a perfect Constitution in all its parts, entirely conservative, and the powers of government were well sustained by checks and balances, whereby one branch of the government was forbidden to trench upon the powers of either of the other branches. It was perfect in all its forms; its language clear and perspicuous; each line had its appropriate meaning, and each word in the line its appropriate place. So that the whole instrument manifested itself to be the work of an able and accomplished statesman, well acquainted with the condition of the people who were to be governed by it. The Constitution lasted not quite nine years. Under it the people of Kentucky enjoyed law and liberty; no people ever obeyed their constitutional injunctions more faithfully, and under the laws of their land lived more happily; but in some evil hour, for some objections to minor parts in the Constitution, the people consented to go into a Convention to amend their Constitution. The Convention assembled, but Nicholas was not there, but in his grave. His Constitution went into the hands of the new Convention, and did not come out of it until juvenile lawyers and unfledged politicians made sad work of its most valuable and conservative principles.

"During the continuance of the old Constitution, Kentucky knew nothing but thrift and prosperity, and, as far as a people could be under any form of government made, happy. During all which time Colonel Nicholas seemed to take but little part in the State government; but by his conversation and conduct indicated that he thought it was best to let well enough alone.

"About the year 1796 he retired from the practice, sold his

farm in the county of Mercer, removed his family to the Iron-Works Company's property, of which company he was a member—hoping by a residence on the property to give a change to the administration of its affairs by the company, which were then in a bad condition. He remained there, however, little more than a year, when he took up his final residence in the town of Lexington. General Washington's administration had expired, and his successor, Mr. Adams, had put his administration in hostile array against the Republic of France by calling into existence a standing army, passing alien and sedition laws, and, to sustain the extraordinary expenses of his administration, bringing to his aid stamp acts and direct taxation; and, to deter the friends of the Constitution and human liberty from resisting his tyrannical and unconstitutional measures, caused prosecutions against those who wrote or published what were deemed seditious libels, until the jails were not only filled with citizens, but some members of Congress. Early in the year 1797 George Nicholas took the field against these high-handed and tyrannical measures of the Federal Government. He not only spoke to the people and brought unto his aid the co-operation and much of the talent and worth of the country, but kept the few papers then published well supplied with his essays arraigning the conduct of the administration, and forewarning the people of the imminent danger in which their liberties were, and calling upon them to wake up to their danger.[276]

"These calls were not lost upon the people of Kentucky. Public meetings were held in the most prominent parts of the State, and by proper preambles and resolutions the measures of the administration were denounced as unconstitutional and tyrannical. These proceedings in Kentucky were justly ascribed by the administration to George Nicholas, and the administration, it is said, contemplated having him arrested for sedition; but before proceeding to execute their designs President Adams sent the Hon. James Ross, then a member of the Senate of the United States, a confidential agent, to Kentucky to ascertain and find out the extent and nature of the opposition, who were its

---

[276] One of his essays was signed "A Friend to Peace," in six numbers; another series was signed "By a Lawyer Who Does Not Wish to Be a Judge."

leaders, and what were their designs, especially to ascertain the purposes Nicholas had in view; and what acts of a seditious character, if any, he had been guilty of. Ross, who was an honorable gentlemen, of great legal knowledge, and the original friend to the administration, possessed a character too elevated to be its dupe or instrument. Fortunately for him and the country he was an old and intimate friend of Colonel James Morrison. Morrison was a friend and relation of Nicholas, and in daily communication with him. Ross frankly disclosed to Morrison the object of his visit, and received from him perfect satisfaction that Colonel Nicholas was sincerely attached to the Union, and that his only object was a reformation of the policy of the administration and to produce a repeal of the laws which he believed to be unconstitutional; and, in addition to other facts, he communicated in still confidence that he had it from Colonel Nicholas himself that the Spanish Government, through their agent, Thomas Perrei, tendered to Colonel Nicholas and two other gentlemen two hundred thousand dollars—one hundred thousand to be to their own use, and the rest to be used in carrying out the measure—to use his and their influence in producing a separation of Kentucky from the Union and annexing it to the Spanish province; that Colonel Nicholas and the other gentlemen not only refused it, but positively assured the agent that no considerations could induce them to desire a separation from the Union or accept a compensation for their political services from any foreign government. When Morrison communicated to Nicholas his conversation with Ross Nicholas replied that he was glad Morrison had made the communication of the facts to Ross, and that the Government would now be informed through its agent of the designs of Spain.

"Colonel Nicholas was continually assailed by the administration papers, particularly by that of Cobbett, and the essays of anonymous scribblers and pamphleteers of the Federal party, in which threats of arrest and punishment were not unfrequent. He, however, sustained himself by letters to his friends and appeals to public opinion through newspapers, until about the month of August, 1798, when he made an appointment through the newspapers to address the people of Kentucky on the condition of the country. On the day of appointment a vast assemblage of people from all parts of the State met at Lexington in pursuance of the notice. There being no house, public or private, large enough to contain the crowd, the people were assembled to the amount of thousands on the College lawn, when Colonel Nicholas addressed them for four hours in a strain of eloquence and power scarcely ever equalled, and certainly never surpassed. In his speech he laid open to the people their Federal Constitution, the nature of their Union, their value and importance to the protection of the States and the liberties of the people of the States; then laid bare the maladministration of President Adams, its crimes, its follies, and its cruel oppressions. He drew a strong picture of the sufferings of the country, and the victims under the alien and sedition laws. He, however, warned them against violence as a means of redress, but urged them to take the constitutional means through the ballot-box, their only remedy of changing the administration and restoring the Constitution to its supremacy, thus relieving the country of their oppression under the Stamp Act, direct taxation, and unconstitutional persecutions.

"This speech overwhelmed the Federal party in Kentucky, and established the cause of the opposition. Colonel Nicholas was now at the highest of his popularity; but his political difficulties were not yet at an end. The Federal administration had infused into most of the religious societies a horror of French infidelity, and denounced Nicholas, Jefferson, and others of the opposition as infidel Democrats. And while Nicholas was engaged in overturning the power of the administration, his adversaries, and those of the Democratic party, set on foot an opposition to the State Constitution, principally on the ground that it tolerated negro slavery, and finally succeeded in having acts passed to call a Convention; and for a season it appeared obvious that the Abolitionists would throw a majority of their party into the Convention, and the slaves would be emancipated. From some cause Colonel Nicholas seemed to pay no attention to the movements of the Abolitionists until the month of February preceding the election of members to the Convention, which, by law, was to take place on the first Monday in May. Seeing that an effort upon the town of Lexington would be ineffectual, the Abolitionists being too strong in the town, he called a meeting of the people in the county, at Bryan's Station, where he had a meeting of the country people, and addressed them at large upon the propriety of their voting for conservative men, and particularly for supporting men opposed to turning the negroes loose upon the country. This speech was well received by the thinking classes of the community north of the Kentucky, and was decisive of the question with the people in every part of the State; so that when the people met there was but one emancipator elected.[277]

"Colonel Nicholas was not only a politician, and exerted, as such, a great influence over the public men of Kentucky; he was also an agriculturist and a political economist; and by his moral writings, lectures, and conduct contributed much to regulate public sentiment in favor of all the branches of labor. He not only devoted himself to this object, but had his office filled with students of law, to whom he lectured and whom he prepared for the profession with a success rather astonishing, as scarcely one of his students failed in the profession, and most of them rose to high eminence, both at the bar and in the councils of the State and the nation. He did not live to reap his full share of the benefits resulting from his labors for his country. He died in the month of June, 1799, in the forty-sixth year of his age,[278] and in the midst of his usefulness, to the loss of his country and the irreparable misfortune of his widow and numerous family. He was a man of low stature, not exceeding five feet seven inches high, of a fair complexion, large, glowing blue eyes. His head was very large for his stature; his hair (what remained of it) was red. He became before his death almost entirely bald, from which circumstance, and from other indications of age, for more than six years before his death, he was called Old Nicholas.[279] He was a man of taciturn habits in mixed company, but in private circles, and especially at his own house and fireside, he was a most interesting companion, and sometimes both humorous and witty. He was remarkable for his hospitality, and in all the relations of husband, father, and master his character was perfect. He was universally loved by the gentlemen of the bar, and

[277] The reader will regard these views of Mr. Wickliffe as embracing the opinions of himself and of Nicholas only.

[278] Forty-four only, if born in 1755.

[279] Every clever fellow by the name of Nicholas soon gets the title of "Old Nick."

looked up to by the greatest lawyers and sages of the age. His eloquence was of a very high order, and his reasoning most powerful. As a criminal advocate in his day he had no equal in Kentucky. This is proved by his success both as a civil and criminal advocate. At the time of his death he was the employed counsel of the unfortunate Fields, who was accused of the murder of his wife. Nicholas died before his trial, and the unfortunate man was condemned to the gallows, although he was ably defended by the late Chief-Justice Marshall. Fields was a man possessed of many able qualities, and had many friends out of his own family; and his family in Kentucky and Virginia among the most numerous and respectable in America, many of whom loved him and stepped forward to rescue him from the fate that awaited him. He continued to declare himself innocent from the moment of his arrest to the moment of his death; and the last words he uttered under the gallows were that he was innocent, and knew not how his wife came by her death. Had Nicholas survived, no one acquainted with his powers and influence as a counsellor doubts that the fate of the unhappy man would have been very different. Nicholas was not only a benevolent and kind-hearted man, but an encourager of every branch of labor; and to the poor he was courteous and kind. The whole State was shocked at his death, and the Legislature that succeeded his death, in gratitude and remembrance of his great talents and services, named the county of Nicholas after him.''

I have only a few words to add to these reminiscences. It was to Nicholas Mr. Jefferson communicated the celebrated Kentucky resolutions, which received the sanction of that State, and played an important part at a memorable crisis.[280] The course of Nicholas in the Virginia Assembly may be seen in the review of their sessions heretofore given.

His last days were serene and honorable. On his removal to Lexington he occupied a commodious house, which became the centre of refined and intellectual society. Here his relatives and friends from abroad received a courteous and cordial welcome, and formed a favorable opinion of the West; and many were induced to make that land of promise their permanent abode.

---

[280] *Jefferson's Works* (Randolph's edition), Vol. IV, 344, and *Randall's Life of Jefferson*, Vol. II, 448.

Few men excelled him in the graces and courtesies of social life. His varied experience in human affairs, his intimate familiarity with all the great men and great questions of his times, his sterling practical sense, and his easy flow of speech made him most instructive and most interesting in conversation. A long and honored life seemed to stretch away before him. Although, like most of his family, he lost his hair in early life, and appeared older than he was, his constitution was unbroken, and when he smiled his pure white teeth displayed the freshness of youth. He died after a short illness, and was buried in the family burial-ground, in the eastern part of the city of Lexington, about a quarter of a mile from the court-house. His grave has no stone, but is enclosed by a substantial wall; and within that enclosure, seven years later, was deposited the body of his wife. It is said that the mourning and wailing of his slaves (who were mostly native Africans), as his coffin was lowered in the grave, was a strange and startling sight. The wild gestures and frantic sounds with which they gave vent to their sense of bereavement on the death of their master, we are told, inspired a supernatural awe.

He left several sons, of whom Colonel Robert Carter and Major Cary Nicholas engaged in the war of 1812; Smith was bred a merchant in the house of Smith & Buchanan, in Baltimore, and died young on a trip to the East Indies; John Nelson studied law, and died at the age of thirty-three; George Wilson, a naval officer, died at sea; Samuel Smith studied law, and is the present Judge Nicholas of Louisville, Kentucky, and is the only son who ever married. Colonel Nicholas left also seven daughters—Maria, Anne, George Anne, Margaretta, Elizabeth Randolph, Hetty Morrison, and a seventh, whose name has not reached me.[281]

Length of life is sometimes as important an element in constituting the reputation of the statesman as in amassing the wealth of the capitalist. George Nicholas died at the age of forty-four.

---

[281] The Saunders paper in the Nicholas manuscripts. I confess my obligations to Miss Ellen Wayles Randolph (now Mrs. William B. Harrison, of "Brandon,") for valuable materials relating to the life of George Nicholas, especially for the Wickliffe and Saunders manuscripts, and some printed documents.

Had he attained the term reached by some of his associates at the bar and in the Assembly—by Marshall, by Monroe, and by Madison—how different might have been the story which the historian would be required to record! What he might not or might have been, it is impossible to divine. He might not have been other than he was—the master-spirit of the young Commonwealth (which was mainly fashioned by his hands, and which holds his dust), moulding her young men to his own high standard of abilities and character, and guiding her politics by his judicious and temperate counsels. He might have been placed on a loftier pedestal, and have transferred the sceptre of the presidency a quarter of a century earlier to the West. Had Marshall died in 1799, what a blank there would be in that career which now looms so grandly before us! He would have been remembered by a few old men as a clear-headed lawyer of slovenly appearance, or as an unlucky minister plenipotentiary. The fame of the great speech in the case of Jonathan Robbins would not have been his.[282] Had Monroe died in the same year his name would be found on the list of the Governors of Virginia, and of the Ministers to France and to England, and there only. Had Madison died at the same time, the report of ninety-nine would have been unwritten; his part in the General Federal Convention and in the present would be remembered by the studious, and his career in the House of Representatives for a few years would be known to some of the higher order of politicians, but all else of his long and honored life would be wiped away. And fully as fair as any of these stood George Nicholas when he descended to the tomb.

---

[282] This speech was delivered in the House of Representatives on the 7th of March, 1800.

WILSON CARY NICHOLAS.

If the sun of George Nicholas was eclipsed at meridian, the light of the genius of his brother, Wilson Cary Nicholas, if less dazzling, shone not less effectively for a score of years to come. The course of George, except in a military capacity, never extended beyond the limits of Virginia and Kentucky; but much of the career of his younger brother was spent abroad in one or other of the houses of Congress; and from the adoption of the Federal Constitution almost down to the close of his natural life he was the main-spring of the party organizations of the day. He exerted, directly or indirectly, no little influence on all the political questions that arose in the interval above defined, either in a minority, as was the case in the earlier part of his course, hanging heavily on the skirts of his foes, or when in a majority, as he was from the commencement of the century, arranging the tactics of the hour, composing the tender griefs of great men who sometimes thought themselves overlooked by their party, and bidding them soothingly to bide their time, assigning the tasks of duty to each individual with a strict regard to his tastes and to the breadth of his shoulders—believing, as he did, that the rule of Horace was quite as applicable to politics as to poetry; engaging in debate with his strongest opponents with sound arguments, with practical rather than with figurative or learned illustrations; and, above all, with that delicate tact which made him say neither more nor less than was needful at the time, and which prevented him from offending an adversary who might be likely to be won over at no distant period, any more than seemed indispensable to the conduct of his argument, to the gravity of his theme, or to the bounding pulses of his more fiery coadjutors. If his life could have been written in full, there would be seen the history of the most adroit political management of the last or the present century. His manners and deportment contributed to his success. In his apparel he was exceedingly plain; he was serious and even solemn in his aspect; his words were few, unless in the presence of intimate friends, but they were well studied, were never uttered to the wrong person, always sank deep in the minds of men, and were never forgotten. He read at a glance the thoughts of men; and when he saw a young recruit, and had looked into his performances, he at once allotted him a special place in the machinery of his party, and made him an active and willing adjutant. The talents of Nicholas were invaluable to his party at a time when coalitions were the order of the day; when a numerous and able party, but recently triumphant, and though wincing under a terrible defeat, ready to coalesce with old friends and with their old enemies, were dogging the footsteps of his own, and when members of his own party even, which had become too strong and was beginning to fritter, were courting their Federal enemies and were looking to them for smiles and votes, Nicholas was equal to the emergency. He could not prevent a small squad of clever friends, who could not be satisfied with anything short of despotic rule and a full enjoyment of choice offices, from starting a little opposition of their own, nor could he control their forked tongues; but he utterly deprived them of all influence in affairs, forced them to doff their uniform and to drop the glorious war-cry of past victories, and drove them in the face of the country to take shelter in the camp of the enemy. His management was altogether successful. If he could not extract the fangs of the asp, he neutralized its poison. Its very victims, instead of dying, flourished fairer than ever, grew fat, laughed at the sinuous motions of their recreant enemy, and at last put their heels upon its head. The leading measures advocated by Nicholas were founded on the best interests of his country; and it was the fault of his enemies that his singular skill in the tactics of party were called into exercise. And wherever these qualities of his were required there they were instantly brought into play. Yesterday he was in the Senate of the United States; to-day he is in the House of Delegates; to-morrow would find him in the House of Representatives, and the day after he would be the Governor of Virginia. If lesser spheres were to be looked into, he became the president of the branch bank of the United States at Richmond, or the collector of the port of Norfolk; loving no office for its own sake, holding none but for a short time,[283] and always eager to return to "Warren," his seat on the banks of the James, and surpass his practical neighbors in making corn, wheat, and tobacco.

He carried the State with him and the people in all his movements. He seemed to combine in a wonderful degree the good qualities of Sir Robert Walpole and of Talleyrand without their bad. Like the former, his policy was as pacific as it was practicable; and in a time of extraordinary embarrassment in our foreign affairs, which appeared to render warlike demonstrations essential to the interests and honor of the country, he cooled down the bellicose and the demonstrative of his own party, outwitted the machinations of his wily opponents, and secured the adoption of measures which, while they postponed actual war, tended seriously to incommode and annoy our foreign enemies. Like Talleyrand, he was versatile or inscrutable, as the occasion required—a weigher of mystic words and of looks more weighty than words, or indulging in a honeyed flow of transparent talk; retentive of his own secrets, but disclosing enough to secure the secrets of others; in debate on topics of great concern frequently silent, or speaking but little, but turning with fatal facility the fairest flowers of speech, yet fragrant with the dew of hostile lips, into dust and ashes; and in the various complications of parties and of circumstances, purposely designed to put him off his guard and to confound him, so much a master of himself, so entirely poised, as not only to circumvent the schemes that were laid to betray him, but to lead his opponents into the belief that he thought them much better and wiser than they felt themselves to be; and, unlike Talleyrand, he never used other weapons than those with which truth, reason, and honor supplied him. He would have been a prince among diplomatists; and every foreign mission was open to him, but his family engagements and his tastes bound him to his home.

In the business of ordinary life he was very generally regarded as an infallible, almost an inspired, oracle. The confidence of the people was as unlimited in his integrity as in his wisdom; his friends shared liberally in his ventures; and although he was,

---

[283] The political enemies of Nicholas used to say that he held the different offices to keep unpopular candidates out of them and until the right man of the party should turn up.

from peculiar circumstances which were beyond the control of
individual action, but rather the results of political arrangements,
unforeseen or improbable at the time, to the last degree unfortunate, and more unfortunate still in involving his friends in misfortune, he retained their sympathy and confidence to the end.
And when the cloud burst, had he thrown off the trammels of
politics and position and directly engaged in commercial affairs,
he might have retrieved a false step, reimbursed his own losses
and those of his friends, and established his character by the not
unfrequently false but ever-flattering test of success, instead of
affording, by his conduct, an ever-memorable example of the
extreme danger which the most prudent and the wisest men
incur when they turn their backs upon their regular business,
and, forsaking the farm and the rostrum, embark in schemes
which, if successful, may add to their thousands, but which will,
if unfortunate (as such schemes, from the nature of the case, are
almost always apt to be), overwhelm them and their friends in
one universal ruin.

But it is time that we begin to trace more minutely the events
in the life of Wilson Cary Nicholas. He was the son of Robert
Carter Nicholas and Anne Cary, of both of whom some mention
has already been made.[284] The characteristics of his revered
father were integrity, wisdom, piety, and unalloyed devotion to
his country—qualities which environ this name to this hour with
a bright and unfading halo. The mother of Nicholas was a
sister of Archibald Cary, that fierce and daring man, who bore
the sobriquet of "Old Iron"; who reported to the Convention of
1776 the resolution instructing the delegates of Virginia in Congress to propose independence; who brought forth in the Convention the Declaration of Rights and the first Constitution of
an independent Commonwealth; who threatened to plant his
dagger in the bosom of any man who should assume the office
of dictator ere the setting of the first day's sun; who, at the time
of his death in 1786, when he was the Speaker of the Senate of
Virginia, was heir-apparent[285] of the English barony of Huns-

---

[284] In the sketch of George Nicholas, *ante.*

[285] *Discourse on the Virginia Convention of 1776*, page 91, where the
fact is stated, as well as other things concerning Colonel Cary. The
late Richard Randolph, Esq., is my authority about the position of
Cary in respect of the barony in question.

don—a man and a statesman whom neither interest, fear, nor favor could swerve from the cause of his country.

Wilson Cary Nicholas was born in the city of Williamsburg on the 31st day of January, 1761, when Governor Fauquier had fairly inaugurated his popular reign. He saw, in his eighth year, the august obsequies which were performed at his grave; had attended with his father—the Treasurer—the meetings of the Council when the mild and enlightened John Blair, the elder, sat as its president; had seen the splendid equipage in which Botetourt drove up the York road when he made his first entrance into the city; had visited with his father that amiable nobleman, and been driven in his coach drawn by his spanking grays, and had been present when the body of that lamented man, in the presence of a weeping audience, was lowered into the sepulchre of the Randolphs, to await its transportation to England; had seen William Nelson take the seat of the departed peer in the Council; had gone with his father to pay his respects to the Earl of Dunmore and his interesting family on their arrival from the old country, and had heard the uproar when it was known one bright April morning that the Earl had purloined the power of the Colony and conveyed it on board a man-of-war. Before fourteen he had wrestled with the sons of Dunmore on the palace green, had hunted hares and gathered chinquapins with them, and at the dancing school had tripped a hornpipe or cut a pigeon-wing in the presence of his popular and pretty daughters.[286]

Meantime Wilson attended the grammar school of William and Mary College, and was about to enter that institution when, in 1775, the troubles of the Colony began in earnest, and the tramp of armed men began to be heard in the hitherto peaceful metropolis. The delicate health of his mother required a less exciting scene, and she removed, with her younger sons, to the "Retreat," an estate of her husband's in Hanover, and there superintended their education. When Wilson Cary attained his eighteenth year—a gloomy period of the war—he entered the army, and, having served several campaigns, returned to

---

[286] The residence of Judge Nicholas was opposite the public green and in the rear of the magazine from which the powder was taken. Lord Dunmore had three sons at William and Mary in 1775—George Viscount Fincastle, the Hon. Alexander, and John Murray.

"Warren," a paternal seat in Albemarle, to which his mother had removed after the visit of Cornwallis to the "Retreat," an account of which has been detailed in the life of George. Under the guidance of his mother he spent his time in reading, his father having died in 1780 at the "Retreat" before the departure of his mother. Such was the progress which he made in his studies, and so high did he stand with the people of his adopted county, that in 1784—in his twenty-third year—he was chosen by a flattering vote to a seat in the House of Delegates. When his mother, who had probably returned to her home in Williamsburg, heard of the election of her son, she addressed him a letter which, with the allowances every intelligent reader will make for her early prejudices and prepossessions, may be studied at the present day by politicians, old as well as young. It is in these words:

"DEAR WILSON,—I congratulate you on the honor your county has done you in choosing you their representative with so large a vote. I hope you are come into the Assembly without those trammels which some people submit to wear for a seat in the House—I mean, unbound by promises to perform this or that job which the many-headed monster may think proper to chalk out for you; especially that you have not engaged to lend a last hand to pulling down the Church, which, by some impertinent questions in the last paper, I suspect will be attempted. Never, my dear Wilson, let me hear that by that sacrilegious act you have furnished yourself with materials to erect a scaffold by which you may climb to the summit of popularity; rather remain in the lowest obscurity; though, I think, from long observation, I can venture to assert that the man of integrity, who observes one equal tenor in his conduct—who deviates neither to the one side nor the other from the proper line—has more of the confidence of the people than the very compliant time-server, who calls himself the servant—and, indeed, is the slave—of the people. I flatter myself, too, you will act on a more liberal plan than some members have done in matters in which the honor and interest of this State are concerned; that you will not, to save a few pence to your constituents, discourage the progress of arts and sciences, nor pay with so scanty a hand persons who are eminent in either. This parsimonious plan, of late adopted, will throw us behind the other States in all valuable improvements, and chill, like a frost, the spring of learning and spirit of enterprise. I have insensibly extended what I had to say beyond my first design, but will not quit the subject without giving you a hint, from a very good friend of yours, that your weight in the House will be much greater if you do not take up the attention of the Assembly on trifling matters nor too often demand a hearing. To this I must add a hint of my own—that temper and decorum are of infinite advantage to a public speaker, and a modest diffidence to a young man just entering the stage of life. The neglect of the former throws him off his guard, breaks his chain of reasoning, and has often produced in England duels that have terminated fatally. The natural effect of the latter will ever be procuring a favorable and patient hearing, and all those advantages that a prepossession in favor of the speaker produces.

"You see, my son, that I take the privilege of a mother in advising you, and be assured you have no friend so solicitous for your welfare, temporal and eternal, as your ever affectionate mother,

"ANNE NICHOLAS.[287]

" *Williamsburg, 1784.*"

It now remains to be seen how far he followed, in a political career of thirty-five years, the suggestions of his estimable parent.

The first act on taking his seat in the House of Delegates in May, 1784, was to vote for the re-election of John Tyler as Speaker, whom he had frequently seen in his childhood in Williamsburg, who had long known and esteemed his father, and with whom he was to be associated under a new Federal Government for many years to come. The nomination of Tyler was seconded by French Strother, whom our young politician had also seen in his early youth, who had proved himself a sterling patriot in our civil conflicts, and with whom he was to fight under the same standard many a sharp battle before the close of the century. As he looked over the House, he recognized many faces which he had seen in his youth, and beheld a number of young men who, like himself, were new members, and with whom he was to engage earnestly on the field of politics for more than the third of a century to come. Among the older

---

[287] *Old Churches*, Vol. I, 184.

members were Patrick Henry, Richard Henry Lee, William Grayson, Henry Tazewell, Madison, John Taylor (of Caroline), Jones (of King George), and others; and among the younger ones were John Marshall, Alexander Stuart, and others who were destined to acquire reputation in the Assembly, in the Congress, and under the new Federal Government. His brother John was his colleague, and sat by his side. His relative, Wilson Miles Cary, was chairman of the Committee of Religion, which at that particular conjuncture was the most interesting of the standing committees. Nicholas was placed on the Committee of Propositions and Grievances, of which Tazewell was chairman, and on the Committee of Courts of Justice, in which Jones (of King George) presided.

As a general outline of the proceedings of this session has already been given, it will be only necessary to state the occasion when some test question of the times was presented for his vote. The first test question was on the engrossing a bill for adjusting claims for property impressed or taken for public service. As the bill was lost, we cannot ascertain its details; for it is plain that it was in some detail of the bill and not in its nominal object that it was disapproved by the House. Nicholas voted for the rejection with Henry, Madison, Taylor (of Caroline), Marshall, Jones (of King George), and his brother, John. The bill was defeated by five votes.

The next test question was one of the most exciting that was agitated in the Assembly before the adoption of the present Federal Constitution. The definitive treaty with Great Britain stipulated that the debts due British subjects before the Revolution should be paid in full. The right of a State to confiscate a debt due to the public enemy was as clear as the right to take any other kind of property, or even life itself, if it were deemed expedient so to do; and Virginia had exercised this right by requiring the British debtors to pay their several amounts into the public treasury. The subject had been deliberately acted upon, and was regarded as settled forever; to open it afresh was thought by the majority of the people of that era as imprudent and as unjustifiable as it would be to require the restoration of any other property taken from the British. But the public aversion to the measure was increased by the absence of all reciprocity on the part of the British, though that reciprocity was enjoined by the treaty. Negroes had been taken off at the evacuation of New York not only in violation of the treaty, but in spite of the demands of their owners, who were present in person at the time of their embarkation. The payment of the debts due by the citizens of Virginia to British subjects was, beyond dispute, decreed by the treaty; yet it was urged by the majority that, though those debts would have to be paid, it was prudent to delay payment until every fair effort could be made to secure the rights of our own citizens. Great Britain could not complain, unless she consented to perform her own part of the bargain; and it was plain that she not only did not intend to pay for our slaves, but designedly kept possession of those fortified places which she had agreed to evacuate, and from which she could annoy us most readily in case of war. On the other hand, it was urged by the members of the minority, of whom Nicholas was one, that our first office was to do justice, and that if England did not fulfil her part of the treaty in good faith we should adopt the means of redress which the laws of nations pointed out. The form in which the present question came up was this: A motion was made that the House adopt a resolution declaring that all acts of Assembly incompatible with the definitive treaty ought to be repealed. The previous question, "Shall the question to agree to the resolution be now put?" was called, and was negatived by a vote of thirty-seven to fifty-seven. In other words, the House refused to come to a direct vote on the resolution at that time. Nicholas voted in the minority with Madison, Marshall, Richard Henry Lee, Corbin, White, Tazewell, and Edmunds (of Brunswick); while the majority included Patrick Henry, Crocker, Strother, John Trigg, Vanmeter, Zane, Ruffin, Edmunds (of Sussex), Matthews, Porter (the colleague of Madison), Riddick, Thomas Smith—members who came from the extreme West as well as the extreme East, and who clearly voted on general grounds.

The proper site for the seat of government of the Commonwealth was long a subject of dispute in our early councils. It had been removed from Williamsburg during the war, when, from the position of that city (between two navigable streams), an attack might at any moment be made upon it, and lands had been purchased in Richmond; but Richmond was far from being in the centre of the State, and, at a time when men could travel on horseback only, it was deemed a long distance from the interior to the falls of the James. At the present session a resolution was reported from the Committee of the Whole, declaring that all the public lands in Richmond not necessary for the purposes of government should be sold, and the proceeds thereof applied to the erection of public buildings in Richmond, pursuant to the act for the removal of the seat of government. When it came up a motion was made to strike it out and insert that it was expedient that measures should be taken to ascertain the opinion of the people as to the place to be fixed on for the seat of government. The amendment was negatived, and the original resolution was agreed to by a vote of sixty-three to fifty-seven. It is probable that the vote on the adoption of the resolution was the direct reverse of the vote in favor of the amendment; and if this supposition is true, then Nicholas voted with Patrick Henry, Madison, Marshall, and Strother, and against White, Tazewell, Prentis, Richard Henry Lee, King, Ruffin, and Matthews—in other words, against the Williamsburg interest, which on such occasions was always upheld with ability by the delegate from that city, who was generally an able and clever tactician, and who at this time was the mild and venerated Prentis.

I now come to a vote given by Nicholas on a subject which seriously perplexed the thoughts of our early statesmen during the period which elapsed between the close of the war and the adoption of the Federal Constitution. In that interval Virginia was truly and practically a sovereign State. In main respects she regulated her own commerce at her own discretion; laid duties on exports and imports; had or might have a navy of her own; did have her revenue cutters, and collected her marine dues in her custom-houses or by her officers on board the ships. This independent position involved important responsibilities, none of which was greater than that of building up a commercial marine. From the earliest times the British vessels traded up our bay and the larger streams, and discharged and received their cargoes at the landings, and sometimes almost at the barn-doors of the planters; and the result was a virtual proscription of the existence of any ships owned by Virginians, and a facility for smuggling which a large navy—if a large navy had been practicable—could not have entirely prevented. When, at the close of the war, it became necessary to levy duties on imports, and also on exports, it was seen that the facility of eluding all the regulations of revenue was such that the State would be compelled either to establish innumerable places of deposit and entry—the expense of which would almost entirely consume the amount derived from the customs—or, in justice to the fair dealer, who would be ruined by the smugglers, to give up the scheme of a revenue from commerce altogether. At this conjuncture it was determined that a few places of deposit and entry should be chosen, as such a policy would not only secure the safe and speedy collection of the revenue, but tend to rear a commercial marine of our own. The transportation of freight to and from the specified ports would soon call into existence a class of men accustomed to the water and ready to man our ships, when they should be built, to foreign ports, and especially able to defend our coasts in time of war. The sagacity of Madison had embraced the whole subject, and he determined to bring the matter before the Assembly.[288] But there were many strong prejudices and powerful local interests to encounter. It is a trait of the Anglo-Saxon family—derived, perhaps, from their piratical ancestors—to hate taxes of all sorts, especially those accruing from the sea, and to love smuggling; and it was also a trait of our British forefathers of a later day, who were mainly agricultural, to hate towns, as interfering with their interests in more regards than one. Even since the accession of the Prince of Orange to the British throne there have been repeated efforts in Parliament by the county members to prevent the growth of London, and severe taxes have been proposed on every new building in the metropolis. The same prejudice existed in Virginia, and, from obvious geographical considerations, to a much greater extent than in England. Our noble bay and our numerous rivers, though affording invaluable advantages to the farmer, are fatal to the existence of any large town, unless their naviga-

---

[288] I have no authority derived from the Journals to sustain my assertion of the primacy of Madison on this subject; but I have often heard old men, who lived thirty years ago, speak of Madison's scheme for building up towns and creating a coasting trade, etc. The present bill passed both houses, but was assailed and amended at every session, until the whole subject was transferred to the Government under the Federal Constitution.

tion is controlled by stringent laws; and a large majority of a rural people, in deciding between the personal and immediate benefit derived from the free use of their streams by ships, foreign as well as domestic, and the apparently remote advantages springing from an economical collection of the revenue, and an efficient marine in case of war, appeared to dread a change.

At the present session—on the 17th of June—the subject was presented on the passage of a bill to restrict foreign vessels to certain ports within the Commonwealth. The bill passed by a vote of sixty-four to fifty-eight; Patrick Henry, Madison, Strother, Corbin, Eyre, Mann Page, Jones (of King George), Edward Carrington, Philip Barbour, Prentis, Matthews, and others in the affirmative, and Nicholas, with Grayson, Marshall, Ruffin, White, and others in the negative. Tazewell and Richard Henry Lee were absent. I wish I could have recorded the name of Nicholas on that side of the question which posterity has substantially approved, but it must not be forgotten that he strenuously upheld the adoption of the Federal Constitution, which established the existing arrangement; as it was, I can only say that he voted in very decent company.

The next vexed question which he had to encounter was the propriety of calling a Convention to revise the Constitution of the State. A few weeks after the adjournment of the Convention which formed that instrument, Wythe, in a letter to Jefferson, expressed himself in a way that would lead at first sight to the opinion that he believed an ordinary Legislature competent to amend that instrument at pleasure, and a design was seriously meditated during the war of undertaking the office of revisal.[289] The attack made on the Constitution in the *Notes on Virginia* was not yet generally read, but it is probable that the opinions of Mr. Jefferson had been uttered freely in conversation, and that his friends—and among them Nicholas—knew what they were. The question now came up in

[289] In a review of the *Life of Jefferson* by Randall, in the Richmond *Enquirer* of 15th of January, 1858, the language of Wythe is examined, and shown to be the result of forgetfulness for the moment, and not conflicting with the doctrine afterwards laid down by him, that an act of Assembly in conflict with the Constitution is void. A letter of George Mason's, deprecating the attempt to revise the Constitution by the Assembly, may be seen in the *Virginia Historical Register*.

the House on agreeing with the opinion of the Committee of the Whole, to which the Augusta petition in favor of calling a Convention had been referred, and which opinion was adverse to the prayer of the petition. The resolve set forth that the petition should be rejected, "such a measure (as the call of a Convention) not being within the province of the House of Delegates to assume; but, on the contrary, it is the express duty of the representatives of the people, at all times and on all occasions, to preserve the same inviolable until a majority of all the free people shall direct a reform thereof."

A motion was made to strike out the part quoted above, and was negatived by a vote of forty-two to fifty-seven. Nicholas was so much interested in the question that he rose and demanded the ayes and noes. He voted in the minority—that is, in favor of striking out—with John Taylor (of Caroline), Madison, Marshall, Stuart, Jones (of King George), Prentis, and Tazewell; while Henry, White, Strother, King, Eyre, Ruffin, Matthews, and his brother John were in the majority. The decision of the majority was that the Assembly had no right to call a Convention, or to meddle with the matter, unless instructed by a majority of all the free people of the State; and it is presumed that the minority thought that the Assembly did possess the power of calling one without any formal instruction from the people. The opinion held forty-four years later, when a Convention was called, seems to be intermediate between the opinions held by both parties on the present occasion. The Assembly then passed an act affording facilities for the expression of the wishes of the people on the subject, and, having learned that a majority of votes was cast in favor of calling a Convention, carried the public will into effect.

He voted with the majority on the passage of the bill to amend the several acts concerning marriages, which was opposed by an able minority, headed by Tazewell, Grayson, Matthews, and others; and he witnessed the amusing scene, already described, which occurred when John Warden was brought before the House for a contempt. And he had the pleasure of voting for that statue to Washington, with the inscription on its base by Madison, which, so finely executed by Houdon, has for more than seventy years adorned the Capitol of Virginia. The session adjourned on the 30th of June.

The House of Delegates reassembled on the 18th day of October, but could not obtain a quorum for several days. The roll was called, the absent members were noted, and the sergeant-at-arms was instructed to take them into custody. In due time Nicholas, Henry, Madison, Adam Stephen, and Grayson were produced at the bar in custody of the sergeant, and were required to make their excuses for their delay in attending the session. Nicholas appeared on the 30th, and was placed on the Committee of Religion—of which Norvell was chairman—and on the Committee of Propositions and Grievances, with Tazewell at its head.

The great question concerning religion came on the 11th of November in the shape of a resolution from the Committee of the Whole, "that the people of the Commonwealth, according to their respective abilities, ought to pay a moderate tax or contribution annually for the support of the Christian religion, or of some Christian church, denomination, or communion of Christians, or of some form of Christian worship." It has been common to regard the assessment recommended by this resolution as the evidence of a lingering attachment to a church establishment; but nothing can be further from the true state of the case. To require all the sects of a Christian community, such as Virginia then was, to make a contribution to their respective churches was a measure which, so far from tending to consolidate the sects and rear an establishment, was the most efficient that could be devised for rendering an establishment impracticable. It was essentially a measure of moral police, deemed advisable at a time when the voluntary system had not been tried, except on a very small scale, and no more trenched on religious freedom than the setting apart of the first day of the week, under severe penalties, as a day of rest alike to Jew and Gentile, can be regarded as an infringement of religious liberty. The House happened to be thin when the question was taken, but the resolution was carried by a vote of forty-seven to thirty-two; Patrick Henry, Jones (of King George), Tazewell, Prentis, Coles, King, Wray, Edmunds (of Sussex), Edmunds (of Brunswick), Riddick, Eyre, and Allen voting in the affirmative, and Nicholas, with Madison, Strother, Johnston, Stuart, Spencer Roane, John Breckenridge, Porter, Russell, and Matthews, in the negative. A committee was appointed to bring in a bill in pursuance of the resolution, consisting of Henry, Corbin, Jones (of King George), Coles, Norvell, Wray, Jones (of Dinwiddie), Carter H. Harrison, Tazewell, and Prentis.

On the 17th of November the question concerning religion came up a second time on two resolutions, reported by the Committee of the Whole, which declared, first, that so much of the petition of the Presbytery of Hanover, and of the Baptist Association, as prays that the laws regulating the celebration of marriage, and relating to the construction of vestries, may be altered, is reasonable; and, secondly, that acts ought to pass for the incorporation of all societies of the Christian religion which may apply for the same. The first passed without a division, but the second excited a warm debate. White called for the ayes and noes, and we are thus enabled to learn how each member voted on the subject. The resolution, enforced as it was by the eloquence of Henry, passed by a vote of sixty-two to twenty-three—largely over two to one; Patrick Henry, Stuart, Spencer Roane, Jones (of King George), and Matthews voting for its passage, and Nicholas, with Madison, John Taylor (of Caroline), Strother, White, Johnston, and John Trigg, against it. Of this resolution it may be said that it contained nothing exclusive. It offered equal facilities to all Christian sects. Matthews, Henry, Madison, and others were appointed a committee to bring in a bill pursuant to the first resolution; and leave was immediately granted to bring in a bill to incorporate the clergy of the Protestant Episcopal Church, and Carter H. Harrison, Henry, Thomas Smith, William Anderson, and Tazewell were ordered to prepare it.

A bill was reported from the Committee of the Whole on the 26th respecting the extradition of criminals, when a motion was made to strike out all after the enacting clause and insert a more explicit enactment instead. The motion prevailed; Madison, Tazewell, Eyre, Ruffin, Marshall, and Matthews in the affirmative, and Nicholas, with John Trigg, Strother, and Prentis, in the negative. The amended bill then passed without a division.

It was on the 22d of December, 1784, that the engrossed bill incorporating the Protestant Episcopal Church came up on its passage; and as soon as the blanks were filled the question was taken, and the bill passed by a vote of forty-seven to thirty-eight; Madison, Marshall, Grayson, Tazewell, and Jones (of King

George) voting in the affirmative, and Nicholas, with Johnston, Porter, Stuart, and Roane, in the negative. John Taylor (of Caroline) was absent. To have a true notion of this bill, the reader will remember that it sprang from a resolution which accorded equal privileges to all sects, and that he has only to strike out the words "the Protestant Episcopal Church" and insert "the Baptist" or "the Presbyterian," and the case will be identically the same. Madison was doubtless the author of the bill, and while drawing it had in his possession (certainly under his guardianship) the famous bill concerning religious freedom, and a few months later drew the celebrated memorial, which was signed by thousands and returned to the Assembly by a large number of counties; and it is plain that if he had deemed the present bill hostile in any respect to the cause of religious freedom, instead of drafting it and of voting for it, he would have been its warmest opponent.

On the 24th another aspect of the religious question was presented. The bill establishing a provision for the teachers of the Christian religion came up on its passage, and a motion was made to postpone its consideration until the fourth Thursday of November next, and was carried by a vote of forty-five to thirty-eight; Nicholas, with Madison, Johnston, Trigg, Stuart, Strother, Spencer Roane, Porter, and Matthews, voting in favor of postponing, and John Marshall, Cropper, Benjamin Harrison, Jones (of King George), Eyre, Ruffin, Corbin, Willis Riddick, and Tazewell against it. The postponement was made with a view of consulting the opinions of the people upon it; and the bill was published in hand-bills, with the ayes and noes on postponing it annexed, copies of which were furnished to every member, who was instructed to obtain full information of the public will on the subject.

It has been seen that Nicholas encountered all the leading religious questions of the day, and, although attached to the Episcopal Church, and urged by the eloquent persuasion of his pious mother against all hostile movements aimed at the Church of her affections, he steadily upheld in its broadest sense the doctrine of a disconnection of the State with religious affairs, passing a bowshot beyond Madison himself, and deserves all the credit that flows from such a course of action. On the other hand, it is due to the cause of justice to say that the policy of the majority was not only fair and liberal, but tended to multiply and strengthen individual sects instead of aggrandizing any one of them at the expense of others; and that in affording the people an opportunity of deciding whether a contribution should be levied for the support of any particular form of Christian worship which the tax-payer preferred, they acted with deliberation, prudence, and wisdom.

Although the session was occupied with many interesting subjects, those already specified embrace the only occasions on which the vote of Nicholas was recorded in the list of ayes and noes. It may be said, however, that in the main he belonged to the younger branch of the great party, of which Henry had long been the leader, engrafting upon the old trunk certain vigorous and fruitful scions from the gardens of "Montpelier" and "Monticello."

He was returned to the House of Delegates at the April election of 1785, and in the following October took his seat in the body. He was now to be present and to bear an honorable part in the deliberations of a session which, in the number of distinguished men who composed the House, in the variety and magnitude of the subjects which were discussed and settled, and in the absorbing interest which it naturally excited among the people of all conditions and denominations, civil and religious, was hardly ever exceeded in our annals. It was, indeed, a glorious school for a young politician. We can readily imagine the sense of responsibility felt by Nicholas when, a few days after taking his seat, he saw Madison rise in his place and report, from the Committee of Courts of Justice (of which he was chairman), a budget of one hundred and seventeen bills, contained in the Revised Code, and not of a temporary nature, and heard him recite deliberately the title of each.[290] To maintain and defend so many important bills was a gigantic task, which no statesman had hitherto attempted, but which Madison, then in his thirty-fifth year, and in the prime and pride of his great powers—and flushed with the glory he had won in the Congress

---

[290] This happened on the 30th of October, 1785. The bills were severally read a second time, says the Journal; but, as a matter of fact, they were not read at all, except in a parliamentary sense, and were referred to a committee of the whole House on the following day.

of the Confederation—not only undertook, but carried through, with the skill and tact and that ever-abounding illustration that he always brought to bear upon every serious public exhibition of his life. These bills involved almost the entire policy of domestic legislation, and their critical examination and discussion were calculated to call forth the finest faculties of the mind and all the wisdom of human experience. Among his associates, beside Madison, the Corypheus of the group, were the veteran Harrison, who, lately Governor, now filled the Speaker's chair, and his old colleague John Tyler, John Taylor (of Caroline), and his namesake (of Southampton), Joseph Prentis, Meriwether Smith, James Innes, French Strother, Cuthbert Bullitt, Stuart (of Augusta) and his venerable colleague Zachariah Johnston, Turberville, Henry Lee (of the Legion), S. Jordan Cabell, Isaac Coles, the Bowyers, the Carys, and many others, who had either attained to distinction or were soon to win it.

Having already reviewed the proceedings of this session, I shall confine myself to a notice of the votes given by Nicholas on the different questions as they arose. His two first votes reflect credit upon his independence, as he voted to send back to the people two prominent men whose elections were contested on just and legal grounds. He succeeded in sending Arthur Lee home; but he failed in the case of Harrison, who, having been beaten by Tyler in Charles City on the first Monday in the past April, moved over with a pot-boiler's outfit to Surry, and on the fourth Monday offered himself as a candidate for the House of Delegates, and was elected. As soon as Harrison took his seat in the House he became a candidate for the chair of the Speaker, which Tyler had filled the year before, and for which his name was now presented to the House, and defeated him. Harrison had no title to a seat in the body, and any other person in his position would have been ejected unanimously; but his public services and the Speakership saved him from the fate of Lee.

The subject of the manumission of slaves was discussed on the 13th of December. A report was made from a standing committee, which recommended that so much of the petition of sundry citizens of Halifax as prayed for the repeal of the act to authorize the manumission of slaves was reasonable. A motion was made to strike out the words "is reasonable" and insert "be rejected," which was lost by the casting vote of the Chair, the House being equally divided; Nicholas voting against striking out (that is, in favor of the repeal of the act to authorize the manumission of slaves) and Madison voting for striking out (that is, against the repeal). The main question was then put on the resolution as reported, and, some two or three members coming in, it was decided in the affirmative by a vote of fifty-one to fifty-two—a majority of a single vote. This decision would seem to show how equally divided the politicians of that day were on the subject of manumission. Present public sentiment sustains the vote which Nicholas gave on this occasion.

The same subject was renewed on the 24th of December. The bill carrying into effect the report of the committee, which had been approved by the House, was read the first time, and when the question was on its second reading, it was rejected by the decided vote of fifty-two to thirty-five—Nicholas in favor of the second reading and Madison against it. There must have been something in the details of the bill offensive to the House; for as soon as it was rejected a committee—of which Nicholas was a member—was ordered to bring in a bill to repeal the act in question, which was duly brought in and passed, under the title of an act concerning slaves, without a division.

When the celebrated bill for establishing religious freedom came up on its second reading,[291] on a motion to strike out the preamble from the pen of Jefferson and insert the sixteenth section of the Declaration of Rights in its stead, Nicholas voted with the majority against the amendment; and when the bill was read a third time, on the following day, he was one of the large majority (seventy-four to twenty) which voted for its passage. And when the bill came back from the Senate again and again, with the amendments of that body, he always voted to retain, as far as possible, the language of its author and its catholic spirit.[292]

Those who voted for the bill for establishing religious freedom merit the applause of their country. They gave to the world a

---

[291] December 16, 1785.

[292] The bill was bandied between the two houses for nearly a fortnight. For a correct view of the original bill, with the amendments in a single view, see *Randall's Life of Jefferson*, Vol. I, 219.

conspicuous and deliberate example of liberal legislation on the question of religion, and showed that, at that early day, they fully appreciated the subject in all its bearings. What could fairly be done by act of Assembly they accomplished. But while history bestows all fair and liberal praise upon the friends of the bill, it is due to justice not to visit with harsh censure the small minority of members whose votes are recorded against it. The truth is that, in a certain sense, the bill came too late. Had it been passed when it was written by its author, its effect would have been original as well as conclusive. But it had been kept back seven or eight years, and until the substantial policy which it prescribed was secured by law. The equality of all sects had already been recognized and established, and the same privileges were offered to all. With this view of the case, those who voted against the bill, while they regarded it as effecting no new or real change in existing laws, were strongly inclined to interpret the language of the preamble as in some instances hostile to the orthodox doctrines of the Christian religion.[293] Hence they sought to substitute for the long preamble, with its questionable theology, the seventh section of the Declaration of Rights, which was succinct, thorough, explicit—covering the whole ground of religious freedom—and, from its origin, imparting dignity and authority to the act, while it was wholly free from religious ambiguity. It is also probable that the minority were favorable to the policy of assessments—a policy which Patrick Henry, George Washington, Richard Henry Lee, and other illustrious patriots approved, and which was not only compatible with the bitterest hostility to an establishment, but actually rendered the existence of such an institution impossible; and though they believed that the bill establishing religious freedom did not necessarily condemn the policy of assessments, as recorded in the bill, to carry that purpose into effect, yet that such a meaning might be placed upon it; and they preferred that the policy of assessments should be decided independently and on its own merits. A glance at the names of the minority will detect those

---

[293] It should be remembered that the bill, as we now have it, was freed by the Senate from some strong objections which pious men might entertain to its details; but when the bill passed the House of Delegates, on the 17th, it contained these objectionable parts.

of some of the purest, most liberal, and most undaunted Republicans of their times.[294]

On the 11th of January, 1786, an engrossed bill to amend the act restricting foreign vessels to certain ports within the Commonwealth was put upon its passage, and was carried by a vote of fifty to forty-six—Nicholas happening to be out of the House at the time. With his usual policy Madison sustained the bill.

Numerous and important as were the subjects discussed and settled during the session, one of the most memorable, not only in our own State but throughout the Union, was reserved to the last day. Soon after the Journal was read John Tyler rose in his place and offered the following resolution:

"*Resolved*, That Edmund Randolph, James Madison, Walter Jones, Saint George Tucker, and Meriwether Smith, Esqs., be appointed commissioners, who, or any three of whom, shall meet such commissioners as may be appointed by the other States in the Union, at a time and place to be agreed on, to take into consideration the trade of the United States; to examine the relative situations and trade of the said States; to consider how far a uniform system in their commercial regulations may be necessary to their common interest and their permanent harmony; and to report to the several States such an act relative to

---

[294] In my assumed character of attorney for the Commonwealth of the past, though I shall not hesitate to condemn any man or measure when it is just so to do, I abhor any indirect reflection on the men and measures of the early days of the Commonwealth. One of the minority against the bill was that sterling patriot, John Page, the classmate of Jefferson and his life long friend—the only member of the Council of Dunmore who stood up for Patrick Henry in his powder foray. Throughout the war he was a true patriot and a thorough Republican. As a member of the first Congress under the present Constitution, and as a Republican elector of 1800, he rendered most efficient service to his country, which was recognized by the Assembly when they conferred the office of Governor upon him. His paper, addressed to Meriwether Jones, when that gentleman was collecting materials for a continuation of *Burk*, is thoroughly democratic. In Church and State he was ever fair and liberal. In private life he was so pure that he was requested, as we are told by Bishop Meade, to take orders, that he might be elected the Bishop of the Episcopal Church of Virginia. He died at Richmond October 11, 1808; aged sixty-four. Peace and honor to his gentle and gracious memory.

this great object as, when unanimously ratified by them, will enable the United States in Congress effectually to provide for the same.''

It was twice read and agreed to without a division. Matthews was ordered to take it immediately to the Senate, which body acted on it forthwith and approved it, with certain amendments. The House concurred in some of the amendments and refused to concur in others. Matthews again took the bill to the Senate, which receded from its amendments, and the resolution was a law.[295] Annapolis was chosen as the place of meeting; and measures were there and then adopted which resulted in the call of the General Convention which formed the present Federal Constitution. How short is the space traversed by the vision of the wisest men! Had Tyler been re-elected at the beginning of the session to the Speaker's chair, the loss of which, under the circumstances, was deeply mortifying to him, he could not have taken the honorable part in debate at this important juncture which now confers so much credit upon his character; nor could he have made a solitary motion on the floor of the House; and he would have forfeited the honor of having offered a resolution which may be said to have laid the corner-stone of the Federal Constitution, and which will cause his remotest posterity to rejoice in the glory of their ancestor. I doubt not that Nicholas, who was the neighbor and the intimate friend of Madison through life, was privy to the plan of presenting the resolution by the hands of a leading member of the majority at this late stage of the session; and though he did not offer it himself, he cordially approved it, and in this way connected his name honorably with an extraordinary epoch.

Having obtained a competent knowledge of the conduct of public bodies and of the prominent politicians of the State, and having been engaged in the adjustment of some of the most delicate and interesting questions of the day, Nicholas now withdrew for a season from public life and devoted his attention to his private affairs. It was not until the assembling of the present Convention, on the 2d day of June, 1788, that he appeared in a public body. He was returned, as the colleague of his brother George, from the county of Albemarle; and, though he

---

[295] See the history of the resolution treated in detail, *ante.*

did not engage formally in debate, he was regarded as one of the most useful and most effective friends of the new Federal system. His votes have already been recorded; and it will suffice to say that he opposed the scheme of previous amendments and voted in favor of the ratification of the Constitution.   When the Convention adjourned he returned to Albemarle and embarked with fresh zest in agricultural pursuits, which, above all the honors of political life which he lived to attain, were the source of his purest enjoyments.

The adoption of the Federal Constitution had wrought a material change in our political system.   The progress of the new administration was watched with the strictest vigilance; but the subject which more particularly attracted the attention of a large majority of the Assembly and of the people was the probable fate of the amendments, which Virginia had proposed by her Convention, to the Constitution.   One session of the new Congress had been held, and some of the amendments had been adopted, but the fate of others was deemed very uncertain. The Assembly met on the 19th day of October, 1789, and Nicholas appeared in the House of Delegates as a member from Albemarle.   He saw in the chair of the Speaker Thomas Matthews, with whom he had previously served in the House and lately in the Convention; and among the members—though Tazewell and Prentis had been translated to the bench, and Grayson, Lee, Madison, Coles, Page, Moore, White, and Bland were in the new Congress—were some of the ablest friends and of the most uncompromising opponents of the new government. Patrick Henry, however, was still a member, and Benjamin Harrison, Edmund Randolph, Dawson, Strother, Henry Lee (of the Legion), Wormeley, Richard Lee, Edward Carrington, Briggs, Edmunds (of Sussex), Norvell, Marshall, and a number of old politicians, who, having flung aside forever (as they supposed) the armor of politics, had determined to venture another campaign and observe the progress of a fresh political organization.

Hitherto, for the most part, the ruling majority, which, since 1765, had usually controlled the local and, at a later day, the Federal politics of Virginia, had remained unbroken by any serious schism; but in the recent struggles consequent upon the formation of the new Federal system some of its younger and more promising members had favored that scheme, and were in a state of isolation in respect of their old friends. Was this state of parties to continue, or were the old majority to unite with the youthful seceders, or were the youthful seceders to return to the fold? In other words, should the brilliant and accomplished Edmund Randolph, who happened to be the latest of the seceders, or Patrick Henry, the old and eloquent oracle of the Republican hosts, be the leader of the majority?

The second day of the session was marked by a deep and ingenious design on the part of the Federalists—as the friends of the Constitution were called. It was proposed that a committee be appointed to prepare an address to President Washington, declaring the high sense felt by the House of his eminent merit, congratulating him on his exaltation to the first office among freemen, assuring him of their unceasing attachment, and supplicating the Divine benediction on his person and administration. It passed unanimously. Henry Lee, who doubtless offered the resolution, was appointed chairman of the committee of eight to prepare the address; Nicholas was one of its members. Of the eight, all were Federalists but two. The address was reported on the 27th, was recommitted, was reported without amendment on the following day, and was unanimously adopted.

On the 5th of November Nicholas was placed on a committee to bring in a bill for the cession of ten miles square for the permanent seat of the Federal Government. Henry Lee, who offered the resolution, was chairman, and Edward Carrington, John Marshall, and Corbin were members. It is remarkable that there was not an opponent of the Constitution on the committee, which was appointed by the Speaker, who was a Federalist. The bill was duly reported, and passed both houses. This was the first connection of Nicholas with the ten miles square, within which, in the process of time, he was to act a conspicuous part. Nicholas opposed the bill for regulating and fixing the salaries of the officers of civil government, which prevailed by a vote of seventy to sixty-five. I hope that the ground of his opposition was the meanness of the salaries. When the test question concerning the payment of the taxes in specie came up on the 13th of November, which seems to have settled the subject in favor of hard money, he happened to be out of the House.

The first regular skirmish between the new parties occurred on the 5th of December on a resolution reported from the Committee of the Whole, which declared that the Assembly ought to call the attention of Congress to the propriety of acting on the amendments to the Constitution proposed by Virginia, not included in those already acted upon. A motion was made to strike out the resolution entirely and insert a more stringent one in its place, and was negatived by the casting vote of the Speaker—the vote being sixty-two to sixty-two. Henry was absent, and Randolph, Marshall, and Nicholas carried the day by the aid of the Speaker.

The act for establishing religious freedom was not altogether conclusive of all the topics connected with the late establishment; and the Baptist Association petitioned for a sequestration of the glebes. Their memorial was referred to the Committee of Religion, which (November 27th) reported that the disposition of church property was a serious question, not to be decided in haste, and that it ought to be referred to the people. A motion was made to amend the report by substituting in its stead an amendment, which declared that the House would uphold the act for establishing religious freedom forever; that the contest for the glebes, churches, and chapels was not a religious question, but should be decided by the rules of private property, etc. The report and amendment were then referred to the Committee of the Whole, which reported (December 9th) a resolution postponing the Baptist memorial, with its appendages, to the 31st day of March next. The resolution prevailed by a vote of sixty-nine to fifty-eight—Nicholas, William Cabell, Jr., Edmund Randolph, John Marshall, Mann Page, Clement Carrington, Norvell, King, Booker, Henry Lee (of the Legion), and others in favor of postponing, and Johnston, John Trigg, James Breckenridge, Prunty, Vanmeter, Green Clay, Crockett, McClerry, McKee, Hugh Caperton, and others against it. The vote plainly indicated a geographical caste, the East voting in the affirmative and the West in the negative. When we estimate the comparatively small value of the property in question—its position, the doubt and uncertainty likely to result from the contest for its possession, during which the houses would be turned into ruins, to say nothing of the public time and money spent therein, and the prejudices engendered during the strife—it would have been wise to adopt the amendment, which referred the right of property in the glebes and buildings to the courts of law, where, at this stage of the contest, it certainly belonged; and it is to the credit of Nicholas that he took this view of so perplexing a question.

Many grave questions were decided during the session, a view of some of which may be seen elsewhere;[296] but I have confined myself to those topics in the settlement of which the votes of Nicholas are recorded. From the number of select committees to which he was assigned it is evident that he was gradually taking his place in the front rank of his political associates; and it is probable that, in the troubled state of domestic and Federal relations existing during his apprenticeship in the Assembly and in the Convention, he imperceptibly acquired that knowledge of the world, and that intuitive tact in composing feuds or in twisting them to his purposes, which the good-natured part of his opponents were wont, at a subsequent day and in a wider scene, to attribute such wondrous effects.[297]

Before we follow Nicholas beyond the limits of the Commonwealth we must trace him in a memorable session of the House of Delegates, in which he held a conspicuous position. It is difficult, at the present day, to estimate the intensity of the excitement which raged during the administration of the elder Adams. Brother was estranged from brother, father from son; the courtesies of life were disregarded, and the stamp of worth was looked for not in the moral qualities that compose a virtuous and honorable character, but in the color of the flag under which an individual fought. There was a strong majority of the Federal party in both houses of Congress; and the administration, having the Legislature in its hands, unwisely determined to use it as a means of curbing the spirit of the people. The sedition law was passed, and it is a known fact in Virginia that every man who made a speech to his neighbors was watched, and his words were weighed by his opponents, in the hope of finding some expression which could be tortured by the Federal courts into an offence to be visited with fine and imprisonment

---

[296] Review of the session, *ante*.

[297] Nicholas held a seat in the House of Delegates from 1794 to 1798, but our limits will not allow us to trace him at length.

in a common jail. The alien law was deemed harsh and unjust, especially on the seaboard; but in the interior, where aliens were comparatively unknown, there were no subjects on which it could operate, and it was discussed on grounds of general policy. Had the counsels of such pure and able statesmen as John Marshall prevailed, the sedition law would not have disgraced the statute-book of a free country.[298] But madness ruled the hour, and the majority in Congress resolved to appeal to the fears rather than to the affections of the people. The minority in both houses was outvoted, but not cast down; and, as all opposition on the floor was of no avail upon legislation, it was determined to transfer the contest from the Federal Capitol to the Legislatures of the several States. Some leading members of Congress vacated their seats and entered the House of Delegates; and resolutions, drawn with eminent skill, and embodying what was deemed the true view of the nature of the Federal compact, as well as a severe analysis of some of the obnoxious measures of the administration, embraced the chart of the campaign. Those adopted by Kentucky were from the pen of Jefferson, and those which produced the memorable debate in the House of Delegates—of which we shall proceed to give an account—though offered by John Taylor (of Caroline), were drafted by Mr. Madison.

It was on the 13th day of December, 1798, that the House of Delegates of Virginia went into Committee of the Whole on the resolutions of John Taylor. James Breckenridge, whose life, protracted almost to our own day, has made his venerable figure known to many now living, and who belonged to the Federal party, was called to the chair.[299] John Taylor then rose and spoke for several hours in support of the resolutions, which were believed to be his own. When he ended George Keith Taylor, an able and excellent man, too soon snatched away from the bar which he adorned by his genius and learning, and from society, of which he was a shining light, moved that the committee rise; but upon an inquiry from Nicholas whether he

---

[298] " He gave his vote to repeal the obnoxious clause of the sedition act." (*Flander's Lives of the Chief Justices*, Vol. II, 395.

[299] In my early youth while travelling on horseback to the West I saw General Breckenridge as I was passing his beautiful seat in Botetourt. I remember his courteous salutation to an unknown lad, covered with the dust of travel. [He died in August, 1846.—EDITOR.]

designed to prevent any one from speaking who might be disposed to take the floor, withdrew his motion. But, as no member seemed inclined to speak, the committee rose and the House adjourned. On the following day (14th) George Keith Taylor replied at great length and with all his accustomed ability to the speech of his namesake from Caroline. Having spoken for several hours he took his seat, and was followed by William Ruffin in support of the resolutions. He was succeeded on the same side by John Pope (of Prince William), who indulged in some humorous remarks. John Allen (of James City) then spoke in favor of the resolutions until the adjournment. On the 17th James Barbour (of Orange), then a very young man, and destined in after life to serve with distinction in the office of Governor at an eventful crisis, of Senator of the United States, of Secretary at War, and of Minister at the Court of St. James, addressed the committee, replying in detail to the arguments of the gentleman from Prince George and in review of the policy of the administration of Adams. His speech was prepared with care, and made a favorable impression upon the House. At its close the House adjourned. Next morning (18th) Archibald Magill (of Frederick) spoke in opposition to the resolutions and in reply to Barbour, and was in turn replied to by Foushee (of the city of Richmond), who was followed by Edmund Brooke (of Prince William) in opposition until the adjournment. On the following day (19th) Pope replied to his colleague Brooke, and was followed by William Daniel, Jr. (of Cumberland), afterwards known as a distinguished judge of the General Court, in an exceedingly able speech, which displayed those characteristics of his mind to which he owed his reputation. He examined in minute detail and with consummate tact and research the arguments of Taylor (of Prince George), and showed an ability in debate that must have led to the highest political preferment. When he concluded his speech, after some conversation between General Henry Lee and Nicholas, William Cowan (of Lunenburg) addressed the committee in opposition to the resolutions until the adjournment.[300]

---

[300] William Cowan is the "Billie Cowan" who was "to show Patrick Henry the law" in the famous beef case at New London. He was an able lawyer, a man of pure morals, and, indeed, of eminent piety, but his manner and the tones of his voice were ludicrously solemn; so that when he spoke he always appeared to be preaching a funeral sermon.

On the 20th General Henry Lee took the floor and spoke with much ingenuity and with sober earnestness in defence of the alien and sedition laws and against the resolutions; and was followed by Peter Johnston,[301] who had fought gallantly in the war of the South under the standard of Legion Harry, whom he now rose to answer, and who was afterwards a judge of the General Court.   He was followed by John Taylor (of Caroline), in reply to the arguments which had been urged by him when last up; and when he concluded, after a short speech from Thomas M. Bayley (of Accomac), against the resolutions, the committee rose, and the House adjourned.

On the 21st George Keith Taylor replied to his namesake of Caroline, and to other speakers who had sustained the resolutions, in a speech of several hours, which was marked by great ability of argumentation and by splendid eloquence, and which closed in the following words: "May He who rules the hearts of men still dispose us to yield obedience to the constitutional acts of the majority; may He avert the mischiefs which these resolutions are calculated to produce; may He increase the love of union among our citizens; may no precipitate acts of the Legislature of Virginia convulse or destroy it; and, to sum up all in one word, may it be perpetual."

When Taylor finished his speech there was a solemn pause for a few moments in the proceedings of the House, when a member rose in his place, who seemed to be in the prime of manhood, and who, elegantly dressed in blue and buff, booted and spurred, and with a riding-whip in his hand, had entered the House just as Taylor rose to speak.   He placed his hat upon his knee, and would now and then use the top of it as a resting-place for a small slip of paper, on which he would scribble a note.   He had entered Congress in 1790, but, until the present session, had never been a member of the Assembly; and though his fame was diffused throughout the Union, he had never spoken

---

He was requested to become a minister of one of the churches, but he wisely declined to change his profession so late in life.   See the *Life of Dr. A. Alexander* by his son, James Waddell Alexander, whose recent death I deeply deplore as I trace these lines.

[301] [Father of General Joseph Eggleston Johnston, late Confederate States Army.—EDITOR.]

on a great public question in his native State.   But on this, as on
all subsequent occasions to the end of a long life, when he was
called upon to address a public body, his simple and sensible
narrative, his clear and plausible reasoning, the tact with which
he either spiked the artillery of his opponents or turned its
thunders against them, and his familiar knowledge of life and
manners in Virginia, from which he mainly drew his illustrations,
produced a great sensation in the House, and abated at once and
by the force of magic the grave argument and the impressive
declamation of Keith Taylor.   Such were the victories William
Branch Giles was wont to win in the pride of his extraordinary
powers.   He was, more than any man of his generation, a natural debater, attaining almost by intuition to the rank which he
soon reached; relied upon as a forlorn hope implicitly by his
friends, wresting victory where victory was not hopeless, and
more dreaded by his ablest opponents than was any other of his
distinguished contemporaries.[302]

At the close of Giles's speech a motion was made by General
Henry Lee to strike out a part of one of the resolutions, when
Nicholas rose and opposed the amendment.   After demonstrating
in some detail the bad effect of the measures of the administration of Adams, he repelled the charge of disunion made by
Keith Taylor, and closed his remarks by declaring "that he had
been a member of the Convention that adopted the Constitution;
that he had been uniformly a friend to it; that he considered
himself as now acting in support of it; that he knew it was the
artifice of those on the other side to endeavor to attach a suspicion of hostility to the Federal Government to those who dif-
fered with them in opinion.   For his part, he despised such
insinuations, as far as they might be levelled at him.   He appealed
to his past life for his justification.   The friends of the resolutions yield to none in disinterested attachment to their country,
to the Constitution of the United States, to union, and to liberty.
He said he had full confidence that the amendment would be
rejected, and that the resolutions, without further alteration,

---

[302] Governor Tazewell, who was a member of the House, informed
me of the appearance of Giles in this debate.   By the way, these two
eminent men never came in collision.   Randolph, in the Convention of
1829, playfully alluded to Giles in debate ; but they never met in a fair
fight, though opposed to each other in Congress in high party times.

would meet the approbation of a great majority of that House." Lee replied, and was followed by Samuel Tyler—afterwards Chancellor—in opposition to the amendment (which was rejected) and in a general defence of the resolutions. The main question was then put, and the resolutions were carried by a vote of one hundred to sixty-three. They were immediately sent to the Senate, and passed that body on the 24th by a vote of fourteen to three. The eighth resolution required the Governor to transmit a copy of the series to the executive authority of each of the other States, with a request that the same may be communicated to the Legislature thereof.[303]

The House of Delegates at its present session contained a large number of men then eminent, or who subsequently attained to distinction in the public service. Besides such as John Taylor (of Caroline), George Keith Taylor, Giles, Breckenridge, Samuel Tyler, Henry Lee, and others of that stamp, there were Littleton Waller Tazewell, James Barbour, William Henry Cabell (afterwards Governor and president of the Court of Appeals), William Daniel, Thomas Newton, Archibald Magill, James Pleasants (afterwards Governor, senator, and judge), Peter Johnston, William McCoy (long a member of Congress), and others of great respectability. A representation of the Convention of 1788 still appeared in both houses of the Assembly. In the Senate were Archibald Stuart, Richard Kennon, French Strother, George Carrington, and Benjamin Temple, all of whom sustained the resolutions; and in the House were Wilson Cary Nicholas, Worlich Westwood, John Prunty, James Johnson (of Isle of Wight, the survivor of the Convention), William O. Callis, Willis Riddick, Henry Lee, and Robert Andrews, all of whom, except the two last named, voted in favor of the resolutions.

While the friends of the resolutions were rejoicing at their triumphant passage through the Assembly, their feelings were shocked by the intelligence of the death of an illustrious statesman, who was regarded as one of the ablest champions of their

---

[303] The resolutions were slightly amended during the discussion. The student who wishes to examine the subject in detail will refer to the valuable little work containing the speeches and proceedings of the sessions on Federal matters, issued in 1850 by J. W. Randolph, of Richmond.

party in the Senate of the United States, and whose ability was greatly relied on to uphold the doctrines of the resolutions on the floor of that body.   Judge Henry Tazewell had been exposed during his journey in mid-winter to Philadelphia, where Congress then held its sessions, but was able to take his seat on the 21st of January, 1799.   His disease, however, resisted the efforts of his physicians, and he died on the morning of the 24th. When the Assembly proceeded to fill the vacancy caused by his death, Wilson Cary Nicholas was chosen to fill the unexpired term.   When we count over the names of the distinguished men who either had been or were subsequently candidates for a seat in the Senate—when we recollect that Madison, Giles, Taylor (of Caroline), Andrew Moore, and others of equal celebrity were within the range of selection—it plainly shows the estimation in which Nicholas was held that he was chosen to execute such an important trust at that extraordinary epoch in the state of parties.

Nicholas took his seat in the Senate of the United States on the 3d day of January, 1800, just after Henry Lee, his associate in the House of Delegates, had delivered his eloquent eulogy on the death of Washington before both houses of Congress.   The first vote which he gave was to strike out from a bill to regulate disputed presidential elections part of the first clause, which assigned certain duties in the premises to the Chief Justice, or, in his absence, to the next oldest judge.   The motion to strike out failed by a vote of eleven to nineteen; and Nicholas had an opportunity of knowing, for the first time, how men feel who vote in a minority.   The next subject he was called to vote upon was a resolution, offered by Tracy (of Connecticut), instructing the Committee of Privileges and Elections to inquire who was the editor of the *Aurora* newspaper, how he came in possession of a copy of the bill prescribing the mode of deciding disputed presidential elections, published in one of the numbers of his paper, and how he knew this and how he knew that; and to report the answers to the Senate.   Cocke (of Tennessee) made a strong, common-sense speech against it, and was followed in a very elaborate harangue by Charles Pinckney, who showed the utter futility and inexpediency of making war upon the press. When several members had spoken, it was moved to postpone the resolution till the following Tuesday; but the motion failed by a vote of nine to nineteen; Nicholas and his colleague, Stevens Thomson Mason, in the minority. Nicholas then rose and asked for information. Was it intended by this resolution to charge the committee with inquiring into a breach of privilege, as it respected a majority of this body? For the resolution itself furnished no correct idea on this point. He wished also to know whether it was intended that the Senate should declare that the publication was a breach of privilege. Tracy, the author of the resolution, made an evasive reply. Humphrey Marshall then proposed to amend it by instructing the committee to make similar inquiries about a publication in a Federal paper, which he pronounced a hundred-fold more outrageous than the article in the *Aurora;* but his amendment was voted down—Nicholas sustaining it.

On the 8th of March the original resolution passed, unamended, by a vote of nineteen to eight—Nicholas and Mason in the minority. The report of the committee was made on the 18th, and concluded with a resolution that pronounced the article in the *Aurora* to be false, defamatory, and scandalous, and tending to defame the Senate and excite against them the hatred of the people of the United States. The resolution was agreed to by a vote of twenty to eight—Nicholas and Mason opposing it. The report in full was adopted on the 20th by a vote of eighteen to ten—Nicholas and Mason in the minority.[304] Then a committee was appointed to prepare a form of proceedings for the trial of Duane, the editor of the *Aurora;* but, as I have already detailed these miserable proceedings in another place,[305] it is only necessary to say that Nicholas voted throughout on the side of the freedom of the press. Indeed, he must have contrasted painfully the freedom of the press and of speech, with which he had been familiar in Virginia, with the odious tyranny which was sought to be visited upon an editor by so grave a body as the Senate of the United States.

The next question which the Senate discussed was the amendment of the judicial system of the Union. A bill to amend the act to establish the judicial courts of the United States was

---

[304] For the report and resolution, and the subsequent proceedings in the case, see *Benton's Debates*, Vol. II, 422.

[305] In the sketch of Stevens Thomson Mason.

brought in by Charles Pinckney on the 5th of March, was explained and enforced by that gentleman with much plausibility and at considerable length, and referred to a committee, which reported certain amendments. Nicholas in vain strove to modify its details, and the bill passed to its third reading. It ultimately passed both houses, became a law, and was repealed in 1802, when Nicholas was present and voted for the repeal. But I must not anticipate.

The Senate resumed its session on the 17th of November, 1799, but Nicholas did not appear until the 25th. One of the first duties to be performed by the Senate was to examine the electoral votes for President and Vice-President. A resolution, which was strongly characteristic of the temper of a majority of the body, that had spent a large part of its last session in perse-cuting a poor printer, was offered February 10, 1800, to pro-hibit any person from being admitted into the gallery when the two houses shall proceed to count the electoral votes for Presi-dent and Vice-President. Why the few people who might hap-pen to be in Washington, in which the session of Congress was now held for the first time, and which was a sheer wilderness, should not be allowed the gratification of overlooking from the gallery so interesting a procedure, can only be explained on the ground that the Federal majority, which was conscious that the sceptre was about to pass from its hands, were fearful of a shout, or a smile, or a sneer from the victors. The proceeding was the more disreputable, as the two houses were to assemble in the Senate chamber, and each had a right to be consulted in the premises. The resolution was carried by a vote of sixteen to ten—Nicholas and Mason voting in the minority, and in favor of that policy which prevails with universal acceptance in our times. The House of Representatives on the same day notified the Senate that they would attend on Wednesday next for the purpose of being present at the opening and counting of the votes, and that they had appointed Rutledge and John Nicholas tellers on their part. The Senate then appointed Wells (of Delaware) their teller. On the 11th the votes were counted, and the result was that Thomas Jefferson and Aaron Burr had received seventy-three each; that John Adams had received sixty-five; that Charles Cotesworth Pinckney had received sixty-four; and that John Jay had received one.

As the number of votes received by Jefferson and Burr was the same, the office of the Senate was performed, and the decision devolved on the House of Representatives. On the 18th that House informed the Senate that Thomas Jefferson had been chosen by them as President of the United States for the term commencing on the 4th of March next. In this decision Nicholas saw the triumph of the party to which he was attached, and in the conduct of which he was to lend his influence till the close of his life.

Though ruled by a stern majority, Nicholas was occasionally placed on important committees that were raised during the session. He was one of the committee to which was referred the bill to prohibit the Secretary of the Navy from carrying on any business of trade, commerce, or navigation. He also reported the bill providing for a naval peace establishment, with amendments, which were concurred in by the Senate. The bill passed unanimously. On the 3d the session terminated, but the Senate was immediately convoked by the new President in its executive capacity, and sat for two days.

When the Seventh Congress assembled in the city of Washington, on the 7th day of December, 1801, Nicholas appeared in his seat on the first day of the session. Heretofore neither himself nor his colleague had been very punctual in their attendance, as it was known that no vote of a Republican member was likely to affect the fate of any question before the Senate; but the case was now altered, and every Democratic vote was needed to sustain the Government. The first reform of the new administration was a personal one, affecting the President as an individual. Up to this period it had been customary for that officer to deliver his opening speech before the two houses in joint session. The speech was responded to by an address from the houses. This address called forth a letter of acknowledgment from the President. But the good sense of Jefferson impelled him to put an end to a custom which, however appropriate in a strictly parliamentary government like that of England, was inconvenient and often embarrassing here, and he accordingly accompanied his message[306] to the heads of the two houses with an explanatory

---

[306] Though the first message to Congress was delivered orally, all other communications from the President during the session were in writing.

note. Henceforth all the communications between the Executive and the legislative departments were to be in writing.

The first regular skirmish between the rival parties occurred on a resolution to admit stenographers within the area of the Senate, at the discretion of the President in respect of the place in which they should sit. The resolution passed at first without a division, but a motion was made to reconsider, which prevailed by a vote of seventeen to nine; all the Federal members, in the hope of curtailing the privilege, and some of the Republicans, in the hope of enlarging it, voting in the affirmative. Nicholas, however, opposed the motion, fearing lest, in the nicely-balanced state of parties, the liberal purpose of the resolution might be trenched upon. Nor were his suspicions vain; for a motion was immediately made by a Federal member to exact from each stenographer a bond in a certain sum, with two sureties for a certain sum, as a pledge for his good conduct. The amendment was lost—nearly all the Federal and wavering members voting for it. The resolution was then amended to include note-takers as well as stenographers, by a vote of sixteen to twelve, and ultimately passed without division.

It is profitable to recur to the various gradations by which we have reached the freedom we now enjoy. Every theory of a republican government should seem to involve a public procedure of its representatives; as otherwise their actions could not be known until it was too late to prevent a mischievous result. But our reasoning and experience on this subject had been derived from England, where, even to this moment, a standing order of the House of Commons, though fallen into disuse, prohibits the publication of their debates without the formal consent of the House itself or of its Speaker. When Lord Campbell was about to publish the first volumes of the *Lives of the Lord Chancellors*, he thought it prudent to move the repeal of a rule of the House of Lords which prohibited any one from writing the life of a lord or officer of that House without the consent of the House or of the representatives of the deceased. As he could not easily learn who were the descendents of Augmendus, the Chancellor of Ethelbert, or even the representatives of William of Wickham, without certainly subjecting himself to the charge of a breach of privilege, he obtained the abrogation of the rule in question. From the commencement of the sessions of the Senate of the United States, in April, 1789, to the 20th of

February, 1794—a space of five years—that body imitated the example of the old Congress, and sat alike in its executive and legislative capacity with closed doors.   Experience is a wise teacher; and we owe much that is permanent and valuable in our institutions to the caution which its lessons have enjoined; yet there is great difficulty in determining what is taught in a given case.   It is honorable to the Republican party that, while experience and prejudice might seem to lean against them, they opened, without hesitation, the doors of the Senate to the people and admitted reporters on its floor.

The repeal of the judiciary act of the last session was now agitated in the Senate.   Mason, the colleague of Nicholas, moved (January 6, 1802) the reading of that part of the President's message relating to the judiciary; and when the reading was ended, Breckenridge rose and moved that the act passed at the last session respecting the judiciary establishment be repealed. The resolution was considered on the 8th of January—a day fatal to the Federal party—when its author explained his views in a speech of unusual ability.   He was followed in opposition by Governor Morris, who was replied to by Jackson (of Georgia). Tracy followed in opposition, and was succeeded by Mason, who, by considerations drawn from the Constitution, from the practice of the States, and from public convenience and expediency, justified the repeal.   He was followed by Olcott in opposition, who was replied to by Cocke.   Morris again took the floor in an elaborate and brilliant oration, mainly in reply to Mason.   It was not until the 3d of February that the debate ended, when the motion to repeal the judiciary act was carried by a vote of sixteen to fifteen—Nicholas and Mason in the affirmative.[307]

When the vote was about to be taken on referring the bill to repeal the judiciary act to a committee—a measure recommended and enforced by its enemies—and after an able appeal by Calhoun (of South Carolina) in favor of reference, Nicholas, whose skill as a party manager was held in high respect, rose to speak

---

[307] I have made this summary of the debate from Benton's second volume; but Mr. Benton's account is very imperfect and cannot convey the faintest impression of the interest excited in the several stages of the bill.   A tolerably fair account may be seen in the little volume published by Bronson in 1802, where the ayes and noes are always given.

to the point. He said he flattered himself that the subject was well understood by the Senate. "What is now the question? The same that has been so often decided. Gentlemen in oppo- sition have said, 'Amend, but do not repeal.' He could say that every vote of that House, in every stage of the discussion, had said, 'Repeal, and do not amend.' He believed the old system required but little amendment. It was the best suited to the interests of the United States and of the States. The law of the last session was in fact a bar to improvement. Gentlemen say why not provide for these judges as you have provided for a judge of the Supreme Court. He would reply that the last operation was simple and easy of execution; but how were we in this new mode to get rid of the circuit judges without having these courts in one part of the Union and not in another? The gentlemen from New Jersey has said this measure is admitted to be bold and violent. By whom is it admitted? Not by me or by gentlemen who think with me. As regards the Constitu- tion, there is no man here—let his boast of federalism be what it may—that can take stronger ground than I hold. Gentlemen profess a great respect for the Constitution; but our principles are not to be evidenced by mere professions. They are to be evidenced by the series of our actions." "My conduct," said Nicholas, "since the formation of the Constitution to this day, is known by those who know me, as well as the conduct of gentlemen is known by those who know them. To the people I appeal. I am not to be alarmed by the tocsin of hostility to the Constitution that is so loudly sounded in our ears. I hope, sir, we shall have the question."

When Nicholas took his seat the question was taken on referring the bill to a committee, and the vote was a tie—fifteen to fifteen—when the Vice-President gave the casting vote on the, affirmative with a distinct declaration that he regarded the purposes of its opponents to be sincere; but that if he saw that it was only meant to defeat the bill he would vote accord- ingly.[308]

At the close of Ogden's speech, after Wright and Jackson had made some explanations, Nicholas again rose to speak, with a copy of the Constitution in his hand, but seeing that Brecken-

---

[308] (*Debates on the Judiciary Bill*, by Bronson, page 256.)

ridge had the floor, took his seat.[309] On the 3d of May the Senate adjourned.

In the December session (1802) Nicholas was early in his seat, and took an active part in the leading questions of the times. The first of a party caste that engaged the attention of the Senate was the memorial of the judges who were appointed under the judiciary act of 1800, which had been repealed at the last session. The form in which it presented itself was that of a resolution from a committee, requesting the President of the United States to cause an information, in the nature of a *quo warranto*, to be filed by the Attorney-General against Richard Bassett, one of the judges, for the purpose of deciding judicially on their claims. The resolution, after a long debate, was rejected by a vote of thirteen to fifteen—Nicholas in the majority. The great political topic of the session was the subject of the Mississippi. Spain had ceded the province of Louisiana to France, and our right of deposit at New Orleans had been suspended. The Executive communicated the facts to the Senate in a message, which at the same time nominated Robert R. Livingston as Minister Plenipotentiary and James Monroe as Minister Extraordinary and Plenipotentiary to France and Spain, to arrange the difficulty by negotiation. In a few days a bill came up from the House of Representatives making further provision for the expenses attending the intercourse between the United States and foreign nations. The object of the bill was to authorize the purchase of the island of New Orleans only; for at this time the purchase of all Louisiana, though doubtless entertained by Mr. Jefferson, had not been communicated to either house. The purpose to be accomplished by the bill was of transcendant importance to the whole country as closing a troublesome question, likely at any moment to lead to war, and to the Western States in particular; but it appealed in vain to the Federal minority. The vote on its passage was fourteen to twelve, Nicholas and his colleague (Mason) ably sustaining it. Mason's speech on its several stages is preserved, but that of Nicholas, though referred to in debate, is probably lost. The subject of the Mississippi called forth the last speech of Mason, who died a few weeks later in Philadelphia; but he could not have spoken

---

[309] *Ibid*, page 312.

on a grander or more glorious topic, and I could have wished
that he had lived to learn that by the present bill the vast domain
of Louisiana was in a few weeks forever secured to his country.

While this wise and politic measure was under discussion,
Ross, of Pennsylvania (a Federal member), introduced a proposition of his own on the Mississippi question, which appeared to
go far beyond the administration in avenging the wrongs and
in securing the rights of the West, but which, in fact, was ingeniously designed either to force the administration into an
immediate war with Spain or France, or to expose it to a for-
feiture of the affection and support of the Western people. No
member of the Senate was more capable of detecting and
exposing such a tortuous policy than Nicholas, who, though
unwell, spoke with his usual tact on the question. The proposition of Ross was met by one from Breckenridge, which made
it acceptable to the administration, and which was adopted by a
strict party vote. Nicholas warmly sustained the amendment,
and, the question recurring on the resolution as amended, it
passed unanimously—a remarkable instance in which the opposition, by seeking to thwart the administration by outdoing it
on its own ground, was forced to play into its hands and to further its most darling purposes.

The Eighth Congress assembled in Washington on the 17th of
October, having been convened by a proclamation of the President in consequence of the purchase of Louisiana. Nicholas
was present on the first day, and must have heard, with a just
pride, the Clerk of the Senate read the message of his friend and
neighbor, which announced in graceful and modest terms the
consummation of that great event. John Taylor (of Caroline)
had succeeded Mason by an executive appointment, and until
the arrival of his successor,[310] and afforded Nicholas the aid of
his great abilities at that difficult conjuncture. The first movement on the subject of the treaty was made by Breckenridge,
who gave notice on the 21st that he would ask leave next day to
bring in a bill to enable the President to take possession of the
territories ceded by France to the United States by the treaty
concluded in Paris on the 20th of April last, and for other pur-

---

[310] Abraham B. Venable, who lost his life at the burning of the Richmond Theatre on the evening of December 26, 1811.

poses, which was brought in accordingly, and in due time became a law.

The proceedings of the House of Representatives during the late presidential election, when it was doubtful for some time whether the person who had received seventy-three votes—a majority of all the votes—for the office of President should be chosen in preference of one who had not received a single *bona-fide* vote for the office, were well calculated to excite alarm, and seem to render an amendment to the Constitution indispensable to prevent the possible recurrence of such a crisis. A resolution was accordingly brought forward by DeWitt Clinton respecting an amendment to the Constitution respecting the election of President, and was referred to a committee, of which Nicholas was a member. When the report came up, on the 23d of November, Nicholas moved to strike out all following the seventh line of the report to the end, and insert an amendment which he held in his hand, and which was substantially the same as that subsequently engrafted upon the Constitution. The motion to strike out was agreed to unanimously, and the amendment was adopted. The bill passed the Senate by a vote of twenty-two to ten, was ultimately ratified by the States, and will effectually prevent the mischief it was designed to remedy. The debate on the bill was very able—John Taylor (of Caroline) making the closing speech, and winding up by quoting the lines recited by a member in the House of Commons in the debate on the bill to exclude the Duke of York (afterwards James the Second) from the succession:

> " I hear a lion in the lobby roar;
> Say, Mr. Speaker, shall we shut the door
> And keep him there ? Or let him in,
> To try if we can get him out again ? "

One of the most interesting debates of the session occurred on the bill authorizing the creation of a stock of eleven million two hundred and fifty thousand dollars for the payment of the purchase-money of Louisiana. It was warmly opposed by White, Wells, Pickering, Dayton, Tracy, and others, and was warmly supported by Wythe, Taylor (of Caroline), Breckenridge, and Nicholas. The bill finally passed by a vote of twenty-six to five, some of the Federal members having changed their minds during the discussion. Nicholas closed the debate as follows:

"The gentlemen on the other side, Mr. President, differ among themselves. The two gentlemen from Delaware say that if peaceable possession of Louisiana is given, this bill ought to pass; the other gentlemen who have spoken in opposition to it have declared that if they believed the Constitution not violated by the treaty they should think themselves bound to vote for the bill. To this Senate it cannot be necessary to answer arguments denying the power of the Government to make such a treaty; it has already been affirmed, so far as we could affirm it, by two-thirds of the body. It is, then, only now necessary to show that we ought to pass the bill at this time. In addition to the reasons which have been so ably and forcibly urged by my friends, I will remark that the treaty-making power of this Government is so limited that engagements to pay money cannot be carried into effect without the consent and co-operation of Congress. This was solemnly decided, after a long discussion of several weeks, by the House of Representatives, which made the appropriations for carrying the British treaty into effect, and such, I believe, is the understanding of nine-tenths of the American people as to the construction of their Constitution. This decision must also be known to foreigners; and if not, they are bound to know the extent of the powers of the Government with which they treat. If this bill should be rejected, I ask gentlemen whether they believe that France would or ought to execute the treaty on her part? It is known to the French Government that the President and Senate cannot create stock, nor provide for the payment of either principal or interest of stock; and if that Government should be informed that a bill authorizing the issue of stock to pay for the purchase ' after possession shall be delivered,' had been rejected by the only department of our Government competent to the execution of that part of the treaty, they would have strong ground to suspect that we did not mean to execute the treaty on our part, particularly when they are informed that the arguments most pressed in opposition to the bill were grounded upon a belief that the Government of the United States had not a constitutional power to execute the treaty. Of one thing I am confident, that if they have the distrust of us which some gentlemen have this day expressed of them, the country will not be delivered to the agents of our Government should this bill be rejected. The gentleman from

Connecticut (Tracy) must consider the grant of power to the Legislature as a limitation of the treaty-making power; for he says that 'the power to admit new States and to make citizens is given to Congress and not to the treaty-making power'; there-fore, an engagement in a treaty to do either of those things is unconstitutional. I cannot help expressing my surprise at that gentleman's giving that opinion, and I think myself justifiable in saying that if it is now his opinion, it was not always so. The contrary opinion is the only justification of that gentleman's approbation of the British treaty, and of his vote for carrying it into effect. By that treaty a great number of persons had a right to become American citizens immediately, not only with-out a law, but contrary to an existing law. And by that treaty many of the powers specially given to Congress were exercised by the treaty-making power. It is for gentlemen who supported that treaty to reconcile the construction given by them to the Constitution in its application to that instrument with their exposition of it at this time.

"If," he continued, "the third article of the treaty is an engagement to incorporate the territory of Louisiana into the union of the United States and to make it a State, it cannot be considered as an unconstitutional exercise of the treaty-making power; for it will not be asserted by any rational man that the territory is incorporated as a State by the treaty itself, when it is expressly declared that 'the inhabitants shall be incorporated in the union of the United States and admitted as soon as possi-ble, according to the principles of the Federal Constitution'; evidently referring the question of incorporation, in whatever character it was to take place, to the competent authority, and leaving to that authority to do it at such time and in such man-ner as they may think proper. If, as some gentlemen suppose, Congress possess this power, they are free to exercise it in the manner they may think most conducive to the public good. If it can only be done by an amendment of the Constitution, it is a matter of discretion with the States whether they will do it or not; for it cannot be done 'according to the principles of the Federal Constitution' if the Congress or the States are deprived of that discretion which is given to the first, and secured to the last, by the Constitution. In the third section of the fourth article of the Constitution it is said 'new States may be admitted by the Congress into this Union.' If Congress have the power, it is derived from this source; for there are no other words in the Constitution that can, by any construction that can be given to them, be considered as conveying this power.[311] If Congress have not the power, the constitutional mode would be by an amendment to the Constitution. If it should be conceded, then, that the admission of this territory into the Union as a State was in the contemplation of the contracting parties, it must be understood with the reservation of the right of this Congress or of the States to do it or not. The words 'admitted as soon as possible' must refer to the voluntary admission in one of the two modes that I have mentioned; for in no other way can a State be admitted into this Union.''

The bill erecting Louisiana into two territories produced a long and most animated discussion, but ultimately passed by a vote of twenty to five—Nicholas sustaining the bill. He also voted with the majority (seventeen to twelve) on the bill to repeal the bankrupt law. Another act of the session—unimportant in itself, but frequently referred to—was the passage of the bill to alter and establish certain post-roads. The last section provided that two post-roads should be laid out under the inspection of commissioners appointed by the President—one to lead from Tellico block-house (in the State of Tennessee), and the other from Jackson court-house (in the State of Georgia), by routes the most eligible and as nearly direct as the nature of the ground will admit, to New Orleans. The bill had been referred to a committee, of which Nicholas was chairman. The vote on adding the last section to the bill was seventeen to ten; the minority voting on anti-Louisiana grounds and not from any constitutional scruple about the laying out of roads by Federal commissioners. It passed without a division.

On the 13th of March John Randolph (of Virginia) and Peter Early (of Georgia) appeared at the bar of the Senate, and, in the name of the House of Representatives and of all the people of the United States, impeached Judge Samuel Chase of high crimes and misdemeanors; and the Senate took the initiatory

---

[311] If Governor Nicholas had lived to read the admirable review of this doctrine in a report on the American Colonization Society by Governor Tazewell, to be found in the United States Senate Documents of 1828, he would have taken broader ground on the subject.

steps for a trial, which took place at the following session. Nor should we omit to say, in closing a review of the session, that the Senate, on the 21st of October, resolved to go into a mourning of thirty days for Stevens Thomson Mason.

At the close of the session Nicholas, from the state of his private affairs, resigned his seat in the Senate. He fondly believed that, in the repeal of the judiciary and bankrupt laws, in the final settlement of the Mississippi question, which had, ever since the Declaration of Independence, harassed our councils—State and Federal—by the acquisition of Louisiana, and in the growing popularity of the administration, which had now secured a predominant majority in both branches of the legislature, a long period of comparative repose was to be enjoyed by his political friends, and that he was fairly entitled to a release from public life. He also knew that his seat in the Senate would be filled by Mr. Giles, his intimate personal friend, who was fully competent to sustain the administration on the floor of that body. But these pleasant anticipations were not to be fulfilled in all their extent. The extraordinary success of the administration in its measures of domestic policy had almost annihilated opposition; but the party which had kept together in the face of an able and relentless foe was now to disagree within itself and to present a divided front to the enemy, which, though overpowered, was ever ready to show itself on the least chance of success.[312]

This is not the place to detail at length the causes which led to a split in the Republican party during the administration of Jefferson. The measures which the administration was compelled to adopt, in consequence of the arbitrary and piratical conduct of England and France, were the ostensible grounds of the schism; but it was then, and is now, believed that private griefs had no little share in making the breach. However this may be, one of the most eloquent friends of the administration became its bitterest enemy, and, leaguing with his old foes, not only opposed the measures of the party to which he still professed to belong, but sought most earnestly to involve the country

---

[312] On resigning his seat in the Senate, Colonel Nicholas accepted the appointment of collector of the port of Norfolk and Portsmouth, but held it for a short time only.

in a war with Spain, and, from the connection then existing between Spain and France, with France also. How far this feud might possibly extend it was difficult to foretell; and it became important—not only in respect of the administration as of the establishment of the party throughout the Union—that the policy of the eloquent and able, though meagre, minority should be counteracted by efficient management in the House of Representatives.

At this crisis it was the general wish of his party that Nicholas, whose popularity made all offices equally open to him, should again appear in Congress. He received intimations of the public will from various quarters, and he was pressed by Mr. Jefferson in the strongest terms to become a member of the House of Representatives, in which "his talents and standing, taken together, would have weight enough to give him the lead." [313] And that standing was indeed high. It was well known that he had repeatedly declined the most honorable and profitable foreign missions, and lately the mission to France, and that he could obtain not only any office in the gift of the Executive for himself, but could exert a great influence in getting offices for other people. He was accordingly returned from the Albemarle district in 1808, and his presence was soon felt to some extent in debate, but mainly by an efficient management which tended to thwart all the cherished plans of the Republican seceders, and to fix the Republicans in power for years to come. The seceders, who were commonly called *tertium quids*, felt that their day was over, that their real influence was henceforth gone, and that their only alternative was, whether they regarded the present or the future, to unite themselves permanently with their Federal allies, or, caps in hand, to beg readmission into the fold from which they had been tempted to stray. But, mean time, their tender mercies, when it was safe to bestow them, fell on Nicholas. He was a cousin of Sir Robert Walpole and a blood-relative of Talleyrand. He was more of an Italian than an Anglo-Saxon, and, if not really descended from Machiavelli—who had not yet been placed *rectus in historia*—he was one of his most dangerous pupils. Posterity can form an opinion of the character of a public man from the caricatures and gibes of his enemies almost

---

[313] (*Jefferson's Works*, Randolph's edition, Vol. IV, 66.)

as well as from the eulogies of friends, and it is the duty of history to preserve the hostile portrait for its reflection and examination. A sketch of Nicholas, which originally appeared in the Washington *Republican*, and is drawn by a bitter but witty enemy, may amuse the reader:

"The opinion is certainly entertained, and has been often confidently advanced by some who knew him well, and who are also acquainted with the character of Talleyrand, that our 'Virginia woodsman' surpassed the French diplomatist in the talent which rendered him most useful to his friends and most formidable to his foes. Though he never gave any great proofs of scholarship within my knowledge, I am satisfied that he enjoyed the advantages of a good classical education, at the least, and that nature gave him a mind of most gigantic power is doubted by none. Mr. Nicholas's ambition knew no bounds; for its gratification he sought popularity 'in his own way' with a perseverance and a clearness of judgment almost unexampled. He was always proverbially plain in his dress and in his manners—two of Wisdom's important steps to reach the hearts of the people. He was, in general, grave and reserved, and sometimes would appear to be even morose and grum—infallible means of establishing with the public a full credit for all the talents he possessed; and the certain means of enhancing, even to fascination, the value of an agreeable smile, or marked familiarity, in which he occasionally indulged with the happiest success. Our country never, perhaps, gave birth to a man better acquainted with all the avenues to the human heart; and few have profited more than Mr. Nicholas for a long while did by the command of that rare and invaluable species of knowledge. The wise and the simple, the learned and the unlearned, were alike at his pleasure—mere automata in his hands. Among other endowments he seemed also sometimes to possess the power of ubiquity; for often has he been politically seen and felt at the same moment in places very different and very distant from one another; and, what almost surpasses belief, he found in our modern hard times, when standing on the verge of bankruptcy, no difficulty in laying the wisest and most cautious of our citizens under contribution. * * * I will conclude this letter with the recital of an anecdote relating to the adroitness with which, while in the House of Representatives, he some-

times managed certain members of that body. It is said that
on some occasion of great importance when a measure was
depending before Congress, the adoption of which Mr. Nicholas
had much at heart, having just recovered, he said, from a fit of
the gout, well muffled in an old-fashioned dress, he sallied forth
in quest of recruits; and no statesman, to be sure, possessed a
happier talent for enlisting speakers and voters by the exercise
of what is called out-of-door influence than he did. The first
boarding-house to which he repaired was filled with members of
Congress from ———— and ————. Upon entering the apart-
ment occupied as a drawing-room by the honorable gentlemen,
very much in the style of a plain, unceremonious farmer, the
members, rising, generally welcome their visitor with great polite-
ness. As soon as he was seated he complained, in a manner
quite familiar and good-natured, that his worthy friends had
neglected him whilst afflicted with the gout, declaring at the
same time he would not have treated them so unkindly. They,
of course, all apologized, and the sufficiency of their excuses
was readily admitted. Next, with the seeming artlessness and
cordiality of a good, well-meaning country gentleman, he inquired
after their families, and then discoursed of plantation matters
and on such other subjects as he found to be most agreeable.
Whilst all were yet charmed by the conversation of their guest
he rose, and, taking a most friendly leave of the gentlemen
individually, obtained from each a promise soon to return his
call. At the threshold of the door, departing, he suddenly
paused, and turning hastily about, as if just then struck with a
new thought, which it was his duty as a friend to communicate,
he exclaimed: 'O! Mr. ————, have you reflected on the great,
the important question now before Congress?' alluding to the
very measure which so deeply interested himself. To which Mr.
———— replied: 'No, Colonel, I confess I have not.' Where-
upon Mr. Nicholas rejoined: 'Good God, sir, is it possible that
a gentleman of your talents, one who ought to take the lead in
every great question discussed in Congress, one whom I had
always believed to be remarkably attentive to all subjects of a
public nature, but more especially to those which immediately
concerned his own district or State—is it possible, sir, that you
have overlooked this question, important, it is true, to the public
at large, but more particularly so to the State from which you

come?' Then, turning to all the members who were listening *auribus erectis*, he added: 'Aye, gentlemen, in the highest degree important to both of your States.' And by a plausible short oration Mr. Nicholas proceeded to convince his delighted hearers that all which he had said to them was perfectly ortho-dox; for the Colonel, like many other politicians of weight, was admirably good at a short speech in a small circle, whilst it is certain that he never did distinguish himself as an orator in either house of Congress. Mr. Nicholas, in fine, had the good fortune to obtain from every member whom he thus addressed an assurance that he would attend whenever the important mea-sure should be called up, and give it, at least, the support of his vote. As to poor Mr. ———, he then for the first time in his life, under the light shed upon the subject by Mr. Nicholas, dis-covered that his endowments were most rich and splendid and his acquirements most valuable and unlimited—fitting him as an orator for the highest niche in the Temple of Fame. He, of course, promised not only to vote, but to speak on the import-ant measure. Highly gratified with the result of his visit and harangue to so many of the members of two influential States, Mr. Nicholas, bowing a second time more profoundly than before, again took an affectionate leave of his friends, reminding them severally of their promise to return his call. In like man-ner, and with like success generally, Mr. Nicholas visited many other boarding-houses where members of Congress lodged, and in several of them, as in the first he had visited, found those whom he convinced by a few judicious remarks and compli-ments, exactly suited to the taste and mind of each, that they were among the most eloquent of all the members of Congress. It was afterwards no difficult task to satisfy each of those inflated orators that it was a sacred duty which he owed to himself and his country no longer 'to hide his light under a bushel.' These *novi homines* promised, of course, to speak as well as to vote in favor of the important measure. Thus had Mr. Nicho-las, after recovering from a fit of the gout, under which he thought much more than he suffered, in very good time made every arrangement necessary to carry his favorite measure.

"'He that hath ears to hear let him hear' is an injunction which is believed to have been always as scrupulously observed by the celebrated statesman 'of Roanoke' as any other precept

contained in the sacred volume; and he saw and heard enough,
in relation to what had passed at the boarding-houses, perfectly
to comprehend the whole game in all its depth which Mr.
Nicholas had been playing. Finally the important measure was
called up, and Mr. Nicholas, his orators, and other friends being
all in their places, Mr. ——— (of ———) rose and addressed
the House at some length in favor of the measure in a neat
speech, but more animated than the occasion seemed to require.
He was followed by Mr. ——— (of ———), who spoke with
considerable ability in opposition. Then, in regular succession,
one after another, rose some half a dozen more of Mr. Nicholas's
orators. Such thundering and declamation! On such a question, too! 'Sure, the like was never heard before!' During all
this time Mr. Nicholas, who felt in reality more solicitude for
the fate of the question than all Congress besides, with muscles
unmoved, sat at his desk folding up newspapers and copies of
documents and addressing them to his constituents, seeming all
the while to be just as unconcerned as if he were entirely ignorant of the subject under consideration. All this was observed
by the statesman 'of Roanoke,' who, sitting in his place with
folded arms, and looking sometimes at Mr. Nicholas and sometimes at his orators, at length touched a friend near him and
said, with a point and an energy peculiar to himself: 'The
master-spirit that acts on this occasion is invisible.' Then,
pointing carelessly to Mr. Nicholas, with a significant look, he
added: ''Tis Signor Falconi who, from behind the curtain, plays
off these puppets upon us' (pointing to Mr. Nicholas's orators).
The hit was so excellent that, ever afterwards, to the day of his
death, Mr. Nicholas was known to many persons by his new
name chiefly. I presume you have not forgotten that, some
years ago, the eminence of Signor Falconi in conducting puppet
shows was unrivalled, and that he was acknowledged to be the
'emperor universal' over all rope-dancers and jugglers wherever
to be found.'' [314]

---

[314] *Letters on the Richmond Party*, page 15—a duodecimo of forty-
eight pages. They were published originally in the Washington *Republican* in 1823. Their design is to show that the active members of the
Democratic party, in office since 1794, were connected by blood or
affinity with one another, and that their true object was rather a love
of the loaves and fishes than any particular affection for the principles

But mark the result! The orator, whose brilliant eloquence, keen wit, and blighting sarcasm held his hearers spell-bound as long and as often as he spoke, and not unfrequently against their will, rarely or never won a vote; was, after years of recruiting, seldom in command of a larger squad than the boat's crew of a custom house tender—and that squad ever ready to run off at any moment when the eye of the basilisk was turned from them; gained whatever victories he may be said to have gained in contests with his own friends, whose general principles he professed to approve, but whom he followed with immortal hate; saw the glittering prizes of successful ambition which he would have delighted to grasp and sport at St. Cloud, and, above all, at St. James's, and, in his excursions through England, at the sepulchres of his sires, casting back upon the ancestral dust the westering radiance of the name—these trophies he saw borne off, one by one, from his reach; was, after years of isolation, again united with his old friends, who, when his last sands were running, when the "church-yard cough" was racking a frame never stout enough for the eagle spirit which it encaged, bestowed upon him the empty office, which he accepted, but which he was unable to discharge, of appearing at the court of men whom he had constantly ridiculed as "ruffians in 'off,'" and of exposing a constitution which required the balm of the tropics to the snows of the arctic zone. How different was the fortune of Nicholas! He was a plain, substantial farmer, not looking to a public career as the staple of life or as a scene of ambition; no orator, in the higher sense of the word, though a strong, well-informed, and ready speaker, always keeping the main point in view and sitting down when he was done, and ever from his sense and position uttering well-weighed words and retaining the erect ear of the House; yet receiving, during a life running through the third of a century, almost every honor which Virginia and the Federal Executive could bestow; declining instantaneously the most dazzling of them all, that would take him abroad from his fireside and from his fields, and holding those at home only long enough

---

which they professed. The letters are written with no inconsiderable ability, and with some force and grace of style, and were the source of much mirth at their date, and of some severe denunciations from those who were honored with the special attentions of the writer. Thirty years ago I heard them attributed to Mr. Macrae.

to accomplish some important result; and by his wonderful fore-
cast, by his broad common sense, by his extraordinary tact, and
by his comprehensive wisdom, composing the stripes and confirming the union of that great party, which, beginning its
triumphs with the opening century, has ruled, with slight intervals, the destinies of the country to the present hour, which has
achieved so many remarkable and glorious results, and which
owes a debt to the memory of Nicholas that it will be ever ready
to acknowledge and ever prompt to pay; and, victorious to the
last, retiring from the chair of the Governor (which he filled at
a remarkable epoch), while he was yet pressed to remain, to the
bosom of his lovely family, there to descend in peace to the
tomb.

In resuming the thread of my narrative, I borrow the pen of a
female descendant of Colonel Nicholas, which touches nothing
that it does not adorn.   Alluding to the reasons which led him
to resign his seat in the Senate, she says:

"All the great changes contemplated by his party having been
accomplished, and the dispute about the right of deposit at New
Orleans adjusted without a war with Spain by the acquisition of
the whole of Louisiana, Colonel Nicholas thought that he might,
without any dereliction of duty, resign his seat in the Senate ;
which step was imperatively demanded by the state of his private
affairs, now seriously embarrassed.   To these he continued to
devote himself for a time with great assiduity—his success in
agriculture bearing witness to the skill and energy with which its
operations were conducted.   In 1806 he refused a special mission
to France to ratify, under the auspices of Napoleon, the treaty
with Spain.   But in 1809 the necessity of having some one
'whose talents and standing, taken together, would have weight
enough to give him the lead,' brought on him such urgent
appeals to his patriotism that he was forced to yield.   He
became a candidate for Congress, and was elected without
opposition.

"The period was momentous and highly critical.   The aggres-
sions of England in the attack on the Chesapeake, and the exten-
sion of the orders of the King in council, and afterwards the
application by France of the Berlin and Milan decrees to our
commerce, imposed upon us the necessity of resistance.   But,
pursuant to the pacific policy which had governed our councils

during a period of unparalleld aggression on the part of Great Britain—a period extending back as far as 1793—our Government proposed an embargo. The country was at that time in a wholly defenceless state; we had but the skeleton of an army, few or no ships in commission, no military stores, with an immense value of property afloat, and our whole seaboard, from north to south, open to attack. Under these circumstances Mr. Nicholas united cordially in support of the embargo, willing to try its efficiency for a while as a coercive measure, but relying on it more as giving us time to prepare for other measures. In 1807 he assured his constituents that, in case of the failure of the embargo to produce some speedy change in the policy of France and Great Britain, the only alternative offered was of base and abject submission or determined resistance. In his circular to them, as well as from his seat in Congress, he urged the necessity of raising men and money, and providing immediately everything necessary for war. In the fall of 1808 he wrote to Mr. Jefferson urging him in the strongest terms, unless there was a moral certainty of a favorable change in our affairs before the meeting of Congress, to announce to them in his message that our great object in laying the embargo had been effected. Having gained that, he said, nothing more was to be effected from it, and it ought to be raised, and other measures, such as the honor of the State required, resorted to; that our people would not much longer bear the embargo, and that we could not and ought not to think of abandoning the resistance we were so solemnly pledged to make.

"In 1809 Mr. Nicholas was again elected to Congress, and served in the spring session, when the agreement with Mr. Erskine produced a delusive calm. In the fall of that year, on his way to Washington, he had so violent an attack of rheumatism that he was compelled to resign his seat, and was confined to his room for four months. He was now so convinced of the impracticability of enforcing any commercial restrictions, of their demoralizing effect upon the people, and their exhausting effect on the finances of the country, that he frequently avowed his determination never again to vote for any measure of the kind, except as preparatory to war, and then to last only a short time.

"In the month of December, 1814—the gloomiest period of the last war with England, when Virginia and the other States

were left much to their own resources—Mr. Nicholas was elected
Governor of the State.   Nothing but patriotism could have
induced any man, at such a time and under such circumstances,
to have undertaken this office; much was risked, with little prospect of anything being gained.   The possibility of being able
to render service to his country vanquished every obstacle suggested by discretion, and the post was accepted.   Fortunately
for the country, peace was announced in about three months;
and the opportunity was not afforded to judge conclusively what
was the capacity of the new Governor for such a state of things.
There is reason to believe, however, that his administration would
have been distinguished by energy, prudence, and indefatigable
industry.   The defence of the State depending mainly upon
militia who could not be kept constantly in the field, an appropriation was made to enable him to erect telegraphs and to raise
a corps of videttes, to be so stationed, at his discretion, as to distribute his orders with the utmost possible dispatch throughout
the State.   A plan for this purpose was digested, but was rendered unnecessary by the peace.

   "As an evidence of the great confidence that was put in
Governor Nicholas by the Legislature, it may be stated that at
the close of the session, and in great haste, they passed a law, of
very complicated character, in reference to raising a force for
the defence of the State.   The execution of this law depended,
in almost every particular, on instructions to be given by the
Governor.   The responsibility thus devolved on him was assumed
in consideration of the object to be gained, though the execution
of the law was rendered unnecessary by the termination of
hostilities.   Loans were necessary to pay and equip this force,
and these were obtained on the most reasonable terms, condi-
tioned upon a clause not authorized in the act ; but, being recommended to the legislature by the Governor, this was done at the
next session, and the desired clause inserted without difficulty,
and much to the honor of the State.

   "After the peace every claim against the State was paid as
soon as the account was adjusted; the militia in service were
discharged in a manner most gratifying to them.   They were
completely paid; provision was made for their return home, and
for the care of the sick until they could be safely removed.
All the military stores of a perishable nature were disposed of,

and the others, including tents and other camp equipage, sufficient for an army of ten thousand men, were deposited in the State arsenal. The closing the accounts for the expenses of the war was pushed on with as much dispatch as was consistent with safety in their after-adjustment at Washington.

"If the war had continued it was the determination of the Governor to urge all the able men of the State, with whom he could take the liberty, to offer for the next Assembly. The return of peace did not prevent this application, but the motive was different. Foreseeing that the State would have command of considerable funds, he believed it was important to make an early effort to induce the Assembly to apply their proceeds to the great purposes of internal improvement and education. This application, it is believed, had some effect, as in the two next Assemblies there appeared many gentlemen who had not been there for several years. At the commencement of the session the Governor pressed these subjects upon their attention with earnestness. They were acted upon, and the means then placed at the disposal of the Board of Public Works and of the President and Directors of the Literary Fund were appropriated to their respective objects, and the foundation laid of a system which has added to the intelligence as well as the wealth and prosperity of the State. In a review of the messages of Governor Nicholas it will be found that most of the objects recommended by him were acted upon by the Legislature, and that they are all strongly marked by an intimate knowledge of the wants and capacity of Virginia. So satisfactory had been the administration of the government that he was re-elected with the loss of but one vote.

"The first act of his second term was an attempt to adjust the claims of the Commonwealth against the United States, all previous efforts at which having proved abortive. After reflecting maturely upon the subject, the Governor believed that a different course ought to be pursued and an additional agent appointed. Upon asking the advice of the Council, some unwillingness was expressed to make the change. It was, however, assented to, and resulted in a speedy adjustment. As President of the Board of Public Works and of the Literary Fund, we find Governor Nicholas displaying the same industry and wise foresight as in the other departments of the government. In all his con-

tracts for the State, of any sort, the utmost economy was practiced and the greatest caution used to preserve the public
interest. A remarkable proof of this was given in the execution
of a law providing for a complete map of the State within limits
which such an object would justify. He anxiously wished it
accomplished; but he could not authorize, in duty to the State,
such an expenditure of public money as the entire execution of
the act would require. After much reflection he gave such
instructions to the county courts, to govern them in their contracts, as would keep them within bounds. Having informed
himself fully as to the value of such surveys, he then divided the
State into districts and made contracts for the general survey.
It is believed that more than one hundred thousand dollars were
saved to the State by this single transaction.

"At the expiration of his second term of office as Governor
he served for a few months as president of the branch of the
United States Bank in Richmond. In the spring of 1819 he
returned to 'Warren.' He had always been of a very delicate constitution, and the bodily fatigue and anxiety of mind
which had marked his later years brought on ill health, and he
was advised to take a journey on horseback. He left home, but
got no further than 'Montpelier,' the residence of Mr. Madison,
when he found himself too unwell to go on, and returned to
'Tufton,' the residence of his son-in-law, Thomas Jefferson
Randolph, Esq. Here he lingered from day to day, each day
hoping to be well enough to return to 'Warren.' Mr. Jefferson
and Mr. Madison (who was then on a visit to 'Monticello'), both
of whom had been his intimate personal friends, visited him frequently here, and all was done which skill or affection could sug-
gest for his recovery, but to no purpose. On the 10th of
October, 1819, he expired suddenly while in the act of dressing.
He was buried in the graveyard at 'Monticello.'

" As regards his wisdom and patriotism, his public life speaks
too plainly to require a word from his biographer. Viewed as a
private individual, none could have been purer from every vice;
and his kind heart and calm temper made him the best father
and the kindest master and neighbor. He owed his influence in
the councils of his country more to his moderation and wisdom
than to his power as a speaker. His style in conversation was
cool, deliberate, sententious, and forcible, replete with the strong-

est views and the wisest opinions. His manners, perfectly moulded in the finest school—viz., the old Colonial Court of Virginia—that we have ever had in the United States, combined a polished dignity and courtesy with a fascination that won its way in the regards of men. His play of feature and its effects were most wonderful; his smile had a charm which threw suspicion off its guard and drew persons irresistibly to him. The rebuke of his cold, stern eye and the withering curl of his lip seemed to congeal the very blood of insolence or arrogance. The posts occupied by Mr. Monroe previous to his election as President, and which proved the stepping-stones to that high station, were all declined by Mr. Nicholas before they were offered to Mr. Monroe. Mr. Jefferson saw in the pecuniary embarrassments in which his endeavors to prop the failing fortunes of a valued friend had involved him the only obstacles to his election to the highest post in the gift of the country."

It would be unfair to close this account of Nicholas without acknowledging the influence wrought on his character by the virtues and graces of that sex which, gentle and shrinking in prosperity, faces the sternest trials and braves the risks of pestilence and war with a firmness rarely exceeded by its manlier counterpart. Of his pious, intelligent, and patriotic mother, who, bereaved of her husband in the darkest period of the Revolution, saw his yet unturfed grave trampled by the myrmidons of Tarleton, and who devoted her time to the education and sustenance of her family, I have already spoken. But Nicholas was blessed not only with a mother worthy of the times in which she lived, and of the gallant sons whom she gave to her country; he was equally fortunate in that lovely woman whom, meeting with her on a military tour, he fell in love with, and whom, when the war was over, he conducted as his bride to his paternal seat at "Warren." Her name was Margaret Smith, daughter of John Smith (of Baltimore), and a sister of General Samuel Smith, whose name for more than the third of a century was connected with Federal affairs, and of Robert Smith, formerly Secretary of the Navy, and Secretary of State during the administration of Mr. Madison. She was born and lived in Baltimore; but, in order to avoid the dangers to which a seaport in time of war was likely to be exposed, she was sent in childhood, when she was old enough to remember the leading incidents of the Revolution, to the town of Carlisle, in the State of Pennsylvania. She was capable of appreciating the dangers to which her father was daily exposed as the active chairman of the Committee of Ways and Means of the State of Maryland; and she saw her three brothers arm in defence of their country. One of them, overcome by the fatigue of war, returned only to die. Samuel at length returned safe, bearing with him the laurels he had earned at Fort Mifflin. "The gentle and amiable André, then a prisoner on parole, was domesticated in her father's family; and, though her childish affections were won by his kindness and her mind dazzled by his varied accomplishments, such was her veneration for the great name of Washington, that she could never be induced to condemn the act of stern and unrelenting retribution which consigned so many virtues to an ignominious grave." [315] The love of country was no mere sentiment in her bosom. It was a principle, inculcated in early childhood, and fixed by the study and reflection of riper years. When, at the age of eighty, she was erroneously informed that her son (Colonel Nicholas, of Louisiana) had changed his politics, she rose from her chair, and, raising her hand, her eye brilliant as in youth and her voice tremulous with emotion, she exclaimed: "Tell my son, as he values the blessing of his old mother, never to forsake the faith of his fathers." [316] She lived to behold and enjoy the honors attained by the husband of her youth, and by her descendants; blending to the last all the gentleness of woman with a masculine judgment and intellect which had enabled her to understand and advise with her husband in all the difficulties that arose in the complicated political career of his eventful life.

'Such was Wilson Cary Nicholas. Embarking early in public life, he exerted a various influence in the passage of many of the most important measures, from the treaty of peace with Great Britain, in 1783, to the treaty of peace with the same Power in 1815; and his life extended from the governorship of Francis

---

[315] If my correspondent does not confound Asgill with André, the abode of André in Carlisle must have been after his capture by Montgomery in 1775, at St. John's, and before he was exchanged.

[316] This anecdote is in fine keeping with a similar one told of the mother of Lord-Chancellor Erskine in respect of George the Fourth, by Lord Cockburn in the *Memorials of His Time*.

Fauquier to the presidency of James Monroe—one of the grand-est stretches of American history. If he had devoted more of his time to letters and had learned to put his thoughts on paper, what a charming narrative could have been unrolled before the coming ages! Born in Williamsburg, he might, in early youth, have seen his father, and Peyton Randolph, and Wythe bearing the pall of Fauquier, and might have told us where the bones of that skilful dealer in cards, and elegant scholar, were laid away. He had seen the members of the House of Burgesses quit their hall and march in procession to the "Raleigh"; and he might have peeped in and seen them sign the memorable non-importa-tion agreement. He might have seen the statue of Lord Bote-tourt, which had been voted to his memory by a grateful people, as it was dragged in huge boxes from the James and placed upon its pedestal; and he might have seen that nobleman as he dis-tributed, in the chapel of William and Mary, his golden medal-lions to the students of each term who excelled in the languages and in science, and he could have told us whether the deceased Baron was really committed to the vault of Sir John. Nicholas was a nephew of Archibald Cary, and was not far from five-and-twenty when the old patriot departed. Indeed, when Nicholas was a member of the House, Cary was Speaker of the Senate. How much he must have heard from "Old Iron"! He must have heard from his lips all about the dictator scheme of 1776, and whether that famous threat was ever made. Nicholas must have heard, again and again, from his brother George, all about the inquiry that that brother moved into the conduct of Governor Jefferson, and the second scheme of a dictatorship which was said to have been meditated at the same session. What an interesting account of the state of parties, from 1783 to 1789, he could have written out, and, when the new Federal Government went into operation, how many things he could have told that now we may never know. Was it here that a party existed which sought to put aside Jefferson as the leader of the Republi-can party, and as the successor of Washington, and take up Edmund Randolph in his stead? Why did Nicholas allow himself, in 1794, to be brought out for the Senate against that tried champion of the Republicans, Stevens Thomson Mason? Or was this the first overt act of the new party? Did Patrick Henry really send a challenge to Edmund Randolph by the

hands of Colonel Cabell?[317]   What were the precise grounds of the
charges urged by Randolph against Henry, and afterwards by
George Nicholas, still more doggedly, on the floor of the Convention?   Who was the author of those eloquent, but bitter and
contumelious, letters addressed to Patrick Henry, the first number of which appeared in the *Virginia Independent Chronicle* of
the 7th of January, 1789?   Who wrote those other libels on
Henry under the signature of a "State Soldier"?   And who
was the writer that dared the authors of those papers to the
proof of their charges?   And then, at a later day, how many
questions we would like to ask him: Was Jefferson really
understood by his own party to include Washington in his
Mazzei letter?   Did the Republican party of 1800 intend to
resist the election of Burr or Adams by force of arms?   At
what precise moment did the scheme of purchasing the entire
broad domain of Louisiana enter the mind of Jefferson?   What
was the true cause of the hostility of John Randolph to the
administration of Mr. Jefferson?   What negotiations preceded
the visit of Mr. John Quincy Adams to Mr. Jefferson on the
embargo business, and was not there some other negotiator than
Mr. Giles?   What was the cause of the temporary hostility of
Mr. Giles to the administration of Madison?   Did Clay and
Calhoun really bully Madison into a war and afterwards into a
bank?   These, and a thousand other questions, no man could
have answered more authoritatively than he.

   As to his public acts, they embraced the most interesting and
the most stirring events of the age.   He voted to abolish all
hindrances to the execution of the British treaty of 1783.   He
voted to keep the seat of government in Richmond, but refused to
sustain the policy of Madison in building up commercial marts in
the Commonwealth.   He saw John Warden before the House of
Delegates for a contempt, and, after laughing at the shrewdness
of the wily Scot, voted to discharge him.   He voted the statue
to Washington which Houdon fashioned with such exquisite

---

   [317] I attach not the slightest blame to the friends of Edmund Randolph for seeking to elevate him to the presidency. His position in
the Virginia Federal Convention, as well as in the General Federal
Convention, was eminently splendid; and abroad he was regarded as
the most efficient person in securing the ratification of the Constitution
by Virginia.

skill. He voted on all the exciting religious questions that agitated our early councils, always leaning to the side of liberty, and recorded his name in favor of the glorious act establishing religious freedom. He voted for the resolution convoking the meeting at Annapolis, and for the ratification of the Federal Constitution, to which that resolution may be said to have given birth. He was one of the committee to bring in a bill to cede ten miles square to the Federal Government as a permanent seat of the capital. He sustained the resolutions of 1798-'99, and voted to repeal the judiciary act of 1800. He took an active part in securing the ratification of the treaty which ceded Louisiana to the Union. On these and many other occasions he rendered most valuable and efficient service; yet all that he could have told about them is lost!

A friend of Nicholas, in a letter addressed to me in answer to one which I had written to him making inquiries of Mr. Nicholas, says:

"I have no anecdotes of Mr. Nicholas. He was too wise to be eccentric, and too calm and prudent in his conduct to excite remark. He was on one occasion elected from his county by a unanimous vote; and in high political excitements his vote always greatly exceeded his party strength. He was loved and admired by many of his political opponents. His manners, whenever he chose, were playful and bewitching in the extreme."

Another letter from a most competent judge presents the following characteristic traits:

"Mr. Nicholas's private character was most amiable and exemplary, and was such as to attach to him with unbounded devotion his family and friends. His manners were of that polished character of the old Williamsburg Colonial school—a mixture of grace, benignity, and dignity—which won all hearts. His powers of countenance were beyond those of any man I have ever known. His smile won the confidence and love of all on whom it beamed; his sternness repelled all approach or familiarty without the utterance of a word. As a listener he was unsurpassed. His conversation was calm, deliberate, imperturbable, forcible, sententious, and pregnant with thought and wisdom. He never spoke without reflection. If asked a question he was not prepared to answer, he would reflect until his queriest might suppose that he had forgotten his question, and then his reply would come in the exposition of the wisest and most profound views. As a debater in public bodies he spoke rarely, but concisely, deliberately, and with great force.[318] As a manager of men he had few equals. When in the House of Representatives or in the Senate of the United States during the presidency of Mr. Jefferson, I have often heard Mr. Jefferson say that he (Mr. Jefferson) had no trouble; that Mr. Nicholas wielded such controlling influence in the party as to keep it in perfect agreement with the administration; and that he esteemed him capable of filling the highest stations. In early life he became embarrassed in some speculations in Western lands, into which he had been drawn by General Henry Lee. This, added to losses sustained in efforts to aid his brother, George Nicholas (of Kentucky), and his brother-in-law, Edmund Randolph, marred his ability to accept office; and, finally, the financial catastrophe of 1819 completed his ruin. He died at the house of his son-in-law, Thomas Jefferson Randolph, Esq., and was buried at 'Monticello'; and was attended to the grave by his friend, Mr. Jefferson, who made the remark on that occasion that had it not been for his pecuniary embarrassments he would have been the President in Monroe's place; that the mission to France, and other offices which led to the presidency, had been first pressed upon him for acceptance. Of this fact the letters of Mr. Jefferson, among the papers of Mr. Nicholas, furnish abundant proof. Mr. Jefferson regarded him as one of the ablest and purest public and private characters he had ever known. Judge William Cabell, President of the Court of Appeals, in speaking of Mr. Nicholas to a friend after his decease, said that he would except no man he ever knew, not even Mr. Jefferson, Judge Marshall, or Mr. Madison; but that Mr. Nicholas was the man of the most sense he had ever known. Had fortune combined with nature to place him in the position to which his virtues and abilities entitled him, he would have ranked among the wisest and most distinguished of Virginia's sons. Of those who were unfriendly towards him he never spoke or alluded to; they were as forgotten or dead.''

---

[318] Colonel Nicholas spoke oftener than my correspondent is aware of, but always in the manner described by him.

APPENDIX.

DELEGATES RETURNED

Convention of March, 1788.

The editor has added the following brief and unpretentious biographical notes, in the hope that they may serve those interested somewhat as data in the preparation of more adequate presentations of the careers of the worthies thus comprehended:

Accomac—EDMUND CUSTIS,[319] GEORGE PARKER.[320]

Albemarle—GEORGE NICHOLAS, WILSON CARY NICHOLAS.

Amelia—JOHN PRIDE, EDMUND BOOKER.[321]

Amherst—WILLIAM CABELL, SAMUEL JORDAN CABELL.

Augusta—ZACHARIAH JOHNSTON, ARCHIBALD STUART.

Bedford—JOHN TRIGG,[322] CHARLES CLAY.

Berkeley—WILLIAM DARKE,[323] ADAM STEPHEN.[324]

Botetourt—WILLIAM FLEMING, MARTIN McFERRAN.

Bourbon—HENRY LEE,[325] NOTLAY CONN.

Brunswick—JOHN JONES,[326] BINNS JONES.

Buckingham—CHARLES PATTESON,[327] DAVID BELL.[328]

Campbell—ROBERT ALEXANDER, EDMUND WINSTON.[329]

Caroline—Hon. EDMUND PENDLETON, JAMES TAYLOR.[330]

Charlotte—THOMAS READ,[331] Hon. PAUL CARRINGTON.[332]

Charles City—BENJAMIN HARRISON, JOHN TYLER.

Chesterfield—DAVID PATTESON,[333] STEPHEN PANKEY, JR.

Cumberland—JOSEPH MICHAUX,[334] THOMAS H. DREW.[335]

Culpeper—FRENCH STROTHER,[336] JOEL EARLY.[337]

Dinwiddie—JOSEPH JONES,[338] WILLIAM WATKINS.[339]

Elizabeth City—MILES KING,[340] WORLICH WESTWOOD.[341]

Essex—JAMES UPSHAW,[342] MERIWETHER SMITH.[343]

Fairfax—DAVID STUART,[344] CHARLES SIMMS.[345]

Fayette—HUMPHREY MARSHALL,[346] JOHN FOWLER.

Fauquier—MARTIN PICKETT,[347] HUMPHREY BROOKE.[348]

Fluvanna—SAMUEL RICHARDSON, JOSEPH HADEN.

Frederick—JOHN S. WOODCOCK, ALEXANDER WHITE.

Franklin—JOHN EARLY, THOMAS ARTHUR.

Gloucester—WARNER LEWIS,[349] THOMAS SMITH.[350]

Goochland—JOHN GUERRANT,[351] WILLIAM SAMPSON.

Greenbrier—GEORGE CLENDENIN, JOHN STUART.

Greenesville—WILLIAM MASON, DANIEL FISHER.

Halifax—ISAAC COLES,[352] GEORGE CARRINGTON.[353]

Hampshire—ANDREW WOODROW, RALPH HUMPHREYS.

Hanover—PARKE GOODALL,[354] JOHN CARTER LITTLEPAGE.[355]

Harrison—GEORGE JACKSON, JOHN PRUNTY.

Hardy—ISAAC VANMETER, ABEL SEYMOUR.

Henrico—Governor EDMUND RANDOLPH, JOHN MARSHALL.

Henry—THOMAS COOPER, JOHN MARR.

Isle of Wight—THOMAS PIERCE,[356] JAMES JOHNSON.

James City—NATHANIEL BURWELL,[357] ROBERT ANDREWS.[358]

Jefferson—ROBERT BRECKENRIDGE,[359] RICE BULLOCK.

King and Queen—WILLIAM FLEET,[360] JOHN ROANE.[361]

King George—BURDET ASHTON, WILLIAM THORNTON.

King William—HOLT RICHESON,[362] BENJAMIN TEMPLE.[363]

Lancaster—JAMES GORDON,[364] HENRY TOWLES.

Loudoun—STEVENS THOMSON MASON, LEVIN POWELL.[365]

Louisa—WILLIAM OVERTON CALLIS,[366] WILLIAM WHITE.

Lunenburg—JONATHAN PATTESON, CHRISTOPHER ROBERTSON.

Lincoln—JOHN LOGAN,[367] HENRY PAWLING.[368]

Madison—JOHN MILLER, GREEN CLAY.[369]

Mecklenburg—SAMUEL HOPKINS, JR., RICHARD KENNON.[370]

Mercer—THOMAS ALLEN, ALEXANDER ROBERTSON.

Middlesex—RALPH WORMELEY, JR., FRANCIS CORBIN.

Monongalia—JOHN EVANS, WILLIAM McCLERRY.

Montgomery—WALTER CROCKETT, ABRAHAM TRIGG.

Nansemond—WILLIS RIDDICK,[371] SOLOMON SHEPHERD.

New Kent—WILLIAM CLAYTON,[372] BURWELL BASSETT.[373]

Nelson—MATTHEW WALTON, JOHN STEELE.

Norfolk—JAMES WEBB, JAMES TAYLOR.

Northampton—JOHN STRINGER, LITTLETON EYRE.

Northumberland—WALTER JONES,[374] THOMAS GASKINS.

Ohio—ARCHIBALD WOODS, EBENEZER ZANE.

Orange—JAMES MADISON, JR., JAMES GORDON.

Pittsylvania—ROBERT WILLIAMS, JOHN WILSON.

Powhatan—WILLIAM RONALD,[375] THOMAS TURPIN, JR.

Prince Edward—PATRICK HENRY, ROBERT LAWSON.[376]

Prince George—THEODORIC BLAND,[377] EDMUND RUFFIN.[378]

Prince William—WILLIAM GRAYSON, CUTHBERT BULLITT.[379]

Princess Anne—ANTHONY WALKE,[380] THOMAS WALKE.

Randolph—BENJAMIN WILSON, JOHN WILSON.

Richmond—WALKER TOMLIN, WILLIAM PEACHY.

Rockbridge—WILLIAM McKEE, ANDREW MOORE.

Rockingham—THOMAS LEWIS, GABRIEL JONES.

Russell—THOMAS CARTER, HENRY DICKENSON.

Shenandoah—JACOB RINKER, JOHN WILLIAMS.

Southampton—BENJAMIN BLOUNT, SAMUEL KILLO.

Spotsylvania—JAMES MONROE, JOHN DAWSON.[381]

Stafford—GEORGE MASON, ANDREW BUCHANAN.

Surry—JOHN HARTWELL COCKE,[382] JOHN ALLEN.[383]

Sussex—JOHN HOWELL BRIGGS,[384] THOMAS EDMUNDS.[385]

Warwick—COLE DIGGES,[386] RICHARD CARY.[387]

Washington—SAMUEL EDMISTON, JAMES MONTGOMERY.

Westmoreland—HENRY LEE, BUSHROD WASHINGTON.[388]

York—Hon. JOHN BLAIR,[389] Hon. GEORGE WYTHE.

Williamsburg—JAMES INNES.

Norfolk Borough—THOMAS MATTHEWS.

BIOGRAPHICAL NOTES.

[319] EDMUND CUSTIS was a descendant from John Custis, who, by tradition, was a native of Ireland; had been for some years an innkeeper in Rotterdam, Holland, and settled in Northampton county in the earlier half of the seventeenth century, his name appearing in the records of that county as early as 1649. The first husband of Mrs. George Washington, John Parke Custis, was of the same descent. Edmund Custis was a member of the House of Delegates in 1787, and perhaps other years.

[320] Of the family of GEORGE PARKER were Robert, George, and John Parker, who received patents of land in Northampton county, respectively, in 1649, 1650, and 1660. Captain George Parker was a Justice of the Peace for Accomac county in 1663, and Major George Parker, probably his son, a Justice in 1707 and Sheriff in 1730-'31. It was the unwritten law of Virginia, down to 1850, that the prerogative of the sheriffalty was vested in the senior magistrate of the county, in rotation, and thus, doubtless, Major George Parker succeeded. Sacker Parker, Burgess from Accomac county, died in June, 1738. Colonel Thomas Parker, of Accomac county, served with distinction in the Revolution as Captain in the Fifth Virginia regiment; was taken prisoner at the battle of Germantown, and died in December, 1819. George Parker, probably the member of the Convention, for many years a Judge of the General Court of Virginia, died July 12, 1826; aged sixty-five years. John A. Parker, member of the House of Delegates from Accomac county, 1802-'3; General Severn Eyre Parker, member of the House of Delegates and member of Congress, 1819-'21; and John W. H. Parker, State Senator, 1852 and later, are other representatives of the family.

[321] Members of the BOOKER family frequently represented Amelia and the neighboring counties in the House of Burgesses and the State Legislature. Samuel Booker was a Captain, and Lewis Booker a Lieutenant, in the Revolution.

[322] The progenitor of the TRIGG family of Virginia was Abraham Trigg, who emigrated from Cornwall, England, about the year 1710. He had issue five sons: ABRAM, a Colonel in the Virginia line in the Revolution, and member of Congress 1797-1809, and, it is presumed, the member of the Convention from Montgomery county; Stephen,

went to Kentucky as a member of the Land Commission in 1779; commanded a regiment in the battle of Blue Licks, and fell there gallantly leading a charge; his gallantry is commemorated on the monument at Frankfort, and Trigg county was named in his honor; JOHN, the member of the Convention, was a Major of artillery in the Revolution; was present at the surrender of Cornwallis, and was a member of the House of Delegates 1784-'92; a member of Congress 1797-1804, and died June 28, 1804; William and Daniel were the remaining sons. Hon. Connally Findlay Trigg, Judge of the United States District Court of Tennessee—died in 1879—was descended from William Trigg, as are Hon. Connally F. Trigg, member of Congress from Virginia, and Mrs. Edmund D. T. Myers and William Robertson Trigg, Esq., of Richmond, President of the Richmond Locomotive and Machine Works.

[323] WILLIAM DARKE was born in Philadelphia county, Pennsylvania, in 1736. In 1740 his parents moved to Virginia. He was with the Virginia troops at Braddock's defeat, in 1755, and was made a Captain at the beginning of the Revolutionary War. He was taken prisoner at the battle of Germantown, but being released, was Colonel Commandant of the regiments from Hampshire and Berkeley counties at the surrender of Cornwallis. He frequently represented Berkeley county in the Virginia Assembly; was Lieutenant-Colonel of a regiment of "Levies" in 1791, and commanded the left wing of St. Clair's army at its defeat by the Miami Indians, November 4, 1791. He made two gallant and successful charges with the bayonet in this fight, in the second of which his youngest son, Captain Joseph Darke, was killed, and he himself wounded, narrowly escaping death. He was subsequently a Major-General of Virginia militia. He died in Jefferson county November 26, 1801.

[324] GENERAL ADAM STEPHEN died in November, 1791. His granddaughter, Ann Evelina, daughter of Moses Hunter, married Hon. Henry Saint George Tucker, and was the mother of the Hon. John Randolph Tucker.

[325] HENRY LEE, Kentucky pioneer, was born in Virginia in 1758; died in Mason couhty, Kentucky, in 1846; well educated, and studied surveying, which he pursued for several years; represented the district of Kentucky in the Virginia Legislature; member of the Convention which met at Danville in 1787; was one of the Commissioners that located the seat of government at Frankfort, and County Lieutenant for all the territory north of Licking river. Studied law, and was appointed Judge of the Circuit Court for Mason county; was also for many years President of the Washington branch of the Bank of Kentucky. He was a sagacious man, of excellent business habits, and amassed a large fortune. He was tall and powerfully built, and his personal appearance was imposing.

[326] COLONEL JOHN JONES was probably a descendant of Captain Peter Jones, the founder of Petersburg. He was a Burgess from Dinwiddie county in 1757-'58; member of the State Senate 1776-'87, and Speaker 1787-'88; County Lieutenant of Brunswick county 1788, and later. Hon. John Winston Jones (Speaker of the United States House of Representatives), son of Alexander and Mary Ann (daughter of Peter Winston) Jones, was his grandson.

[327] CHARLES PATTESON was probably of the same lineage as David Patteson, of Chesterfield county. He was a member of the Buckingham County Committee of Safety, 1775-'76, of the Convention of 1776, and of the House of Delegates of 1787-'88. Other members of the family have been prominent in the State annals. Captain Camm Patteson, of Buckingham, and S. S. P. Patteson, Esq., of Richmond, are present representatives.

[328] DAVID BELL was a son of David and Judith (sister of Archibald Cary of "Ampthill") Bell.

[329] EDMUND WINSTON, of "Hunting Tower," Buckingham county, Judge of the General Court of Virginia, was a first cousin of Patrick Henry, under whom he studied law, whose joint executor he was, and whose widow he married. He was the son of William Winston and grandson of Isaac and Mary (Dabney) Winston. Isaac, William, and James Winston emigrated from Yorkshire, England, in 1704, and settled near Richmond, Virginia. From them have descended the distinguished Winston family, whose ramifications include nearly every family of worth in the Southern States. Edmund Winston wore the ermine worthily. He was a sound lawyer, and his character was spotless. He died in 1813, aged more than four-score. A number of his descendants reside in Missouri.

[330] COLONEL JAMES TAYLOR was of the family of President Zachary Taylor. He was a Burgess 1762-'64, member of the Committee of Safety of Caroline county 1774-'76, and of the Conventions of 1775-'76.

[331] THOMAS READ, the son of Colonel Clement Read (see *Grigsby's Convention of 1776*, page 106, *et seq.*), began life as a surveyor; studied at William and Mary College, and was Deputy Clerk of Charlotte county, when it was set apart from Lunenburg in 1765, becoming Clerk in 1770, holding the office until 1817, "to the approbation of all." He was of fine physique, his stature approaching six feet. He died at his seat, "Ingleside," February 4, 1817.

[332] PAUL CARRINGTON was the eldest son of Judge Paul Carrington, and by the early laws of primogeniture, his father dying intestate, inherited the whole estate of the latter. He nobly divided the estate

equally with his brothers and sisters. He was a member of the House of Burgesses and of the Conventions of 1775-'76; appointed, in 1779, the second Judge of the General Court of Virginia; was Chief Justice in 1780; 1789, Judge of the Court of Appeals; resigned 1807, at the age of seventy-five; died, aged ninety-three years.

[333] DAVID PATTESON, a descendant of David Patteson, who received a patent of land in Henrico county (then including Chesterfield county) in 1714; was Colonel commandant of Chesterfield county in 1785 and a member of the House of Delegates, 1791-'93. Of his descent are Mrs. Branch, the widow of the late Colonel James R. Branch, and Mrs. McCaw, wife of Dr. James Brown McCaw, of Richmond.

[334] The emigrant ancestor of the MICHAUX family of Virginia was a Huguenot, Abraham Michaux; born at Cadent, France, in 1672, and died in Henrico county, Virginia, in 1717. He married Susanna Rochet (who escaped from France, in a hogshead, to Holland, and was subsequently known by the *soubriquet* " Little Night-Cap," from having been thus mentioned to friends by her sister to avoid attention and religious persecution). Of their issue was JACOB MICHAUX, a Captain in the Revolution, who died in 1787. He married Judith Woodson, and had, among other issue, the member Joseph Michaux, who died in 1807.

[335] A son of the member, of the same name, THOMAS H. DREW; born May 13, 1785, at "Clifton," Cumberland county; died at Richmond, Virginia, at the residence of his son-in-law, William D. Gibson, Esq., October 9, 1878; was an interesting link with the past. He came to Richmond in 1803, and was first employed as a collector by the old Mutual Assurance Society, which was founded in 1794, and, though the oldest in Virginia, is still among the staunchest. He was deputy United States Marshal in 1807, and summoned the famous jury which tried Aaron Burr for treason. He subsequently engaged in mercantile pursuits, and was the senior member of the firm of Drew, Blair & Carroll. He was one of the audience in the Theatre at its lamentable burning on Saturday night of December 26, 1811, and one of the movers in the building of the Monumental Church on its site. His memory was very clear as to the moving events of his long life, and he was a delightful *raconteur*. The family was seated in York county as early as 1657, and has been numerously represented in Eastern Virginia.

[336] Slaughter, in his *History of St. Mark's Parish*, page 169, cites General Richard Taylor, late Confederate States Army, son of President Zachary Taylor, whose mother was Sarah Strother, as having visited the old family burying-ground of the Strothers in the Isle of Thanet, County Kent, England, and noted the name in its various transitions from its original form, Straathor, to its present authography. Anthony Strother, of this derivation, patented, in 1734, a tract of land under the Double-top mountain, in what was then St. Mark's Parish, and is now

Bromfield, in Madison county; Jeremiah Strother died, in that part of Orange county which now forms Culpeper, in 1741, leaving wife, Eleanor, and children, James, William, Francis, Lawrence, Christopher, Robert, and several daughters, the marriages of whom are recorded in preceding sketches. James, the eldest son, married Margaret, daughter of Daniel French, of King George county. Of their issue was FRENCH STROTHER, who married Lucy, daughter of Robert Coleman. He was a vestryman and church warden of St. Mark's Parish, and as such "made himself very popular by releasing a Baptist minister, who had been imprisoned at night, substituting his servant man, Tom, in his place." He represented Culpeper county in the General Assembly for nearly thirty years; was a member in 1776 and also in 1799, when he voted against the celebrated resolutions of 1798-'99. He was solicited to oppose James Madison for Congress, but James Monroe became the candidate, and was badly beaten. Monroe had only 9 votes in Orange, Madison 216, Culpeper, Monroe 103, Madison 256. One of his daughters married Captain Philip Slaughter, of the Revolution. A son, George French Strother, was a member of Congress, 1817-'20.

[337]The distinguished Jubal A. Early, late Lieutenant-General Confederate States Army, has written me that his ancestor emigrated from Donegal, Ireland, early in the eighteenth century, settled in Culpeper county, and married a Miss Buford. They had issue three sons: Joshua, the great-grandfather of General Early, whose father was Joab, and grandfather Jubal Early, "who established his son-in-law, Colonel James Callaway, in Franklin county, with the first iron furnace in the Piedmont region; JOEL EARLY, the member, who removed to Georgia, and was the ancestor of Governor Peter Early of that State; JOHN EARLY, member from Franklin county, ancestor of Bishop John Early, of the Methodist Church South.

[338]JOSEPH JONES, "of Dinwiddie," probably served in the House of Burgesses. He was a member of the House of Delegates 1784-'87; Postmaster of Petersburg; a General of militia. He married Jane, daughter of Roger Atkinson, of "Mansfield," and left issue.

[339] The WATKINS family of Virginia has been supposed to be of Welsh origin. James Watkins was among the emigrants to Virginia in 1608. John Watkins was granted 850 acres of land in James City county July 3, 1648. An account of the family was prepared by the late Hon. F. N. Watkins. He commences his deduction with Thomas Watkins, of Swift Creek, Cumberland county, whose will bears date 1760. He had issue eight children, the eldest Thomas. Another son, Benjamin, married Miss Cary, of Warwick county. He was the first Clerk of Chesterfield county, in 1749, until his death, in 1779. He was a member of the Conventions of 1775-'76, and took an active part in the affairs of the Revolution. One of his daughters was the wife of

Rev. William Leigh, and the mother of Judge William Leigh and of United States Senator Benjamin Watkins Leigh. Another daughter, Frances, married William Finnie, of Amelia county, and her descendants include the names also of Royall, Worsham, Sydnor, and others. WILLIAM WATKINS, member, is presumed to have been the brother of Benjamin Watkins.

[340] MILES KING was a member of the House of Delegates from Elizabeth City county in 1784, 1786-'87, '91, '92-'3, and 1798, and resigned in the latter year to accept the county clerkship. Henry King was a member of the Virginia Convention of 1776 from Elizabeth City county.

[341] WORLICH WESTWOOD was a Burgess in 1774; member of the Committee of Safety of Elizabeth City county 1774-'76; member of the Conventions of 1775-'76; member of the House of Delegates 1785, 1790, 1798-1800, 1802-'3, and Sheriff in 1790.

[342] JAMES UPSHAW was a signer of the Resolutions of the Westmoreland Association against the Stamp Act, February 27, 1766. His ancestor. John Upshaw, probably from England, born July 21, 1715, was a Burgess from Essex 1758-'65. Forest Upshaw, who served as Captain in the French and Indian war; Captain James Upshaw, of the Revolution, a member of the Virginia branch of the Order of the Cincinnati; John H. Upshaw, member of the House of Burgesses 1809-'10, were all of this lineage.

[343] MERIWETHER SMITH was born about the year 1730 at " Bathurst," Essex county. His mother was a daughter of Launcelot Bathurst, a patentee of nearly 8,000 acres of land in New Kent county, Virginia, in 1683, who was appointed, August 1, 1684, by Edmund Jenings, Attorney-General of Virginia, his deputy for Henrico county. The name Bathurst appears as a continuously favored Christian name in the Buckner, Hinton, Jones, Randolph, Skelton, Stith, and other families. Meriwether Smith married twice—first, about 1760, Alice, daughter of Philip Lee, third in descent of the emigrant Richard Lee, and widow of Thomas Clarke; and, secondly, September 29, 1769, Elizabeth, widow of Colonel William Daingerfield, of Essex county, member of the House of Burgesses. Meriwether Smith served Virginia with zeal and distinction through a long series of years, and in important stations. He appears as a signer to the Articles of the Westmoreland Association of February 27, 1766, which, in opposition to the odious Stamp Act, was pledged to use no articles of British importation; and on May 18, 1769, was a signer also of the Williamsburg Association, which met at the old Raleigh Tavern, in that city, and who bound themselves to abstain from the use of the proscribed British merchandise, and "to promote and encourage industry and frugality and discourage all luxury and extravagance." In 1770 he represented Essex

county in the House of Burgesses. He was a member of the Conventions of 1775-'76, and in the latter body prepared a draft of the Declaration of Rights. He was a representative of Virginia in the Continental Congress from 1778 to 1782. He represented Essex county in the House of Delegates 1786-'88. He died January 25, 1790. His wife, Mrs. Elizabeth Smith, surviving him, died January 24, 1794. They are both buried at "Bathurst." A son by the first marriage, George William Smith, born at "Bathurst" 1762; married February 7, 1793, Sarah, fourth daughter of Colonel Richard Adams, the elder, member of the Convention of 1776, an ardent patriot throughout the Revolution, and one of the most enterprising, public-spirited, wealthy, and influential citizens of Richmond. Colonel Adams was a large property-holder, and the Assembly considered for a time the erection of the State Capitol upon a site in Richmond, on Church Hill, owned by him, and proffered as a gift to the State. George William Smith represented Essex county in the House of Delegates in 1794. Soon thereafter he made Richmond his residence, and in his profession of the law speedily took high rank and enjoyed a lucrative practice. He represented the city in the House of Delegates from 1802 to 1808, inclusive, and in 1810 was appointed a member of the State Council, and as senior member of that body, or Lieutenant-Governor, upon the resignation of Governor James Monroe to accept the position of Secretary of State in the Cabinet of President Madison, succeeded, December 5, 1811, as the Executive of the State. His term was lamentably brief, he being one of the victims of the memorable calamity, the burning of the Richmond Theatre, December 26, 1811.

[344] Dr. DAVID STUART, of "Hope Park" and "Ossian Hall," Fairfax county, was the son of Rev. William Stuart, of King George county, and a correspondent of Washington. He was a member of the House of Delegates 1785-'87; married Eleanor, widow of John Parke Custis, and daughter of Benedict Calvert, of Maryland.

[345] CHARLES SIMMS is presumed to have been the gallant Colonel of that name of the Revolution.

[346] HUMPHREY MARSHALL, born in Virginia, about 1756, was a pioneer to Kentucky in 1783; married, 1784, Mary Marshall, born in Virginia 1757; died 1827. He was a relative of Chief-Justice John Marshall. He was a member of the Convention which assembled in Danville in 1787, preliminary to the formation of the State Convention; a member of the Kentucky Legislature for many years, and United States Senator 1795-1801. He fought a duel with Henry Clay, in which the latter was wounded. Author of the first history of Kentucky, published in one volume in 1822, and enlarged to two volumes in 1824. He was the father of John J. and the Hon. Thomas A. Marshall, and died at the residence of the last named July 1, 1841.

[347] MARTIN PICKETT was a member of the Convention of 1776, and a great-uncle of the late General George E. Pickett, Confederate States Army; Sheriff of Fauquier county 1789-'90.

[348] ROBERT BROOKE is said to have come to Virginia about 1660. Robert Brooke was a Justice of the Peace of King William county in 1691. Robert Brooke, Sr., William Brooke, Humphrey Brooke, and George Braxton, Sr., had a joint patent of land in 1720. Brooke married Elizabeth, daughter of George Braxton, Sr. (who died 1748, aged seventy-one), and their son was George Brooke. Robert Brooke was Sheriff of King and Queen county in 1723. Humphrey Brooke, a Justice of the Peace of King William county, died in October, 1738. Colonel George Brooke was Burgess from King and Queen 1772-'75; member of the Committee of Safety 1774-'76; of the Conventions of 1775-'76; State Treasurer 1781; Member of the House of Delegates 1792, and later. Walter Brooke was a Commodore in the Virginia Navy of the Revolution, and George Brooke a Colonel, and both received bounty lands. HUMPHREY BROOKE, member, was the Clerk of Fauquier county and later of the State Senate, 1791-1802. General George M. Brooke, United States Army, and Commodore John Mercer Brooke, United States and Confederate States navies, were of this lineage.

[349] This is presumed to be WARNER LEWIS (died December 30, 1791, aged forty-four years) son of Warner Lewis, of "Warner Hall," and his wife, Eleanor (widow of William, son of Sir William Gooch, and daughter of James Bowles), great-grandson of Robert Lewis, from Brecon, Wales, and grandson of Augustine Warner.

[350] THOMAS SMITH was a member of the House of Delegates from Gloucester county almost continuously from 1784 to 1840. Whether it was the same individual or not, I do not know. Colonel Thomas Smith, of "Airwell," Gloucester county, was dead in 1841.

[351] JOHN GUERRANT, of Huguenot descent, was born March 23, 1760; member of the House of Delegates 1787-'93, and probably later; member of the State Council, and for a time its President, and as such Lieutenant-Governor, in 1805. He married Mary Heath, daughter of Robert and Winifred (Jones) Povall, and had issue.

[352] COLONEL ISAAC COLES was the son of Major John Coles an Irishman, who settled in Henrico county early in the eighteenth century, and engaged in merchandising. The house in which he resided in Richmond, a frame building on Twenty-second between Broad and Marshall streets, was demolished in 1871. He was a worthy citizen and was long a vestryman of St. John's Church, beneath which he was buried. He married Mary, daughter of Isaac Winston, one of the three emigrant brothers from Yorkshire, England. Colonel Coles was

thus a first cousin of Patrick Henry. He was a member of Congress 1780-'89 and again 1793-'97, and voted for locating the seat of government on the Potomac. He married Catherine Thompson, of New York, whose sister married Elbridge Gerry. Coles's Ferry, Halifax county, perpetuates the name and seat of Colonel Isaac Coles.

[353] LIEUTENANT GEORGE CARRINGTON of the Revolution, and a member of the Virginia branch of the Cincinnati; born June 21, 1758; died May 27, 1809. He was the son of George Carrington, born in Barbadoes 1711 ; died in Virginia February 7, 1785 ; married, 1732, Anne Mayo.

[354] The name GOODALL appears early in the annals of Virginia. Michael Goodall patented lands in 1662, and James Goodall in 1740. Charles Goodall died in Hanover county in 1766, Samuel Overton administering on his estate. PARKE GOODALL, member, was the son of Richard Goodall, of Caroline county, a British subject, whose estate was vested in the son by statute. He was an Ensign in the company of Captain Samuel Meredith, of Hanover county, which marched under Patrick Henry (to whom the command was resigned) to Williamsburg, in 1775, to demand restitution of the powder removed from the magazine by Lord Dunmore; was a Justice of the Peace for Hanover county in 1782; member of the House of Delegates 1786-'89; Sheriff in 1809, and subsequently proprietor of the Indian Queen Tavern, in Richmond. He was latterly termed Major Goodall—probably a militia title. His two daughters, Martha Perkins (died May 1, 1809) and Eliza, married, respectively, Parke and Anthony Street, brothers. A son, Colonel Charles Parke Goodall, who married Elizabeth, daughter of Isaac Winston, and died at "Mayfield," Hanover county, October 5, 1855, aged seventy years, and a grandson, Dr. Charles Parke Goodall, each frequently represented Hanover county in the Virginia Assembly.

[355] JOHN CARTER LITTLEPAGE was of the family of the famous adventurer, Lewis Littlepage, Chamberlain to Stanislaus Augustus, King of Poland; served as Captain in the Revolution, and several times represented Hanover county in the Assembly. He may have been of the descent of the emigrant, John Carter.

[356] By my venerable friend, Dr. John Robinson Purdie, of Smithfield, whose dimmed vision caused him to avail himself of the kind services of Captain R. S. Thomas as amanuensis, I am enabled to add some particulars as to the members from the Isle of Wight county, CAPTAIN JAMES JOHNSON and THOMAS PIERCE. The age of the former at death is given me as ninety-one years. He was long a Justice of the Peace of the county, and in court was always the presiding magistrate. Dr. Purdie states that he sat on the bench of magistrates with him as

late as 1843. He was tall and muscular, and retained his vision in a remarkable degree. He was fond of field sports and an excellent shot. Up to his death he was accustomed to go out deer hunting "with the boys," and would drop a buck as often and as surely as any of them. Neither he nor his colleague were remarkable for mental vigor, and it was matter of surprise that they should have defeated competitors of such ability and experience as General John Scarsbrook Wills and Colonel Josiah Parker. The former had frequently been in the Assembly, and was a member of the Conventions of 1775 and 1776. He was a Brigadier-General of militia, and resided in the Carroll's Bridge section of the county, where are now descendants of his, and his name is commemorated in a venerable church formerly held by the Episcopalians, called Wills's Old Meeting-House. Wills and Parker were devoted adherents of Patrick Henry, and with him opposed to the ratification of the Constitution. They were badly beaten by Johnson and Pierce, who favored ratification. (*VI Hening*, page 450.) Joseph Bridger, a great-grandson of Colonel Joseph Bridger (died 1688), who superintended the building of the historic church at Smithfield, erected, it is claimed, in 1632, married Mary, daughter of Thomas Pierce, and had issue Judith, who married Richard Baker, of Burwell's Bay, Clerk of Isle of Wight county. They were the parents of Judge Richard H. Baker (father of Richard H. Baker, Esq., of Norfolk, Virginia). After the death of Thomas Pierce his widow, Mary, married Colonel Josiah Parker, and had issue a daughter, Nancy, who married Captain William Cowper, and had issue : i, Joseph Parker ; ii, Leopold P. C., Lieutenant-Governor of Virginia, died unmarried ; iii, T. F. P. P. (whose children are residents of Smithfield and Norfolk); and iv, William Cowper, died unmarried. Josiah Parker Cowper's name was changed by an act of the Assembly to Josiah Cowper Parker to enable him to inherit the estate of his grandfather, Colonel Josiah Parker. Thomas Pierce owned a large landed estate, and resided just beyond the limits of Smithfield—the lands of Smith and Pierce adjoining for the whole length of what is now Main street and beyond it. Pierce was wealthy and of excellent social position. Both he and Johnson have descendants living in the county. Colonel Josiah Parker was also a member of the Conventions of 1775-'76. He commanded a regiment in the Revolution, and distinguished himself at the battle of Brandywine. He was, unfortunately, of irascible temper. After the battle, applying to General Washington for a furlough, and being denied, in irritation he resigned his commission—an impulsive action, which was ever regretted by him. He was subsequently a Judge of the General Court of Virginia and a member of Congress 1789-'91, and voted for locating the seat of government on the Potomac.

[357] NATHANIEL BURWELL, subsequently of "Carter Hall," Clarke county, Virginia, fourth in descent from Major Lewis Burwell (who

settled, about 1640, on Carter's Creek, Gloucester county,) and his wife, Lucy, daughter of Robert Higginson ; student at William and Mary College in 1766; married, first, his cousin, Susanna Grymes; second, Mrs. Lucy (Page) Baylor.

[358] REV. ROBERT ANDREWS, Professor of Moral and Intellectual Philosophy at William and Mary College from 1777. In 1784 he served with John Page and Bishop James Madison, of Virginia, and Andrew Ellicott, of Pennsylvania, in fixing the boundary line between the two States.

[359] ROBERT BRECKENRIDGE, pioneer to Kentucky from Virginia ; married the widow of Colonel John Floyd ; representative from Jefferson county in 1792, and Speaker; member of the Convention held in Danville in 1792, and which formed the first Constitution of Kentucky.

[360] A descendant of WILLIAM FLEET, Gent, a member of the Virginia Company, of Chartham, Kent ; married Deborah Scott, daughter of Charles Scott, of Egerton, Kent, by his wife, Jane Wyatt. He had issue seven sons and one daughter, viz.: George, William, Henry, Brian, Edward, Reynold, and John, and Catherine. On July 3, 1622, he transferred to his daughter his three shares in Virginia. At least four of his sons (Henry, Edward, Reynold, and John) were among the early emigrants to Virginia and Maryland. All four of them were members of the Maryland Legislature of 1638—the first Assembly whose records have been preserved. Captain HENRY FLEET was the most noted of this brotherhood in our annals. He, at an early date, was captured by the Indians on the Potomac in 1623; remained a captive until 1627 ; became familiar with the Indian tongue ; an interpreter, trader, and legislator in Maryland ; finally settled at Fleet's Bay, in Lancaster county, and represented the county in the House of Burgesses in 1652. His daughter, Sarah, married Edwin Conway. of Lancaster county, Virginia. Captain Henry Fleet was first cousin to Dorothy Scott, who married, first, Major Daniel Gotherson, of Cromwell's army, and about 1655 became a Quaker preacher. She married, secondly, Joseph Hogben, and, about 1680, settled at Long Island, New York. (*Brown's Genesis of the United States*, Vol. II, p. 892.)

[361] JOHN ROANE was a Presidential Elector in 1809, and a member of Congress from 1815 to 1817, from 1827 to 1831, and from 1835 to 1837.

[362] HOLT RICHESON was a Colonel in the State line in the Revolution.

[363] LIEUTENANT-COLONEL BENJAMIN TEMPLE, a gallant officer of the Revolution.

[364] JAMES GORDON, of an ancient Scotch family, was a member of the Convention of 1776. Of his lineage is the distinguished family of Albemarle county, so often and worthily represented in our legislative annals.

[365] LEVIN POWELL was born in 1738; served through the Revolution, and rose to the rank of Lieutenant-Colonel; was a member of Congress 1799-1801 ; died at Bedford, Pennsylvania, in August, 1810.

[366] COLONEL WILLIAM OVERTON CALLIS, son of William and Mary (Cosby) Callis, was born March 4, 1756, near " Urbanna," Virginia, and died March 14, 1814, at "Cuckoo," Louisa county, Virginia. His mother was third in descent from William Overton; born December 2, 1638, in England; settled in Hanover county, Virginia, in 1682; married, November 24, 1670, Mary Waters, who by tradition was a descendant of the famous Nell Gwynne, mistress of Charles the Second. William Overton Callis served in the Revolution seven years and ten months entering the army as Lieutenant, and promoted Captain, and so badly wounded at the battle of Monmouth as to require a trip to the West Indies to recruit his health. During 1781 he served on the staff of General Thomas Nelson, with the rank of Major, being at the reduction of Yorktown; served in the Virginia Assembly seventeen years, and voted for the Resolutions of 1798-'99 ; was twice married—first to a daughter of John Winston, and second to the daughter of Captain Thomas Price, of Hanover county. Hon. William Josiah Leake, of Richmond, Virginia, is his great-grandson. The descendants of William Overton include the worthy names of Blackford, Barry, Beckley, Carr, Clough, Claybrooke. Campbell. Coleman, Cary, Fontaine, Gilliam, Garland, Hart, Harris, Holliday, Harrison, Leake, Morris, Minor, Nelson, Terrell, Waller, Watson, and others.

[367] COLONEL JOHN LOGAN, a doughty Indian-fighter.

[368] HENRY PAWLING was a representative of Lincoln county in 1792, under the first Constitution of Kentucky.

[369] GREEN CLAY, son of Charles Clay, was born in Powhatan county, Virginia, August 14, 1757. He was of the family of Henry Clay. He went to Kentucky when a youth, entered the office of James Thompson, and became a proficient surveyor. His occupation gave him the opportunity to acquire a large and valuable landed estate. He was a member of the Convention of 1799, which formed the present Constitution of Kentucky, and long represented Madison county in each branch of the Legislature. Appointed a Brigadier-General March 29, 1813, he led 3,000 Kentucky volunteers to the relief of Fort Meigs and forced the enemy to withdraw. General Harrison left him in the com-

mand of Fort Meigs, which he skilfully defended from the attack of a large force of British and Indians, under General Proctor and Tecumseh. He was the father of Hon. Cassius M. Clay. He died October 31, 1826. Clay county, Kentucky, was named in his honor.

[370] GENERAL RICHARD KENNON, third in descent from Richard Kennon, who settled in Virginia, about 1670, at "Conjuror's Neck," about five miles below Petersburg, Virginia; entered the army of the Revolution as Lieutenant in the Fifth Virginia Regiment; promoted at the battle of Monmouth; served throughout the war; appointed by President Jefferson first Governor of Louisiana Territory; died in that State, aged forty-four years; member of the Cincinnati; married Elizabeth Beverley, daughter of Robert and Anne (Beverley) Munford, of "Richland," Mecklenburg county, Virginia.

[371] WILLIS RIDDICK was a member of the Virginia Conventions of 1775-'76, and served long in the Virginia Assembly.

[372] WILLIAM CLAYTON was a descendant of John Clayton, a Burgess from James City county in 1723; Attorney-General of the Colony in 1724; Judge of the Court of Admiralty; died November 18, 1737, in the seventy-second year of his age. A manuscript volume of his opinions has been preserved. William Clayton was a Burgess from New Kent in 1769, member of the House of Delegates 1776, and member of the Virginia Convention of 1776.

[373] COLONEL BURWELL BASSETT, JR., of "Eltham," New Kent county, Virginia, was a nephew of Mrs. George Washington; member of the House of Delegates of Virginia 1789, 1819-'20; of State Senate 1798-'99, 1802-'3; member of Congress 1805-'13, 1815-'19, and 1821-'31; died February 26, 1841, aged seventy-six years and eleven months.

[374] DR. WALTER JONES was born in Virginia in 1745; graduated at William and Mary College in 1760; studied medicine in Edinburgh, Scotland, and received the degree of M. D.; on his return to Virginia he settled in Northumberland county and became eminent as a scholar and physician. In 1777 he was appointed by Congress Physician-General of Hospitals in the Middle Department; was a representative in Congress from Virginia from 1797 to 1799, and again from 1803 to 1811. He was at one time a "Free Thinker," but his views were subsequently entirely changed, and he embraced the Christian faith, after which he wrote a lengthy volume denouncing his former views, and stating with clearness the grounds on which he did so. This was done for the satisfaction and the gratification of his children. He died in Westmoreland county, Virginia, December 31, 1815.

[375] WILLIAM RONALD was a native of Scotland and a brother of General Andrew Ronald, a prominent lawyer of Richmond, Virginia, who was one of the counsel representing the British merchants in the so-called British Debts case, in which the debtors were represented by Patrick Henry.

[376] GENERAL ROBERT LAWSON was a gallant and meritorious officer of the Revolution.

[377] THEODORICK BLAND was born in Virginia in 1742, and was the uncle of John Randolph, of Roanoke. Graduated M. D. in Edinburgh, Scotland, and practiced his profession for a time in Williamsburg, combining with it, as was the custom in the towns of Virginia in that day, the keeping of an apothecary or dispensary. At the commencement of the Revolution he entered the army, and rose to the rank of Colonel of Dragoons. In 1779 he had command of the troops at Albemarle barracks, and continued in that station till elected to Congress in 1780, where he served three years. He was then chosen a member of the Virginia Legislature. He was a representative in the first Congress under the Constitution. He died at New York June 1, 1790, while attending a session of Congress. He was the first member of Congress whose death was announced in that body; and although buried in Trinity church-yard, the sermon in the church was preached by a pastor of the Dutch Reformed denomination. He was present at the battle of Brandywine, and enjoyed the confidence of General Washington. He was of worthy lineage and a man of culture. His correspondence with eminent men, under the title of *The Bland Papers*, was edited by Charles Campbell (author of a history of Virginia), and published in two volumes, 8vo., in 1843.

[378] EDMUND RUFFIN, fourth in descent from William Ruffin, who was seated in the Isle of Wight county in 1666, and died 1693. He was the son of Edmund Ruffin by his first marriage with Mrs. Edmunds, *née* Simmons (he married secondly Elizabeth Cocke, of Surry county), and was born January 2, 1744-'45; died in 1807; was a member of the House of Delegates 1777, 1784, 1786, and 1787; County Lieutenant 1789; Sheriff 1797; married Jane, daughter of Sir William Skipwith, Baronet, of "Prestwould," Mecklenburg county. Their grandson, Edmund Ruffin, of Prince George and Hanover counties, born January 5, 1794, was the eminent agriculturist, who volunteered in the late war between the States, and is said to have fired the first gun in the reduction of Fort Sumter. Under mental depression, caused by the failure of the Confederacy, he committed suicide June 15, 1865.

[379] CAPTAIN THOMAS BULLITT was a meritorious officer under Washington in the French and Indian war. Cuthbert Bullitt was probably of the same family. He was a Judge of the State Court.

[380] The ancestor of the WALKE family of Virginia was Anthony Voelke (anglicized Walke), who accompanied William, Prince of Orange, to England in 1688, and came to Virginia in 1693. His grandson, ANTHONY WALKE, the member, was a worthy citizen and pious churchman. He built the church still standing near Norfolk and known as Old Donation Church He married twice—first, Jane, daughter of William Randolph; second, Mary Moseley, a granddaughter of Bishop Gilbert Burnett. He died in 1794. His colleague, THOMAS WALKE, was of the same lineage.

[381] JOHN DAWSON graduated at Harvard University in 1782; was a Presidential Elector in 1793; member of Congress 1797–1814; was frequently in the Virginia Legislature; was a member of the Executive Council of Virginia; rendered service in the War of 1812 as Aid to the Commanding General on the Lakes, and was appointed bearer of dispatches to France in 1801 by President John Adams. He died in Washington, D. C., March 30, 1814, aged fifty-two years.

[382] The progenitor of the COCKE family of Virginia was Richard Cocke, who emigrated from Leeds, Yorkshire, England, in 1636, and settled at "Malvern Hills," Henrico county, the locality of a sanguinary battle of the name during the late war between the States. Richard, a grandson of the emigrant, married Elizabeth, daughter of Henry Hartwell, who was Clerk of the General Court in 1675, and one of the trustees in the charter of William and Mary College, February 8, 1692, O. S. From this couple was descended the member, JOHN HARTWELL COCKE.

[383] The ancestor of the member, JOHN ALLEN, was Major Arthur Allen, who patented lands in 1649 in Surry county. He was the grandson of Colonel John Allen, of "Clermont." He was a member of the House of Delegates in 1784, '86, '87, '88, and '91; a member of the Council, and died before 1799.

[384] JOHN HOWELL BRIGGS, the son of Gray Briggs, a native of Ireland, was a member of the House of Delegates 1786–'88, and of the Council in 1789. His sister, Eliza, married Colonel William Heth, of the Third Virginia regiment, a gallant officer of the Revolution, who enjoyed the friendship of Washington, by whom he was appointed Collector of the Ports of Richmond, Petersburg, and Bermuda Hundred. He was removed in 1802, being succeeded by John Page. He died in May, 1807. His brother, John Heth, was a Lieutenant in the Revolution; and his sister, Margaret, married General Robert Porterfield.

[385] THOMAS EDMUNDS was the son of John Edmunds, who died February 8, 1770, and who had represented Sussex in the House of Burgesses from the creation of the county. William Edmunds (probably the father of John Edmunds) died in Sussex, March 9, 1739–'40.

[386] COLE DIGGES was the grandson of Cole Digges, a Burgess in 1718; member of the Virginia Council in 1724, and subsequently its President, and who was the son of Edward Digges (fourth son of Sir Edward Digges, of Chelburn, Kent, England, Master of the Rolls and M. P.), President of the Council of Virginia, and Acting Governor of the Colony, 1665-'66. His son, Edward Digges, also served in the Council, and his daughter, Mary, was the first wife of Nathaniel Harrison, of "Wakefield."

[387] RICHARD CARY was born in Elizabeth City county. He is said to have served for a time in the Revolution, on the staff of Washington; Judge of the Court of Admiralty of Virginia in 1777, and subsequently of the Court of Appeals. He was a man of cultivated tastes, and was fond of botanical studies, in which he acquired much proficiency.

[388] It may be of interest to note that of the forty-nine members of the Phi-Beta-Kappa Society, organized at William and Mary College December 5, 1776, nine were members of the Convention of 1788: John Jones, John Stuart, Littleton Eyre, John Allen, BUSHROD WASHINGTON, William Cabell, Archibald Stuart, John Marshall, Stevens Thomson Mason, and a tenth, if Hartwell Cocke and John Hartwell Cocke may be identified as the same individual. Another member, John James Beckley, was the Secretary of the Convention. The Society was an admirable nursery of patriots and statemen, as the distinguished careers of others of its members has given evidence.

[389] JOHN BLAIR was the son of John Blair, President of the Council, and Acting Governor of Virginia in 1758; grandson of Dr. Archibald Blair, a brother of Commissary James Blair, President of William and Mary College. He was born in Williamsburg, Virginia, in 1732; graduated at William and Mary College; studied law at the Temple, London; a Burgess in 1765; and on the dissolution of the House in 1769, he, with Washington and other patriots, drafted the "Non-importation Agreement" at "Raleigh Tavern." He was one of the committee in June, 1776, which drew up the plan for the government of the State; was elected a Judge of the Court of Appeals, then President of the Court, and, in 1780, Judge of the High Court of Chancery. He was a Delegate to the Philadelphia Convention to Revise the Articles of Confederation. He supported the "Virginia Plan." In September, 1789, he was appointed by Washington a Judge of the United States Supreme Court, resigned in 1796; died in Williamsburg August 31, 1800.

ARCHIBALD STUART.

The Hon. A. H. H. Stuart was engaged in the preparation of the following sketch for this work, in emendation and enlarge- ment of that by Dr. Grigsby, given *ante* (pages 10–15), when he was stricken with fatal illness, dying February 13, 1891. Whilst it is to be regretted that it is incomplete, it is invested with peculiar interest as being the final literary and a filial task of his nobly useful life. His son-in-law, Alexander F. Robertson, Esq., writes me that " he made a great effort to complete it." It is received just in time to add finally to the text of the work previously in print.—EDITOR.

R. A. BROCK, ESQ.:

My Dear Sir: Sickness, accompanied by a nervous affection of my right hand, which rendered it impossible for me to write legibly, prevented me during the summer and autumn months from preparing the "sketch" of my father, "Archibald Stuart," which I promised you. I have read with great interest and satisfaction your publication founded on Mr. Grigsby's lecture. But there are some errors and omissions which I desire to correct and supply, and also some notes as to his ancestry.

First, I wish to state that Archibald Stuart, Sr., his grandfather—the first of the family who came to America—was a young Irishman of respectable family, who lived not far from Londonderry. He was a man of good education, as evidenced by the fact that his will, written by himself, and now in the office of Augusta county, dated 1759 and recorded 1761, presents, both in style and handwriting, unquestionable proof that he was a man of education. He was a man of intelligence and deep religious convictions and great energy of character. In early life he married Janet Brown, a sister of John Brown, who afterwards became a Presbyterian minister in Virginia. By her he had two chil- dren while living in Ireland—viz., a son, named Thomas Stuart, and a daughter, named Eleanor.

About 1725–'26 the persecutions of the Presbyterians and other "dis- senters" became so intolerable that Archibald Stuart, with others,

became active promoters of an avowed insurrection or rebellion to defend their rights. The military power of the Government was invoked to suppress it, and when that was done Archibald Stuart was one of those proscribed, and if he could have been arrested would have been executed for treason.

Being thus compelled to fly for his life, he managed with great difficulty to make his escape to the coast, where he contrived to get on board a ship bound for America, leaving his wife and two children behind him. He reached America in safety and took refuge in the wilds of Western Pennsylvania, where he remained in concealment for seven years. Finally there was some act or proclamation of amnesty, which enabled him to send for wife and children to join him in Pennsylvania. During his seclusion in Pennsylvania he had been diligently making provision for his family, so as to be ready to receive them. In 1732 his wife and children came over, under the escort of her brother, John Brown, and joined Archibald Stuart in his new home in Pennsylvania. They remained in Pennsylvania for about seven years, and during that time two other children were born—viz., Alexander and Benjamin.

After the proclamation of the Governor of Virginia in 1738, granting freedom of religious opinions and worship to immigrants who would move to the Valley of Virginia and protect the western frontier of Virginia against the incursions of the Indians, Archibald Stuart, with his family, removed to Virginia, accompanied or followed by John Brown, and settled permanently in Augusta county. Archibald Stuart, being a sagacious business man, acquired large and valuable tracts of land and other property, which not only enabled him to live in comfort, but also to give to his children the best opportunities for education which the circumstances would allow, and to convey to each of them by deed or will a valuable estate in land.

The three sons of Archibald Stuart married in early life daughters of prominent settlers of the Valley. His daughter, Eleanor, also married Edward Hall, the son of a neighbor, and left a large family. Among her descendants were Dr. Isaac Hall, who graduated at Edinburgh Medical College in the latter part of the last century, and settled in Petersburg, Virginia, where he became eminent as a physician; Judge John Hall, of the Supreme Court of North Carolina, and many others who became distinguished. One of her daughters married Captain Andrew Fulton, an officer in the Revolutionary War, and among the offspring of this marriage were Hon. John H. Fulton, of Abingdon, who was for several terms representative of that district in Congress, and Hon. Andrew S. Fulton, for many years judge in the Wythe district.

All the sons of Archibald Stuart, Sr., left large families, the members of which in turn intermarried with families of the vicinage, until they were closely allied to the Pattersons, Moffets, McClungs, Fultons,

Tates, Tylers, Halls, Guthries, Alexanders, Withrows, Watkinses, Douglases, Moores, Steeles, McDowells, and many others of the best standing in this part of the Valley.

John Brown, Mrs. Stuart's brother, also married and settled in Augusta county. His wife was a daughter of John Preston, and the fruit of this marriage was five sons. He studied divinity at Princeton, became pastor of Providence church, and held that position for forty-four years, and was the second rector of Liberty Hall Academy. Late in life he removed to Kentucky, where his sons attained high distinction, one of them (James) having served as United States senator and afterwards as Minister to France; and another was the ancestor of the late B. Gratz Brown, of Missouri.

At an early day, after Archibald Stuart had established himself in Augusta, two of his brothers, named David and John, came over from Ireland. Of them I know but little, except that they were men of high character and intelligence. David was the ancestor of the Stuarts of Greenbrier county. John, after remaining some time in Virginia, removed to Kentucky. Among his descendants were John T. Stuart, of Springfield, Illinois, who was at an early age a prominent member of Congress (having beaten Stephen A. Douglas in an earnestly-contested race), and subsequently a very distinguished lawyer. He was a partner of Abraham Lincoln in the practice of law, and when he died was the subject of a noble funeral oration by ex-Judge David Davis, of the Supreme Court of the United States.

I have thus disjointedly jotted down some of the facts connected with the ancestry and family connections of Archibald Stuart. I have done so because of late years I have received many letters from all parts of the country making inquiries on the subject.

As has been already stated, Archibald Stuart, Sr., left three sons to survive him—viz., Thomas, who was born in Ireland, and Alexander and Benjamin, who were born in Pennsylvania after his wife and children joined him there.

Thomas was a prominent man in Augusta county, and is the person of that name referred to by Mr. Grigsby as one of the founders of Liberty Hall Academy. Benjamin was the youngest son, and is represented to have been a man of admirable character and fine intellect. He inherited the family mansion of his father and lived a quiet life, not taking any active part in public affairs. He married, and left a number of children.

Of these two members of the family I do not deem it necessary to say anything more than that they lived honorable and useful lives.

Alexander Stuart Sr., was the second son of Archibald Stuart, Sr., the fugitive emigrant from Ireland. He was born during the sojourn of his parents in Pennsylvania, and came with them at the age of four years to Augusta county, where he was reared to manhood. He received a common-school education, and his letters show that he wrote and spelled correctly and was versed in arithmetic and the simpler branches of mathematics. At the age of twenty he married Mary Patterson, the daughter of a Scotch-Irish farmer of the neighborhood. By her he had two sons—Archibald and Robert—and a number of daughters. For some time after his marriage he lived in Augusta, about three miles northwest from Waynesboro'. Subsequently he removed to a farm, which his father had given him, lying in what is now Rockbridge county, near Brownsburgh. Having lost his wife, he married a second time. His second wife was a young widow lady, a Mrs. Paxton, whose maiden name had been Moore. By her he had two sons and a number of daughters. The sons were named Alexander and James. Alexander Stuart, Sr., my grandfather, is the person referred to by Mr. Grigsby as Captain Alexander Stuart, one of the founders of Liberty Hall Academy. He seems to have been deeply impressed with the importance of education, and as he had four sons to educate he took an active part in causing the academy to be removed from its original location in Augusta county to a point near Timber Ridge church, which would bring it much nearer to his residence. To that end he and his neighbor, Samuel Houston (the father of President Samuel Houston, of Texas), offered to the trustees a donation of forty acres of land each, and liberal subscriptions in money, if they would remove the academy to the place indicated by them. This offer was accepted and the removal accomplished. The four sons of Alexander Stuart were educated at the academy after its transfer to the new location. Archibald, the oldest son of Captain Alexander Stuart, having exhibited a strong thirst for knowledge while a pupil at Liberty Hall Academy, and more than ordinary capacity to acquire it, he made known to his father his wish to adopt the law as his profession. This suggestion being approved, his father determined to send him to William and Mary College to obtain the best education that could then be had in Virginia. He accordingly went to William and Mary about 1777, and continued there until 1781. During a large portion of his sojourn at college he was an inmate of the family of Bishop Madison, the president of the college. He thus had opportunities of seeing the best society of the city and of becoming acquainted with many of the gentlemen who were prominent in the councils of the State, Williamsburg being the seat of government.

Meanwhile the struggle for independence of the Colonies was progressing, and when the seat of government was transferred to. the South by the invasion of Cornwallis the militia troops of the Valley and Southwestern Virginia were called into active service and ordered to proceed to the South to join the army of General Greene. Among these was the regiment of which Colonel Samuel McDowell, a gallant and distinguished officer, was colonel, and which consisted mainly of troops from Augusta and Rockbridge. Colonel McDowell was a man of high character, a brave and experienced officer, but unfortunately some time before the battle of Guilford Courthouse he had an attack of malarial-fever, which unfitted him for active service in the field, and the command of the regiment devolved on Major Alexander Stuart, who was the senior officer in the absence of Colonel McDowell. This regiment was composed mainly of the flower of the young men of the Valley, who fought with the enthusiasm of patriots and the steadiness of veterans. They were stationed at a point particularly exposed to the fire of the British artillery, and suffered greatly. In my early youth and manhood I was personally acquainted with a number of men who participated in the battle, and heard from their lips many interesting incidents connected with it. Among these was the late General Samuel Blackburn, of Bath county; Rev. Samuel Houston, of Rockbridge; David Steele, of Augusta; and my father, of Augusta.

General Blackburn and my father passed through the fight without injury. Rev. Samuel Houston narrowly escaped death from a musket-ball, which struck the Bible which he had in his knapsack with such force as to penetrate more than half-way through it. David Steele received a sabre-cut, which chipped a small piece from his skull and exposed to view the coating of his brain, which was protected by a small plate of silver attached to the bone. The wound did not seem to have any injurious effect upon him, except perhaps to develop some eccentricities which were observable in his conduct, and he lived to attain the age of seventy-five or eighty years.

Major Alexander Stuart, according to every account, conducted himself with great gallantry, and two horses were killed under him during the battle. The first casualty occurred in an early stage of the conflict, but he was promptly mounted on another horse and resumed his position in the field. At a later period of the fight, when the British artillery were brought to bear on the American troops, a shell exploded so near to Major Stuart that the fragments killed the horse on which he was mounted and inflicted a severe wound on himself. Being thus disabled, and his horse having fallen on him, he had not the strength to extricate himself from his entanglements, and was compelled to lie helpless on the field until he was captured and sent as a prisoner to the British hospital, where his wound was properly attended to. When he was well enough to be moved he was transferred, with other prisoners, to one of the prison-ships on the coast, where he was detained for more than six months, when he regained his liberty by an exchange of prisoners. Meanwhile the condition of things had materially changed. The surrender of Cornwallis soon followed, and active hostilities had ceased.

Archibald Stuart spent the greater part of the next two years in the study of law with Mr. Jefferson. After he had completed his course of reading he returned to the residence of his father, in Rockbridge county, with a view to conference with his friends as to his future settlement in life. Some of them thought that it would be advisable for him to become a candidate for a seat in the House of Delegates at the election which was then near at hand. The elections were then, and continued for half a century later, to be held on the first day of the county courts of April in the respective counties. The April term of the County Court of Rockbridge was then, and I believe still continues to be, held on the Monday before the first Tuesday in April, and all the votes were cast at the court-house. In compliance with the wishes of his friends he became a candidate, but was defeated by a majority of thirteen votes.

On the day after the election he was requested by his father to go to Botetourt county to close some matters of unsettled business which he had with Colonel George Skillern, who resided about two miles from Pattonsburg. Accordingly, on Wednesday, he went to the residence of Colonel Skillern, and on the following day closed up the business which was the object of his visit, so as to enable him to return to his father's on Friday, according to his original plan.

In the mean time an invitation had been sent to him, as the guest of Colonel Skillern, to attend a barbecue to be held on Friday at Pattonsburg. At the urgent solicitation of Colonel Skillern he consented to remain and attend the festival, at which it was expected most of the leading gentlemen of the county would be present.

During the progress of the entertainment a toast was offered in honor of the soldiers of the Revolutionary War, and Archibald Stuart was called on to respond to it. This he did at some length, and apparently to the satisfaction of his audience, to whom he was a stranger. Many inquiries were made about him, and it having been made known that he was the son of Major Alexander Stuart, who had commanded the Valley regiment at Guilford, and that he had left William and Mary College some weeks in advance of the battle to join the army, and had himself actively participated in the fight, the favorable impression made by his speech was strengthened; and some one having referred to the fact that he had been defeated as a candidate for the Legislature in Rockbridge on the preceding Monday, it was suggested that the people of Botetourt should elect him as one of their delegates at the election to be held on the following Monday. The suggestion was promptly adopted, and a committee appointed to wait on Mr. Stuart and communicate to him their wishes and invite him to be a candidate. This action was wholly unexpected by him, and after thanking them for their kind wishes he was obliged to decline their offer, on the ground that he was ineligible for Botetourt, not being a freeholder in the county. Colonel Skillern, who was a man of wealth, promptly replied that he was prepared to remove that objection by conveying to Mr. Stuart a small house and lot which he owned in Fincastle. The proposition was finally accepted, and all the arrangements perfected, and at the close of the barbecue the gentlemen who had been present returned to their homes prepared to announce to their neighbors that Mr. Stuart would be a candidate for a seat in the House of Delegates from Botetourt at the election to be held on the following Monday.

He remained as the guest of Colonel Skillern, who was an old friend of his father, but on Monday morning he appeared at Fincastle, and the deed from Colonel Skillern to him having been deposited in the clerk's office which made him eligible, he was regularly announced as a candidate for the House of Delegates from Botetourt county, and proceeded to address the large crowd, which, attracted by the novelty of the circumstances, had assembled at the court-house, on the political topics of the day, and at the close of the polls he was announced as one of those duly elected.

Thus it happened that the young man who had left his father's house a week before a defeated candidate for the House of Delegates for Rockbridge county, returned a ' delegate-elect " for Botetourt.

These events occurred in April, 1783. In the progress of that year Archibald Stuart removed to Staunton, which presented many inducements to a young man who proposed to follow the profession of law. By diligence and energy he soon acquired a large and lucrative practice. As proof of the activity and industry which he displayed in the pursuit of his profession, I can refer to the fact that, in addition to what may be called his "home practice" in Augusta and the adjacent, he was a regular attendant on what were then called the "district courts," held at New London, Abingdon, the Sweet Springs, and Rockingham.

He represented Botetourt in the session of the General Assembly in the winter of 1783-'84, and was re-elected and served the same county in the sessions of 1784-'85 and 1785-'86.

In 1786 he was elected and served as a delegate from Augusta; was re-elected in 1787. In 1788 he was elected a member of the convention of Virginia which ratified the Constitution of the United States. He was probably the youngest member of that body, as he had barely completed his thirty-first year when he took his seat in it. There he was brought into association with Edmund Pendleton, President, Patrick Henry, George Mason, James Madison, Edmund Randolph, John Marshall, James Monroe, George Nicholas, and many other of the distinguished men of Virginia.

In the presence of men like these, who had inaugurated and conducted the movement for independence, he very properly declined to participate in the debates and was content to remain an attentive and delighted listener to the marvellous displays of wisdom, logic, and eloquence which were made by those who were justly regarded as the fathers of the Republic.

After the close of the session of the Convention Archibald Stuart declined a re-election to any public office, with a view to devote his whole time to his profession. There were other family reasons which concurred in leading him to this conclusion. His father, who was advanced in life, had met with some heavy losses in consequence of a partnership into which he had unfortunately entered. He was, therefore, unable to give to his two younger sons, Alexander and James, the same opportunities of education which he had extended to Archibald. He had been educated at Liberty Hall Academy, which afforded a fine course of instruction. They were both young men of energy and ability, and, stimulated by the success of their brother in the law, evinced a strong desire to adopt the same profession. This fact having been made known to Archibald Stuart, he promptly invited them to come to Staunton and take positions in his office, and study law under his supervision and instruction. A similar invitation was given by him to his cousin, John Hall. These invitations were gratefully accepted, and in due season these three young men became installed as law-students in the office of Archibald Stuart. They all proved to be diligent students, and all successful men in after life.

John Hall settled in North Carolina, where, after a distinguished career at the bar, he was elected Judge of the circuit or district court, and, after a service of some years in that court, he was promoted to the bench of the Supreme Court of that State, where he gained still higher distinction as an able and upright judge.

After Alexander Stuart had completed his course of study of law in the office of his brother in Staunton he removed to Campbell county, where he commenced the practice of his profession. Not long afterwards he was elected a member of the Executive Council of the State and removed to Richmond, where he resided for some years. About this time (but the writer has no information as to the date) he married Miss Ann Dabney, a near relation of the late Chiswell Dabney, of Lynchburg; and when a territorial government was established in Illinois, he was appointed United States Judge for the territory, and settled in Kaskaskia. But, the climate proving unfavorable for the health of his family, he returned to Virginia. Subsequently he removed to Missouri, where he owned valuable real estate, and continued to be a resident of that State until his death, in December, 1832. During his residence there he served as District Judge of the United States, and occupied other positions of honor and responsibility. Two of his children by his first wife (Miss Dabney) survived him— viz., a son, Archibald, and a daughter, Anne. Anne married Judge James Ewell Brown, of Wythe county, Virginia. Archibald Stuart studied law and settled in Patrick county, Virginia, where he became eminent as a lawyer and politician. He represented Patrick county at different times in the House of Delegates, in the Senate of Virginia, in the Congress of the United States, and in the Virginia Constitutional Convention of 1829-'30 and 1850-'51. He married Miss Elizabeth Pannil and reared a large family of sons and daughters. Two of his sons, in after life, attained peculiar eminence in their respective vocations—viz., William Alexander Stuart as one of the most enterprising and successful business men of the State, and General James Ewell Brown Stuart, who is generally recognized to have been the most brilliant and successful cavalry officer of the late war between the States.

James Stuart, after obtaining his license to practice law, removed to one of the southern counties of Virginia (Pittsylvania), commenced his professional career, and soon afterwards married a lady named

Stockton. The result of this marriage was a large family of children. For many years he was successful as a lawyer, but finally he was over- taken by disease which impaired his mind to such an extent as to dis- qualify him for the pursuit of his profession. The family then removed to Mississippi, where they established themselves in good social posi- tion, and their descendants are now to be found in various parts of the State. During the late civil war two young men, the grandsons of James Stuart, who had won for themselves great distinction at the University of Mississippi, came to Virginia with the troops of that State. In consequence of their scientific attainments they were assigned to duty in the signal department; but, when the hour of deadly conflict came, they were unable to restrain their military ardor, and rushed into the thickest of the fight and both were killed—one at the second battle of Manassas, and the other at Fredericksburg.

Passing from this digression from the regular line of narrative—which the writer thought might be interesting to collateral branches of the family connected with Archibald Stuart—he now returns to the con- sideration of the principal events connected with the subsequent career of Archibald Stuart.

On the 4th of May, 1791, Archibald Stuart was married to Eleanor Briscoe, second daughter of Colonel Gerard Briscoe, of Frederick county, Virginia. Colonel Briscoe was a Maryland gentleman, and had served in the Revolutionary War. He lived for many years in Montgomery county, near Rockville, Maryland, but having married Miss Margaret Baker, a Virginia lady, he subsequently removed to an estate which he owned near Winchester, Virginia, where he continued to reside during the residue of his life. After Archibald Stuart's marriage he withdrew from public life and devoted all his time to his professional business interests. But he still felt deep solicitude about the success of the new Federal Government, which he, as a member of the State Convention of 1788, had aided in establishing.

It will be remembered that the Constitution of the United States seemed to contemplate the division of each State into "electoral dis- tricts," corresponding in number with the number of electoral votes which the State was entitled to cast, and the people of each district were allowed to choose their own elector. In the earlier presidential elections the counties of Augusta, Rockingham, and Shenandoah com- posed one electoral district

The writer has not taken pains to inform himself who was elected from that district in the year 1788-'89, when George Washington was first elected, but he has in his possession the original certificate of the election of Archibald Stuart as elector in that district at the second election. This paper is prepared and certified under the hands and seals of And. Shanklin, sheriff of Rockingham, Joseph Bell, sheriff of Augusta, and Jacob Steigal, deputy sheriff for Evan Jones, sheriff of Shenandoah county, dated 12th day of November, 1792. Under this certificate of his election Archibald Stuart qualified as a member of the Electoral College of Virginia and cast the vote of his district for George Washington at his second election in 1793.

It may be added that at each presidential election thereafter, up to and including the election of 1824, he was chosen a member of the Electoral College of Virginia, voting consecutively for Jefferson, Madison, Monroe, and William H. Crawford, of Georgia

In pursuance of a resolution of the General Assembly of Virginia, passed on the 25th of December, 1795, authorizing the Executive to appoint commissioners to ascertain the boundary line between the Commonwealth of Virginia and the State of Kentucky, a commission was——

The manuscript of Mr. Stuart concludes as above. The commissioners on the part of Virginia were Archibald Stuart, General Joseph Martin, and Creed Taylor; and John Coburn, Robert Johnson, and Buckner Thruston on the part of Kentucky. Their report is embodied in " an act for confirming and establishing the boundary line between this State and the State of Kentucky, ascertained and fixed by certain commissions by both States, and for other purposes," passed by the Virginia Assembly January 13, 1800. (*Shepherd's Continuation* of *Hening's Statutes*, Vol. II, pages 234, *et seq.*)—EDITOR.

INDEX.

CRAWFORD, William Harris, I, 61;
II, 392.
Creditors of the Nation, distinction
among the, II, 277.
Creek, applicability of the name,
I, 13.
CROCKETT, Walter, II. 365.
"*Cuckoo*," II, 375.
Cumberland County, II, 71.
Current Money of Virginia, II, 204.
CUSTIS, Edmund, II, 363; descent
of, 367.
John, II, 367.
John Parke, II, 367, 373.
Customs, Revenues from, I, 277.

DABNEY, Ann. II, 390.
Chiswell, II, 390.
Mary, II, 369.
DAINGERFIELD, Elizabeth, II, 372.
Colonel William, II, 372.
DANIEL, Jr., William, II, 326.
DARKE, Captain Joseph, II, 368.
General William, I, 35, 340; II, 9,
363; sketch of, 368.
DAVEISS, Joseph Hamilton, II, 289.
DAVIDSON, Miss Mary, I, vii.
DAVIES, Rev. Samuel, I, 255, 257;
II, 42, 114
DAVIS, Augustine, I, 67.
General, II, 25.
David, II, 385.
DAWSON, John, I, 139, 314; II, 192,
199, 230, 375; sketch of, 381.
DUANE, LL. D., Charles, I. xxiii.
Debtors, bill for the relief of, II,
74; vote on, 74.
Debts of States, I, 90; to be assumed
by the general government, II,
212; vote on, 213; sinking fund
for, 228; of the United States to
foreign governments, 125.
"*Decius*," Letters of, I, 333; II,
358.
Delaware and Catawba Indians,
II, 55.
D'ESTAING, Count, anecdote of,
II, 254.
DICKENSON, Henry, II, 365.
*Dictator proposed for Virginia in
1781*, II, 352, 357.
DIGGES, Cole, II, 366, 382.
Dudley, II, 48.
Edward, II, 382.
Sir. Edward, II, 382.
DINWIDDIE, Governor Robert, His
pistol tax, I, 35; presents mace to
Norfolk, 74, 329; II, 25, 41, 42.

Dirlton's Doubts, I, 258.
Dismal Swamp, canal, II, 176, 228;
lands, I, 161.
Disunion, Apprehensions of, I, 154.
DODDRIDGE, Philip, I, 201, 347.
DOUGLAS, Stephen A., II, 385.
DREW, Thomas H., II, 360, 370.
Will., II, 53.
DRINKARD, Jr., William, I, 66.
Sr., William, I, 66.
DROMGOOLE, George C., I, 24.
DUANE, William, editor of the
Aurora; cited before the United
States Senate for contempt, II,
246, 263
William, J., II, 263.
Duel, between Mason and McCarty,
II, 265; between Marshall and
Clay, 373.
DUNCAN, Rev. James A., I, viii.
Rev. W. W., I, viii.
DUNMORE, Lord, I, 324; II, 46, 61,
303, 375.

Eagle Tavern, I, 347.
EARLY, Joab, II, 364, 371.
Joel.
John, II, 364, 371.
Bishop John, II, 371.
Jubal, II, 371.
General Jubal A , II, 371.
Peter, II, 342, 371.
"*Edge Hill*," I, ix.
EDMISTON, Samuel, II, 366.
EDMOND, Charles, I, vii.
EDMUNDS, II, 380.
John, II, 381.
Thomas, II, 366, 381,
William, II, 381.
Education in Virginia, Early, II,
71, 216, 225, 379, 382.
EGE, Jacob, II, 137
Elections, Federal, I, 118; regula-
tion of State, II, 82.
"*Eltham*," II, 379.
ELTONHEAD, Alice, I, 143.
Emancipation of Slaves, I, 211;
II, 56; vote on, 59, 69, 130, 131,
195, 316.
Entails, question of, II, 72.
Episcopal Church, legislation con-
cerning the, II, 99, 106, 114; II,
313, 323; value of its property,
113; ministers of, their scholar-
ship, 114, 122, 126; free use of
its edifices petitioned for, 210,
323.
Escheats and Forfeitures, II, 96.

MASON, General Stevens Thomson, II, 268.
  Stevens Thomson, I, 24, 36, 327 ; II, 72, 138, 178, 193, 198, 215, 216, 220 ; sketch of, 225 ; death and burial of, 263, 268, 269, 343, 365, 382.
  Temple, II, 223, 264, 268.
  Thomson, sketch of, II, 215 ; personal characteristics of, 224, 262, 268.
  William, II, 215, 364.
MASON family, in New England, II, 215.
Massachusetts Historical Society, action of, on the death of H. B. Grigsby, I, xxv.
Massachusetts, intestine commotions of, I, 82 ; insurgents of, 270.
MATHEWS, George, I, 338 ; II, 80.
  Sampson, I, 338.
MATTHEWS, Major, II, 45.
  Thomas, I, 36 ; notice of, 306, 321, 343, 347 ; II, 80, 105, 173, 179, 198, 211, 366.
MAXWELL, II, 81.
  William, I, vii, xvii.
MAY, David, II, 48.
"*Mayfield*," II, 375.
MAYNARD, Lieutenant, I, 95.
MAYO, Ann, II, 375.
  Joseph, II, 56, 69, 80.
Mecklenburg county, Virginia, petitions for emancipation, II, 131.
MERCER, II, 55.
  General Hugh, II, 53.
  James, I, 66 ; II, 19, 48, 193.
  John Francis, II, 279.
Merchants of Virginia, chiefly foreign, II, 143.
MEREDITH, Colonel Samuel, II, 375.
Messages from the Governor of Virginia, not formal in early days, II, 199.
Methodist Episcopal Church, II, 126.
MICHAUX, II, 370.
  Abraham, II, 370.
  Captain Jacob, II, 370.
  Joseph, II, 364 ; sketch of, 370.
Military officers, influence of, in ratifying the Constitution, I, 160.
Militia of Virginia, intrepidity of, I, 160, 259 ; II, 174.
MILLER, John, I, 7 ; II, 368.
MILO, trial of, I, 269.
MINOR, II, 378.

Mississippi, navigation of the, I, 152, 181 ; discussed, 231, 274 ; II, 169, 171, 194, 237.
MOFFET, II, 384.
Monmouth, Battle of, II, 378, 379.
Monongahela, Battle of, II, 42.
MONROE, II, 392.
  James, I, 36, 64, 75, 102 ; notice of, 167 ; discusses the Federal Government, 175, 203, 211, 234 ; cabinet of, 239, 243, 255, 257, 268, 304, 323, 347 ; II, 214 ; ballad on his election to the United States Senate over John Walker, 214, 337, 366, 371, 373. Spence, I, 203.
"*Monticello*," II, 315.
"*Montpelier*," II, 315.
MONTGOMERY, James, II, 366.
Monumental Church, The, I, 68 ; II, 370.
MOORE, II, 386.
  Andrew, I, 36, 340, 347 ; II, 9 ; sketch of, 31, 271, 274, 279, 345, 365.
  David, II, 32.
  William, II, 36, 63.
MORECOCKE, W. H. E., I, xxvi.
MORGAN, II, 55.
  Daniel, Rifle Corps of, II, 32.
MORRIS, II, 378.
  Gouverneur, II, 249, 254, 335.
  Robert, cited on the poll tax, I, 190.
MORRISON, Colonel James, II, 293.
MOSELEY Mary, II, 381.
MUHLENBURG, General, I, 258 ; II, 97.
MUNFORD, Anne, I, 144.
  Anne Beverley, II, 379.
  Elizabeth Beverley, II, 379.
  Robert, II, 379.
  William G., II, 92.
MURRAY, Hon. Alexander, II, 303.
  George, Viscount Fincastle, II, 303.
  John, II, 303.
  William, Earl of Mansfield, II, 216.
  William, II, 289.
Mutual Assurance Society of Virginia, II, 370.
MYERS, Major E. D. T., II, 368.

Naval Officers of Virginia, legislation regarding, II, 177.
Navy, United States. I, 214 ; its creation due to Jefferson, 214.